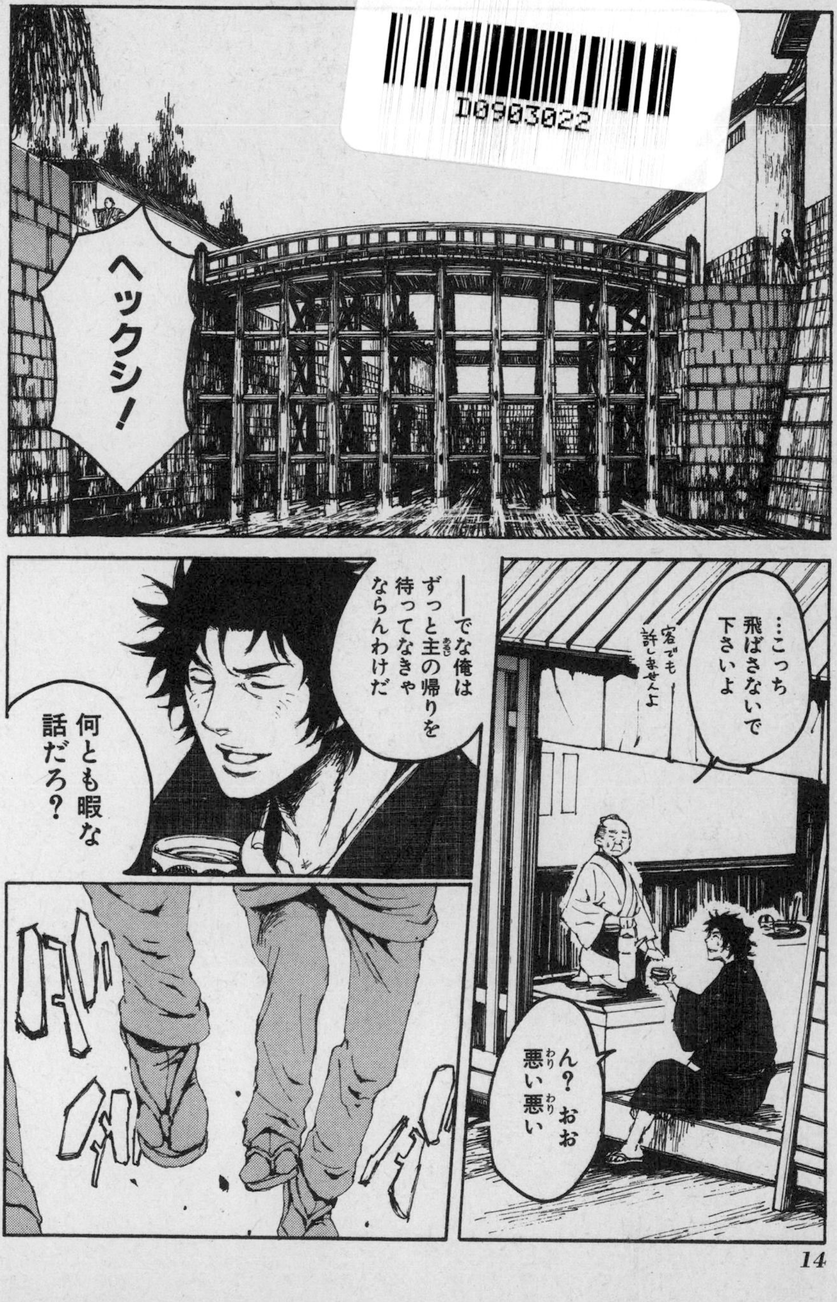
ヘックシ！
…こっち飛ばさないで下さいよ
客でも許しませんよ
ん？おお悪い悪い
――でな俺はずっと主の帰りを待ってなきゃならんわけだ
何とも暇な話だろ？

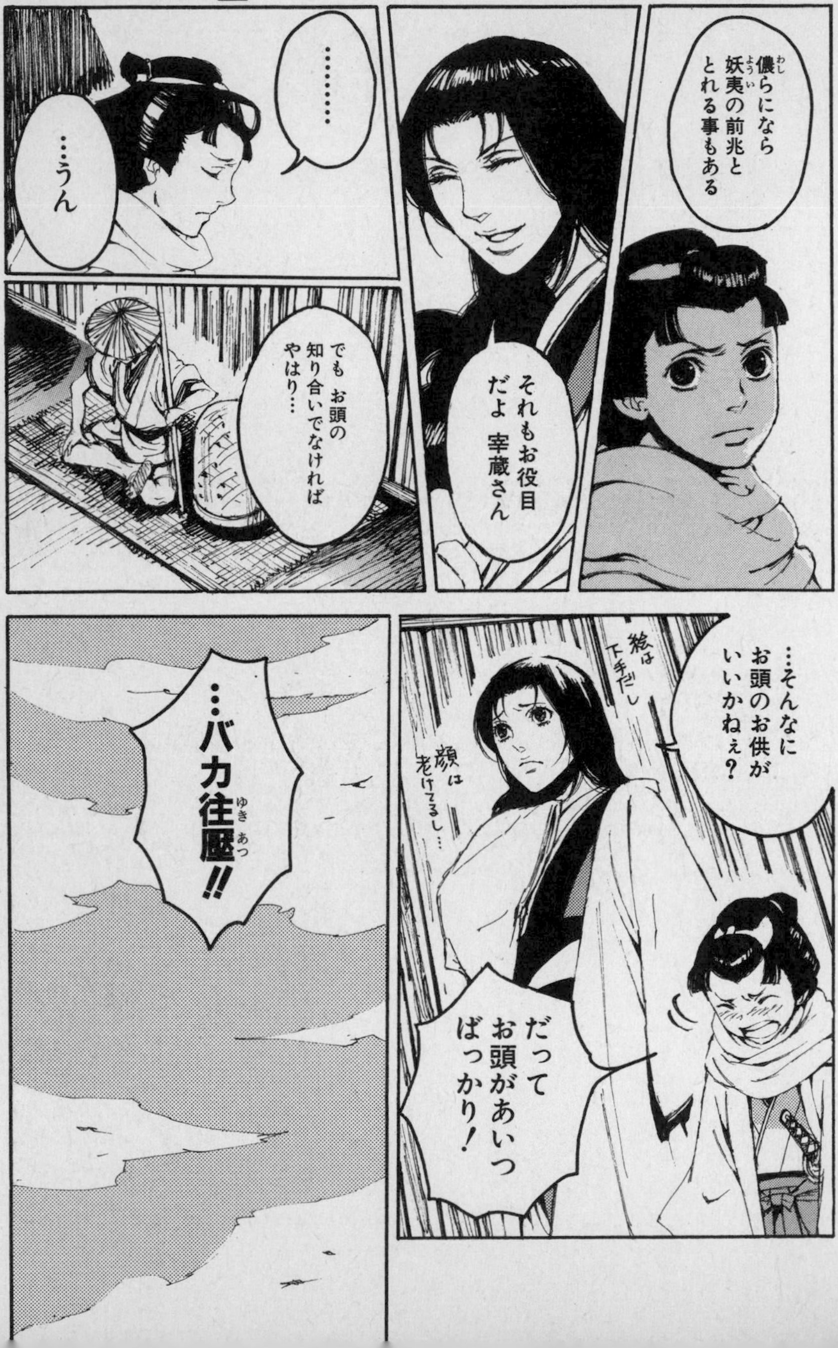
儂らになら妖夷の前兆ととれる事もある
それもお役目だよ 宰蔵さん
………
…うん
でも お頭の知り合いでなければやはり…
…そんなにお頭のお供がいいかねぇ？
絵は下手だし
顔は老けてるし…
だってお頭があいつばっかり！
…バカ往歴!!

HOW NOT TO SUMMON A DEMON LORD

DEMON LORD

2

Story
YUKIYA MURASAKI

Art
NAOTO FUKUDA

Character Design
TAKAHIRO TSURUSAKI

HOW NOT TO SUMMON A DEMON LORD

CONTENTS

5 TRYING TO BE AN ADVENTURER I

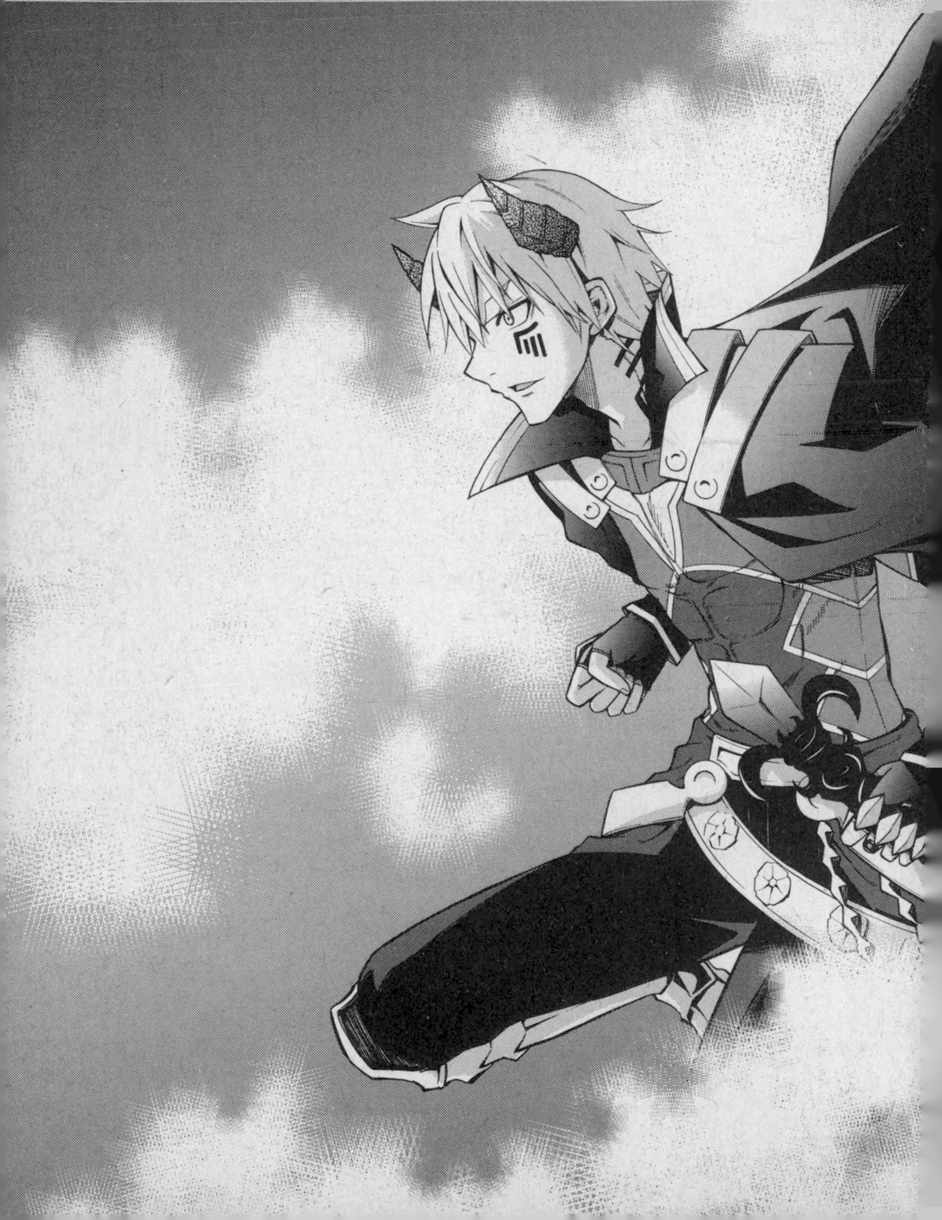

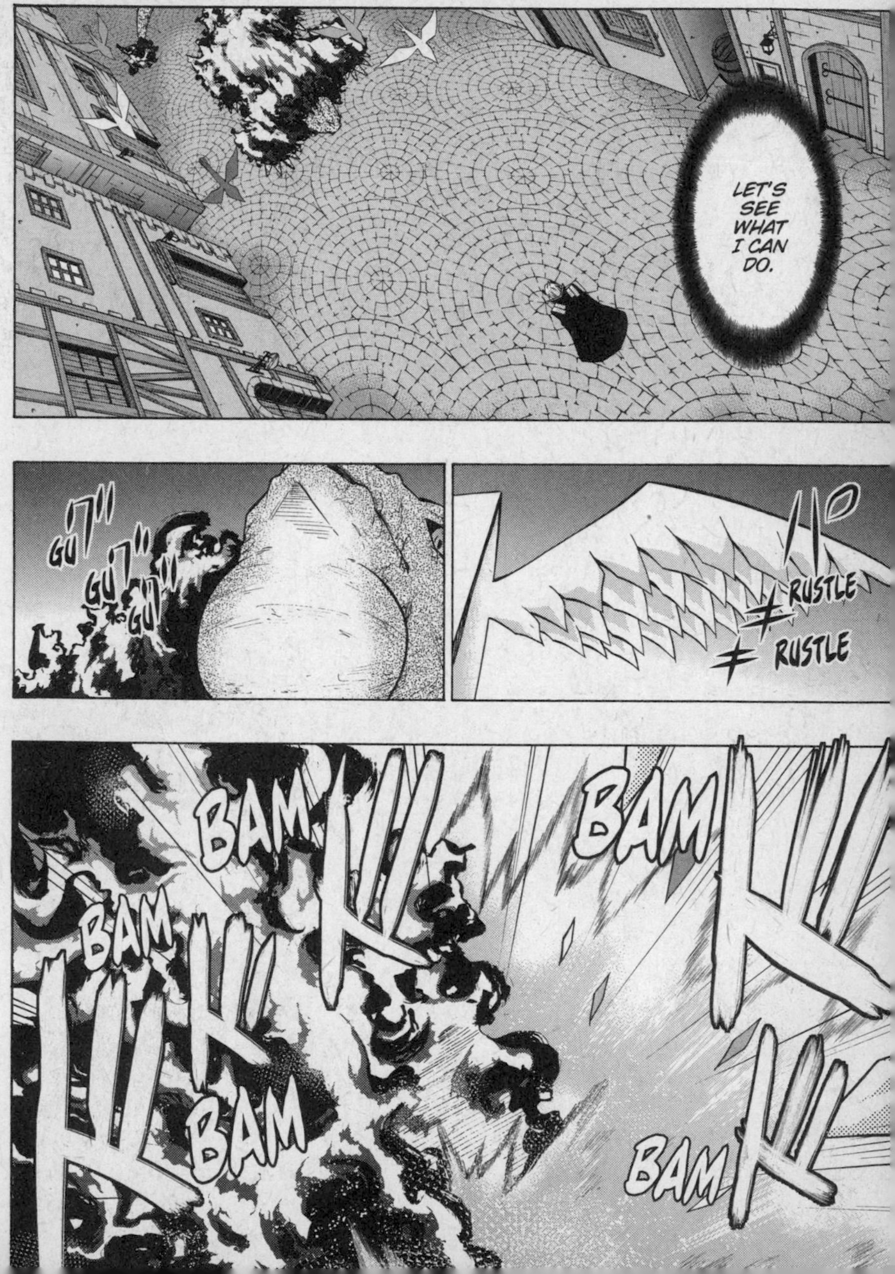
LET'S SEE WHAT I CAN DO.
RUSTLE
RUSTLE
GU
GU
GU
BAM
BAM
BAM
BAM
BAM

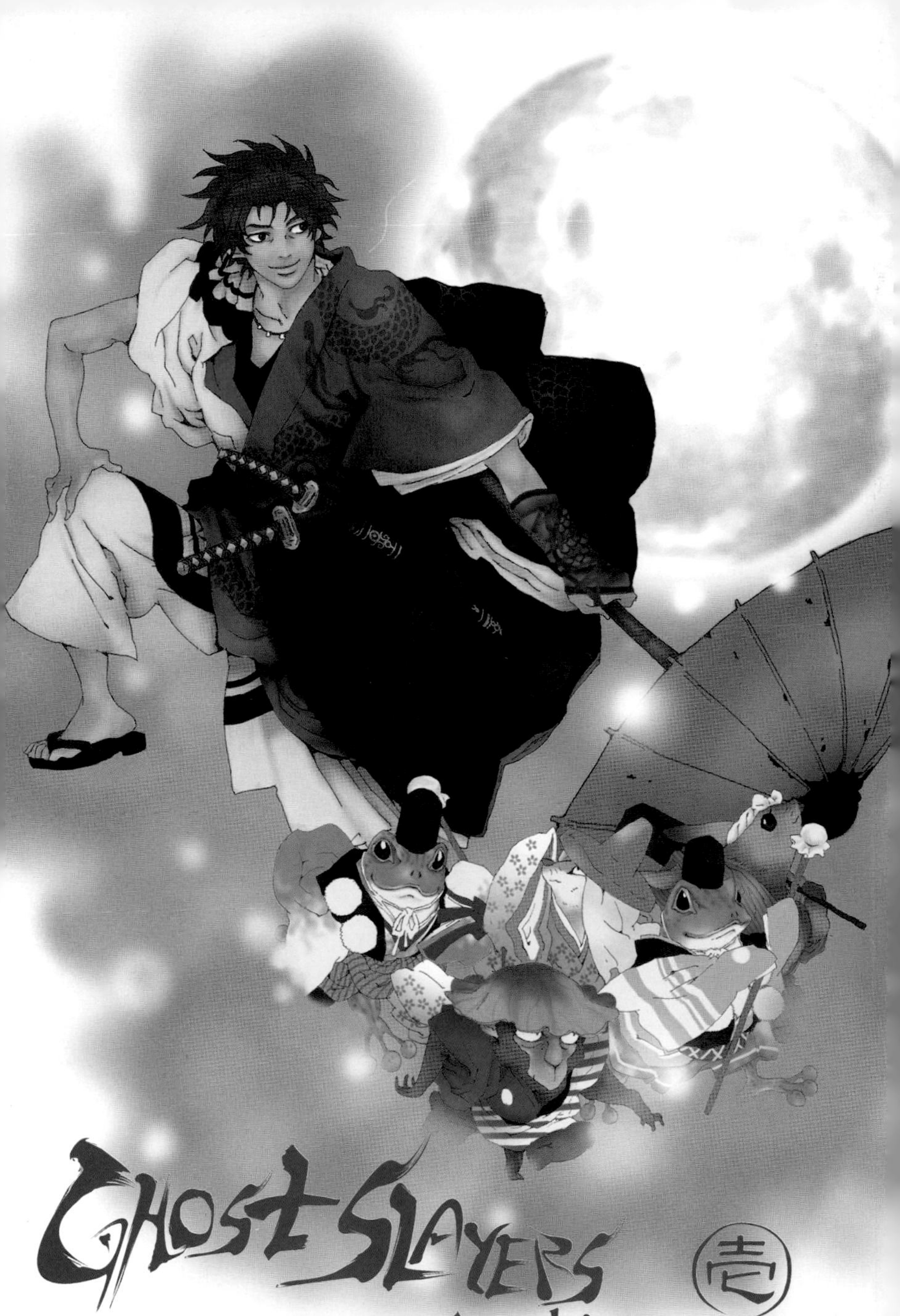

GHOST SLAYERS Ayashi

壱

ONE

GHOST SLAYERS Ayashi

壱

ONE

CONTENTS

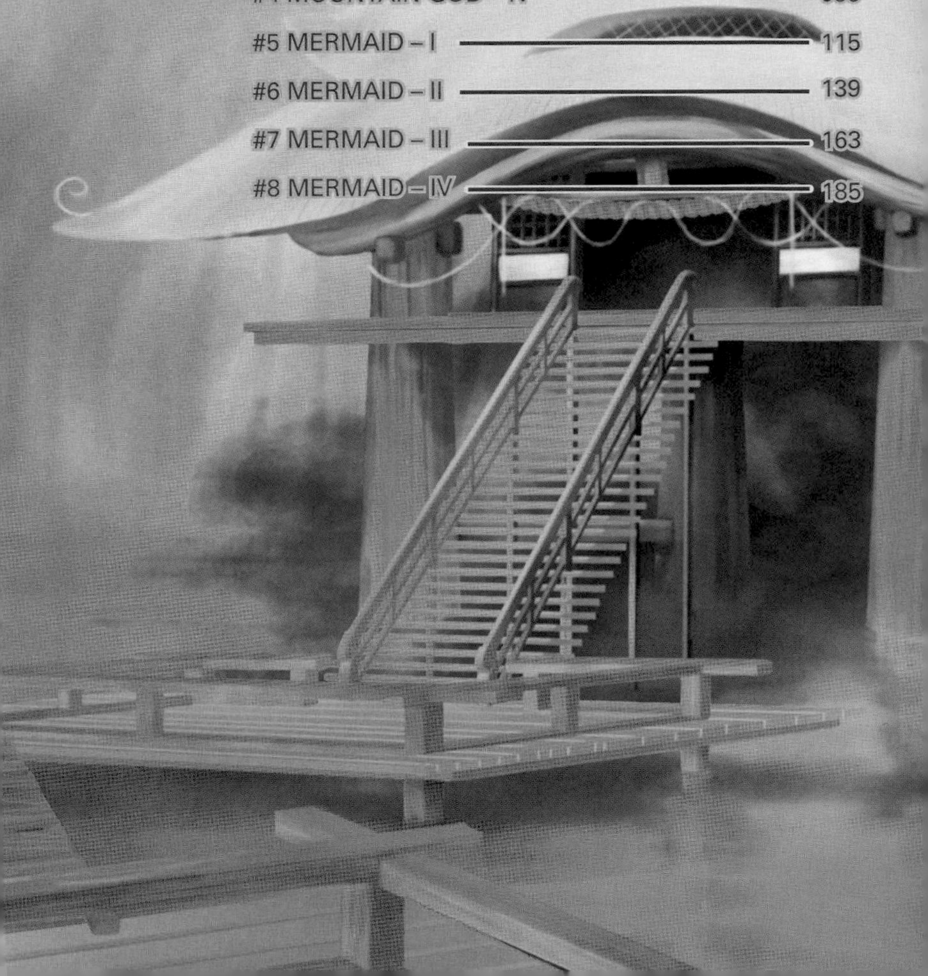

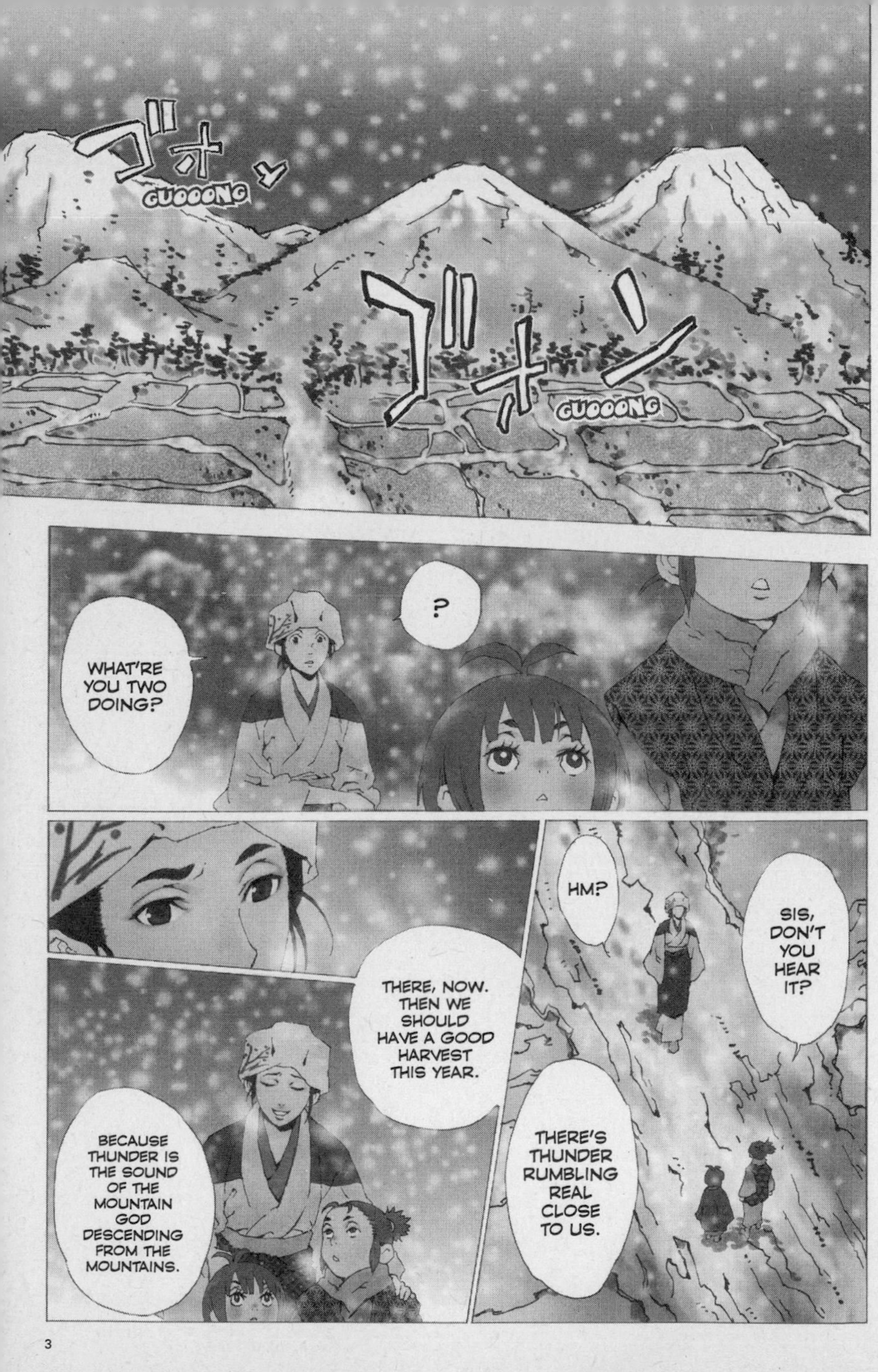
ゴォッ
GUOOONG
ゴォン
GUOOONG
?
WHAT'RE YOU TWO DOING?
SIS, DON'T YOU HEAR IT?
HM?
THERE'S THUNDER RUMBLING REAL CLOSE TO US.
THERE, NOW. THEN WE SHOULD HAVE A GOOD HARVEST THIS YEAR.
BECAUSE THUNDER IS THE SOUND OF THE MOUNTAIN GOD DESCENDING FROM THE MOUNTAINS.

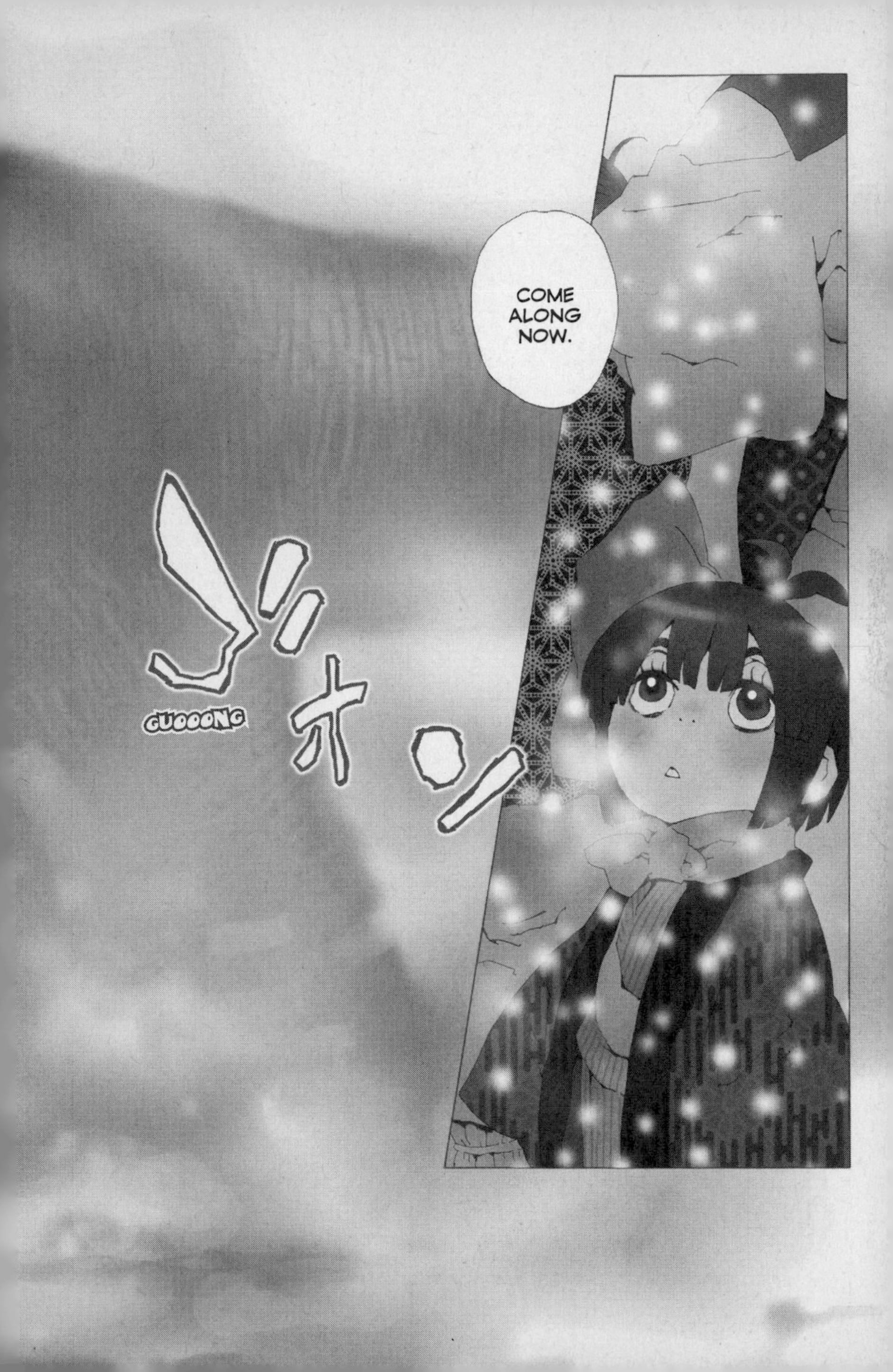
COME ALONG NOW.
GUOOONG

#1 MOUNTAIN GOD - I

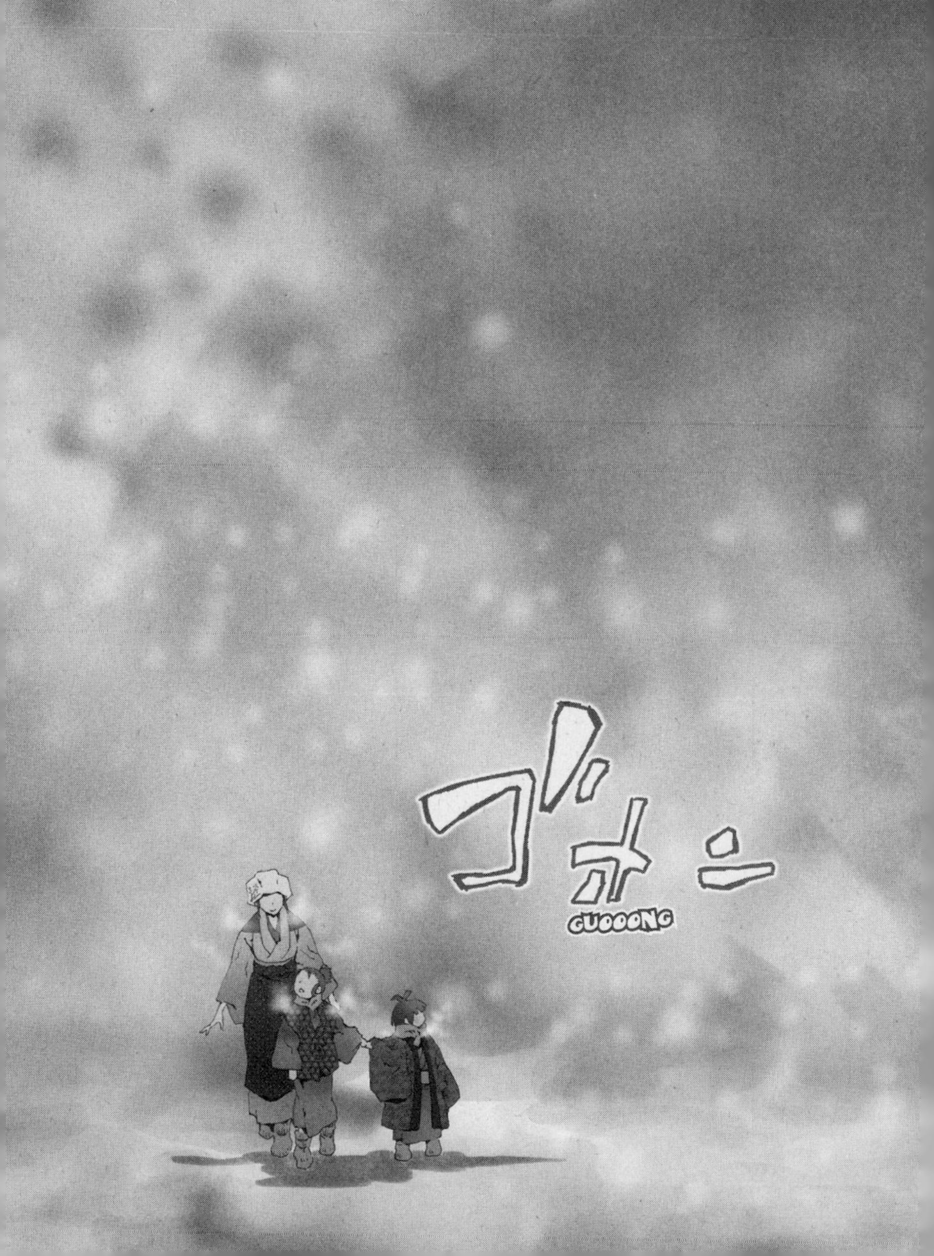
GUOOONG

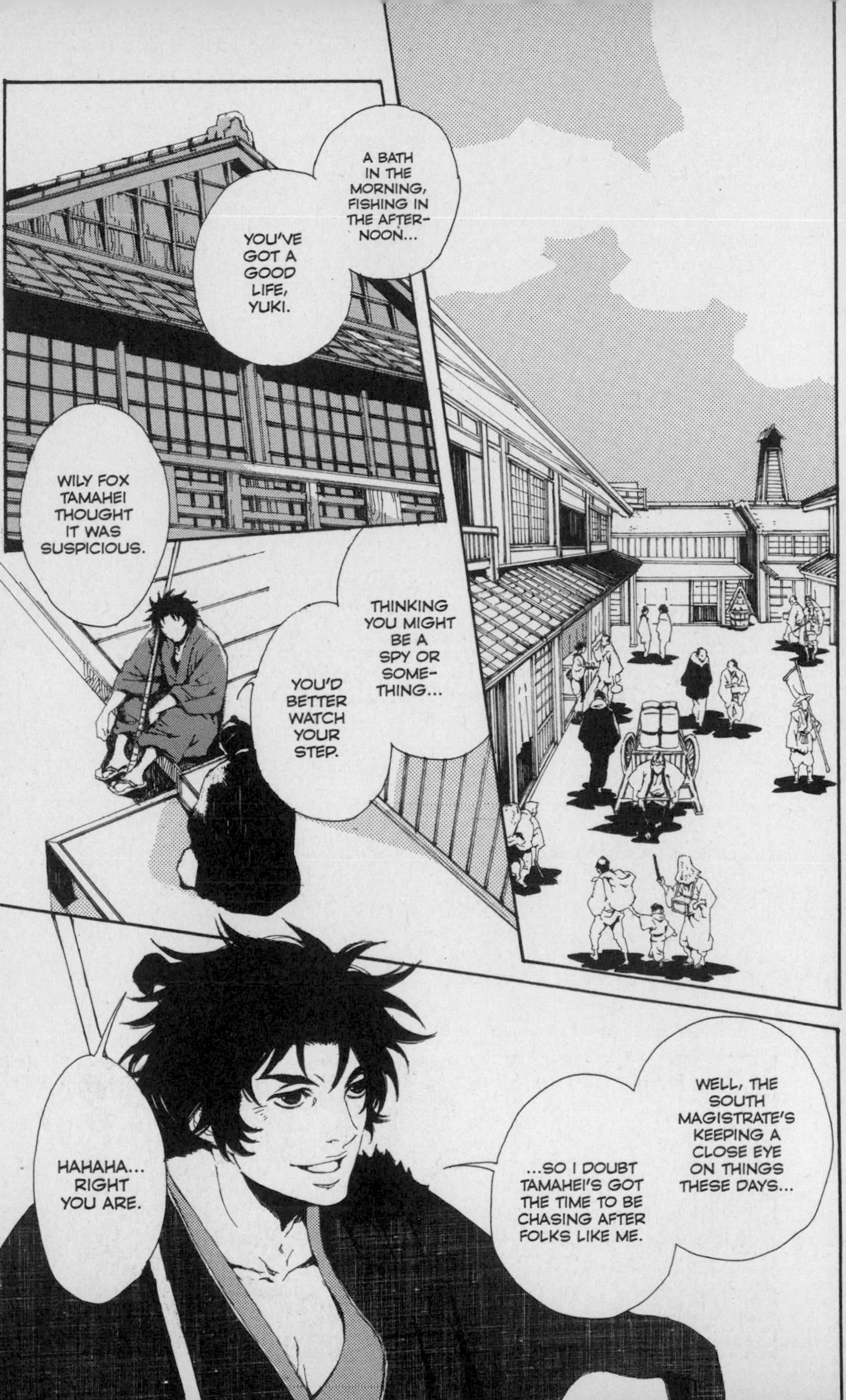
A BATH IN THE MORNING, FISHING IN THE AFTER-NOON...
YOU'VE GOT A GOOD LIFE, YUKI.
WILY FOX TAMAHEI THOUGHT IT WAS SUSPICIOUS.
THINKING YOU MIGHT BE A SPY OR SOME-THING...
YOU'D BETTER WATCH YOUR STEP.
WELL, THE SOUTH MAGISTRATE'S KEEPING A CLOSE EYE ON THINGS THESE DAYS...
...SO I DOUBT TAMAHEI'S GOT THE TIME TO BE CHASING AFTER FOLKS LIKE ME.
HAHAHA... RIGHT YOU ARE.

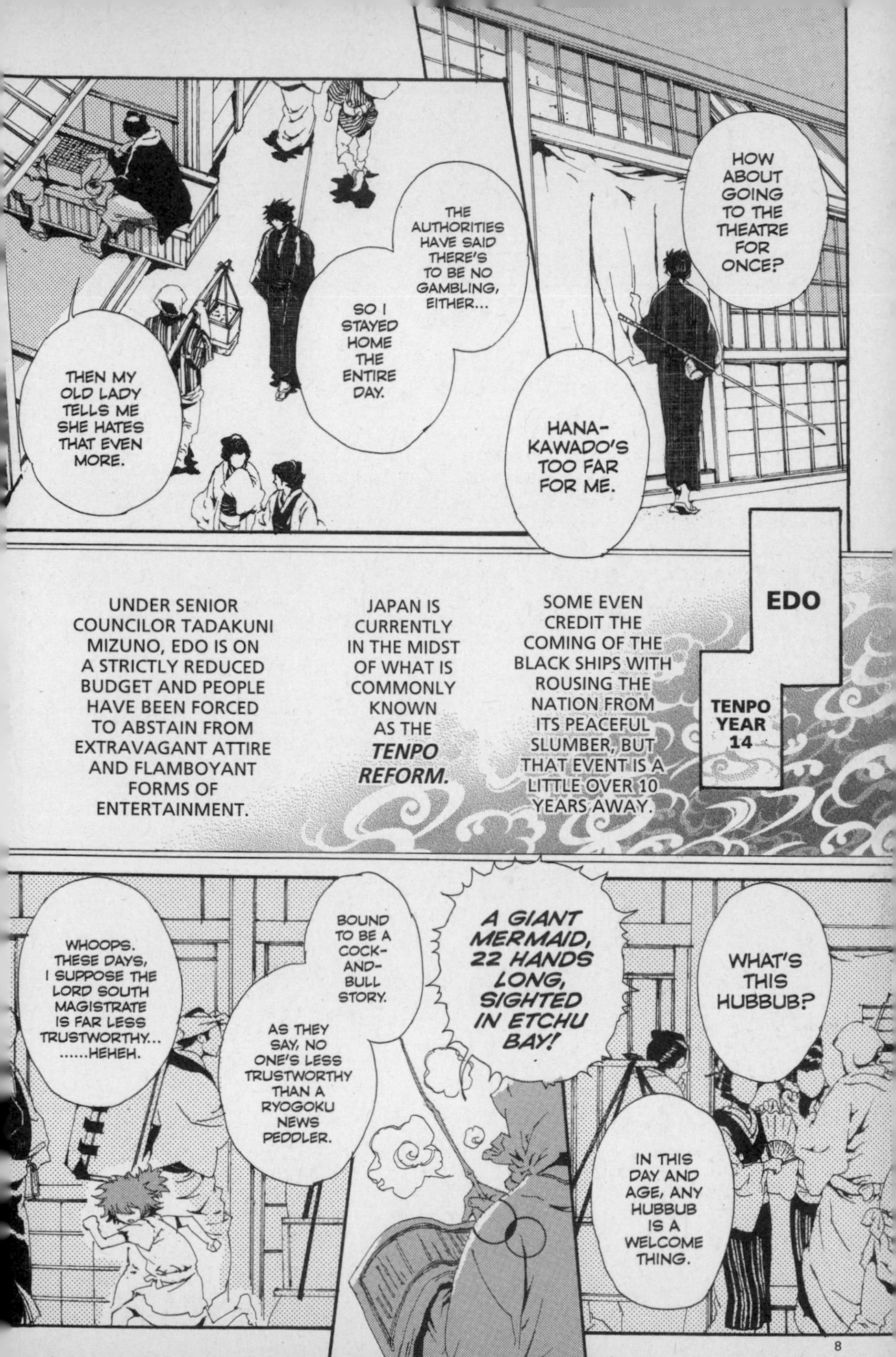
HOW ABOUT GOING TO THE THEATRE FOR ONCE?
HANA-KAWADO'S TOO FAR FOR ME.
THE AUTHORITIES HAVE SAID THERE'S TO BE NO GAMBLING, EITHER...
SO I STAYED HOME THE ENTIRE DAY.
THEN MY OLD LADY TELLS ME SHE HATES THAT EVEN MORE.
EDO
TENPO YEAR 14
SOME EVEN CREDIT THE COMING OF THE BLACK SHIPS WITH ROUSING THE NATION FROM ITS PEACEFUL SLUMBER, BUT THAT EVENT IS A LITTLE OVER 10 YEARS AWAY.
JAPAN IS CURRENTLY IN THE MIDST OF WHAT IS COMMONLY KNOWN AS THE *TENPO REFORM.*
UNDER SENIOR COUNCILOR TADAKUNI MIZUNO, EDO IS ON A STRICTLY REDUCED BUDGET AND PEOPLE HAVE BEEN FORCED TO ABSTAIN FROM EXTRAVAGANT ATTIRE AND FLAMBOYANT FORMS OF ENTERTAINMENT.
WHAT'S THIS HUBBUB?
IN THIS DAY AND AGE, ANY HUBBUB IS A WELCOME THING.
A GIANT MERMAID, 22 HANDS LONG, SIGHTED IN ETCHU BAY!
BOUND TO BE A COCK-AND-BULL STORY.
AS THEY SAY, NO ONE'S LESS TRUSTWORTHY THAN A RYOGOKU NEWS PEDDLER.
WHOOPS. THESE DAYS, I SUPPOSE THE LORD SOUTH MAGISTRATE IS FAR LESS TRUSTWORTHY... ......HEHEH.

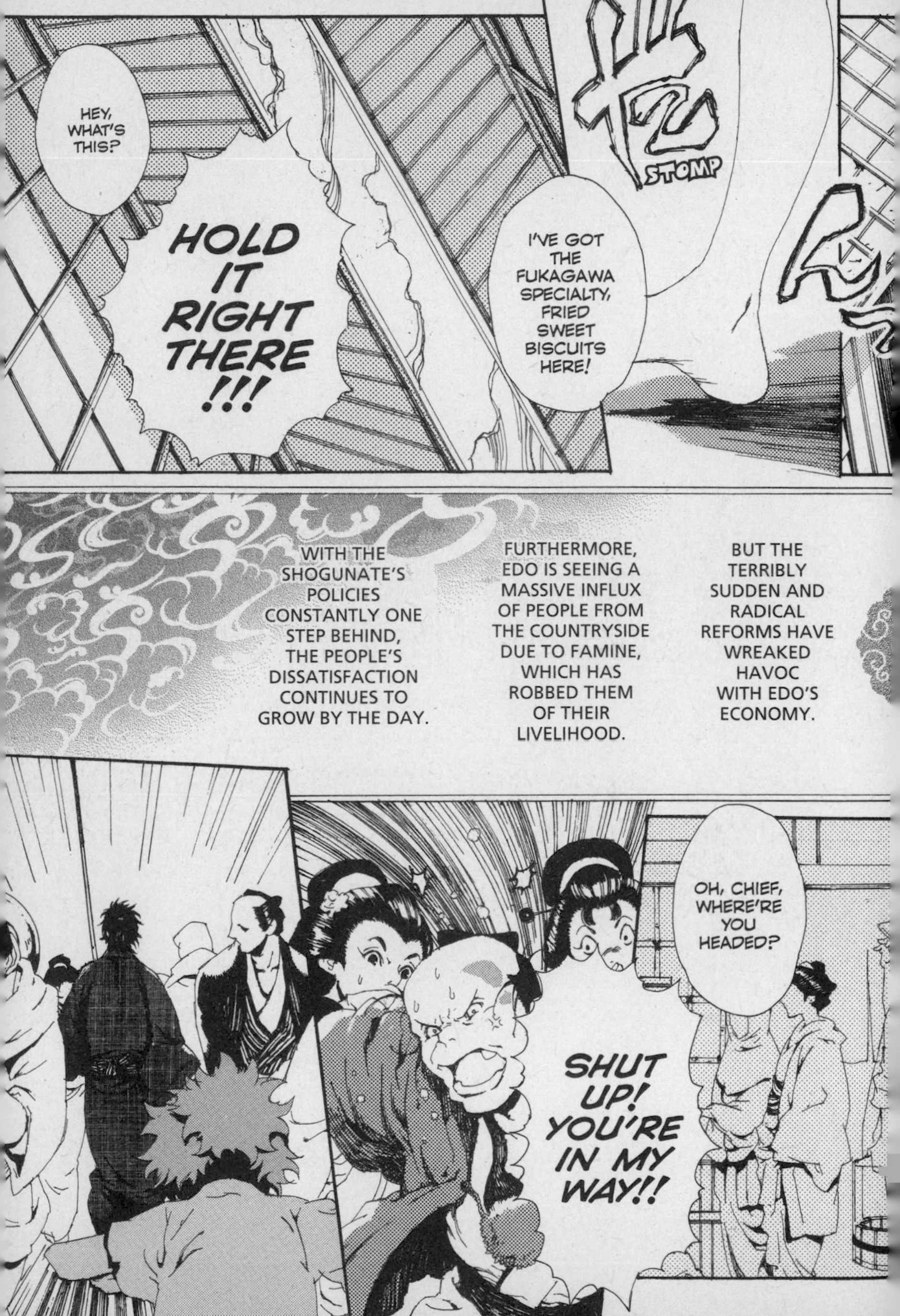
STOMP
I'VE GOT THE FUKAGAWA SPECIALTY, FRIED SWEET BISCUITS HERE!
HEY, WHAT'S THIS?
HOLD IT RIGHT THERE!!!
BUT THE TERRIBLY SUDDEN AND RADICAL REFORMS HAVE WREAKED HAVOC WITH EDO'S ECONOMY.
FURTHERMORE, EDO IS SEEING A MASSIVE INFLUX OF PEOPLE FROM THE COUNTRYSIDE DUE TO FAMINE, WHICH HAS ROBBED THEM OF THEIR LIVELIHOOD.
WITH THE SHOGUNATE'S POLICIES CONSTANTLY ONE STEP BEHIND, THE PEOPLE'S DISSATISFACTION CONTINUES TO GROW BY THE DAY.
OH, CHIEF, WHERE'RE YOU HEADED?
SHUT UP! YOU'RE IN MY WAY!!

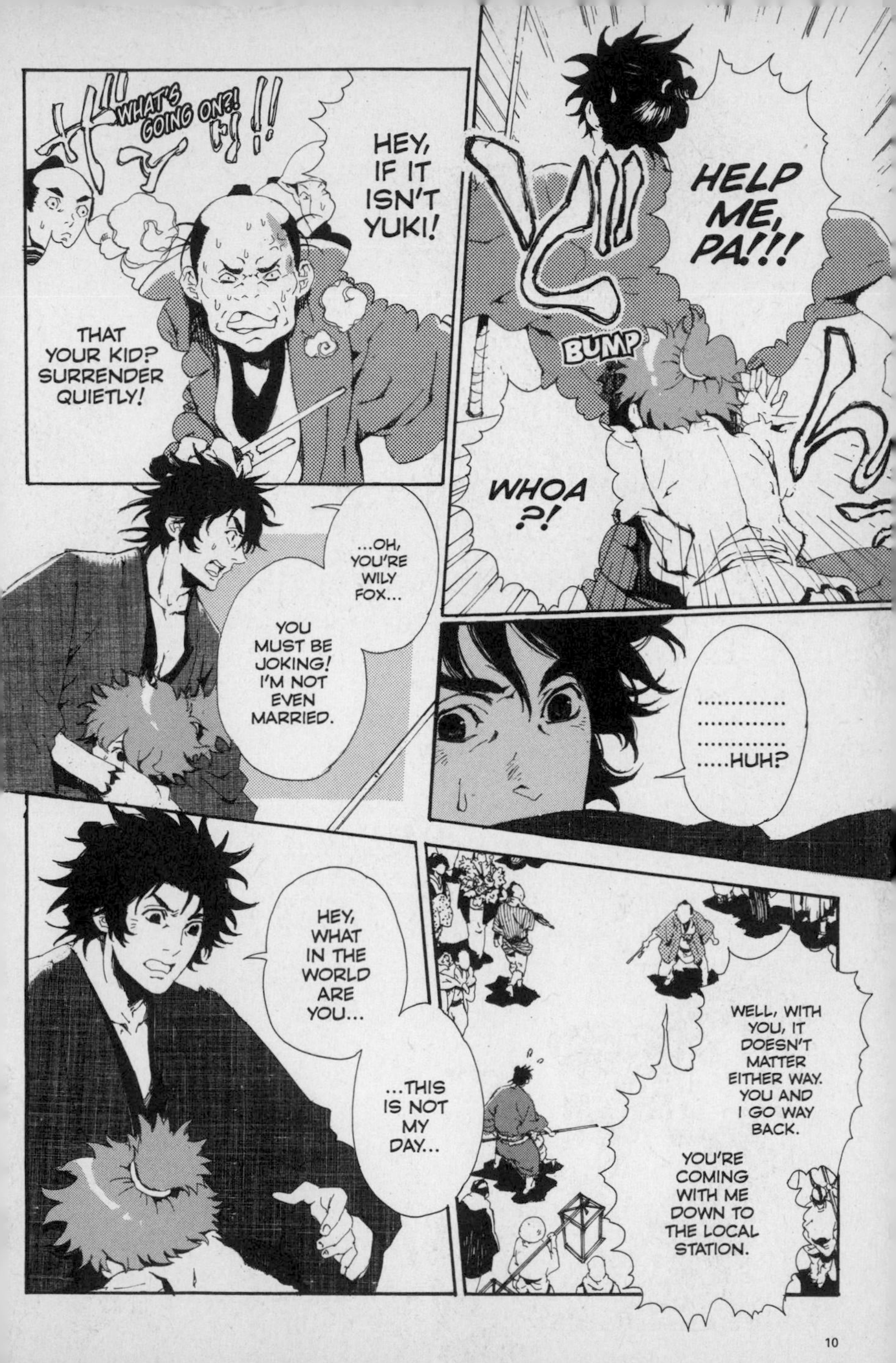
HELP ME, PA!!!
BUMP
WHOA ?!
WHAT'S GOING ON?!
HEY, IF IT ISN'T YUKI!
THAT YOUR KID? SURRENDER QUIETLY!
....HUH?
...OH, YOU'RE WILY FOX...
YOU MUST BE JOKING! I'M NOT EVEN MARRIED.
WELL, WITH YOU, IT DOESN'T MATTER EITHER WAY. YOU AND I GO WAY BACK.
YOU'RE COMING WITH ME DOWN TO THE LOCAL STATION.
HEY, WHAT IN THE WORLD ARE YOU...
...THIS IS NOT MY DAY...

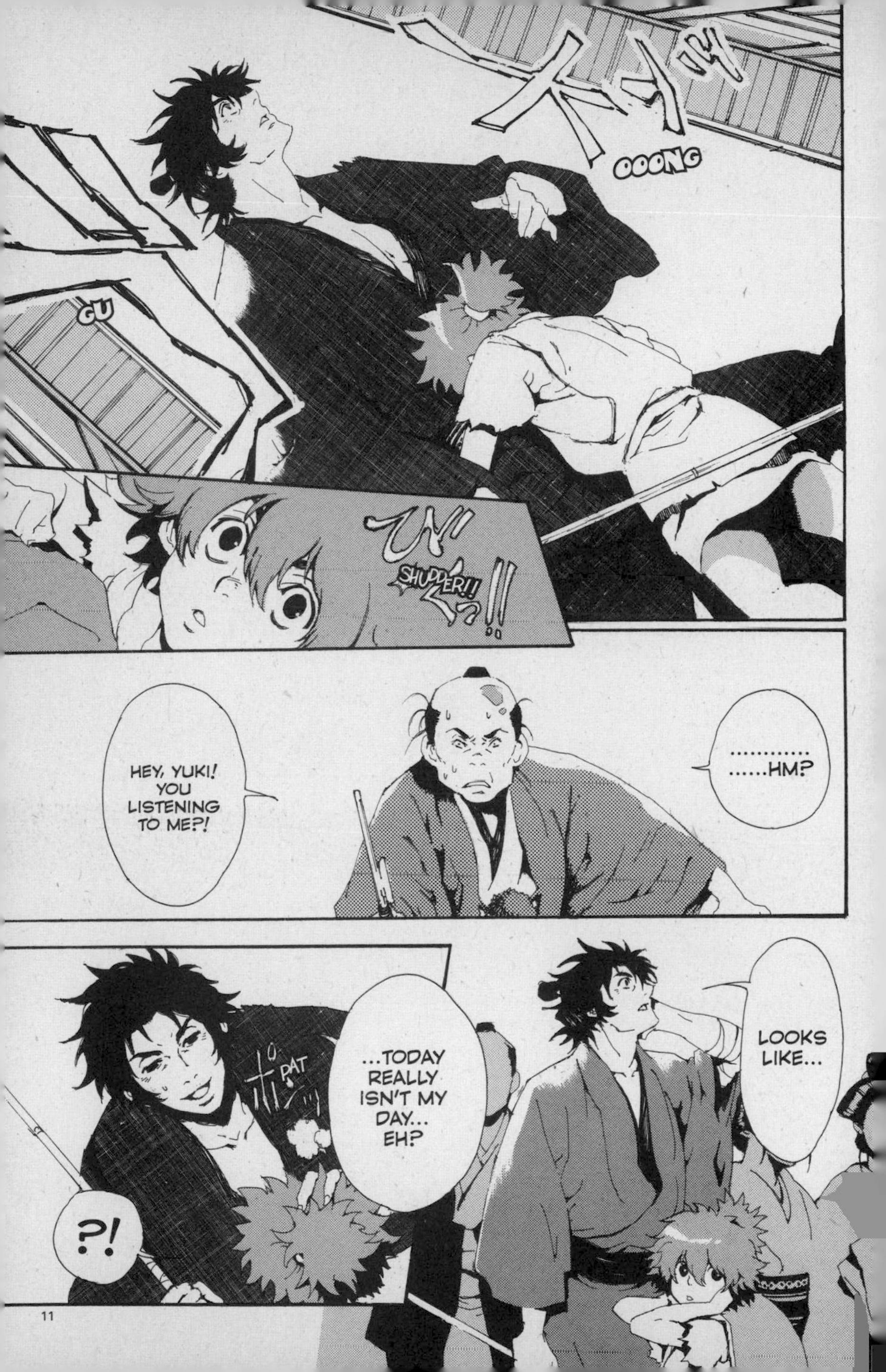

OOONG
GU
SHUDDER!!
....
......HM?
HEY, YUKI! YOU LISTENING TO ME?!
LOOKS LIKE...
...TODAY REALLY ISN'T MY DAY... EH?
PAT
?!

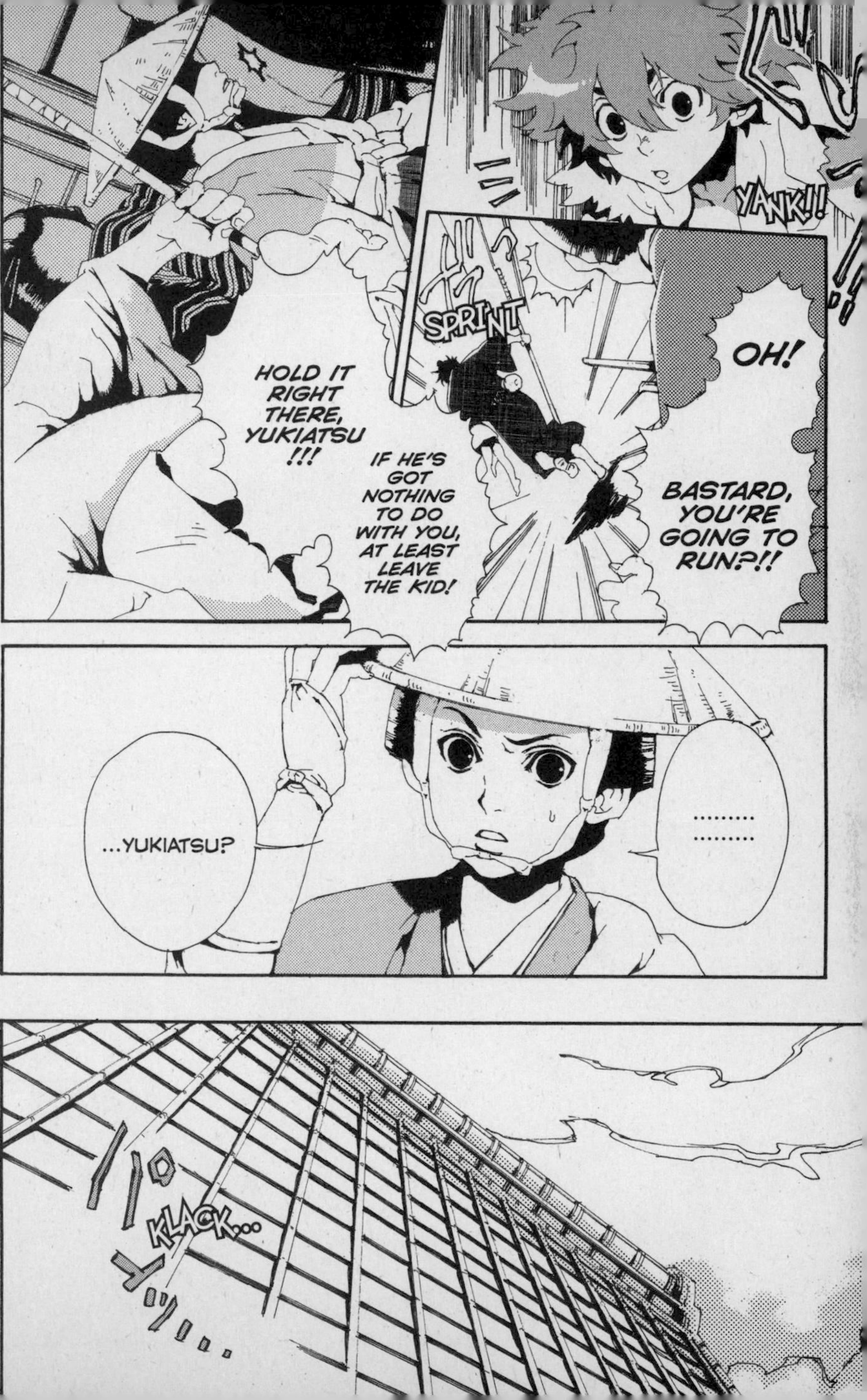
YANK!!
SPRINT
OH!
BASTARD, YOU'RE GOING TO RUN?!!
HOLD IT RIGHT THERE, YUKIATSU!!!
IF HE'S GOT NOTHING TO DO WITH YOU, AT LEAST LEAVE THE KID!
....
....
...YUKIATSU?
KLACK...

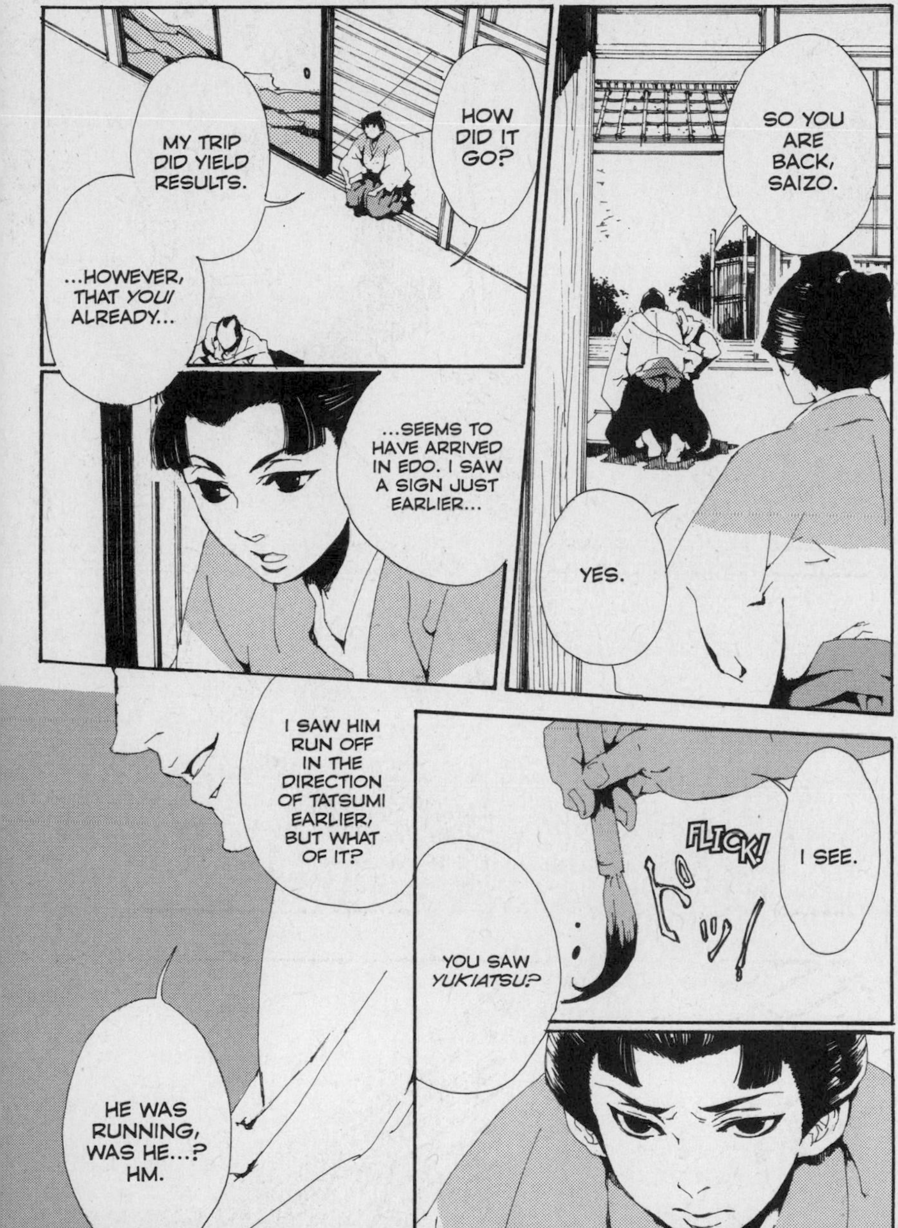

SO YOU ARE BACK, SAIZO.
YES.
HOW DID IT GO?
MY TRIP DID YIELD RESULTS.
...HOWEVER, THAT YOU/ ALREADY...
...SEEMS TO HAVE ARRIVED IN EDO. I SAW A SIGN JUST EARLIER...
I SEE.
FLICK!
YOU SAW *YUKIATSU?*
I SAW HIM RUN OFF IN THE DIRECTION OF TATSUMI EARLIER, BUT WHAT OF IT?
HE WAS RUNNING, WAS HE...? HM.

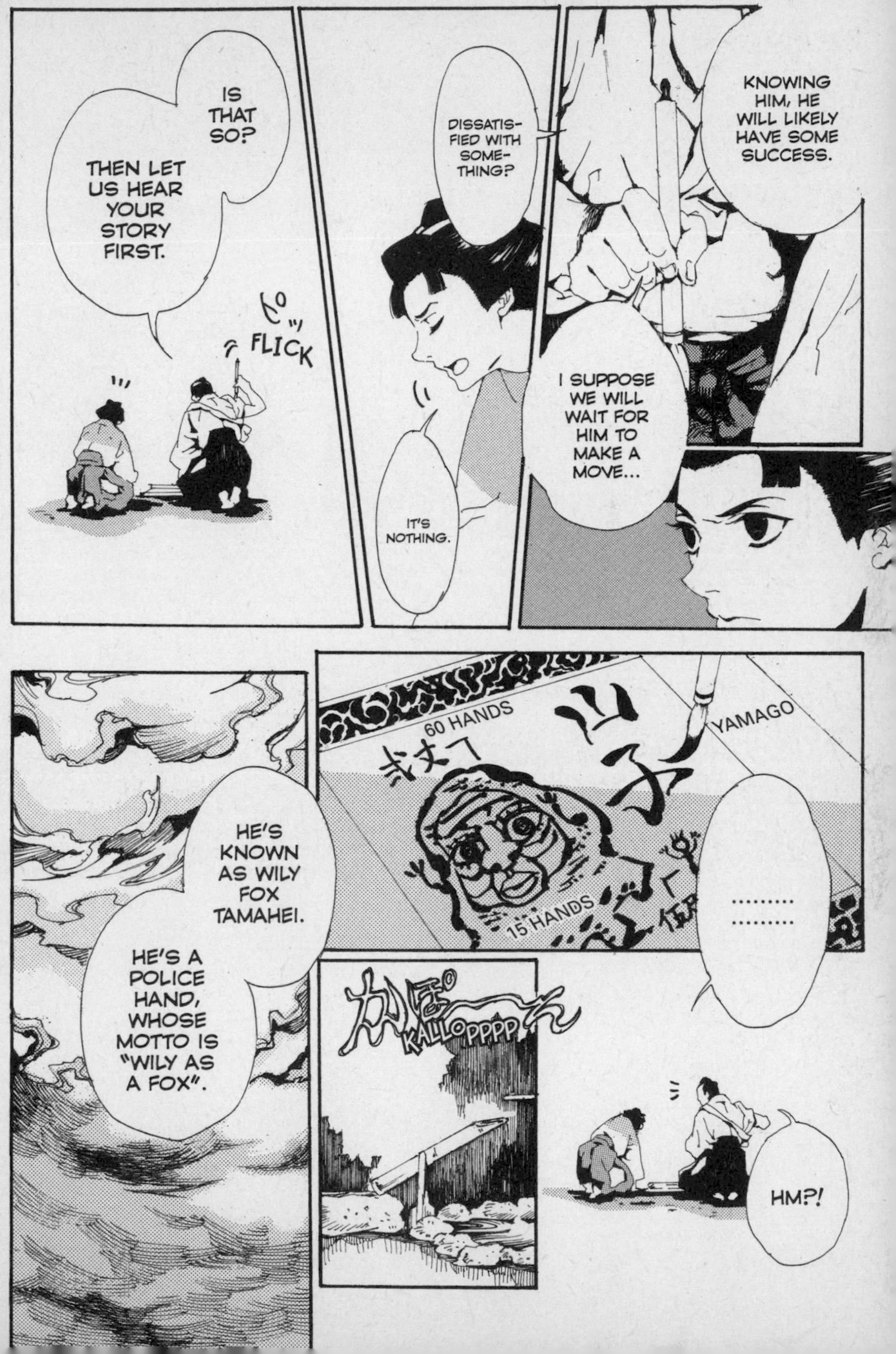
KNOWING HIM, HE WILL LIKELY HAVE SOME SUCCESS.
I SUPPOSE WE WILL WAIT FOR HIM TO MAKE A MOVE...
DISSATIS-FIED WITH SOME-THING?
IT'S NOTHING.
IS THAT SO?
THEN LET US HEAR YOUR STORY FIRST.
FLICK
YAMAGO
60 HANDS
15 HANDS
....
....
KALLOPPPP
HM?!
HE'S KNOWN AS WILY FOX TAMAHEI.
HE'S A POLICE HAND, WHOSE MOTTO IS "WILY AS A FOX".

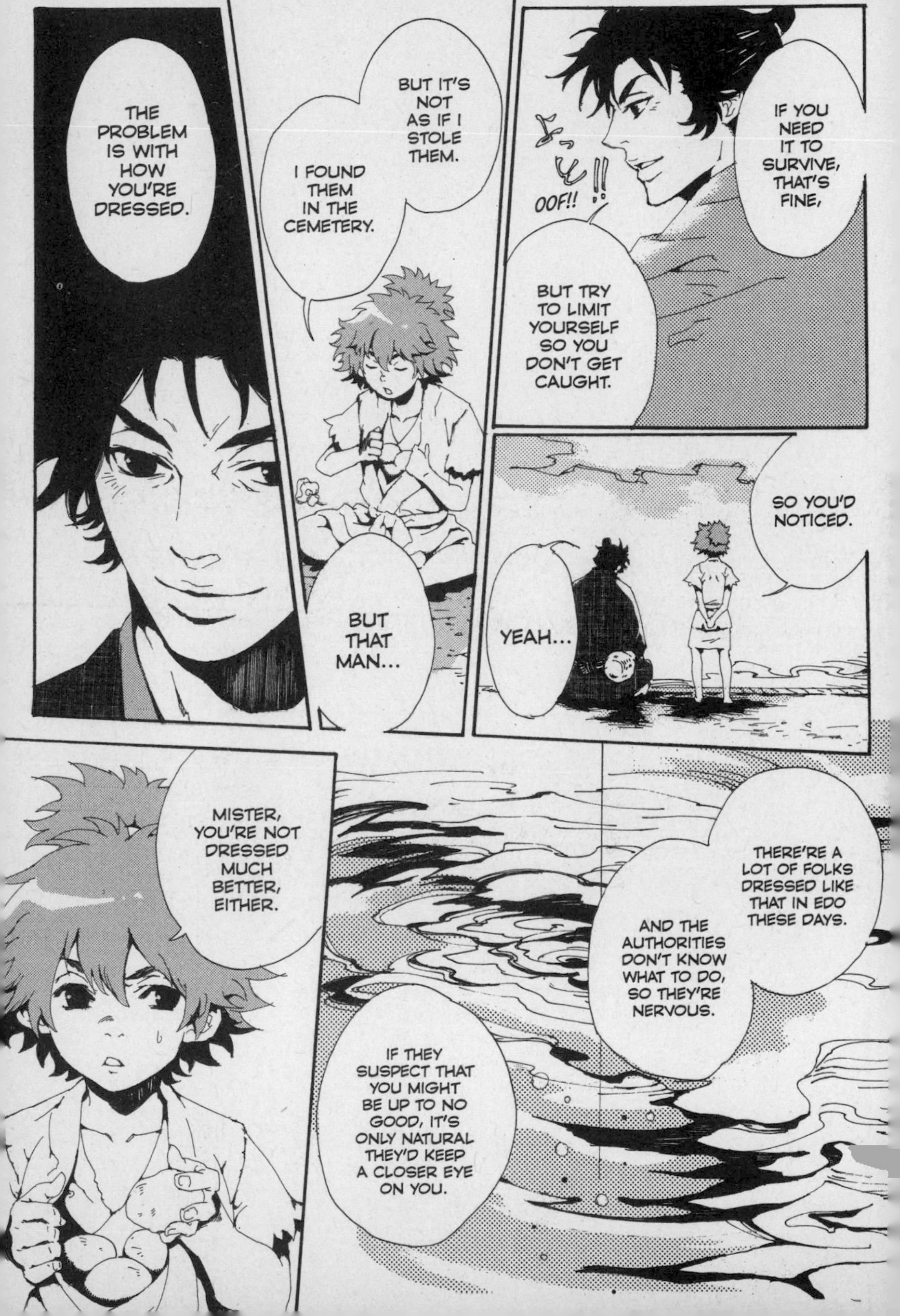
IF YOU NEED IT TO SURVIVE, THAT'S FINE,
OOF!!
BUT TRY TO LIMIT YOURSELF SO YOU DON'T GET CAUGHT.
SO YOU'D NOTICED.
YEAH...
BUT IT'S NOT AS IF I STOLE THEM.
I FOUND THEM IN THE CEMETERY.
BUT THAT MAN...
THE PROBLEM IS WITH HOW YOU'RE DRESSED.
THERE'RE A LOT OF FOLKS DRESSED LIKE THAT IN EDO THESE DAYS.
AND THE AUTHORITIES DON'T KNOW WHAT TO DO, SO THEY'RE NERVOUS.
IF THEY SUSPECT THAT YOU MIGHT BE UP TO NO GOOD, IT'S ONLY NATURAL THEY'D KEEP A CLOSER EYE ON YOU.
MISTER, YOU'RE NOT DRESSED MUCH BETTER, EITHER.

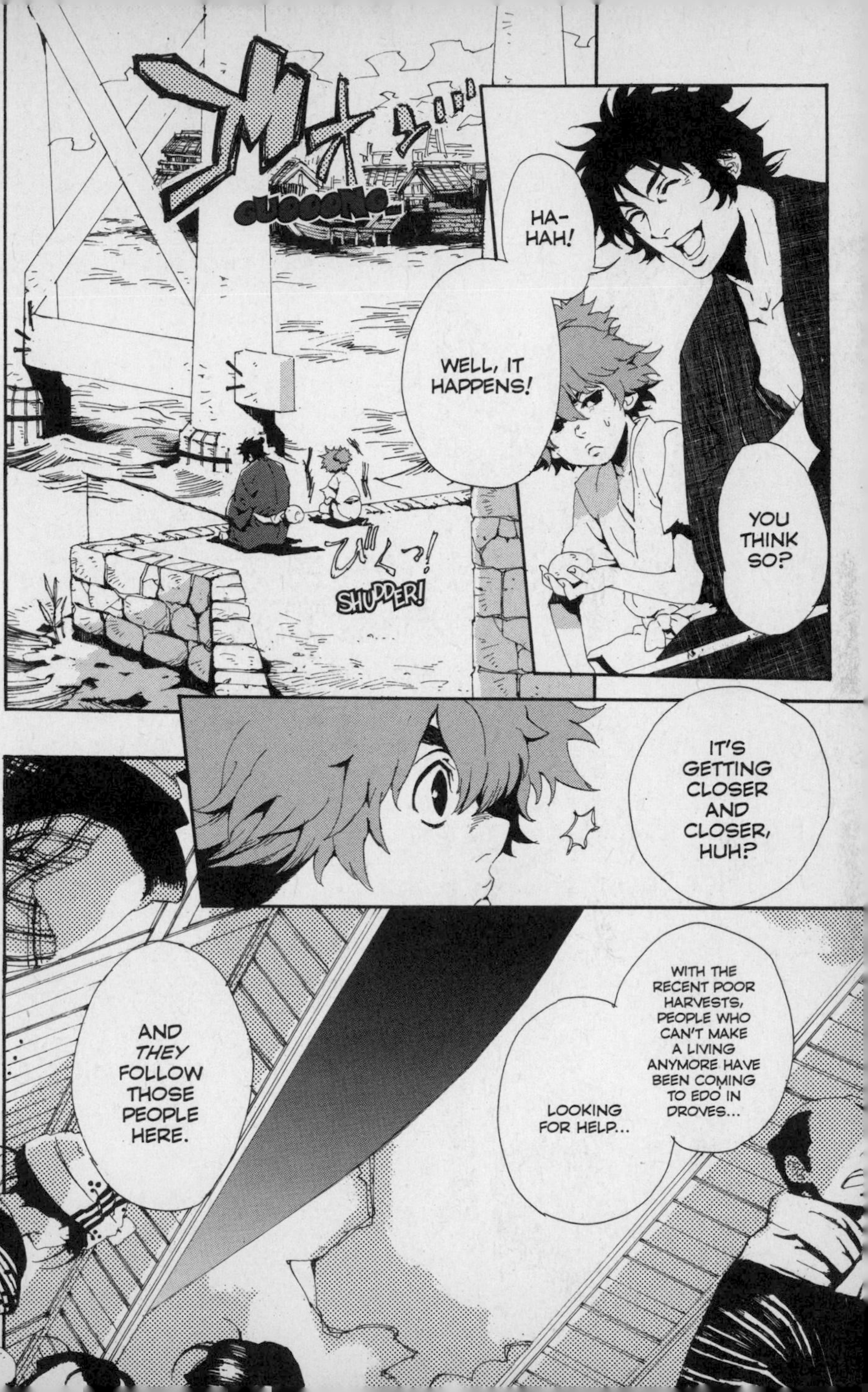
HA-HAH!
WELL, IT HAPPENS!
YOU THINK SO?
びくっ!
SHUDDER!
...
IT'S GETTING CLOSER AND CLOSER, HUH?
WITH THE RECENT POOR HARVESTS, PEOPLE WHO CAN'T MAKE A LIVING ANYMORE HAVE BEEN COMING TO EDO IN DROVES...
LOOKING FOR HELP...
AND *THEY* FOLLOW THOSE PEOPLE HERE.

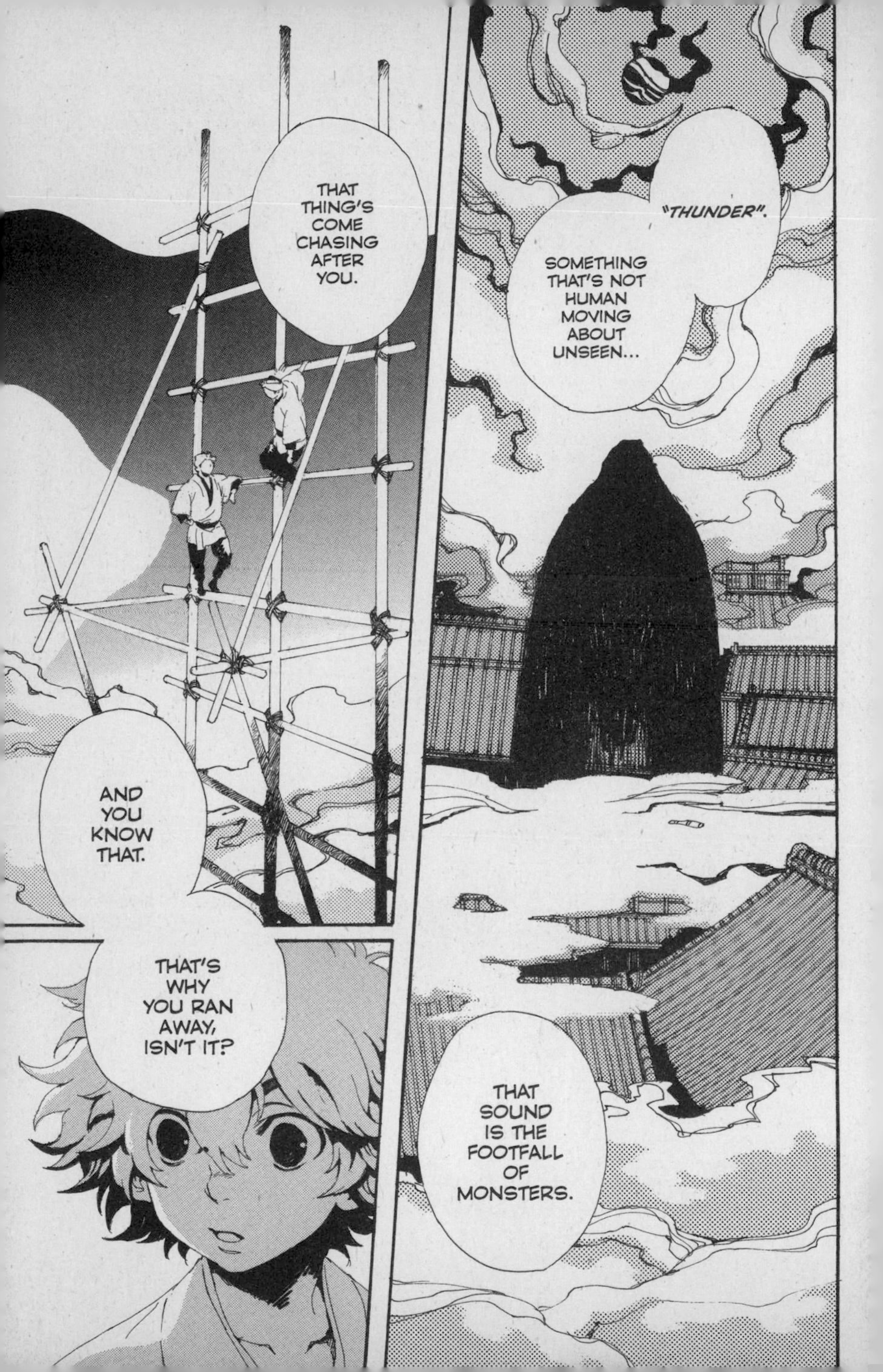
"THUNDER".
SOMETHING THAT'S NOT HUMAN MOVING ABOUT UNSEEN...
THAT SOUND IS THE FOOTFALL OF MONSTERS.
THAT THING'S COME CHASING AFTER YOU.
AND YOU KNOW THAT.
THAT'S WHY YOU RAN AWAY, ISN'T IT?

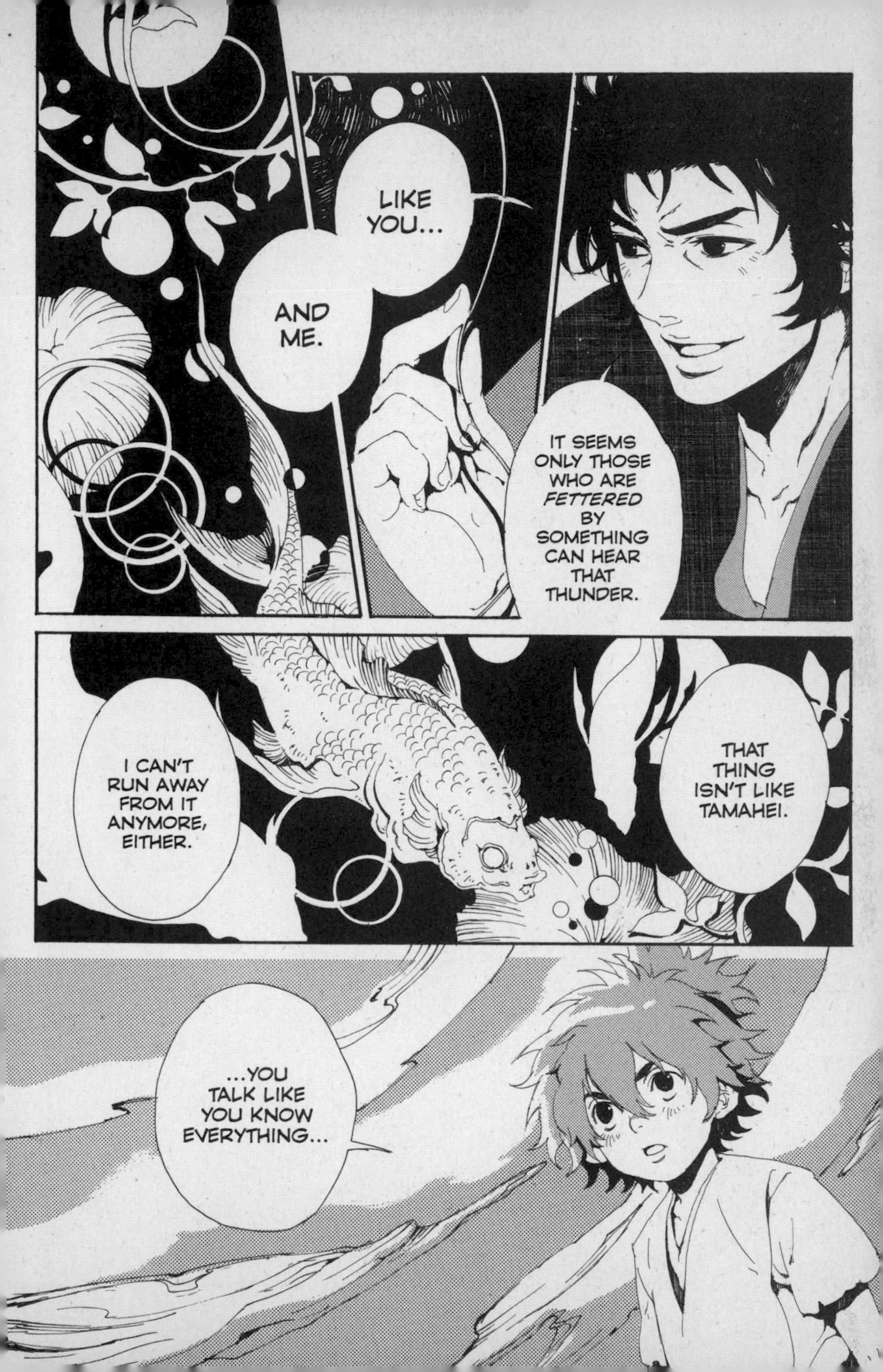
IT SEEMS ONLY THOSE WHO ARE *FETTERED* BY SOMETHING CAN HEAR THAT THUNDER.
LIKE YOU...
AND ME.
THAT THING ISN'T LIKE TAMAHEI.
I CAN'T RUN AWAY FROM IT ANYMORE, EITHER.
...YOU TALK LIKE YOU KNOW EVERYTHING...

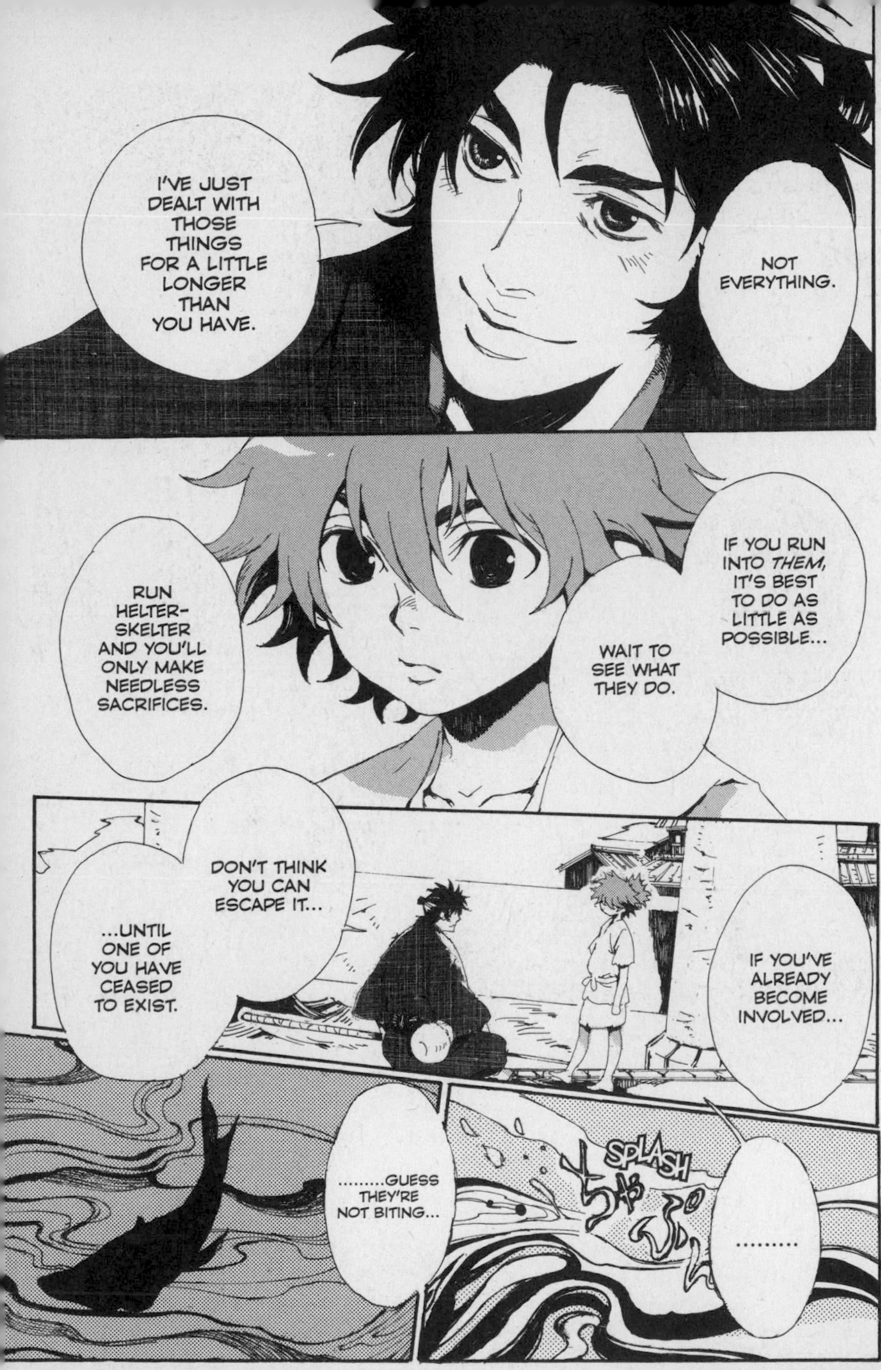
NOT EVERYTHING.
I'VE JUST DEALT WITH THOSE THINGS FOR A LITTLE LONGER THAN YOU HAVE.
IF YOU RUN INTO *THEM*, IT'S BEST TO DO AS LITTLE AS POSSIBLE...
WAIT TO SEE WHAT THEY DO.
RUN HELTER-SKELTER AND YOU'LL ONLY MAKE NEEDLESS SACRIFICES.
IF YOU'VE ALREADY BECOME INVOLVED...
DON'T THINK YOU CAN ESCAPE IT...
...UNTIL ONE OF YOU HAVE CEASED TO EXIST.
....
SPLASH
.........GUESS THEY'RE NOT BITING...

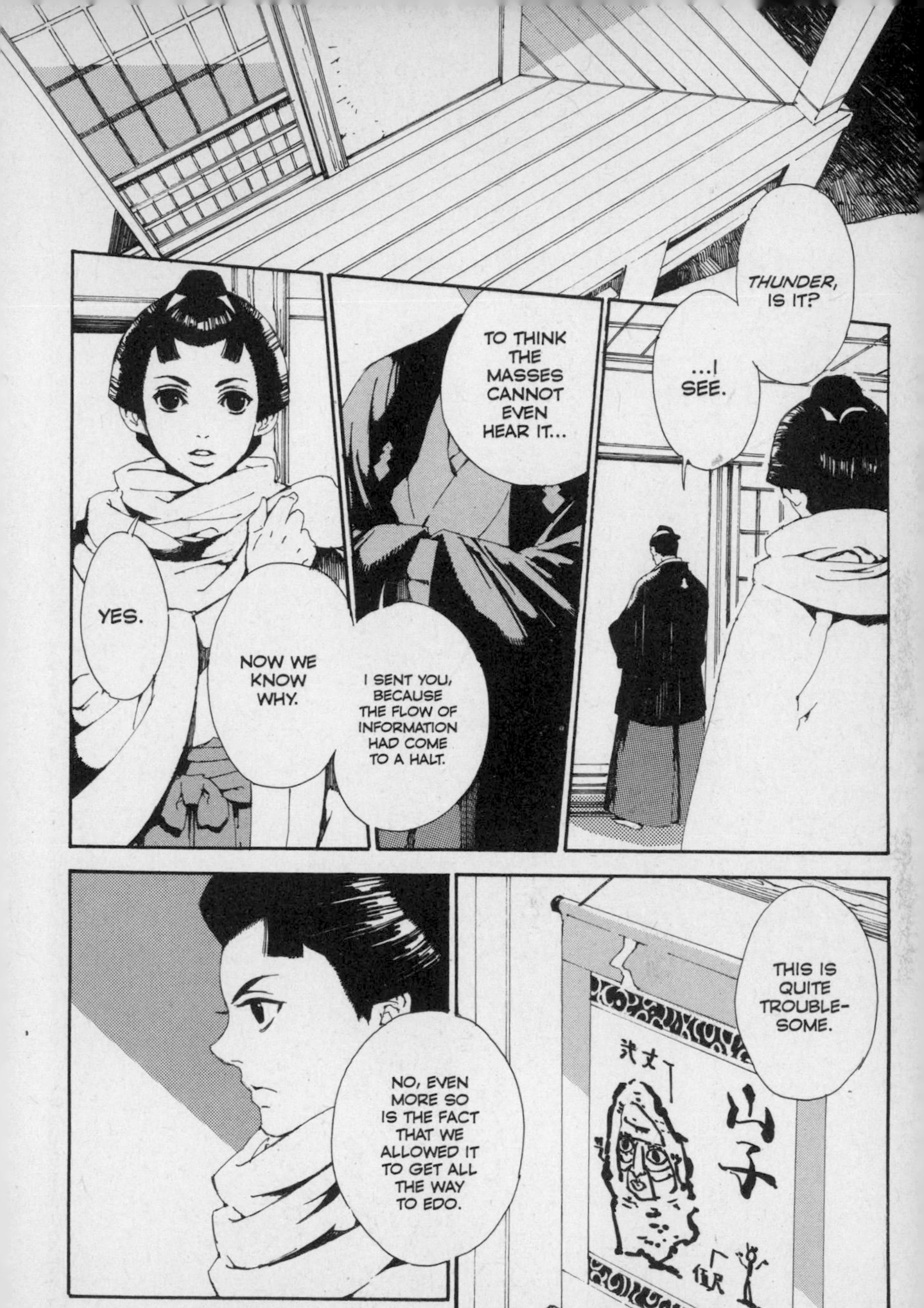
THUNDER, IS IT?
...I SEE.
TO THINK THE MASSES CANNOT EVEN HEAR IT...
I SENT YOU, BECAUSE THE FLOW OF INFORMATION HAD COME TO A HALT.
YES.
NOW WE KNOW WHY.
THIS IS QUITE TROUBLE-SOME.
NO, EVEN MORE SO IS THE FACT THAT WE ALLOWED IT TO GET ALL THE WAY TO EDO.

SIGN: 60 HANDS / YAMAGO / 15 HANDS

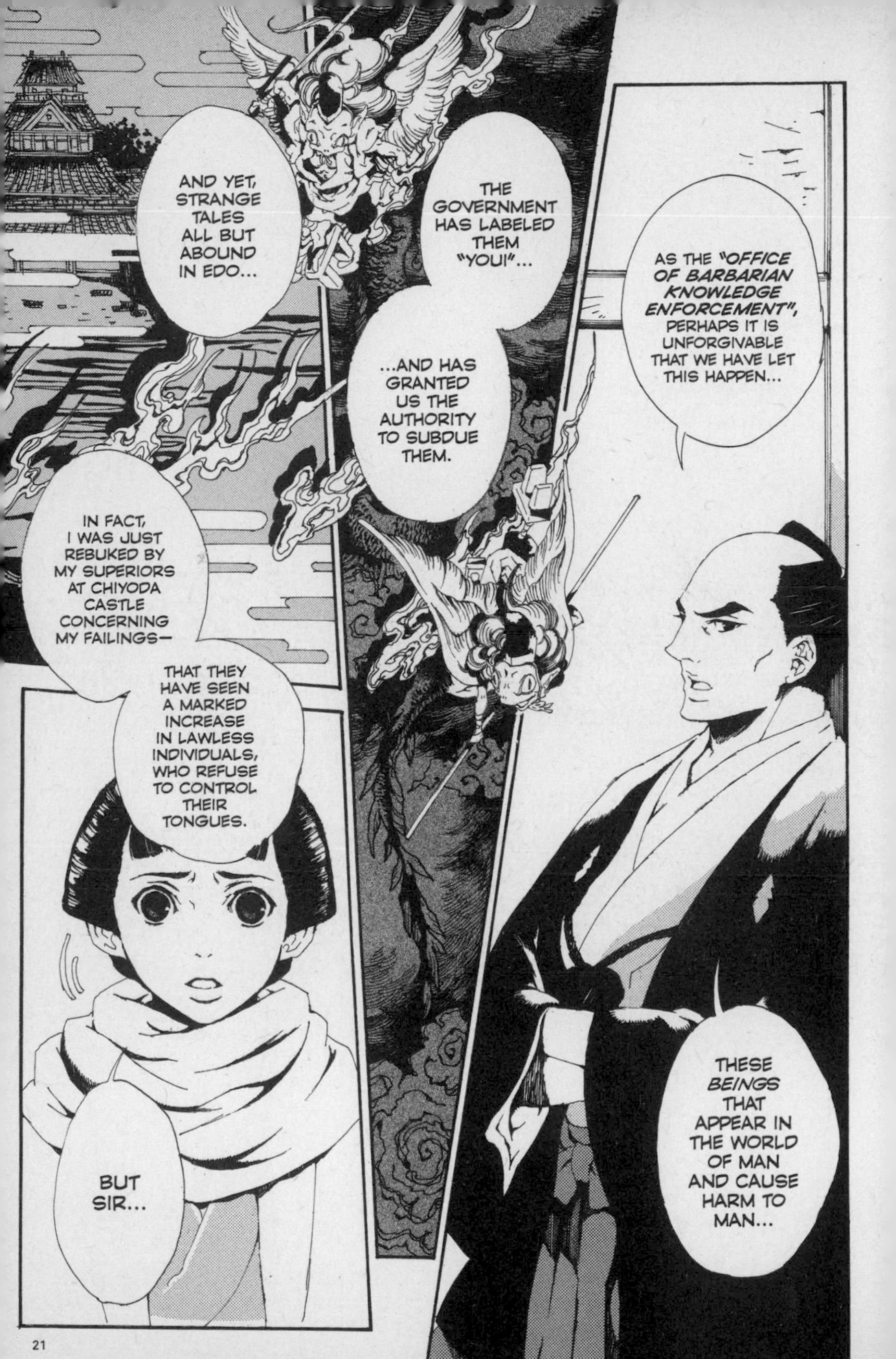
AS THE "OFFICE OF BARBARIAN KNOWLEDGE ENFORCEMENT", PERHAPS IT IS UNFORGIVABLE THAT WE HAVE LET THIS HAPPEN...
THESE *BEINGS* THAT APPEAR IN THE WORLD OF MAN AND CAUSE HARM TO MAN...
THE GOVERNMENT HAS LABELED THEM "YOUI"...
...AND HAS GRANTED US THE AUTHORITY TO SUBDUE THEM.
AND YET, STRANGE TALES ALL BUT ABOUND IN EDO...
IN FACT, I WAS JUST REBUKED BY MY SUPERIORS AT CHIYODA CASTLE CONCERNING MY FAILINGS—
THAT THEY HAVE SEEN A MARKED INCREASE IN LAWLESS INDIVIDUALS, WHO REFUSE TO CONTROL THEIR TONGUES.
BUT SIR...

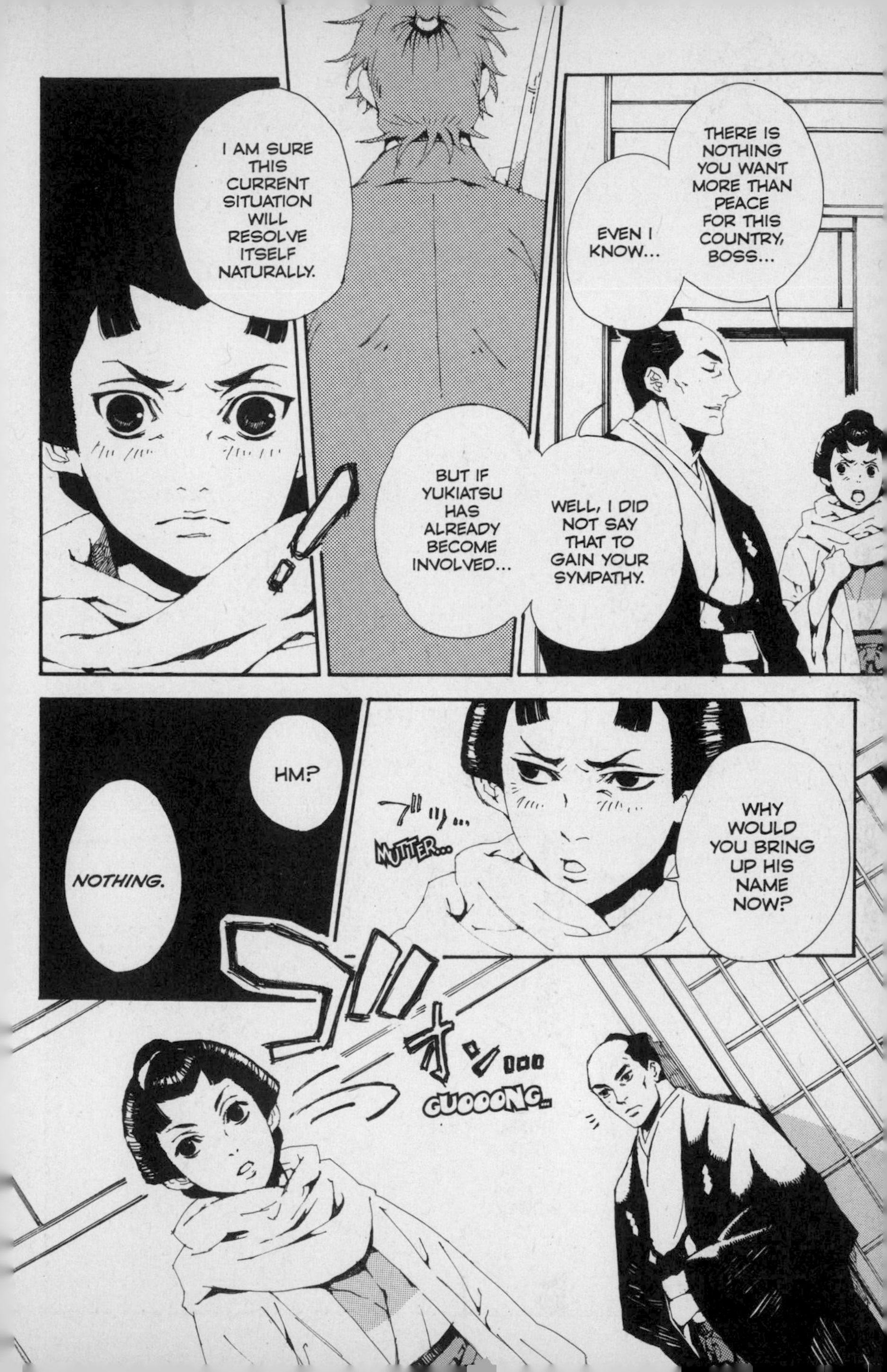
THERE IS NOTHING YOU WANT MORE THAN PEACE FOR THIS COUNTRY, BOSS...
EVEN I KNOW...
WELL, I DID NOT SAY THAT TO GAIN YOUR SYMPATHY.
BUT IF YUKIATSU HAS ALREADY BECOME INVOLVED...
I AM SURE THIS CURRENT SITUATION WILL RESOLVE ITSELF NATURALLY.
WHY WOULD YOU BRING UP HIS NAME NOW?
MUTTER...
HM?
NOTHING.
GUOOONG...

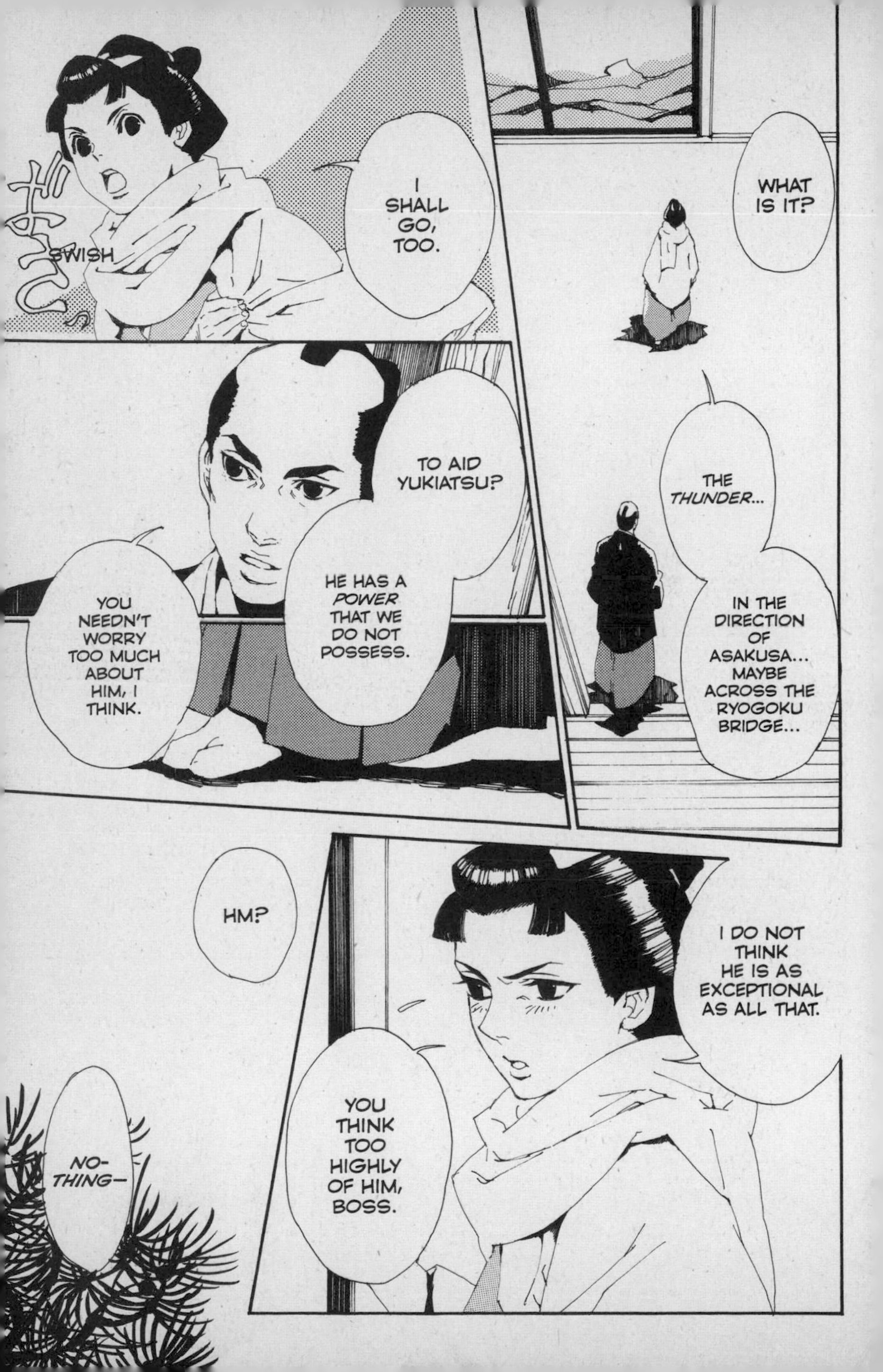
WHAT IS IT?
THE *THUNDER*...
IN THE DIRECTION OF ASAKUSA... MAYBE ACROSS THE RYOGOKU BRIDGE...
I SHALL GO, TOO.
SWISH
TO AID YUKIATSU?
HE HAS A *POWER* THAT WE DO NOT POSSESS.
YOU NEEDN'T WORRY TOO MUCH ABOUT HIM, I THINK.
I DO NOT THINK HE IS AS EXCEPTIONAL AS ALL THAT.
HM?
YOU THINK TOO HIGHLY OF HIM, BOSS.
NO-THING—

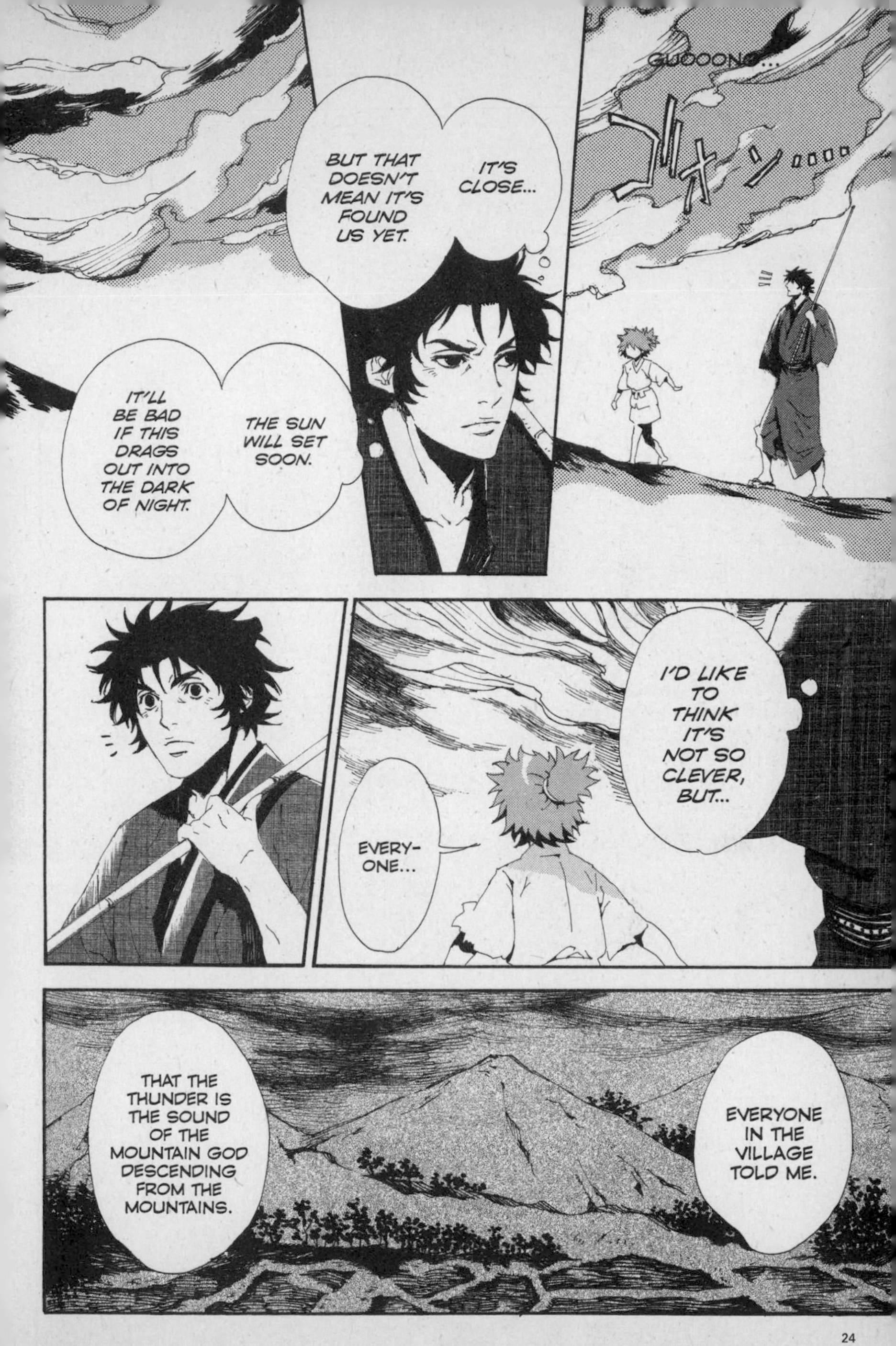
GUOOONG...
IT'S CLOSE...
BUT THAT DOESN'T MEAN IT'S FOUND US YET.
THE SUN WILL SET SOON.
IT'LL BE BAD IF THIS DRAGS OUT INTO THE DARK OF NIGHT.
I'D LIKE TO THINK IT'S NOT SO CLEVER, BUT...
EVERY-ONE...
EVERYONE IN THE VILLAGE TOLD ME.
THAT THE THUNDER IS THE SOUND OF THE MOUNTAIN GOD DESCENDING FROM THE MOUNTAINS.

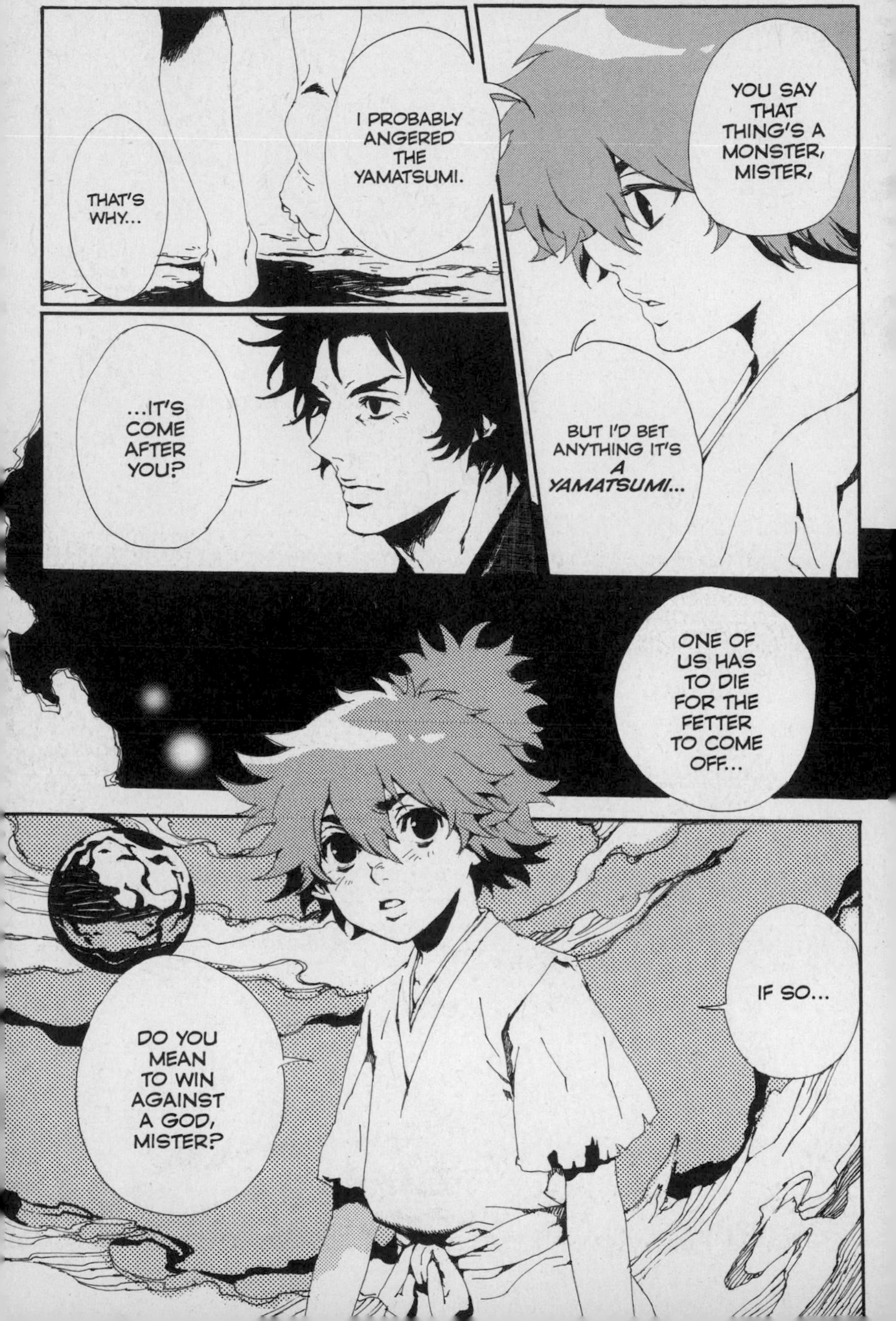
YOU SAY THAT THING'S A MONSTER, MISTER,
BUT I'D BET ANYTHING IT'S A *YAMATSUMI*...
I PROBABLY ANGERED THE YAMATSUMI.
THAT'S WHY...
...IT'S COME AFTER YOU?
ONE OF US HAS TO DIE FOR THE FETTER TO COME OFF...
IF SO...
DO YOU MEAN TO WIN AGAINST A GOD, MISTER?

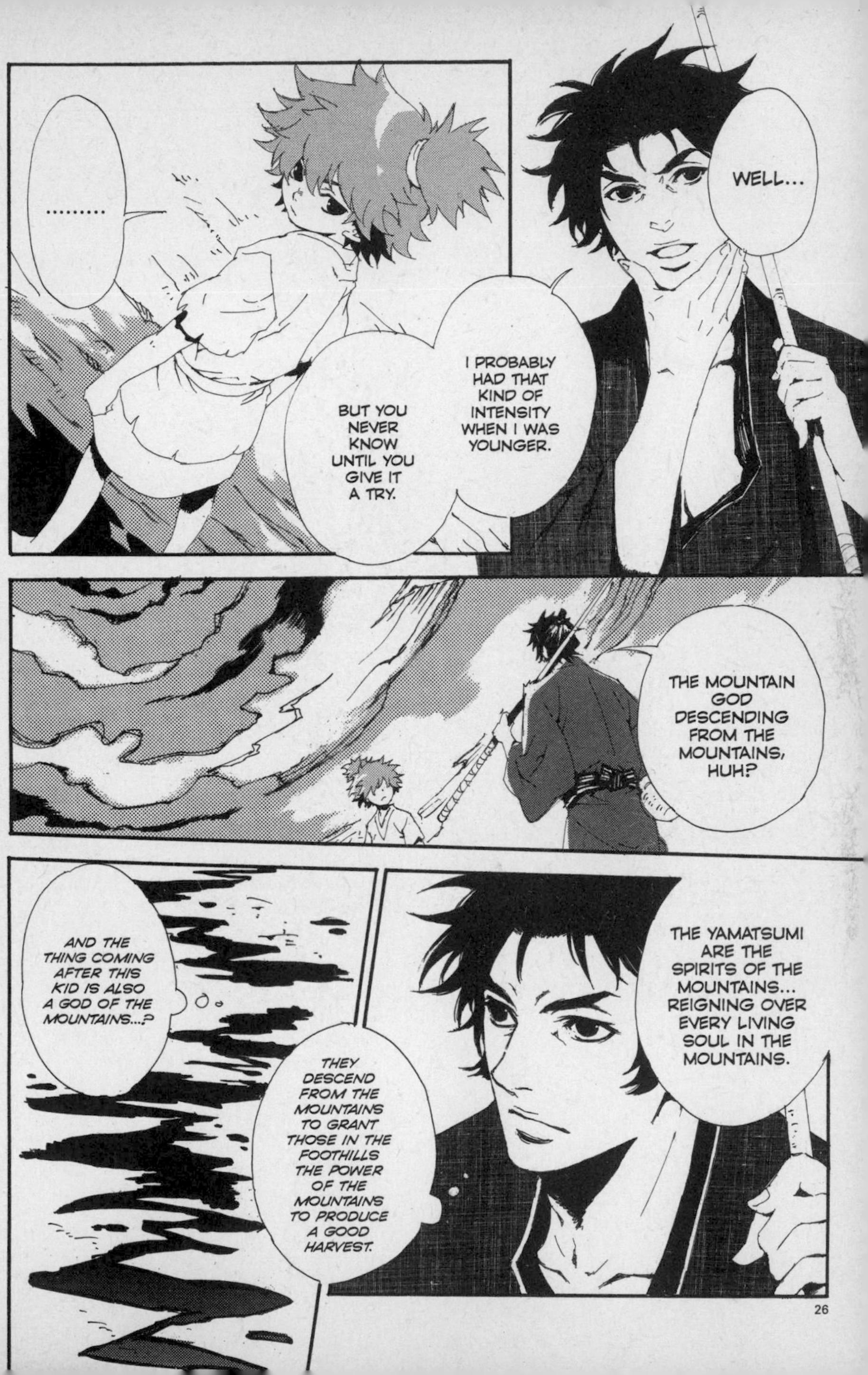

WELL...
I PROBABLY HAD THAT KIND OF INTENSITY WHEN I WAS YOUNGER.
BUT YOU NEVER KNOW UNTIL YOU GIVE IT A TRY.
....
THE MOUNTAIN GOD DESCENDING FROM THE MOUNTAINS, HUH?
THE YAMATSUMI ARE THE SPIRITS OF THE MOUNTAINS... REIGNING OVER EVERY LIVING SOUL IN THE MOUNTAINS.
THEY DESCEND FROM THE MOUNTAINS TO GRANT THOSE IN THE FOOTHILLS THE POWER OF THE MOUNTAINS TO PRODUCE A GOOD HARVEST.
AND THE THING COMING AFTER THIS KID IS ALSO A GOD OF THE MOUNTAINS...?

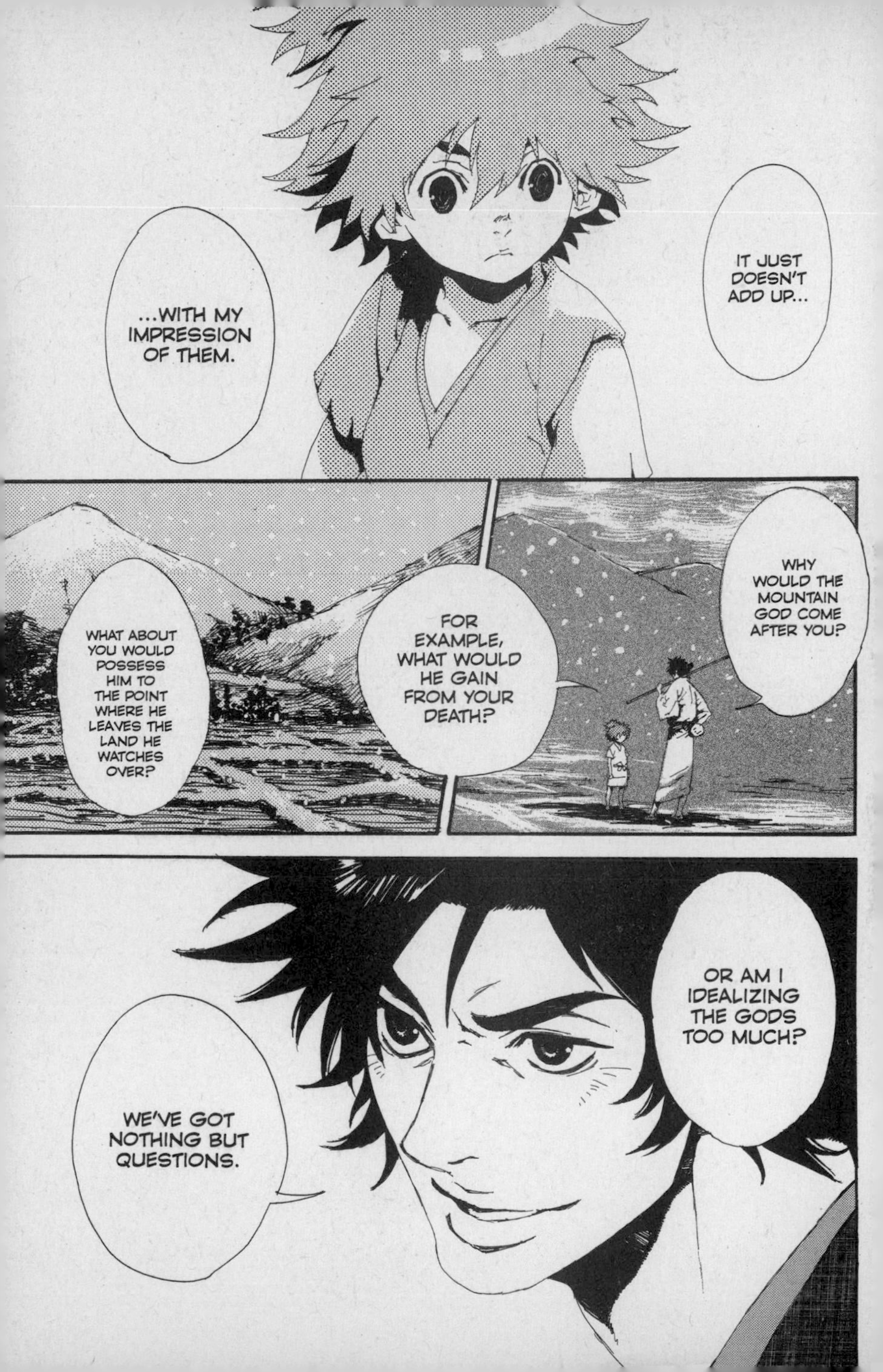
IT JUST DOESN'T ADD UP...
...WITH MY IMPRESSION OF THEM.
WHY WOULD THE MOUNTAIN GOD COME AFTER YOU?
FOR EXAMPLE, WHAT WOULD HE GAIN FROM YOUR DEATH?
WHAT ABOUT YOU WOULD POSSESS HIM TO THE POINT WHERE HE LEAVES THE LAND HE WATCHES OVER?
OR AM I IDEALIZING THE GODS TOO MUCH?
WE'VE GOT NOTHING BUT QUESTIONS.

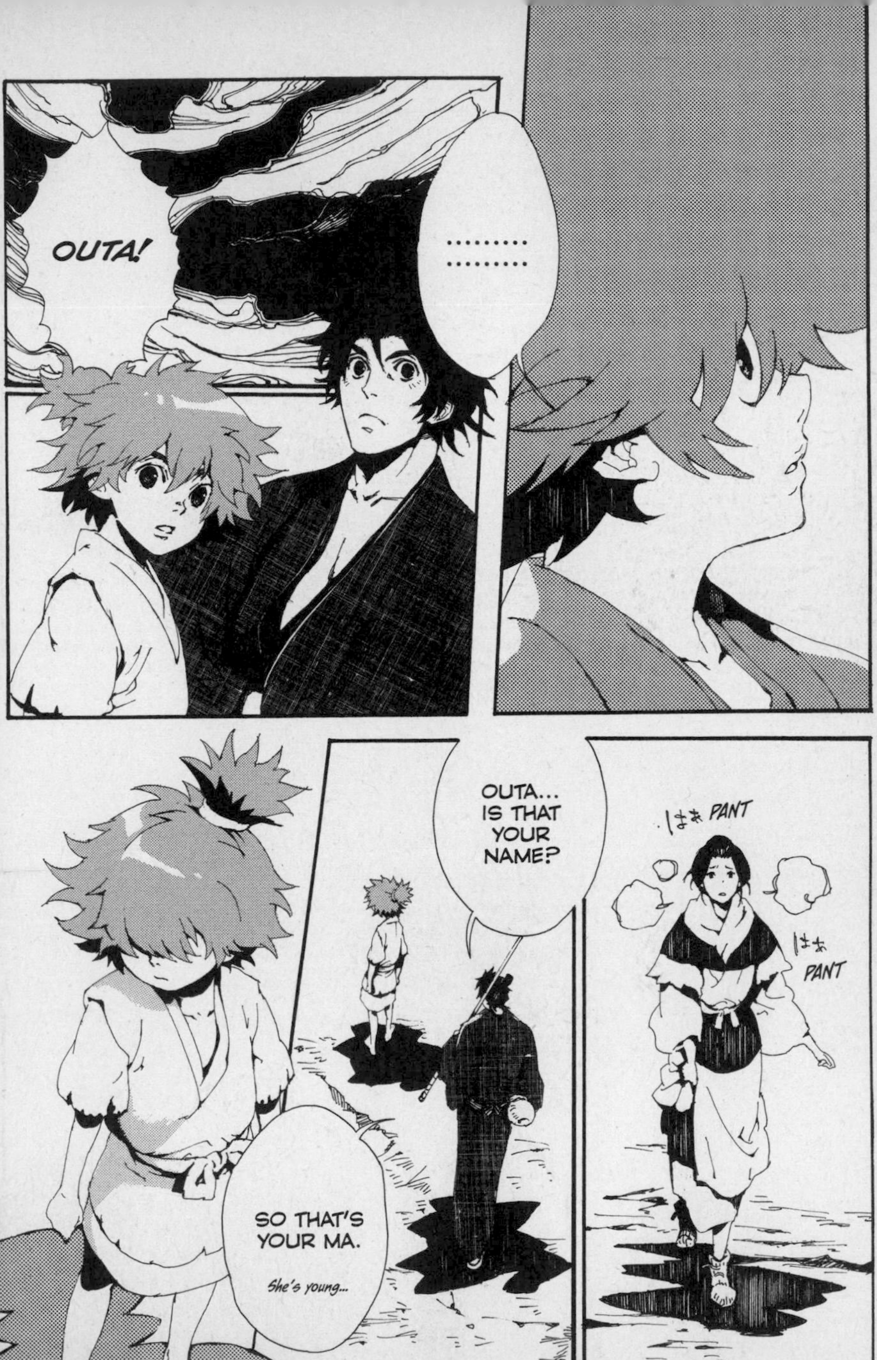
....
....
OUTA!
はぁ PANT
はぁ PANT
OUTA... IS THAT YOUR NAME?
SO THAT'S YOUR MA.
She's young...

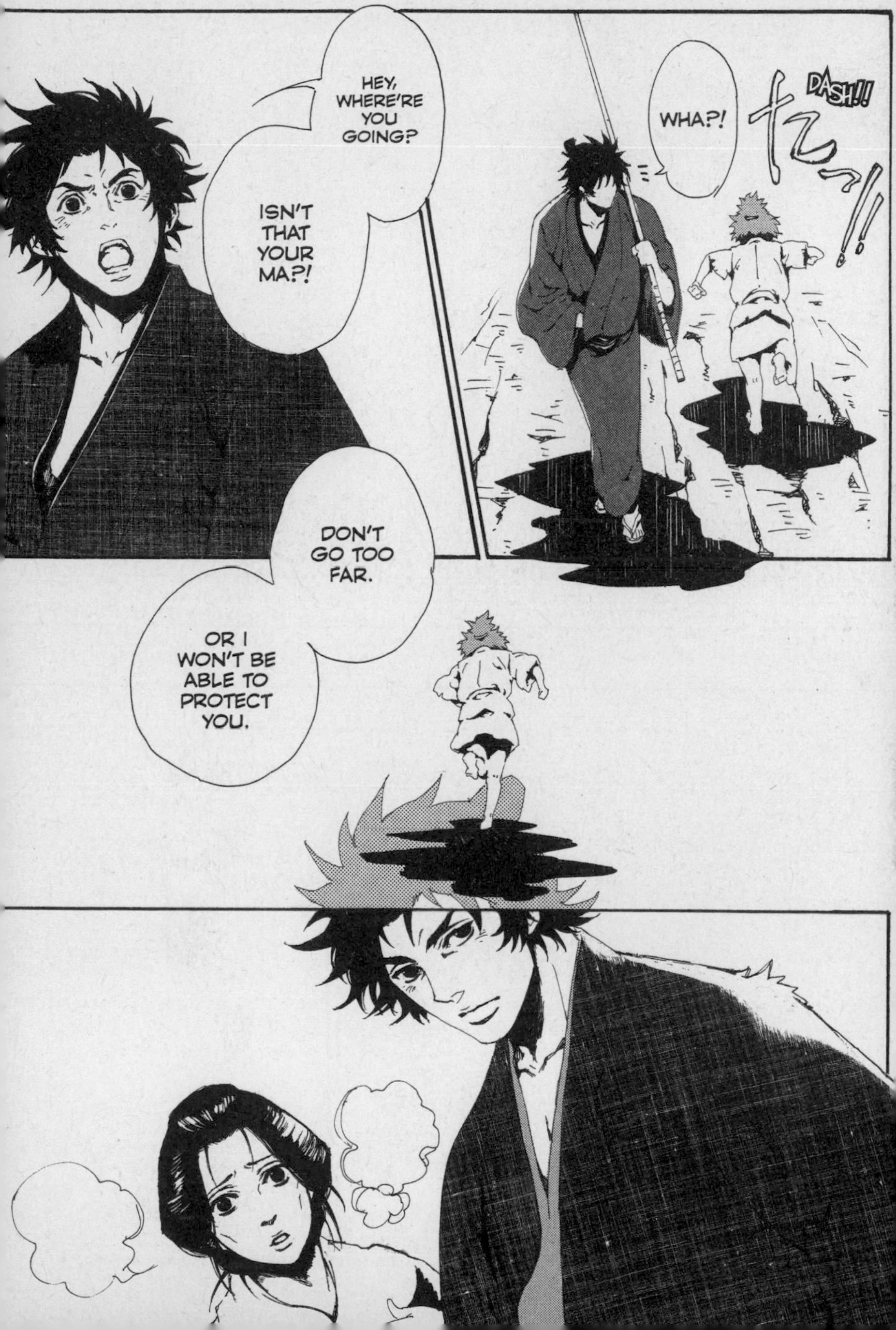
WHA?!
DASH!!
HEY, WHERE'RE YOU GOING?
ISN'T THAT YOUR MA?!
DON'T GO TOO FAR.
OR I WON'T BE ABLE TO PROTECT YOU.

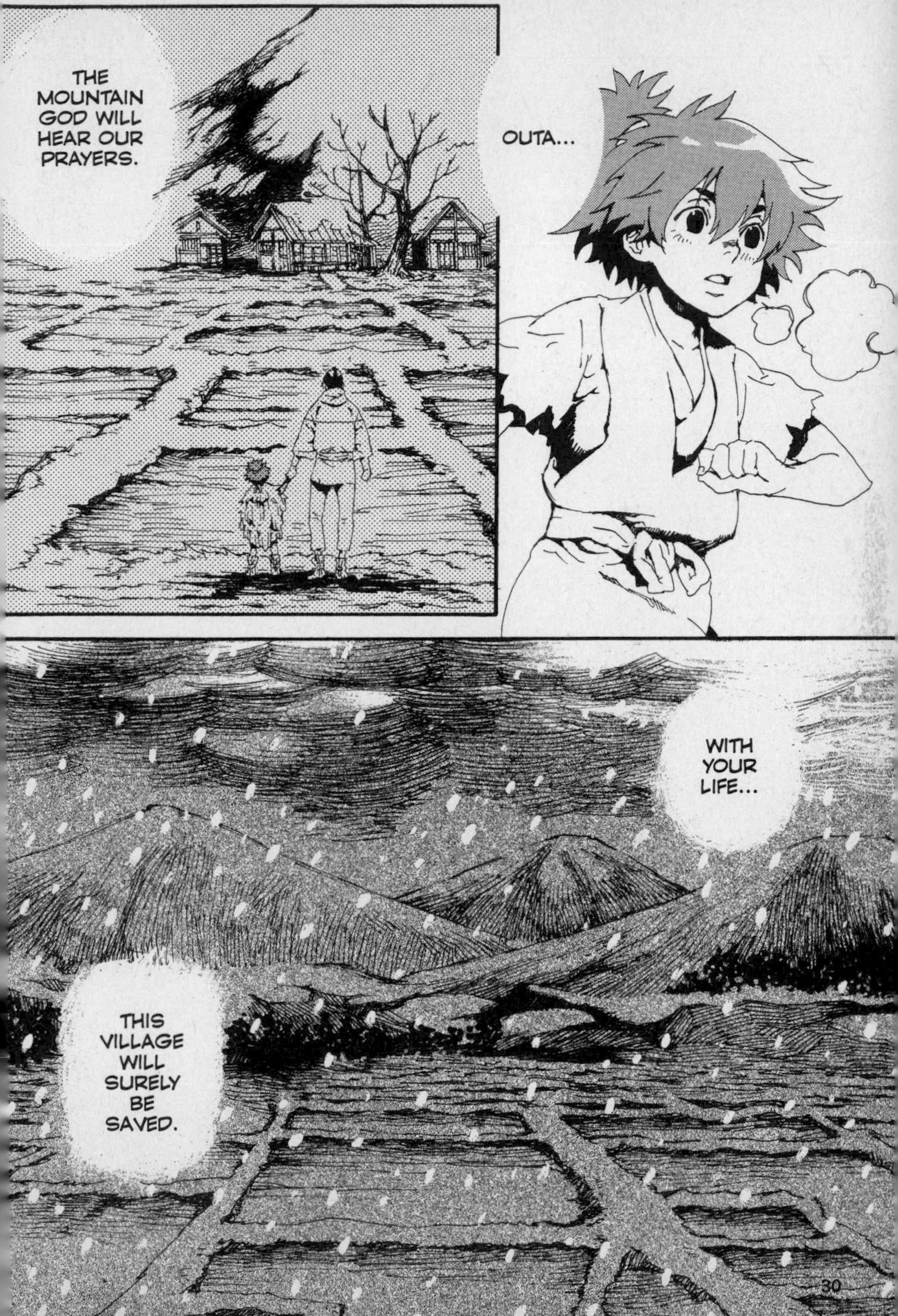
OUTA...
THE MOUNTAIN GOD WILL HEAR OUR PRAYERS.
WITH YOUR LIFE...
THIS VILLAGE WILL SURELY BE SAVED.

#2 MOUNTAIN GOD - II

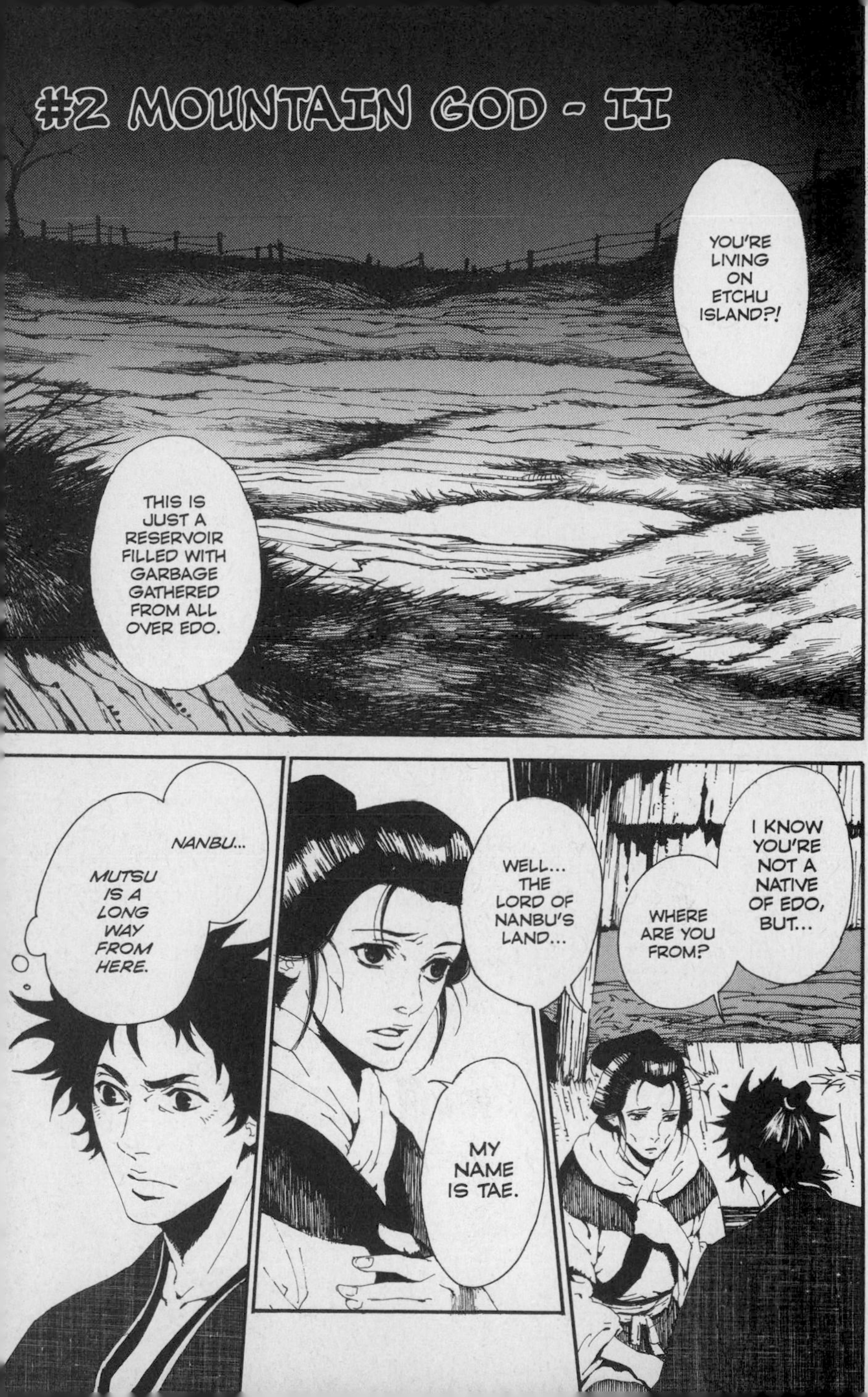
YOU'RE LIVING ON ETCHU ISLAND?!
THIS IS JUST A RESERVOIR FILLED WITH GARBAGE GATHERED FROM ALL OVER EDO.
I KNOW YOU'RE NOT A NATIVE OF EDO, BUT...
WHERE ARE YOU FROM?
WELL... THE LORD OF NANBU'S LAND...
MY NAME IS TAE.
NANBU...
MUTSU IS A LONG WAY FROM HERE.

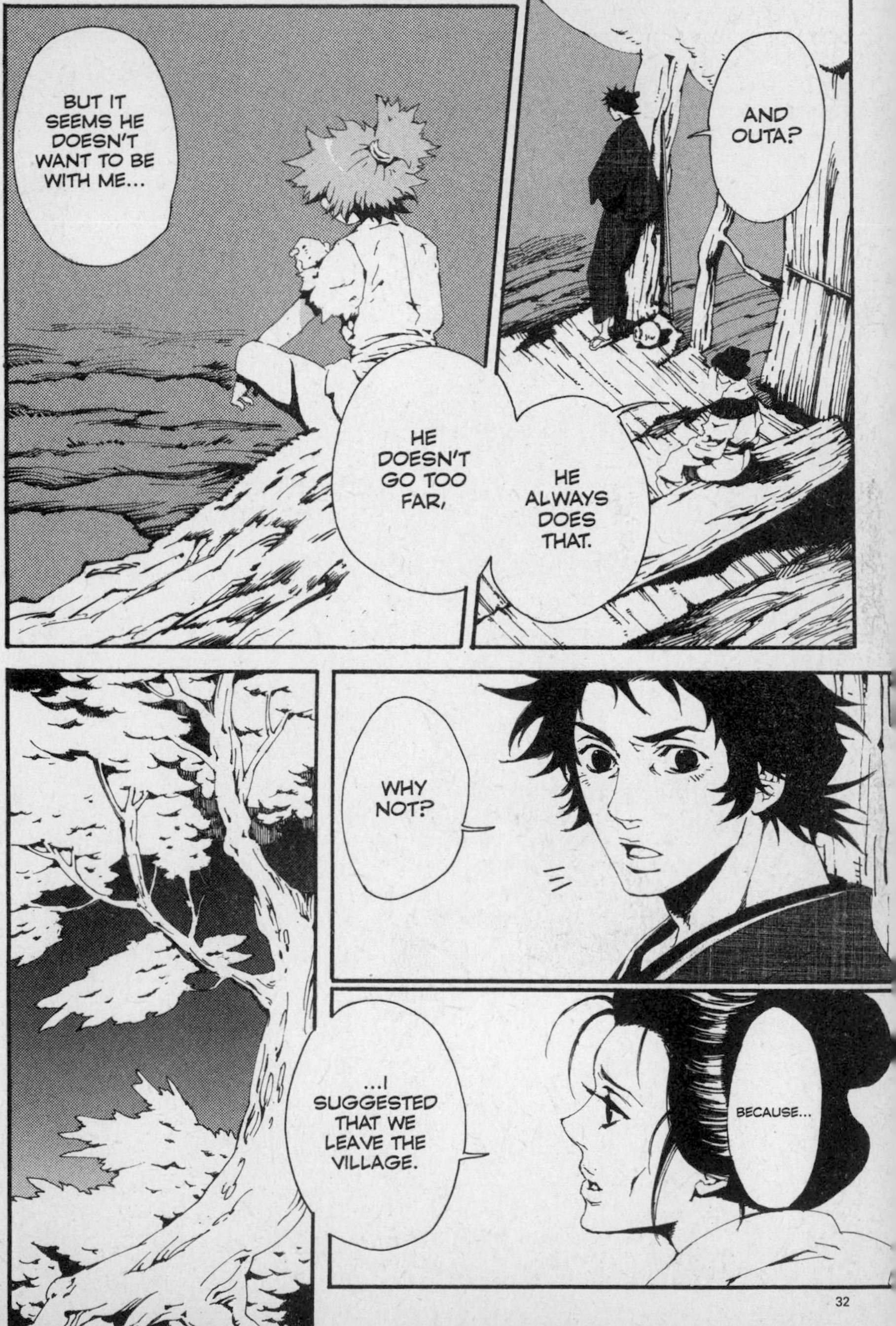
AND OUTA?
HE ALWAYS DOES THAT.
HE DOESN'T GO TOO FAR,
BUT IT SEEMS HE DOESN'T WANT TO BE WITH ME...
WHY NOT?
BECAUSE...
...I SUGGESTED THAT WE LEAVE THE VILLAGE.

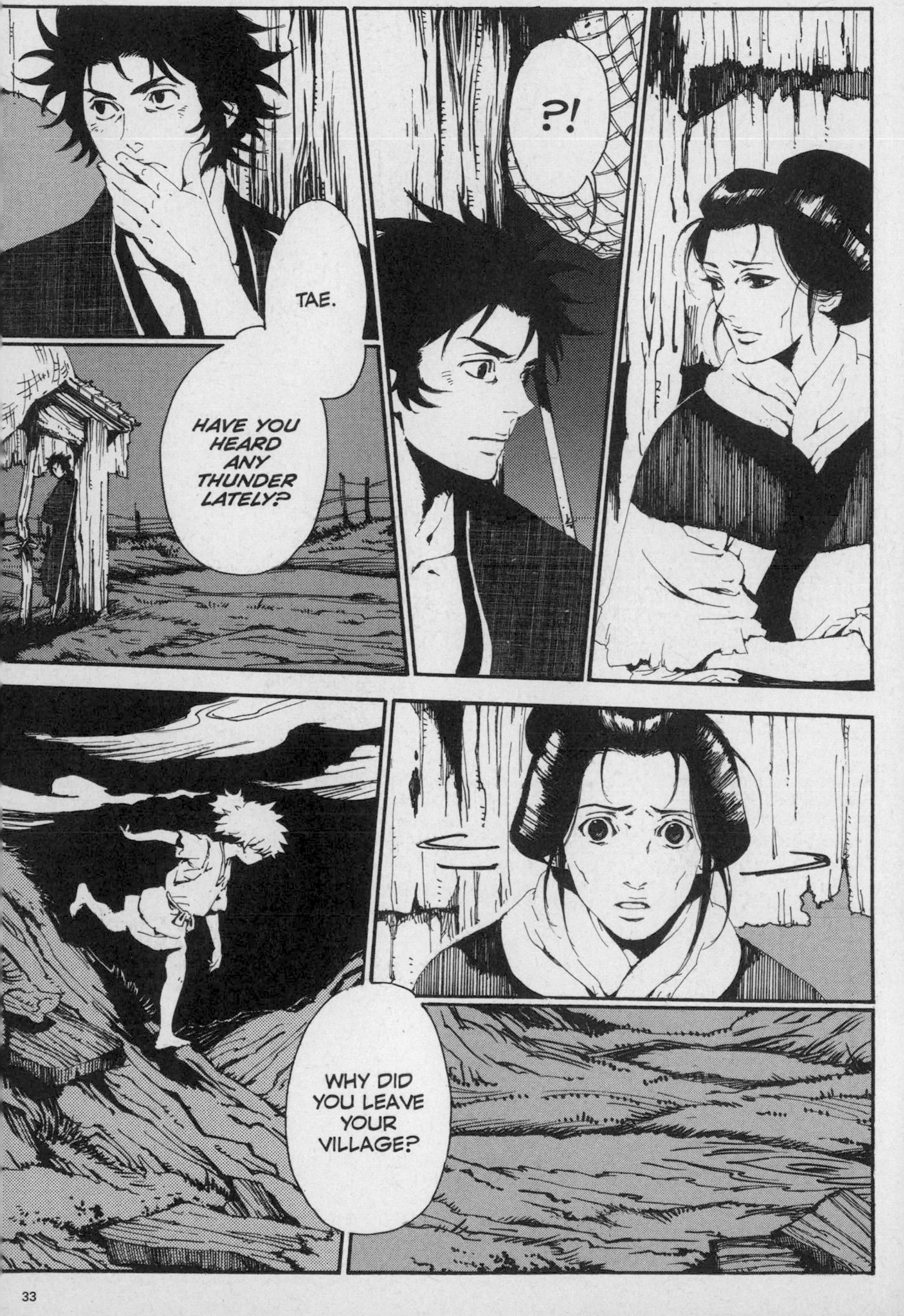
?!
TAE.
HAVE YOU HEARD ANY THUNDER LATELY?
WHY DID YOU LEAVE YOUR VILLAGE?

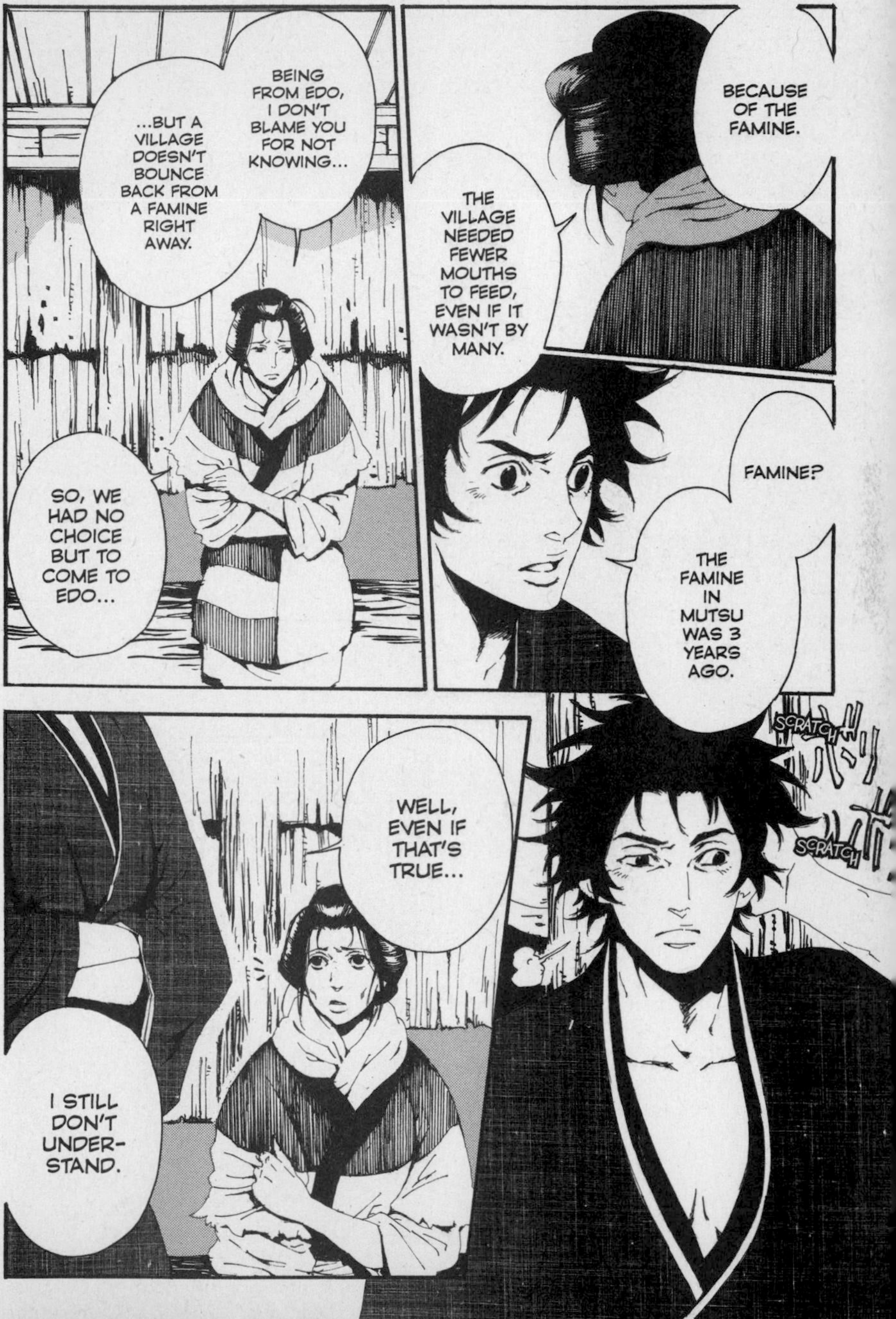
BECAUSE OF THE FAMINE.
THE VILLAGE NEEDED FEWER MOUTHS TO FEED, EVEN IF IT WASN'T BY MANY.
FAMINE?
THE FAMINE IN MUTSU WAS 3 YEARS AGO.
BEING FROM EDO, I DON'T BLAME YOU FOR NOT KNOWING...
...BUT A VILLAGE DOESN'T BOUNCE BACK FROM A FAMINE RIGHT AWAY.
SO, WE HAD NO CHOICE BUT TO COME TO EDO...
SCRATCH
SCRATCH
WELL, EVEN IF THAT'S TRUE...
I STILL DON'T UNDER-STAND.

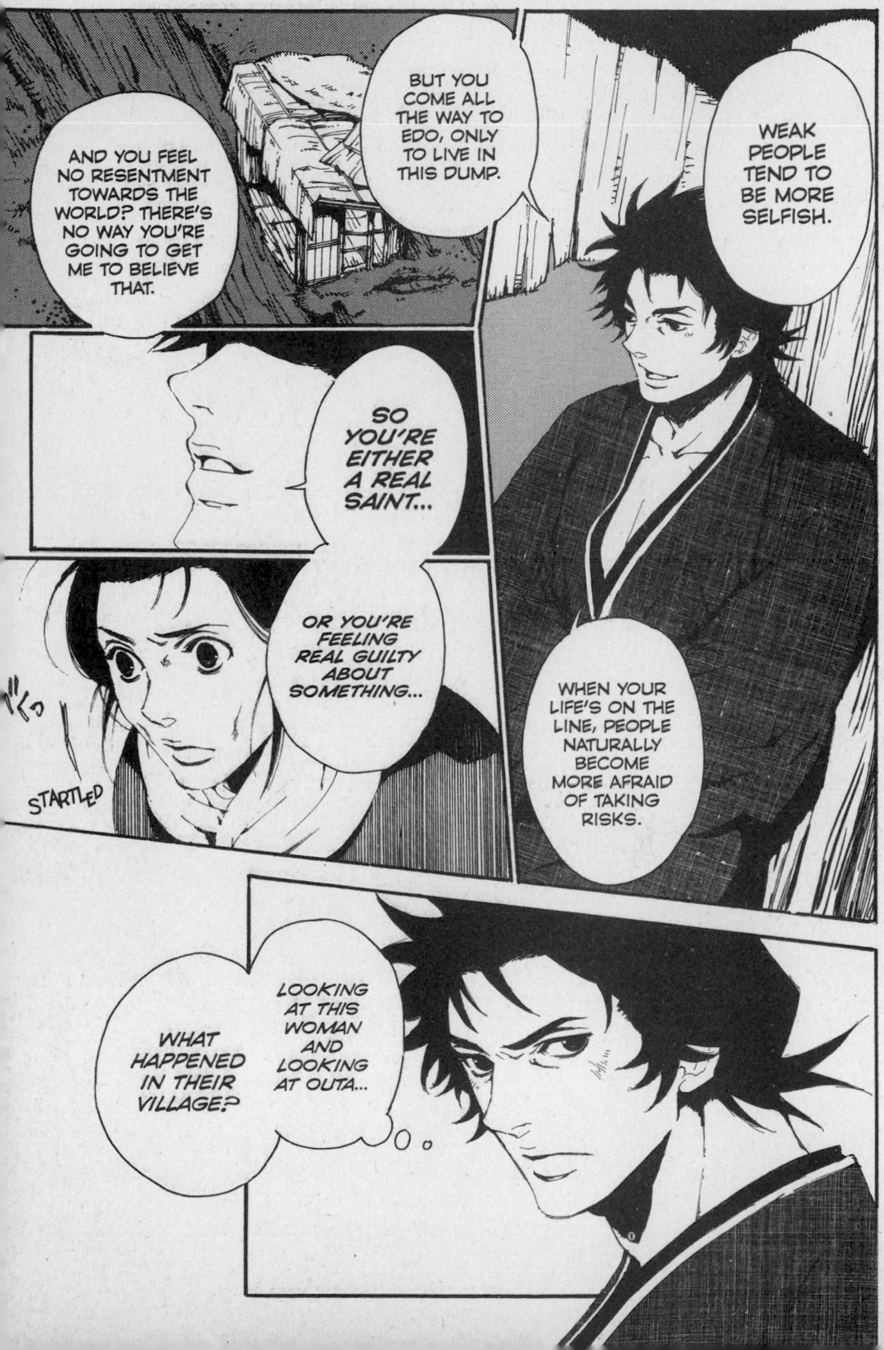
WEAK PEOPLE TEND TO BE MORE SELFISH.
WHEN YOUR LIFE'S ON THE LINE, PEOPLE NATURALLY BECOME MORE AFRAID OF TAKING RISKS.
BUT YOU COME ALL THE WAY TO EDO, ONLY TO LIVE IN THIS DUMP.
AND YOU FEEL NO RESENTMENT TOWARDS THE WORLD? THERE'S NO WAY YOU'RE GOING TO GET ME TO BELIEVE THAT.
SO YOU'RE EITHER A REAL SAINT...
OR YOU'RE FEELING REAL GUILTY ABOUT SOMETHING...
STARTLED
LOOKING AT THIS WOMAN AND LOOKING AT OUTA...
WHAT HAPPENED IN THEIR VILLAGE?

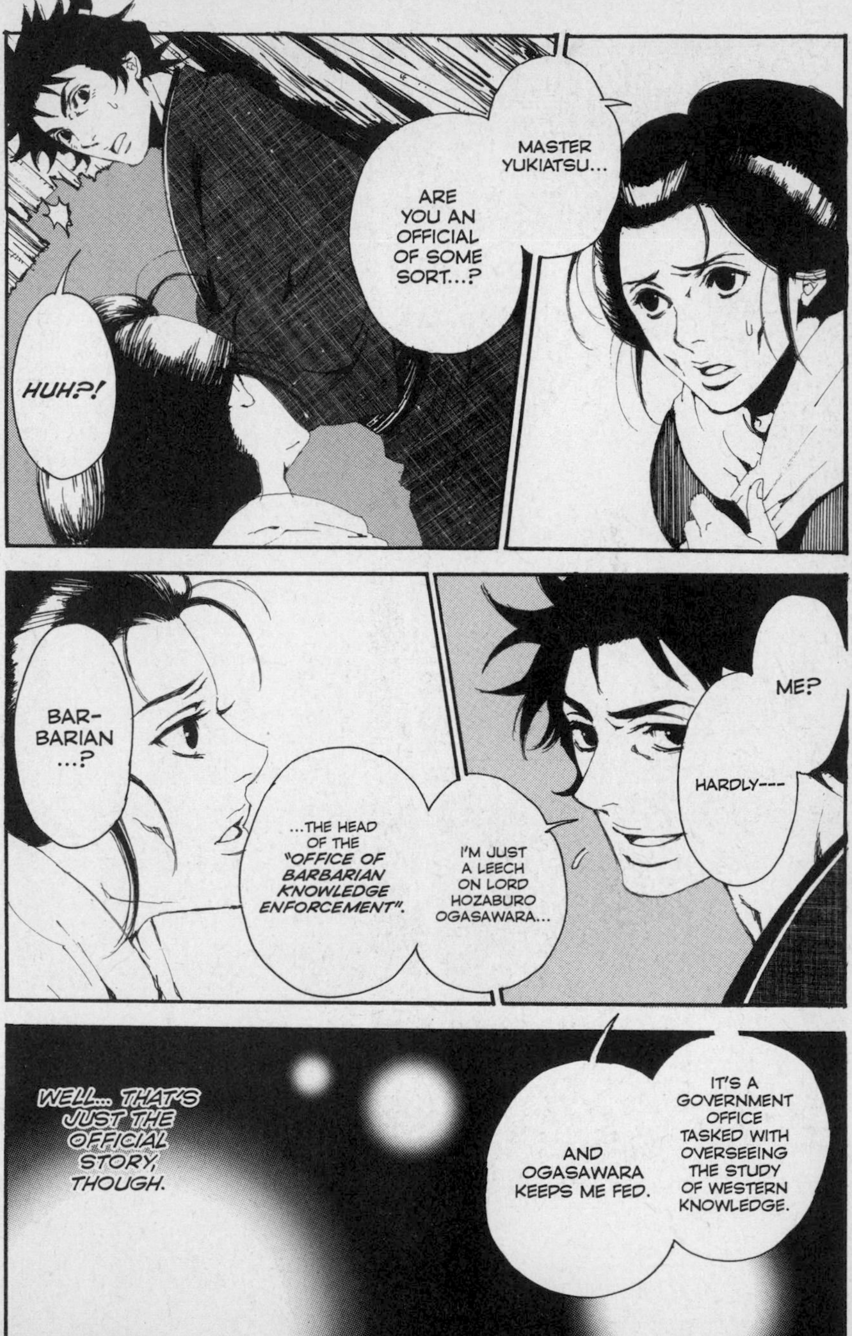
MASTER YUKIATSU...
ARE YOU AN OFFICIAL OF SOME SORT...?
HUH?!
ME?
HARDLY---
I'M JUST A LEECH ON LORD HOZABURO OGASAWARA...
...THE HEAD OF THE "OFFICE OF BARBARIAN KNOWLEDGE ENFORCEMENT".
BAR-BARIAN...?
IT'S A GOVERNMENT OFFICE TASKED WITH OVERSEEING THE STUDY OF WESTERN KNOWLEDGE.
AND OGASAWARA KEEPS ME FED.
WELL... THAT'S JUST THE OFFICIAL STORY, THOUGH.

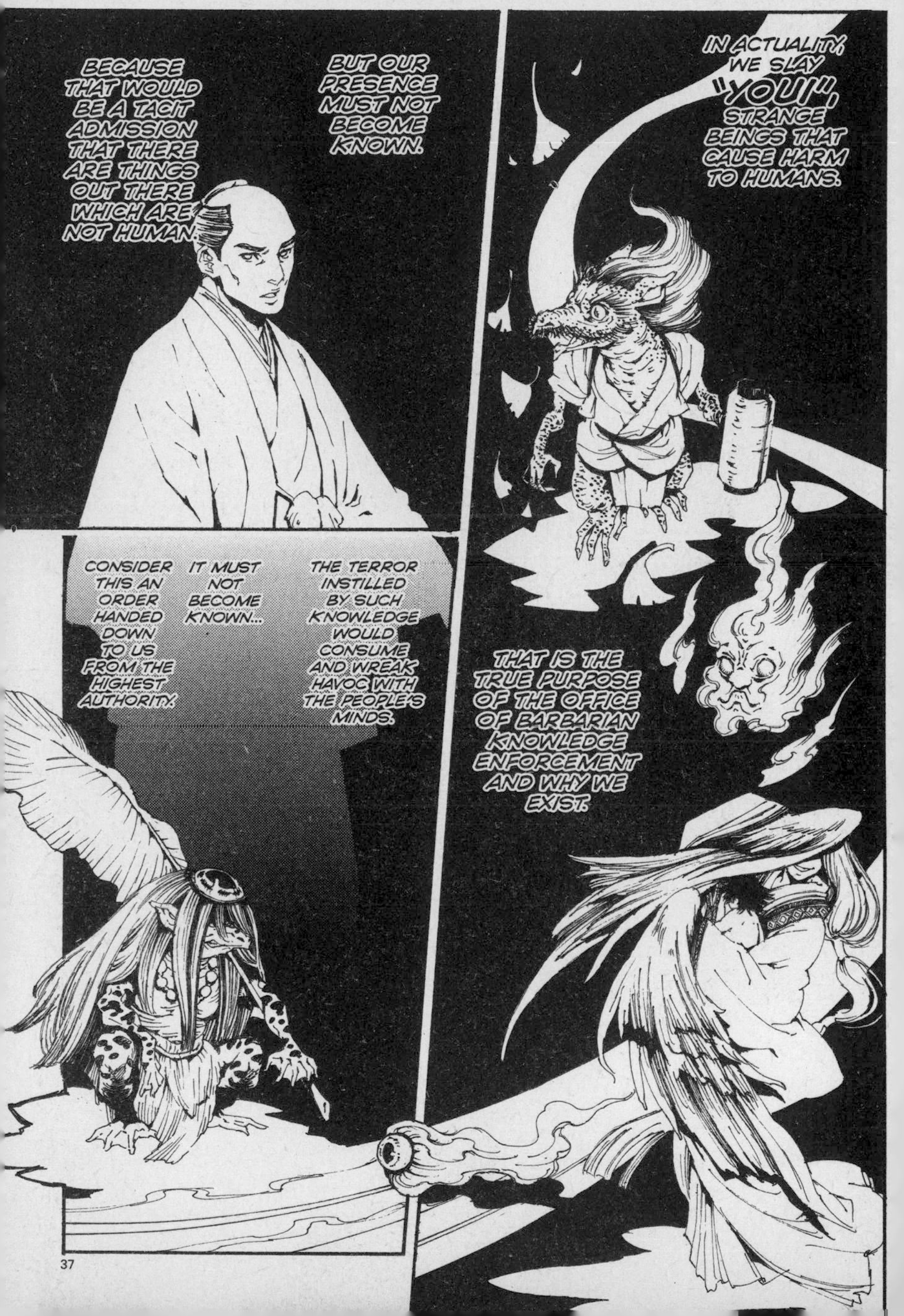
IN ACTUALITY, WE SLAY "YOUI", STRANGE BEINGS THAT CAUSE HARM TO HUMANS.
THAT IS THE TRUE PURPOSE OF THE OFFICE OF BARBARIAN KNOWLEDGE ENFORCEMENT AND WHY WE EXIST.
BUT OUR PRESENCE MUST NOT BECOME KNOWN.
BECAUSE THAT WOULD BE A TACIT ADMISSION THAT THERE ARE THINGS OUT THERE WHICH ARE NOT HUMAN.
THE TERROR INSTILLED BY SUCH KNOWLEDGE WOULD CONSUME AND WREAK HAVOC WITH THE PEOPLE'S MINDS.
IT MUST NOT BECOME KNOWN...
CONSIDER THIS AN ORDER HANDED DOWN TO US FROM THE HIGHEST AUTHORITY.

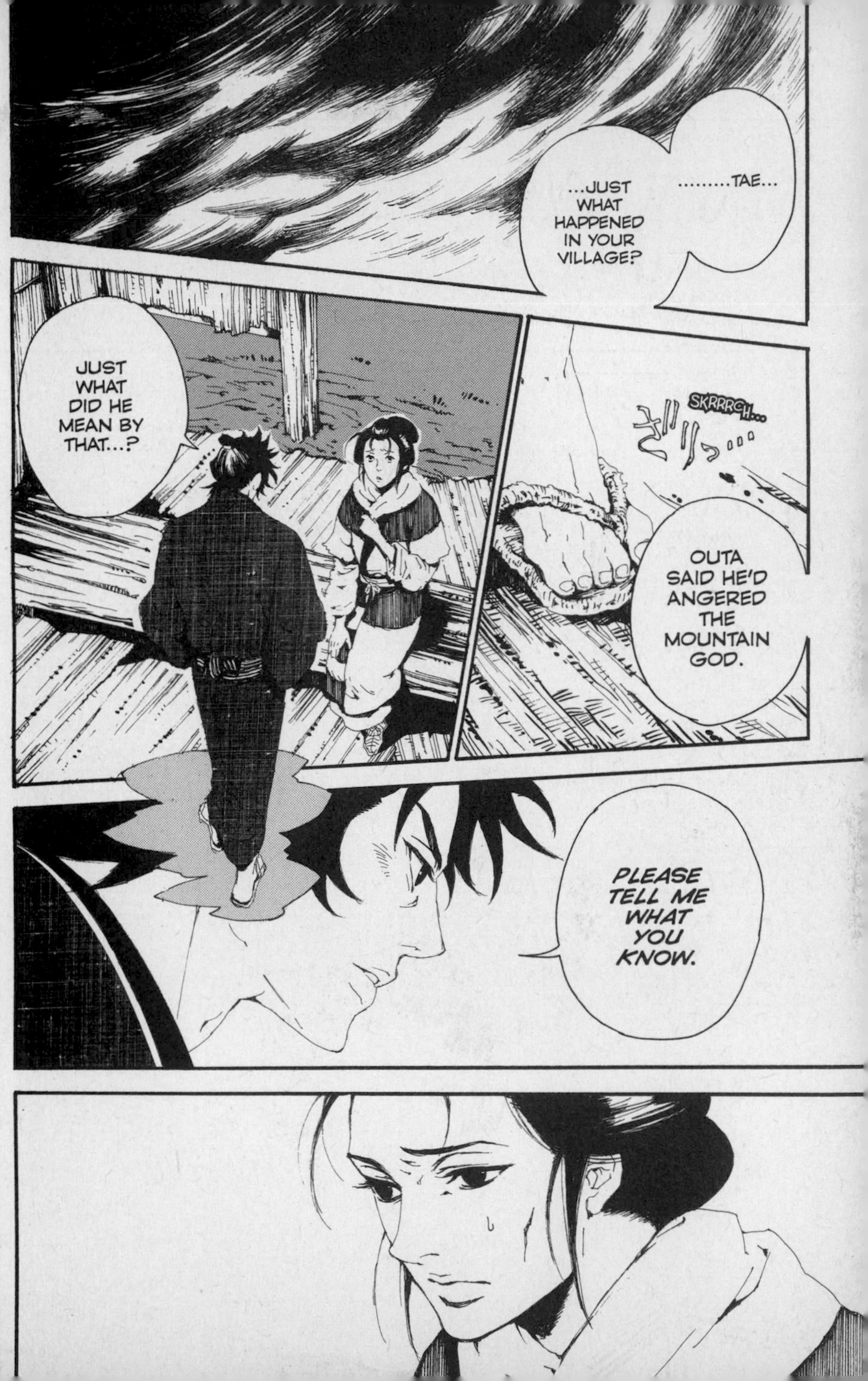
.........TAE...
...JUST WHAT HAPPENED IN YOUR VILLAGE?
SKRRRCH...
ざりっ...
OUTA SAID HE'D ANGERED THE MOUNTAIN GOD.
JUST WHAT DID HE MEAN BY THAT...?
PLEASE TELL ME WHAT YOU KNOW.

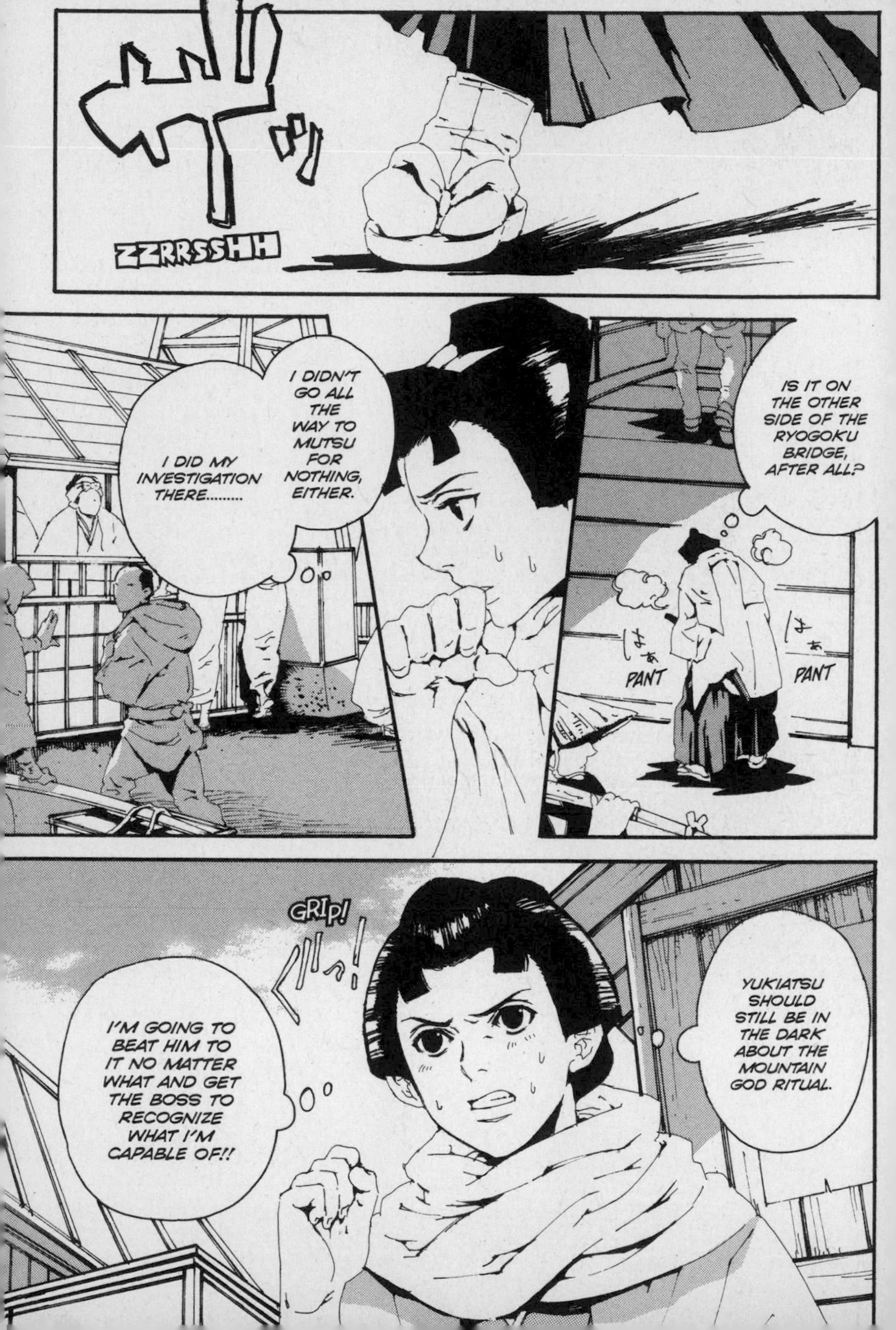
ZZRRSSHH
IS IT ON THE OTHER SIDE OF THE RYOGOKU BRIDGE, AFTER ALL?
はぁ PANT
はぁ PANT
I DIDN'T GO ALL THE WAY TO MUTSU FOR NOTHING, EITHER.
I DID MY INVESTIGATION THERE.........
GRIP!
YUKIATSU SHOULD STILL BE IN THE DARK ABOUT THE MOUNTAIN GOD RITUAL.
I'M GOING TO BEAT HIM TO IT NO MATTER WHAT AND GET THE BOSS TO RECOGNIZE WHAT I'M CAPABLE OF!!

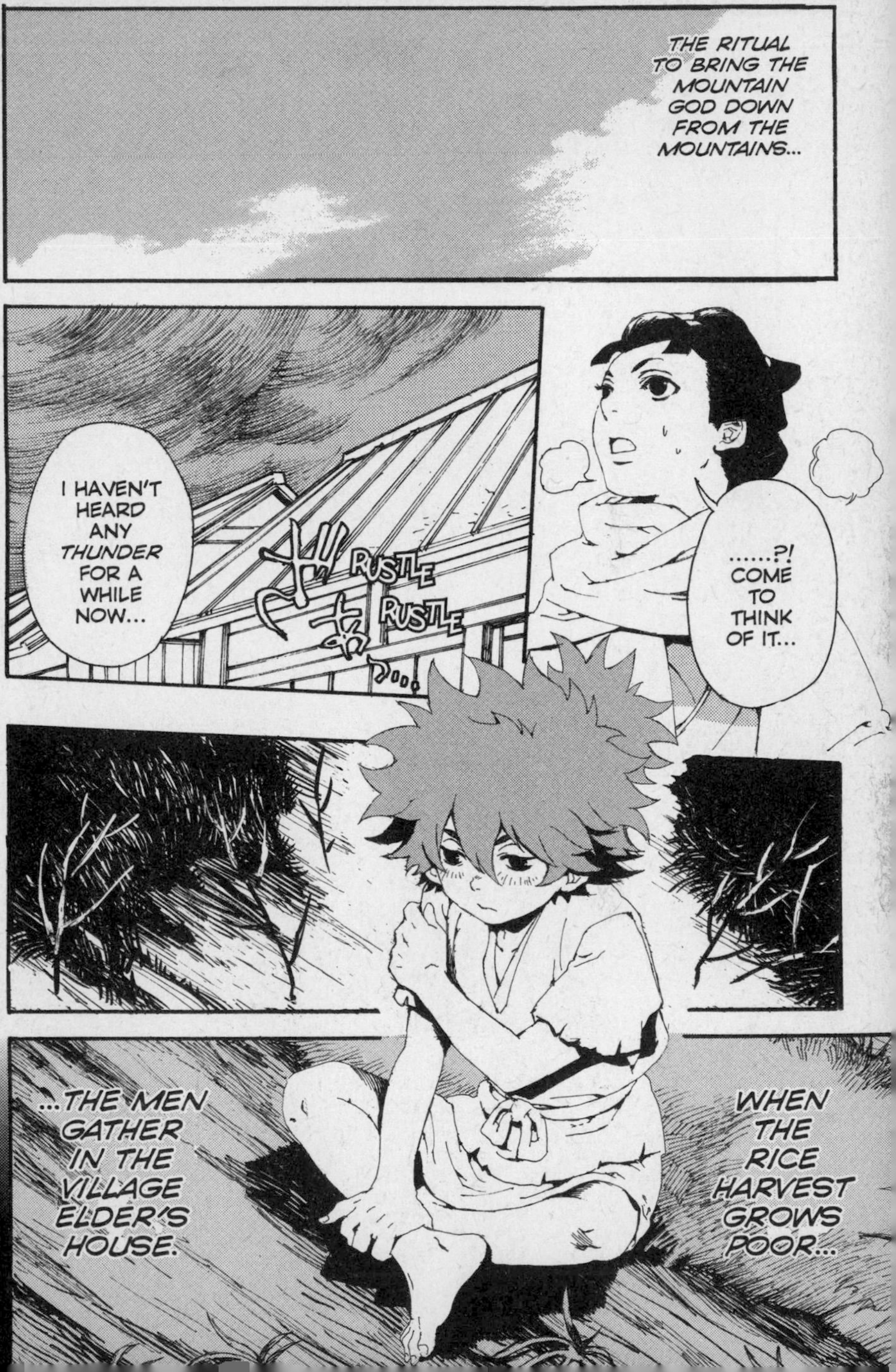
THE RITUAL TO BRING THE MOUNTAIN GOD DOWN FROM THE MOUNTAINS...
......?! COME TO THINK OF IT...
I HAVEN'T HEARD ANY *THUNDER* FOR A WHILE NOW...
RUSTLE
RUSTLE
WHEN THE RICE HARVEST GROWS POOR...
...THE MEN GATHER IN THE VILLAGE ELDER'S HOUSE.

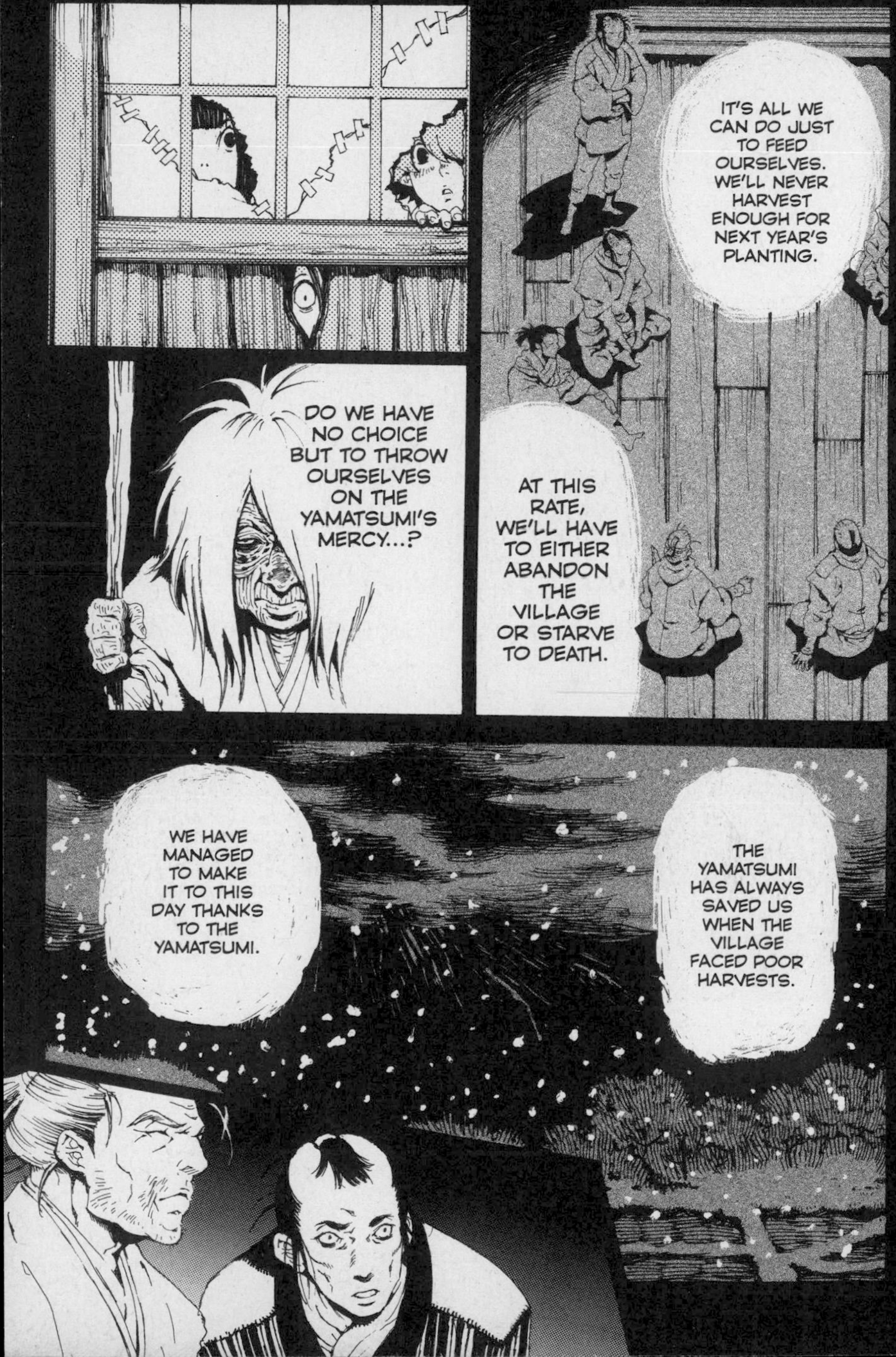
IT'S ALL WE CAN DO JUST TO FEED OURSELVES. WE'LL NEVER HARVEST ENOUGH FOR NEXT YEAR'S PLANTING.
AT THIS RATE, WE'LL HAVE TO EITHER ABANDON THE VILLAGE OR STARVE TO DEATH.
DO WE HAVE NO CHOICE BUT TO THROW OURSELVES ON THE YAMATSUMI'S MERCY...?
THE YAMATSUMI HAS ALWAYS SAVED US WHEN THE VILLAGE FACED POOR HARVESTS.
WE HAVE MANAGED TO MAKE IT TO THIS DAY THANKS TO THE YAMATSUMI.

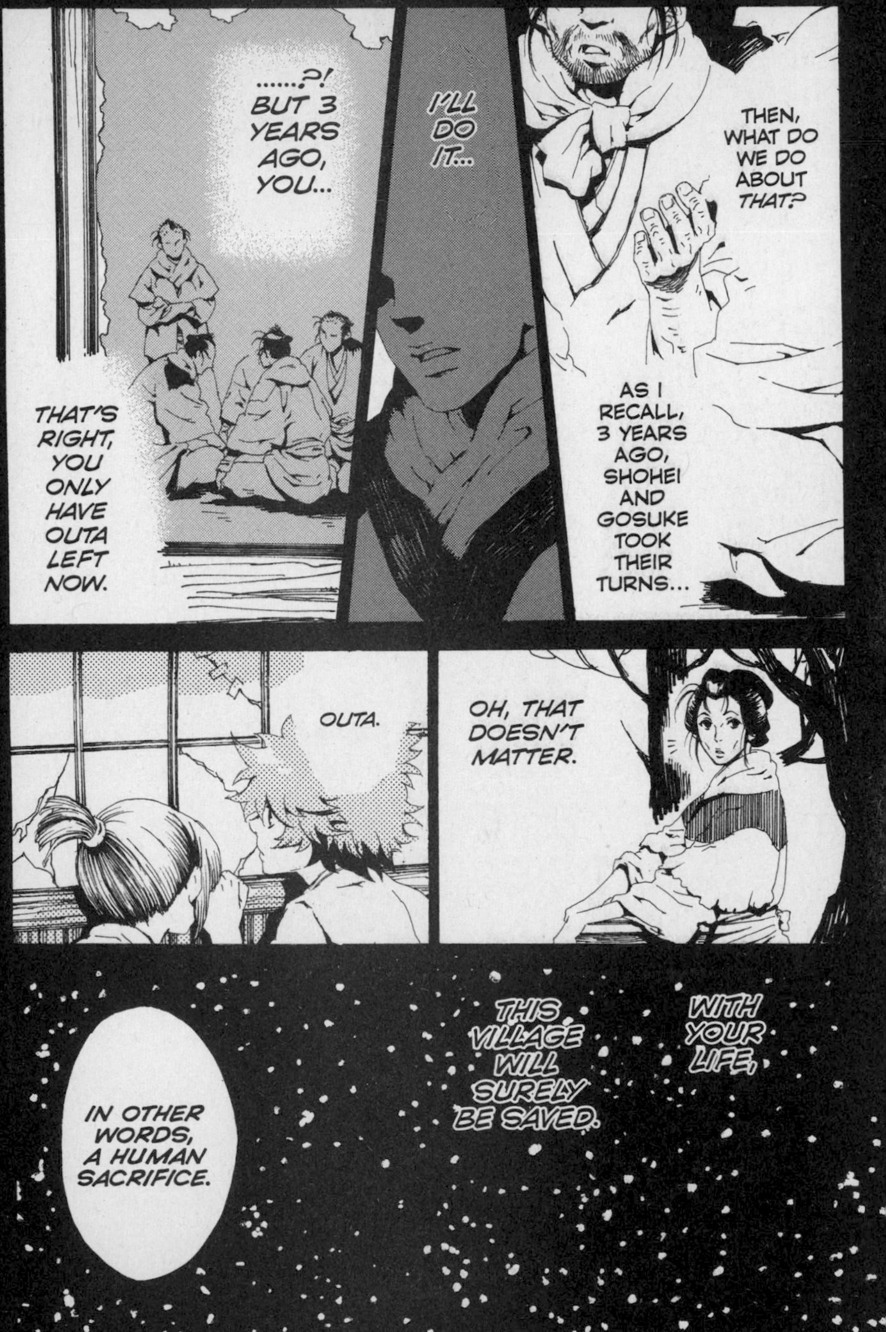
THEN, WHAT DO WE DO ABOUT THAT?
AS I RECALL, 3 YEARS AGO, SHOHEI AND GOSUKE TOOK THEIR TURNS...
I'LL DO IT...
......?! BUT 3 YEARS AGO, YOU...
THAT'S RIGHT, YOU ONLY HAVE OUTA LEFT NOW.
OH, THAT DOESN'T MATTER.
OUTA.
WITH YOUR LIFE,
THIS VILLAGE WILL SURELY BE SAVED.
IN OTHER WORDS, A HUMAN SACRIFICE.

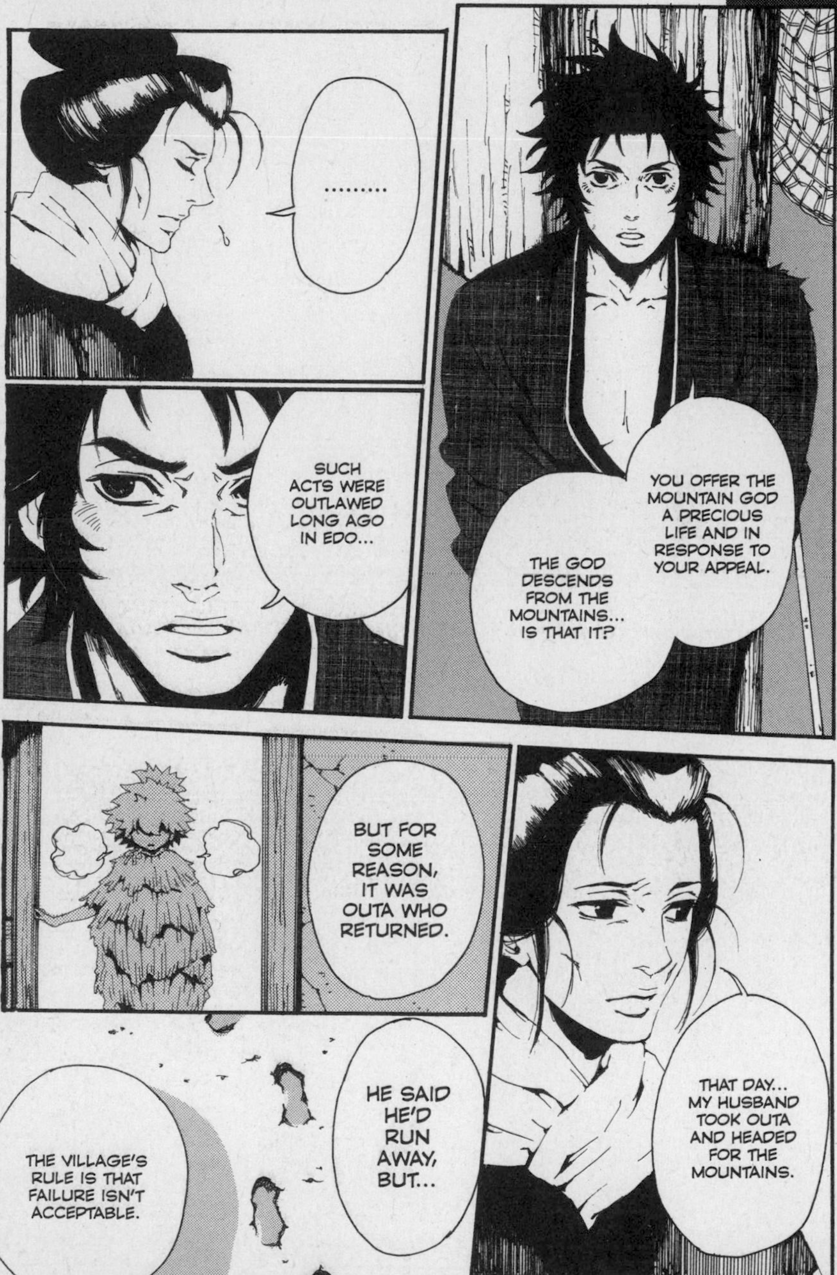
YOU OFFER THE MOUNTAIN GOD A PRECIOUS LIFE AND IN RESPONSE TO YOUR APPEAL.
THE GOD DESCENDS FROM THE MOUNTAINS... IS THAT IT?
....
SUCH ACTS WERE OUTLAWED LONG AGO IN EDO...
THAT DAY... MY HUSBAND TOOK OUTA AND HEADED FOR THE MOUNTAINS.
HE SAID HE'D RUN AWAY, BUT...
BUT FOR SOME REASON, IT WAS OUTA WHO RETURNED.
THE VILLAGE'S RULE IS THAT FAILURE ISN'T ACCEPTABLE.

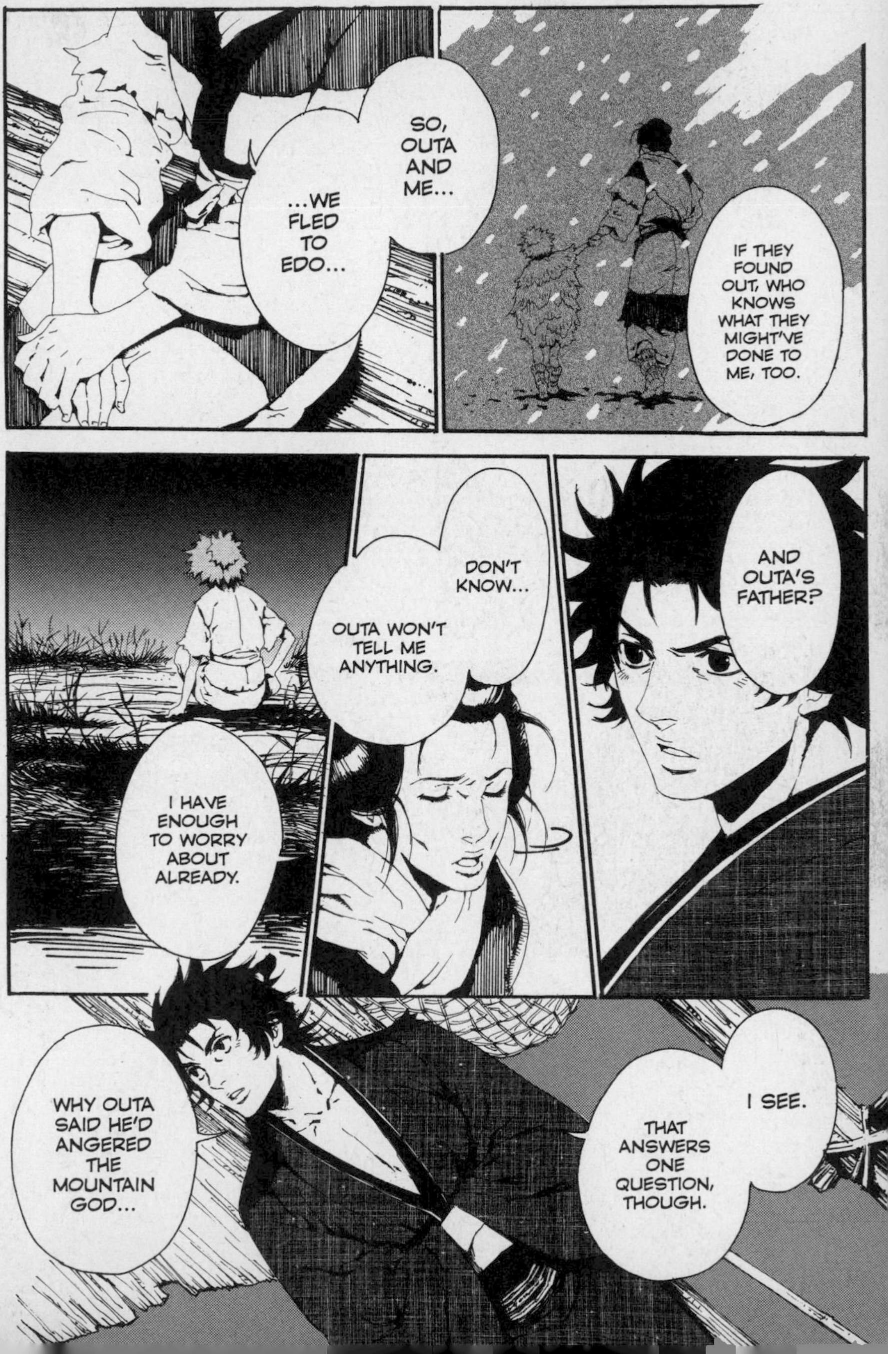
IF THEY FOUND OUT, WHO KNOWS WHAT THEY MIGHT'VE DONE TO ME, TOO.
SO, OUTA AND ME...
...WE FLED TO EDO...
AND OUTA'S FATHER?
DON'T KNOW...
OUTA WON'T TELL ME ANYTHING.
I HAVE ENOUGH TO WORRY ABOUT ALREADY.
I SEE.
THAT ANSWERS ONE QUESTION, THOUGH.
WHY OUTA SAID HE'D ANGERED THE MOUNTAIN GOD...

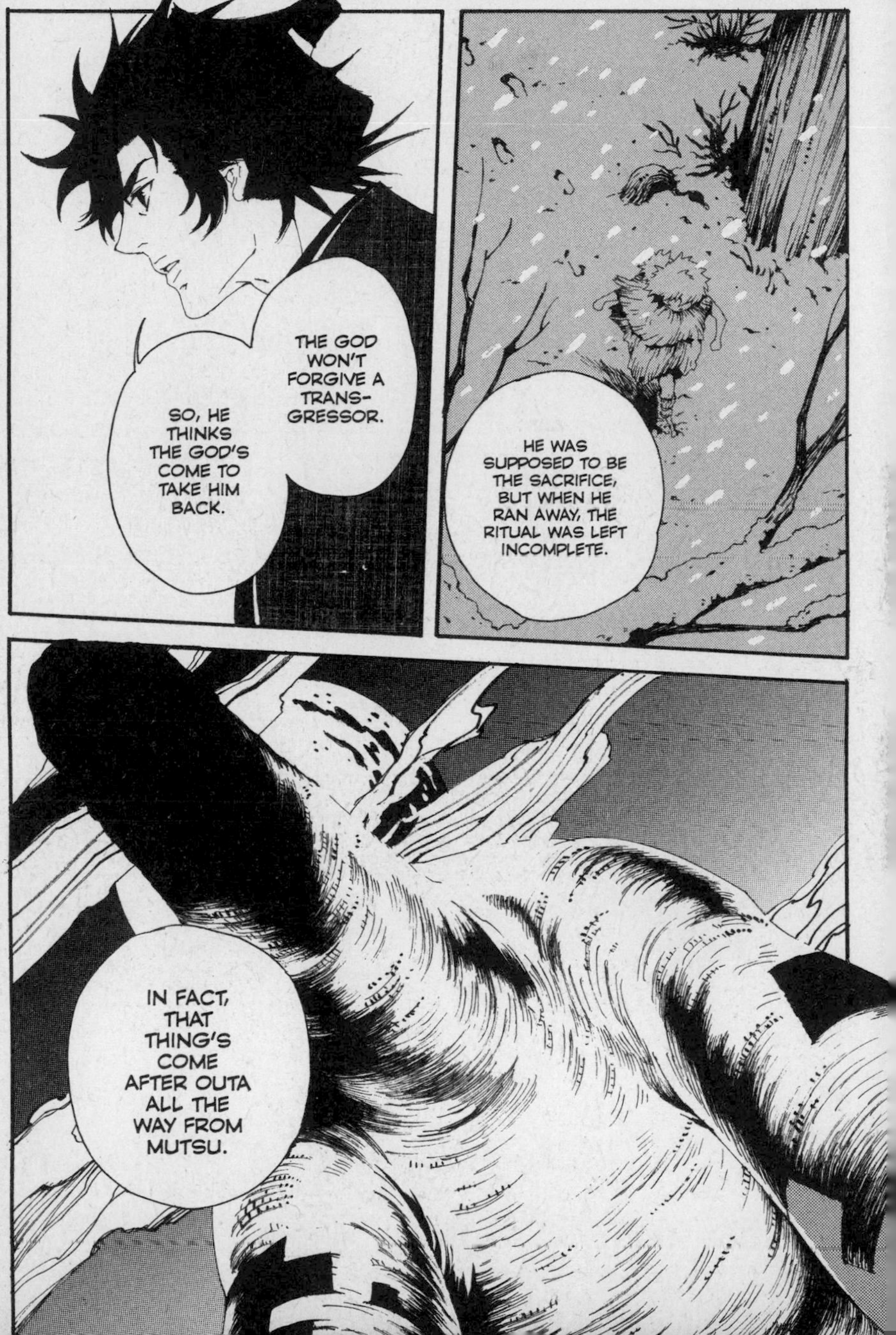
HE WAS SUPPOSED TO BE THE SACRIFICE, BUT WHEN HE RAN AWAY, THE RITUAL WAS LEFT INCOMPLETE.
THE GOD WON'T FORGIVE A TRANS-GRESSOR.
SO, HE THINKS THE GOD'S COME TO TAKE HIM BACK.
IN FACT, THAT THING'S COME AFTER OUTA ALL THE WAY FROM MUTSU.

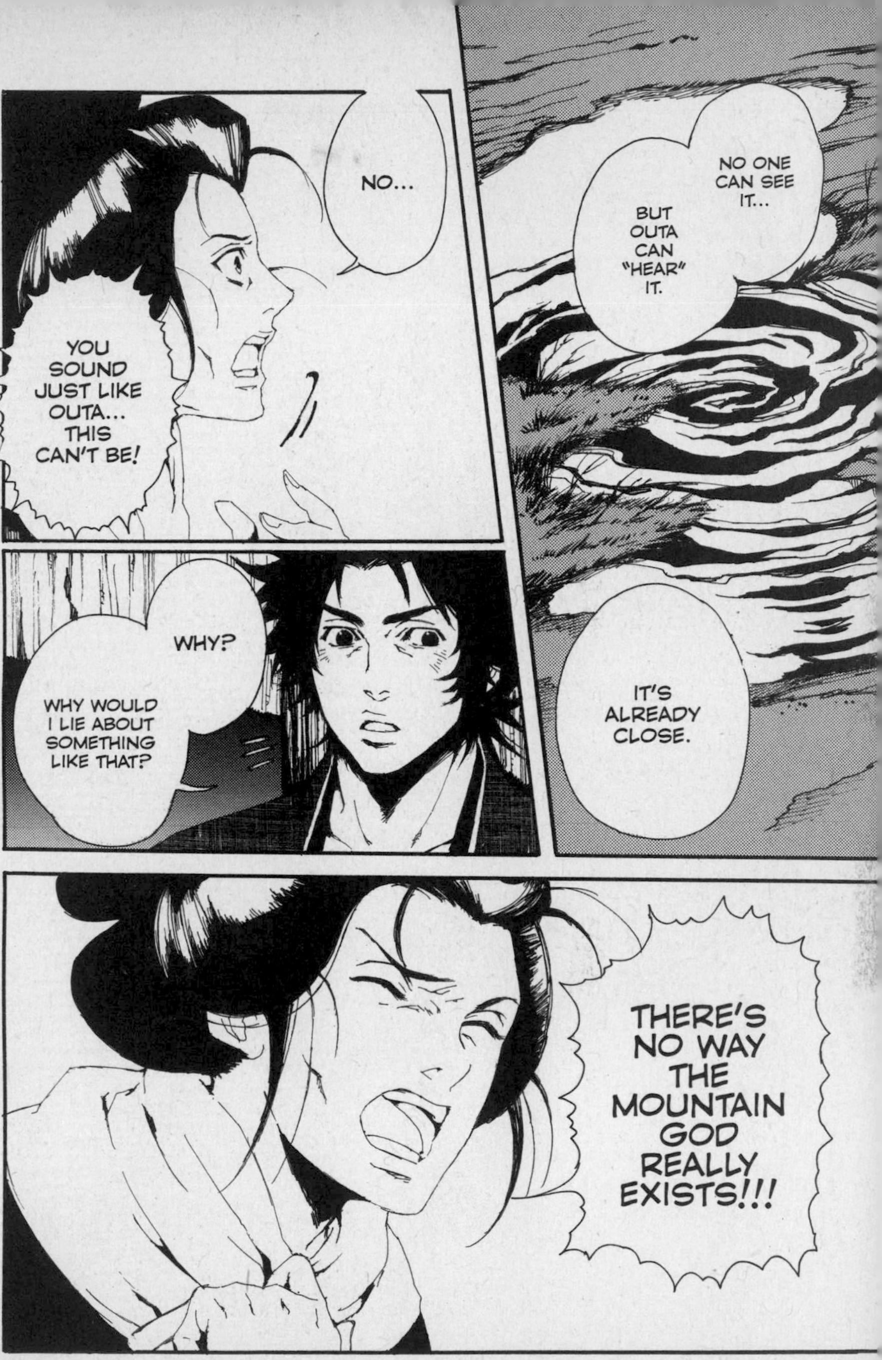
NO ONE CAN SEE IT...
BUT OUTA CAN "HEAR" IT.
IT'S ALREADY CLOSE.
NO...
YOU SOUND JUST LIKE OUTA... THIS CAN'T BE!
WHY?
WHY WOULD I LIE ABOUT SOMETHING LIKE THAT?
THERE'S NO WAY THE MOUNTAIN GOD REALLY EXISTS!!!

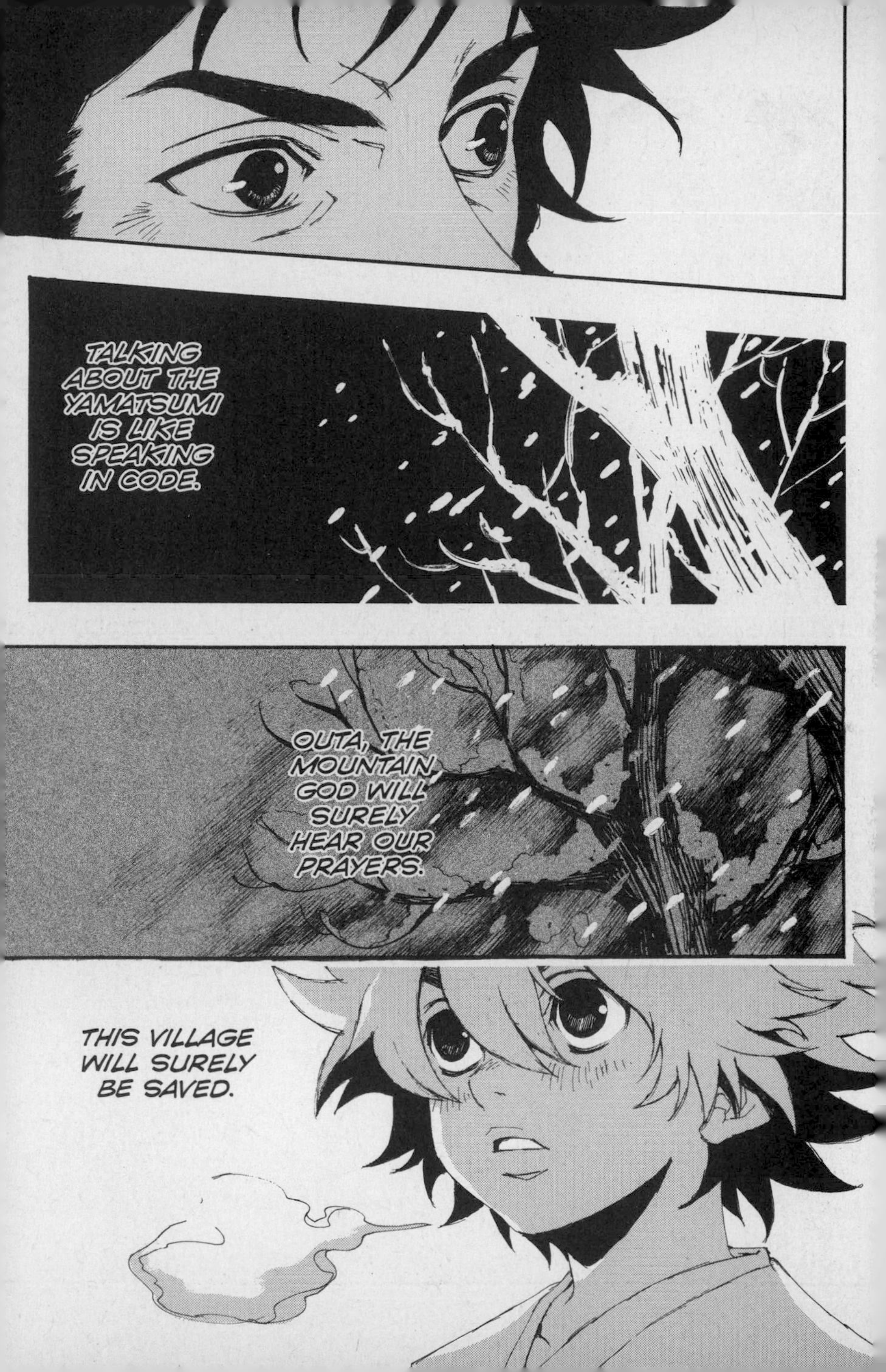
TALKING ABOUT THE YAMATSUMI IS LIKE SPEAKING IN CODE.
OUTA, THE MOUNTAIN GOD WILL SURELY HEAR OUR PRAYERS.
THIS VILLAGE WILL SURELY BE SAVED.

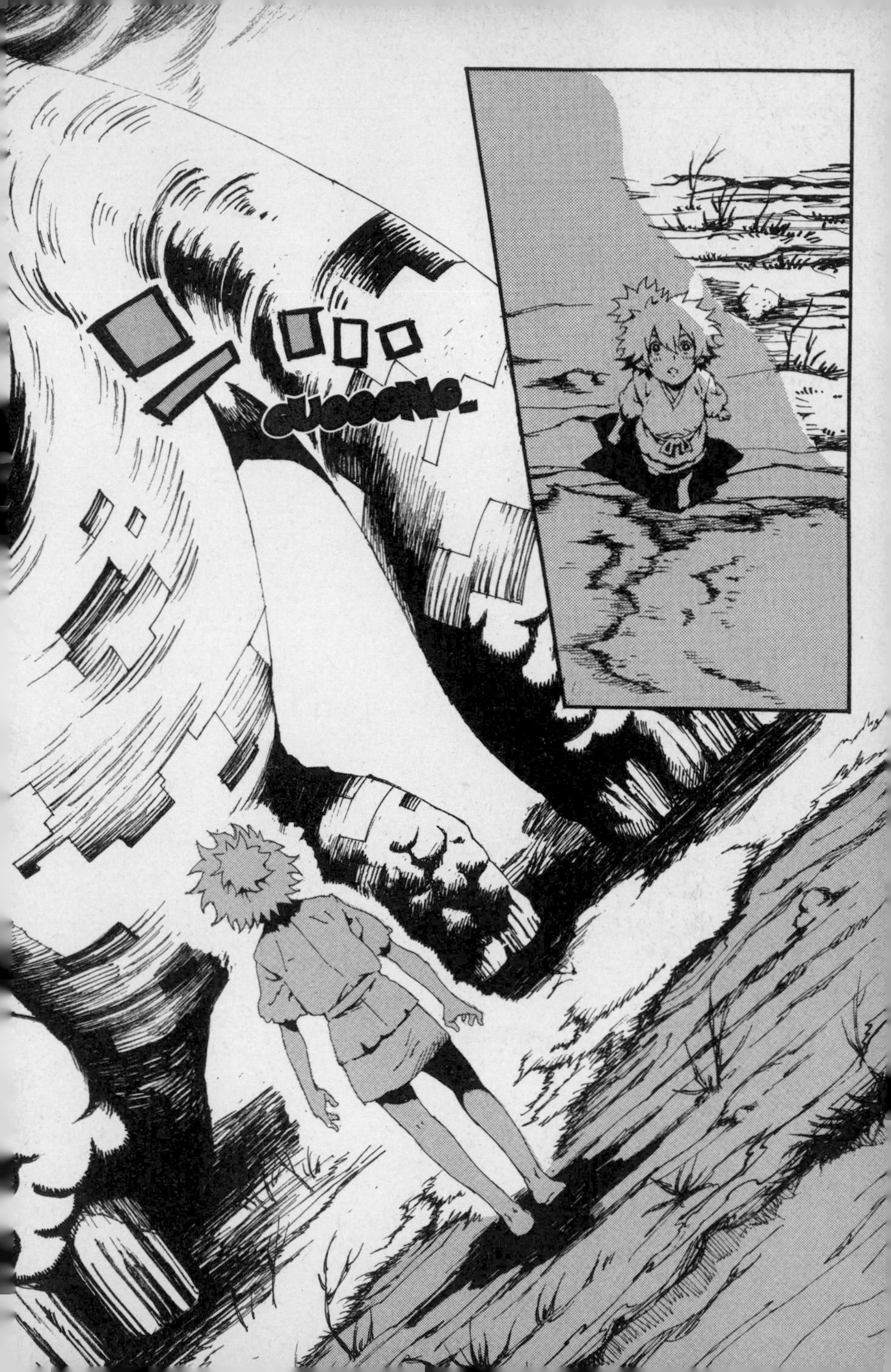

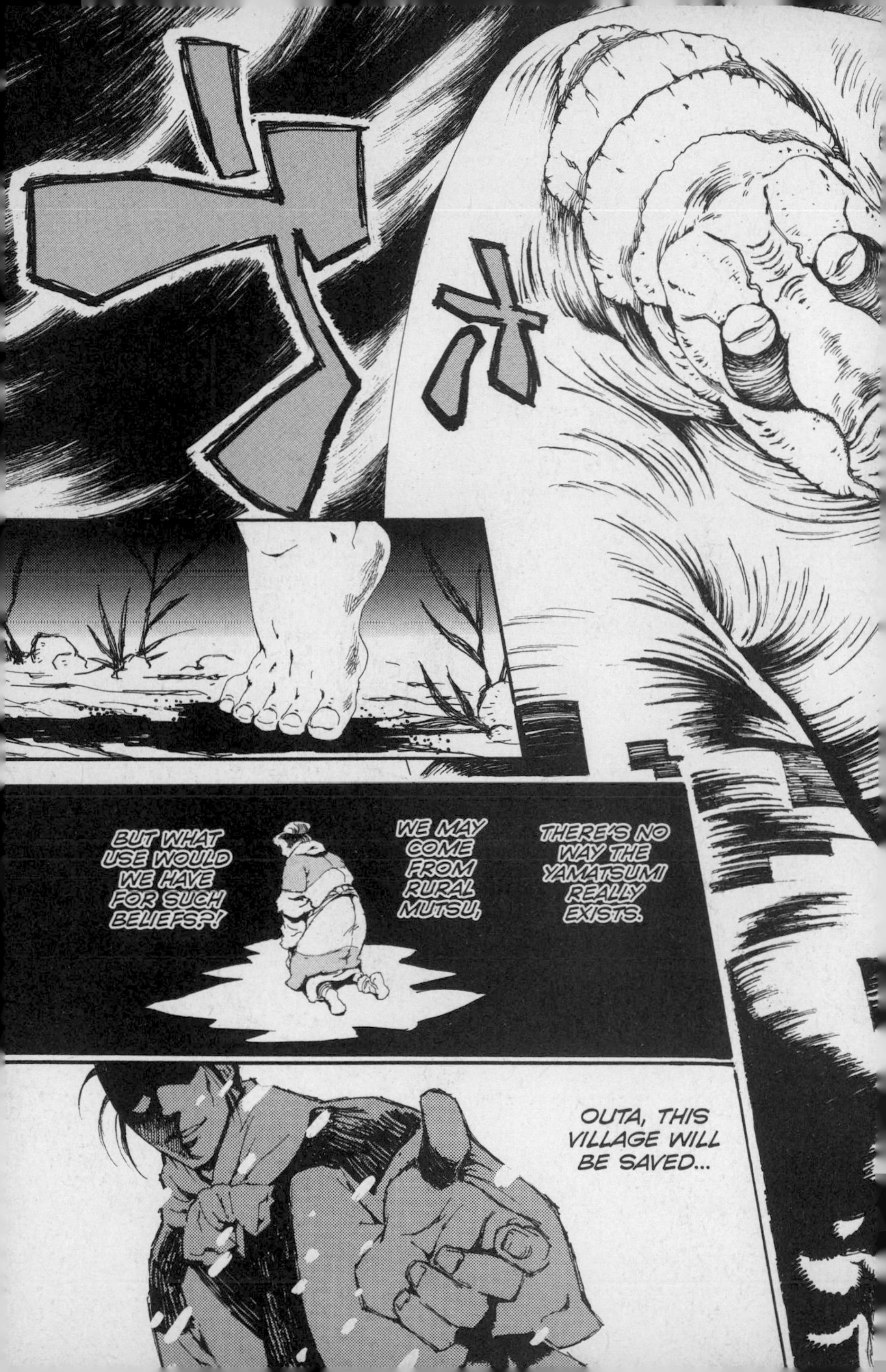
THERE'S NO WAY THE YAMATSUMI REALLY EXISTS.
WE MAY COME FROM RURAL MUTSU,
BUT WHAT USE WOULD WE HAVE FOR SUCH BELIEFS?!
OUTA, THIS VILLAGE WILL BE SAVED...

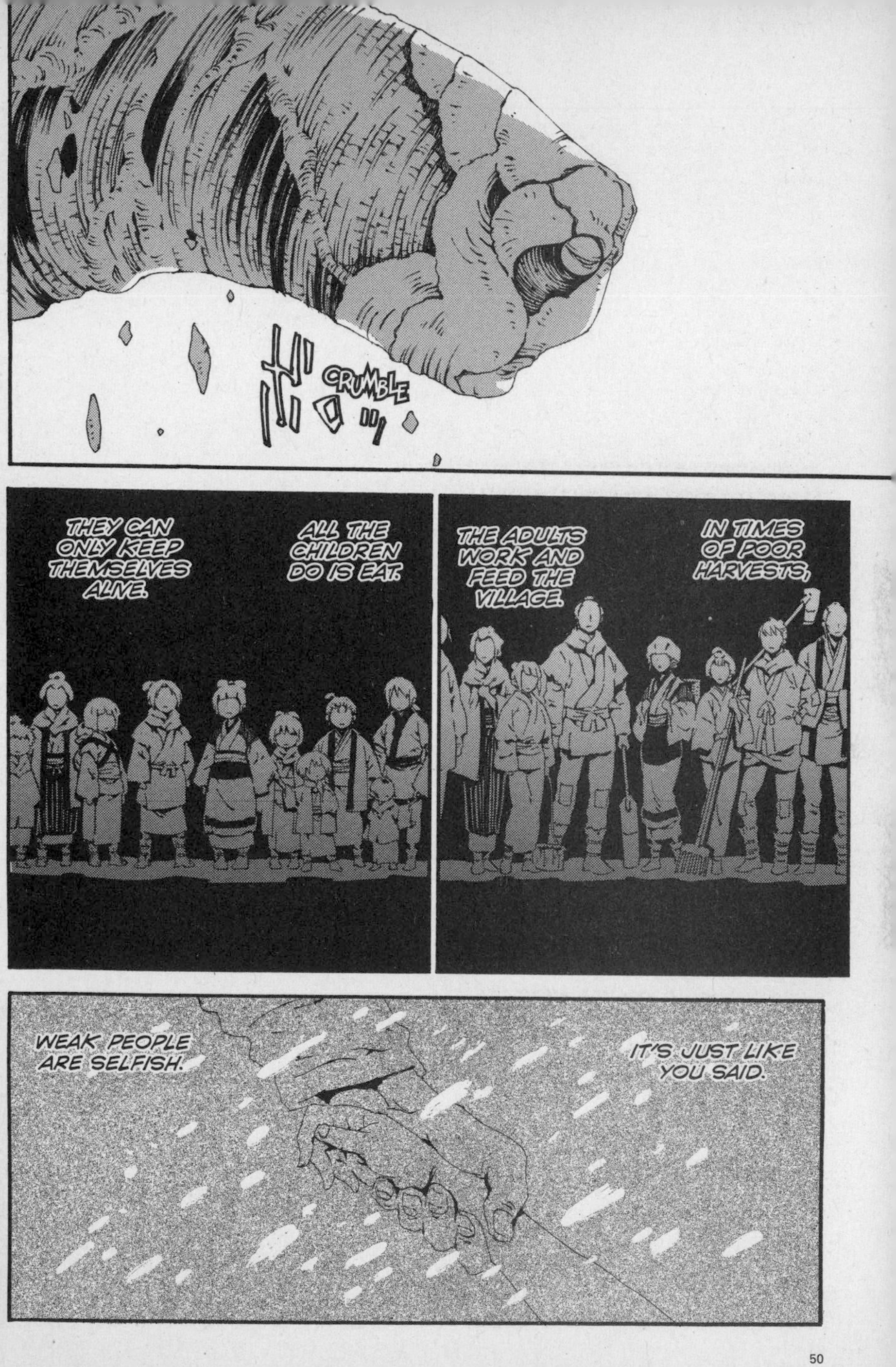

CRUMBLE
IN TIMES OF POOR HARVESTS,
THE ADULTS WORK AND FEED THE VILLAGE.
ALL THE CHILDREN DO IS EAT.
THEY CAN ONLY KEEP THEMSELVES ALIVE.
IT'S JUST LIKE YOU SAID.
WEAK PEOPLE ARE SELFISH.

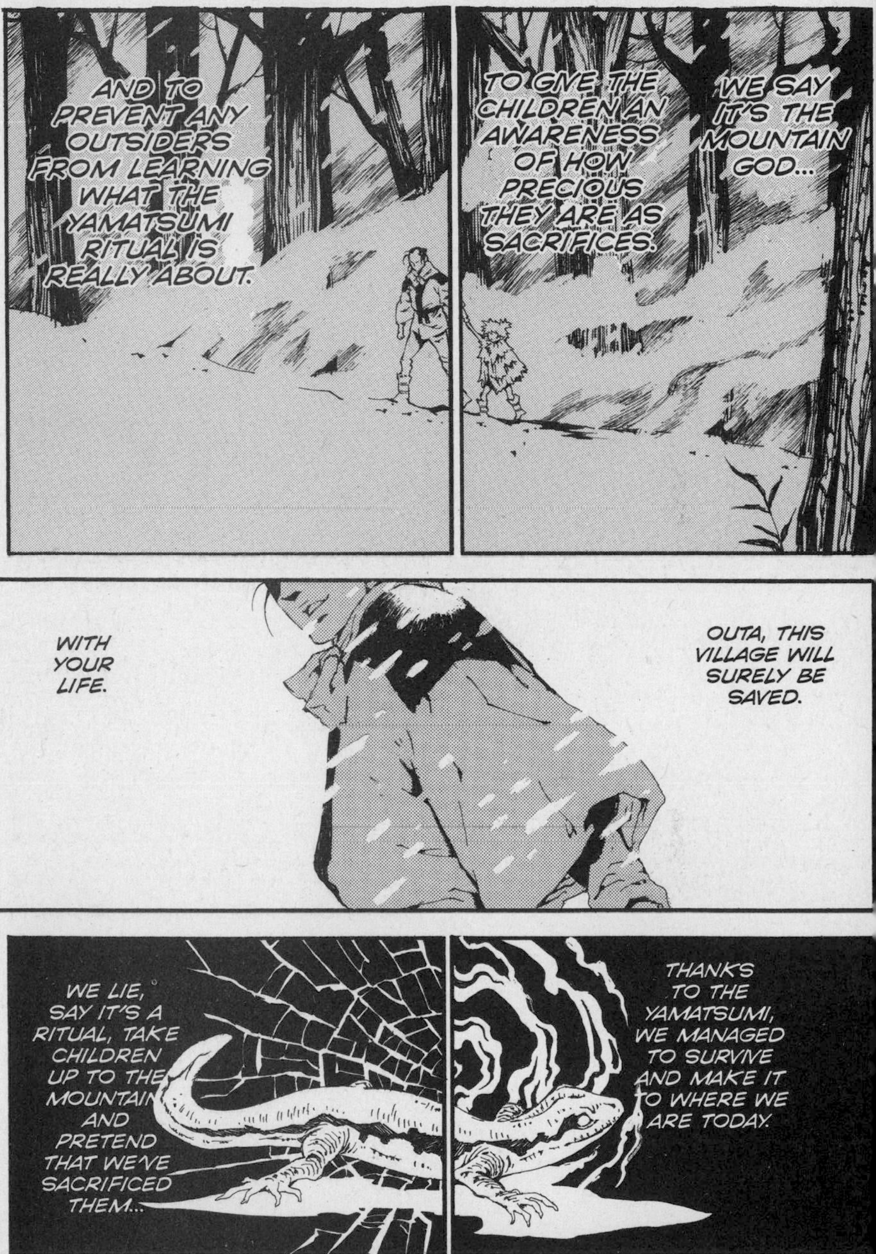
WE SAY IT'S THE MOUNTAIN GOD...
TO GIVE THE CHILDREN AN AWARENESS OF HOW PRECIOUS THEY ARE AS SACRIFICES.
AND TO PREVENT ANY OUTSIDERS FROM LEARNING WHAT THE YAMATSUMI RITUAL IS REALLY ABOUT.
OUTA, THIS VILLAGE WILL SURELY BE SAVED.
WITH YOUR LIFE.
THANKS TO THE YAMATSUMI, WE MANAGED TO SURVIVE AND MAKE IT TO WHERE WE ARE TODAY.
WE LIE, SAY IT'S A RITUAL, TAKE CHILDREN UP TO THE MOUNTAIN AND PRETEND THAT WE'VE SACRIFICED THEM...

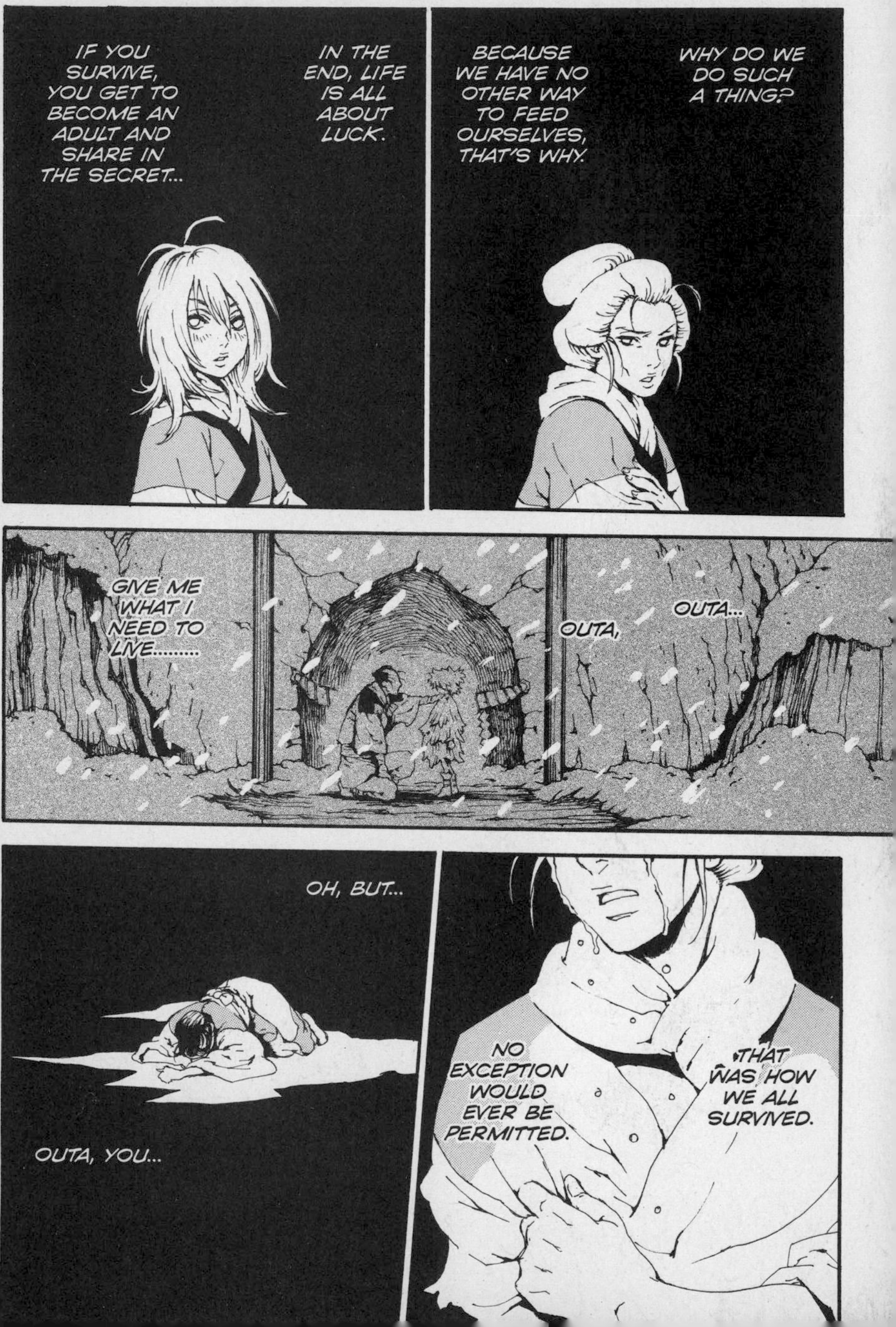
WHY DO WE DO SUCH A THING?
BECAUSE WE HAVE NO OTHER WAY TO FEED OURSELVES, THAT'S WHY.
IN THE END, LIFE IS ALL ABOUT LUCK.
IF YOU SURVIVE, YOU GET TO BECOME AN ADULT AND SHARE IN THE SECRET...
OUTA...
OUTA,
GIVE ME WHAT I NEED TO LIVE.........
THAT WAS HOW WE ALL SURVIVED.
NO EXCEPTION WOULD EVER BE PERMITTED.
OH, BUT...
OUTA, YOU...

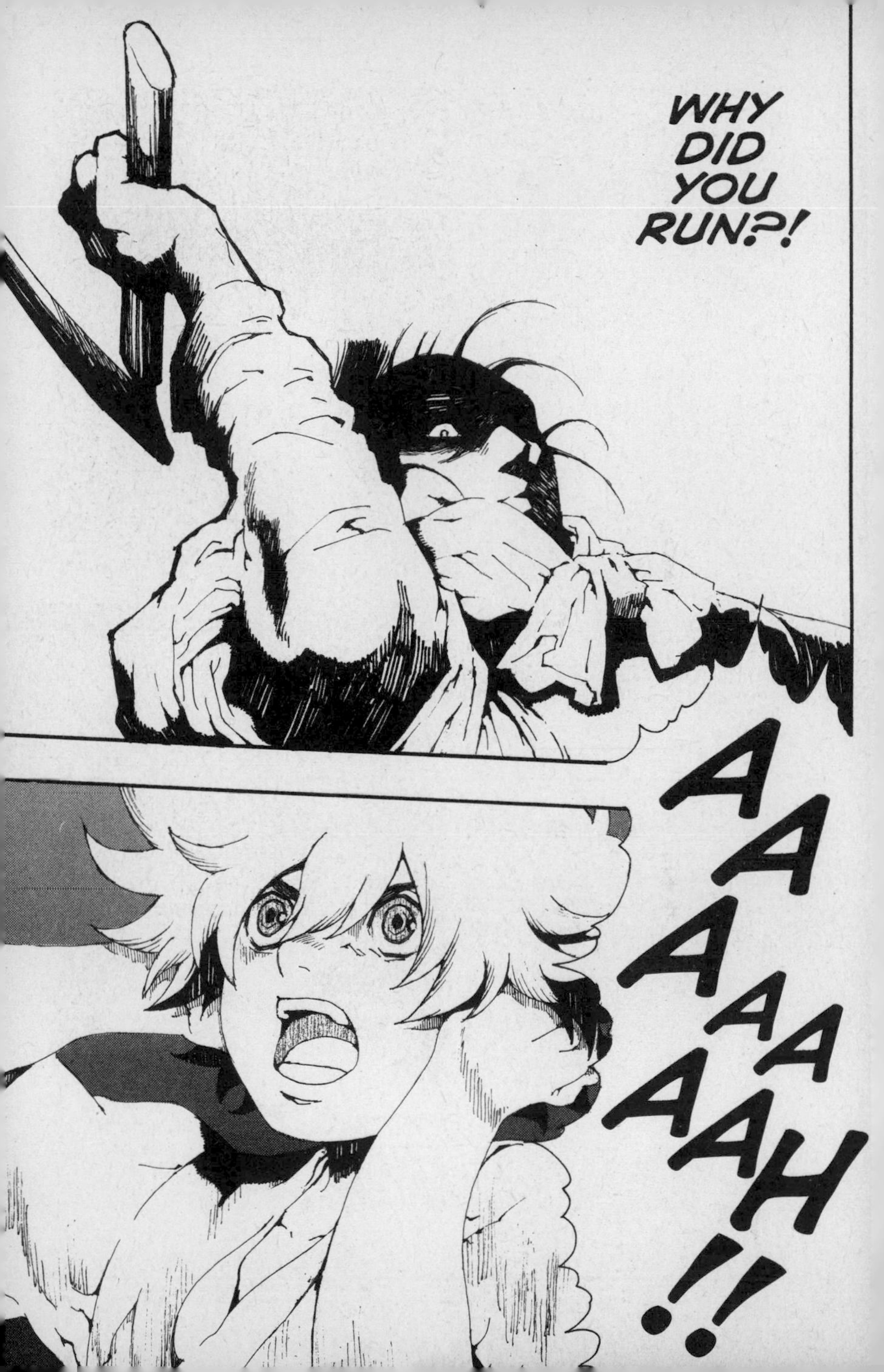
WHY DID YOU RUN?!
AAAAAAAH!!

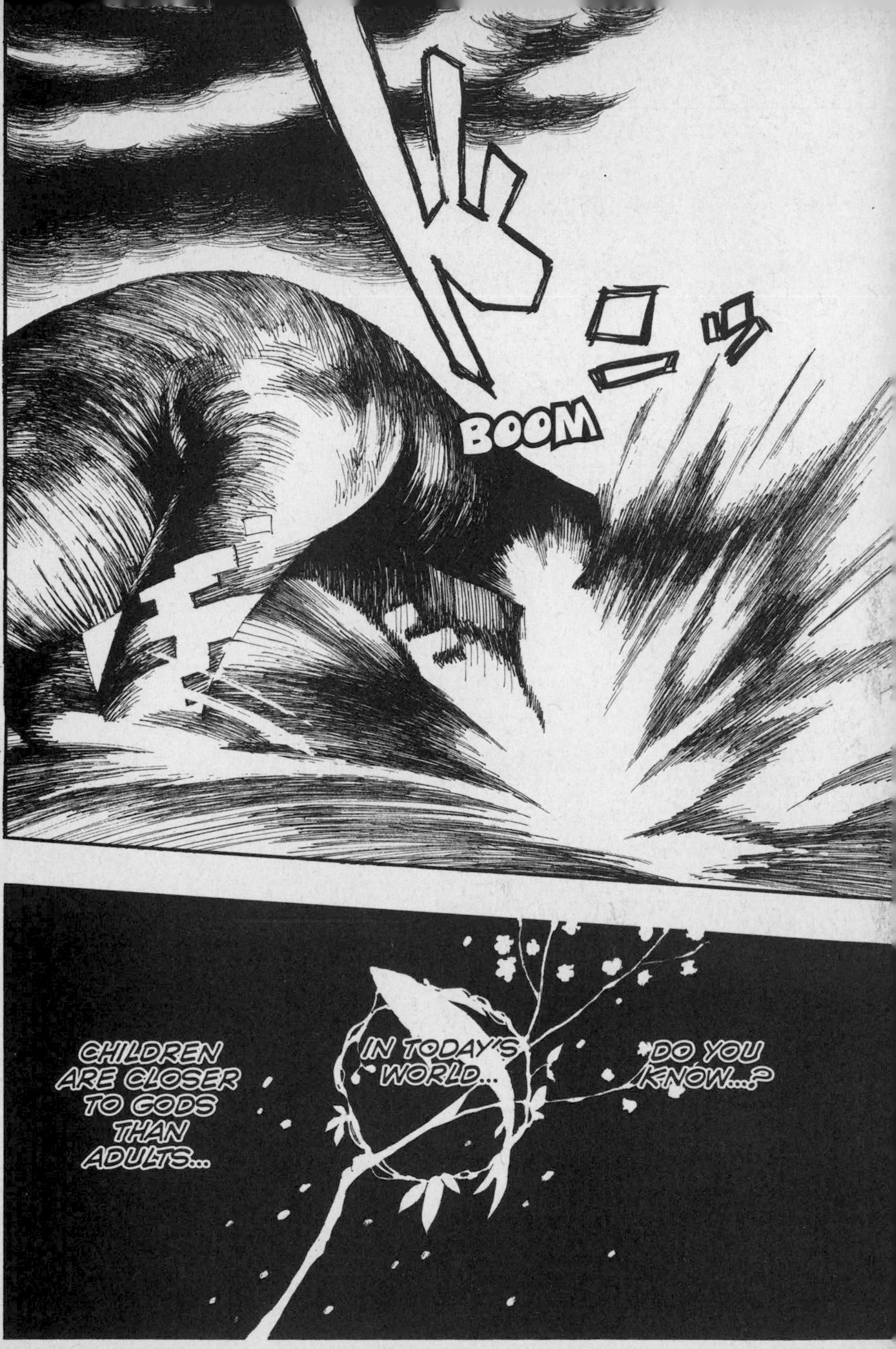
BOOM
DO YOU KNOW...?
IN TODAY'S WORLD...
CHILDREN ARE CLOSER TO GODS THAN ADULTS...

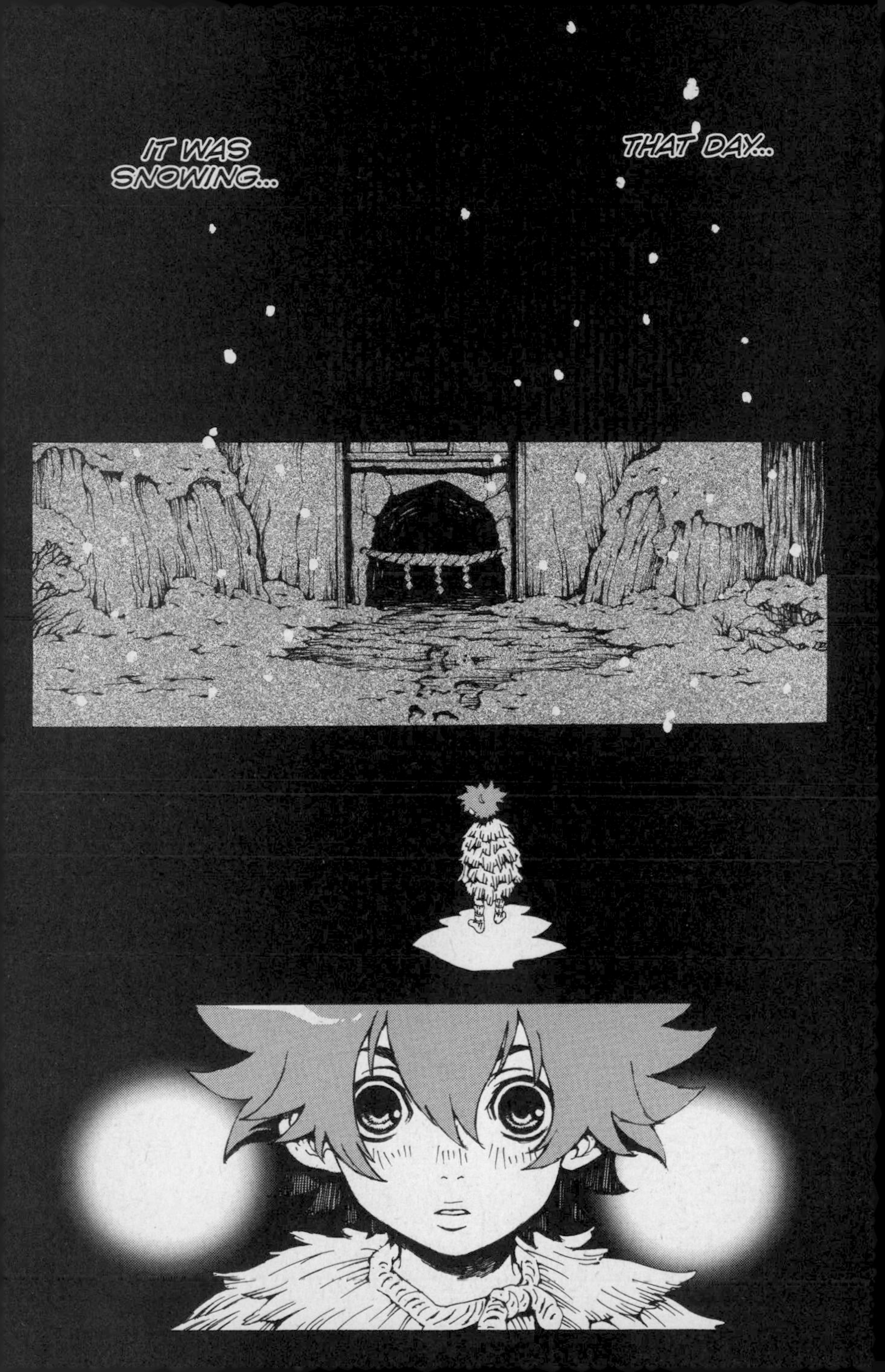
THAT DAY...
IT WAS SNOWING...

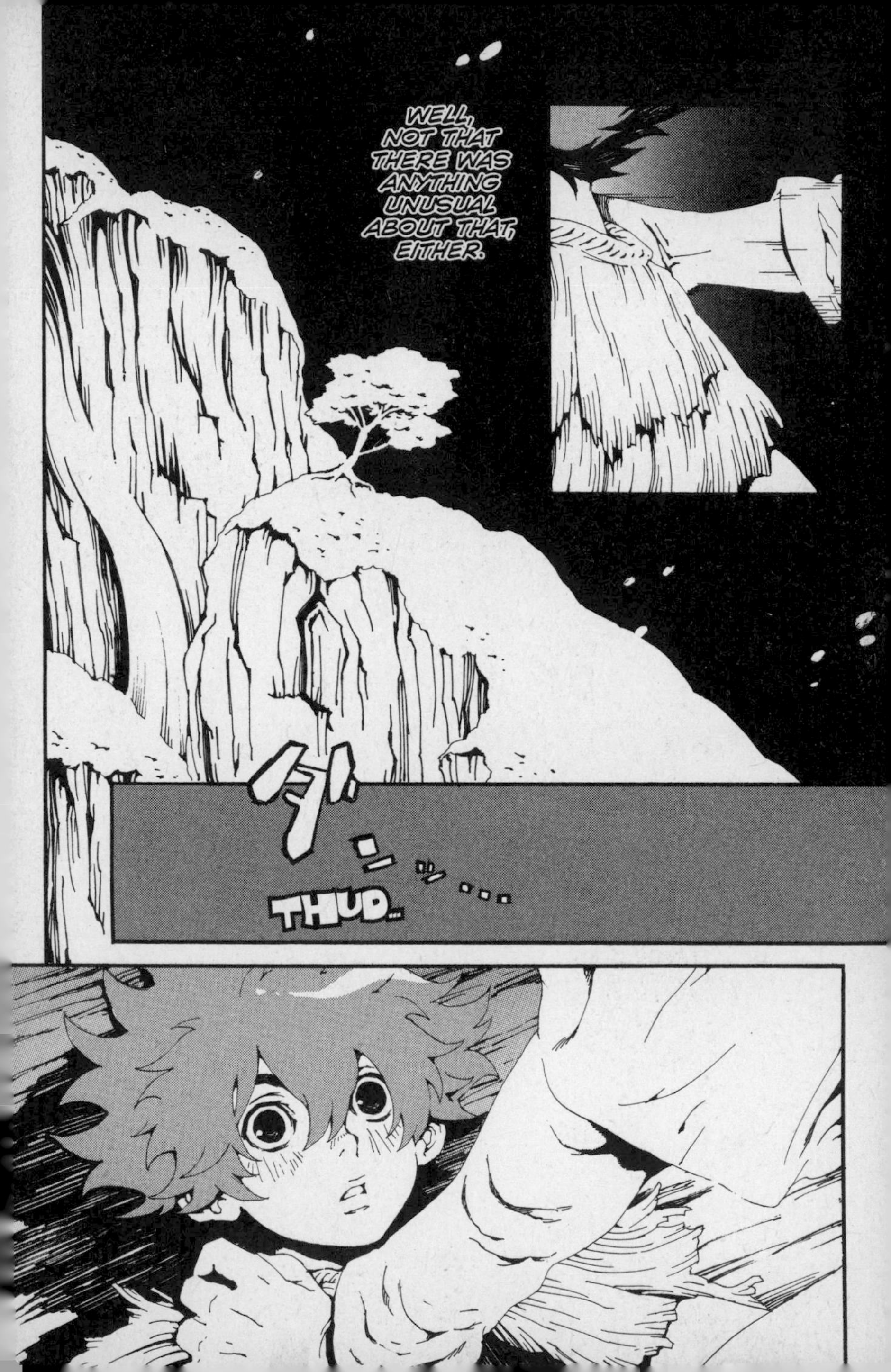
WELL, NOT THAT THERE WAS ANYTHING UNUSUAL ABOUT THAT, EITHER.
THUD...

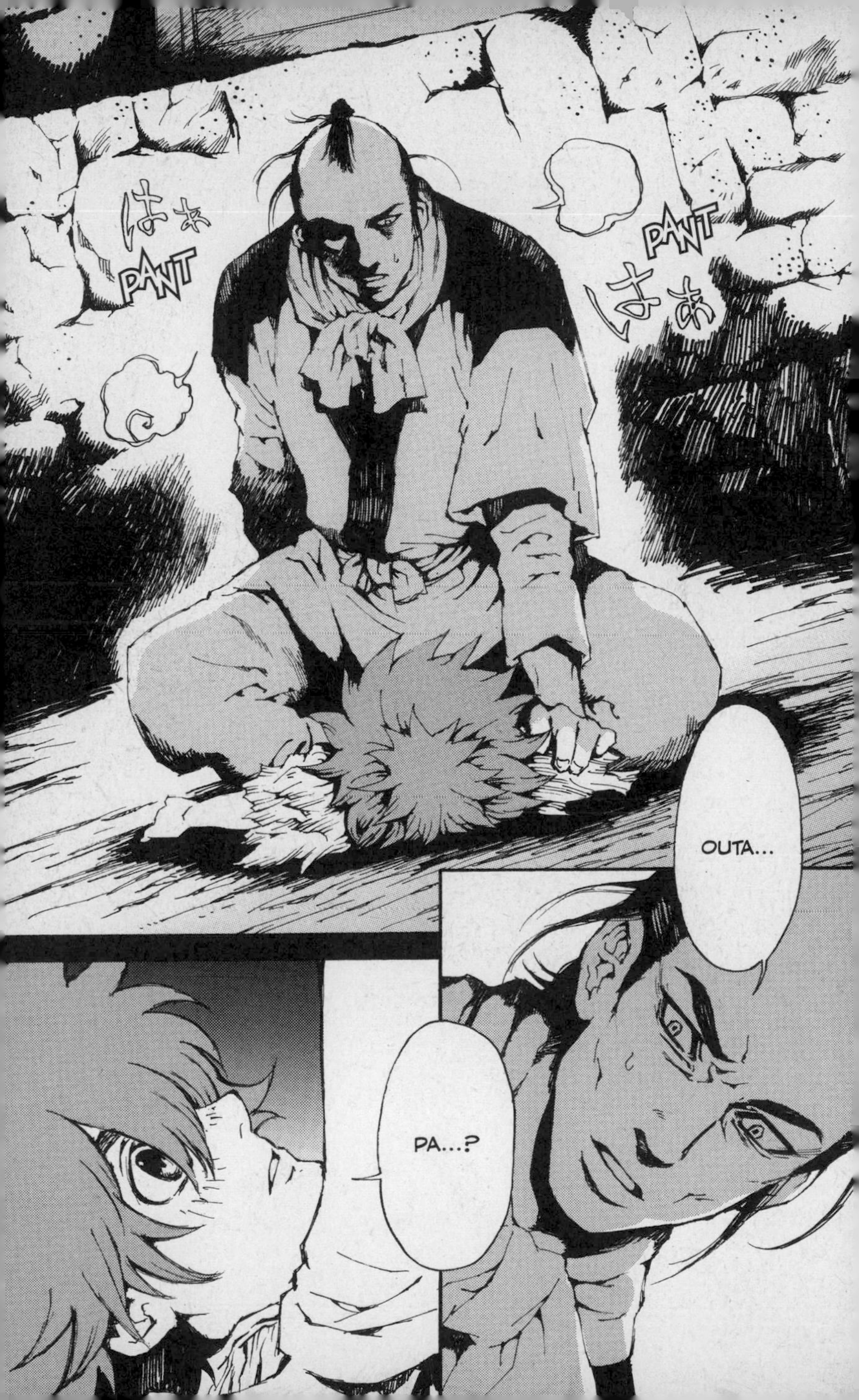
PANT
はぁ
はぁ
PANT
OUTA...
PA...?

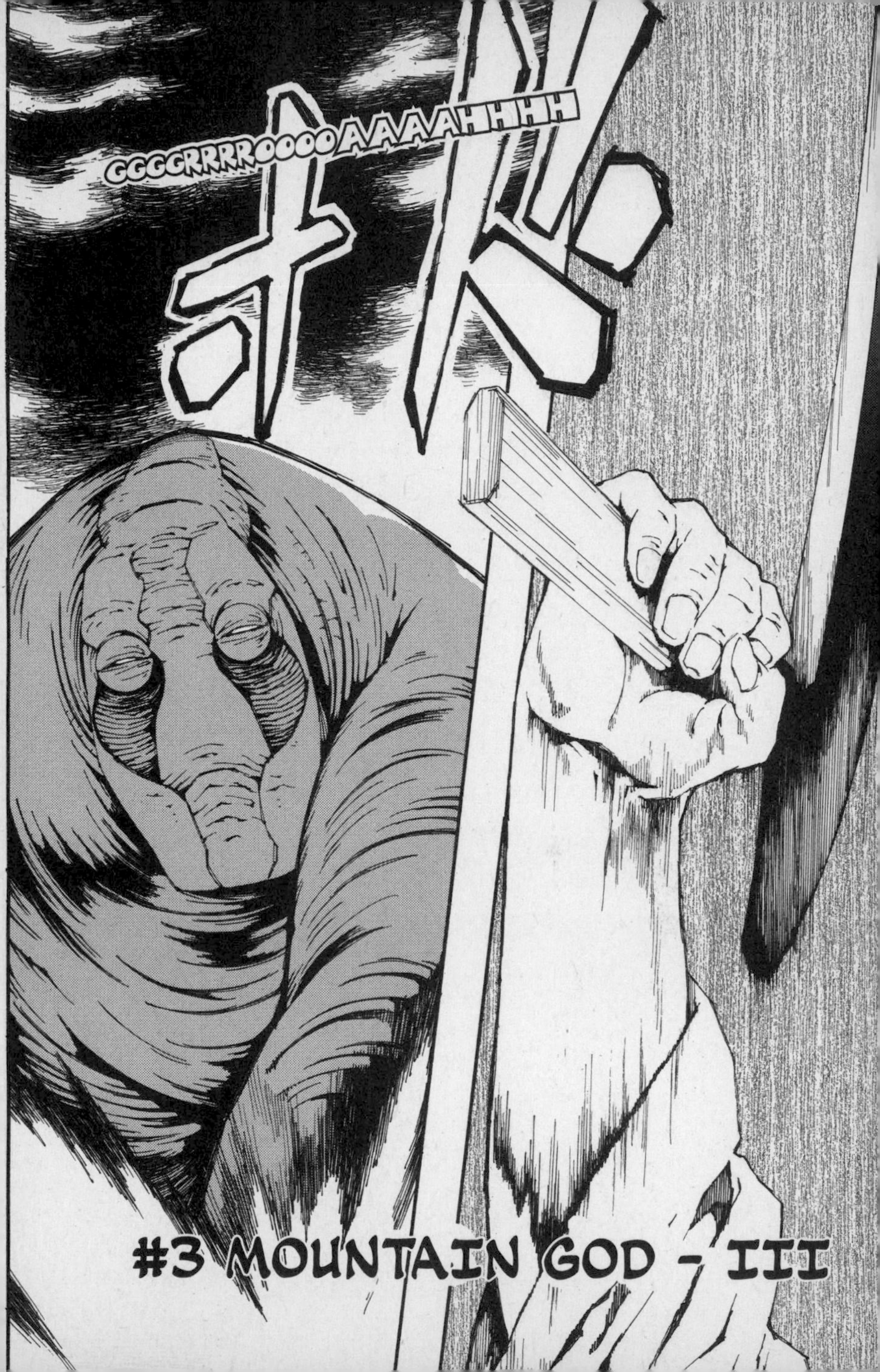
GGGGRRRROOOOAAAAAHHHHH
#3 MOUNTAIN GOD - III

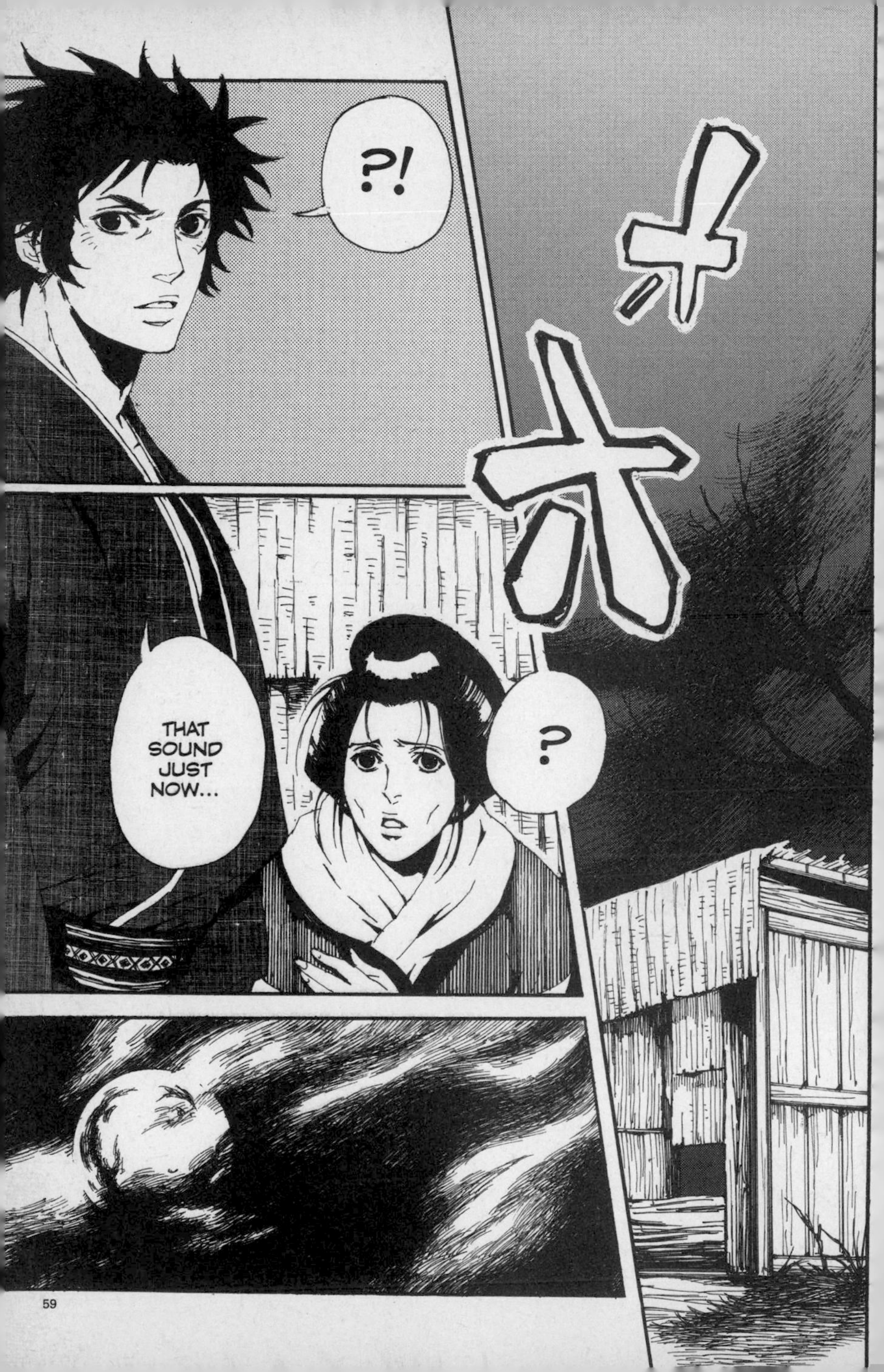
?!
?
THAT SOUND JUST NOW...

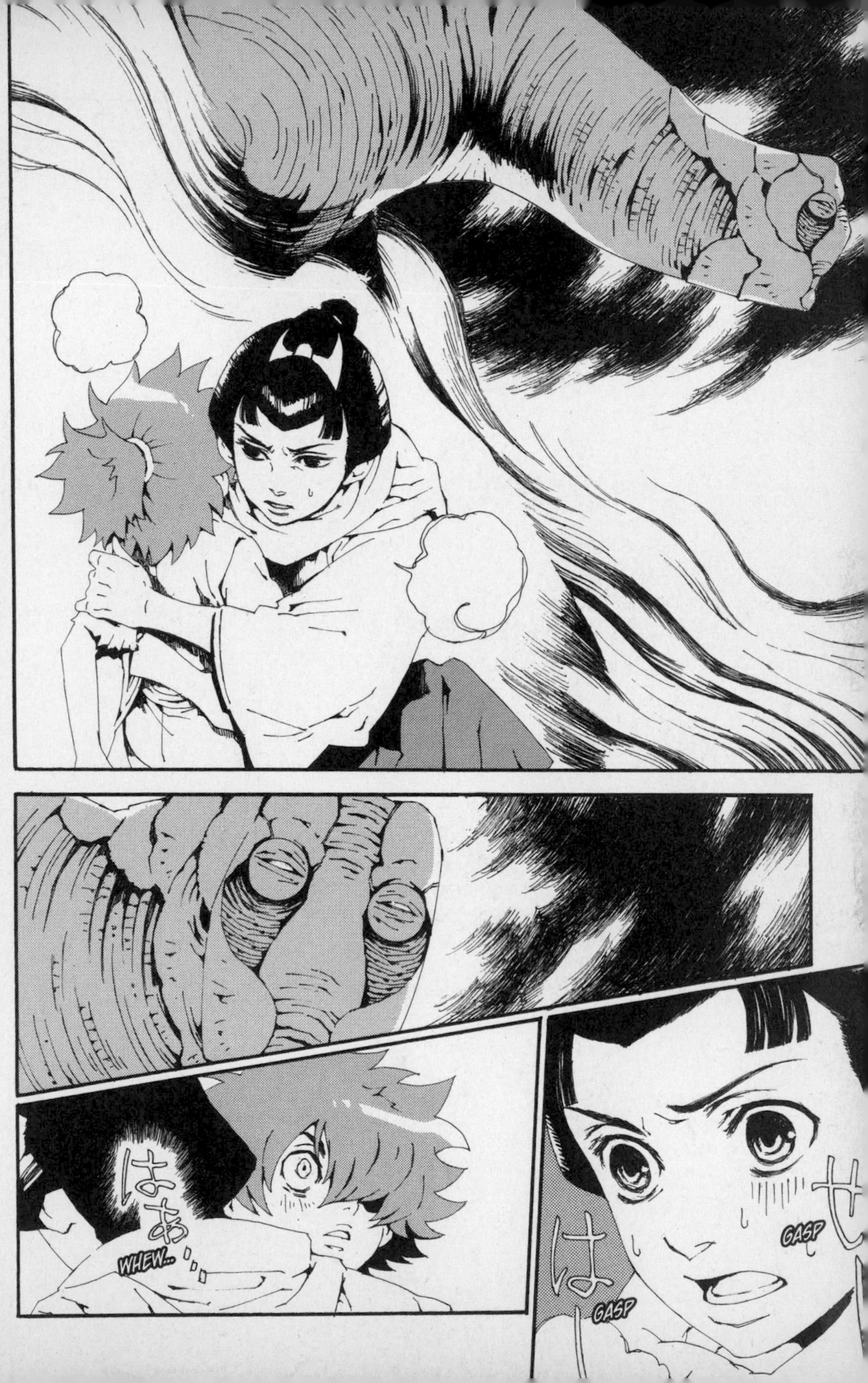
せ
GASP
は
GASP
はあ
WHEW...

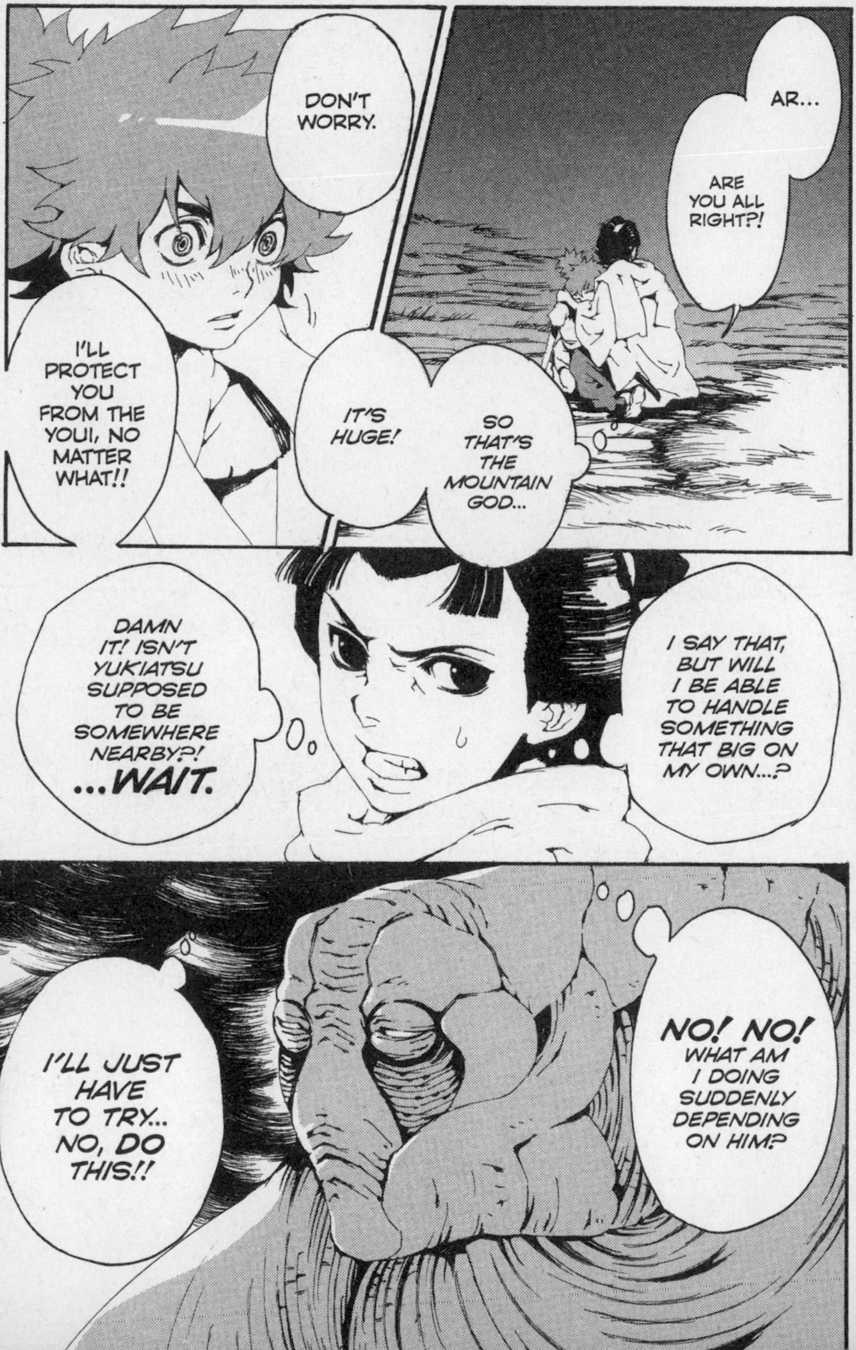
AR...
ARE YOU ALL RIGHT?!
SO THAT'S THE MOUNTAIN GOD...
IT'S HUGE!
DON'T WORRY.
I'LL PROTECT YOU FROM THE YOUI, NO MATTER WHAT!!
I SAY THAT, BUT WILL I BE ABLE TO HANDLE SOMETHING THAT BIG ON MY OWN...?
DAMN IT! ISN'T YUKIATSU SUPPOSED TO BE SOMEWHERE NEARBY?! ...WAIT.
NO! NO! WHAT AM I DOING SUDDENLY DEPENDING ON HIM?
I'LL JUST HAVE TO TRY... NO, DO THIS!!

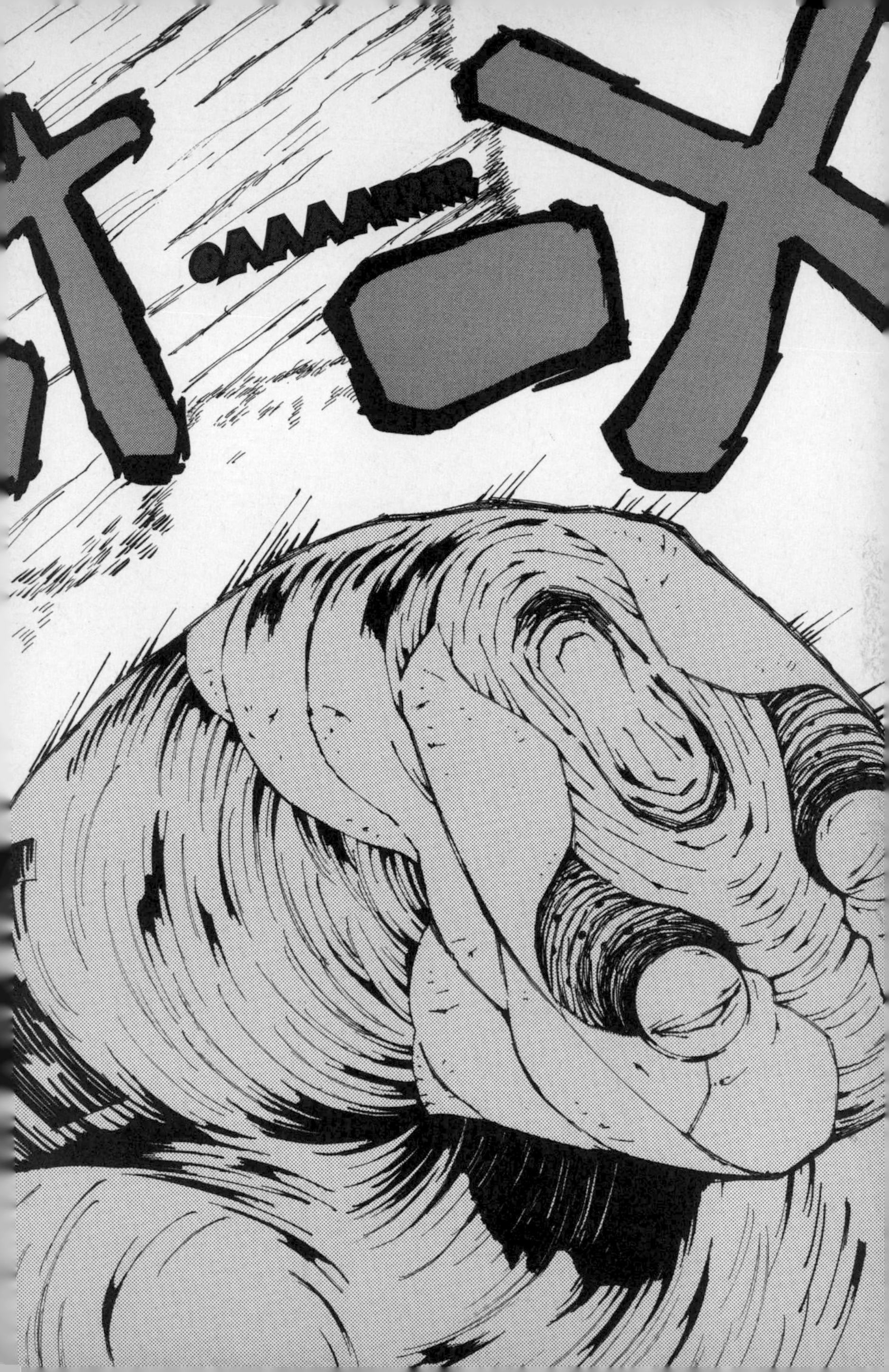
GAAAARRRR

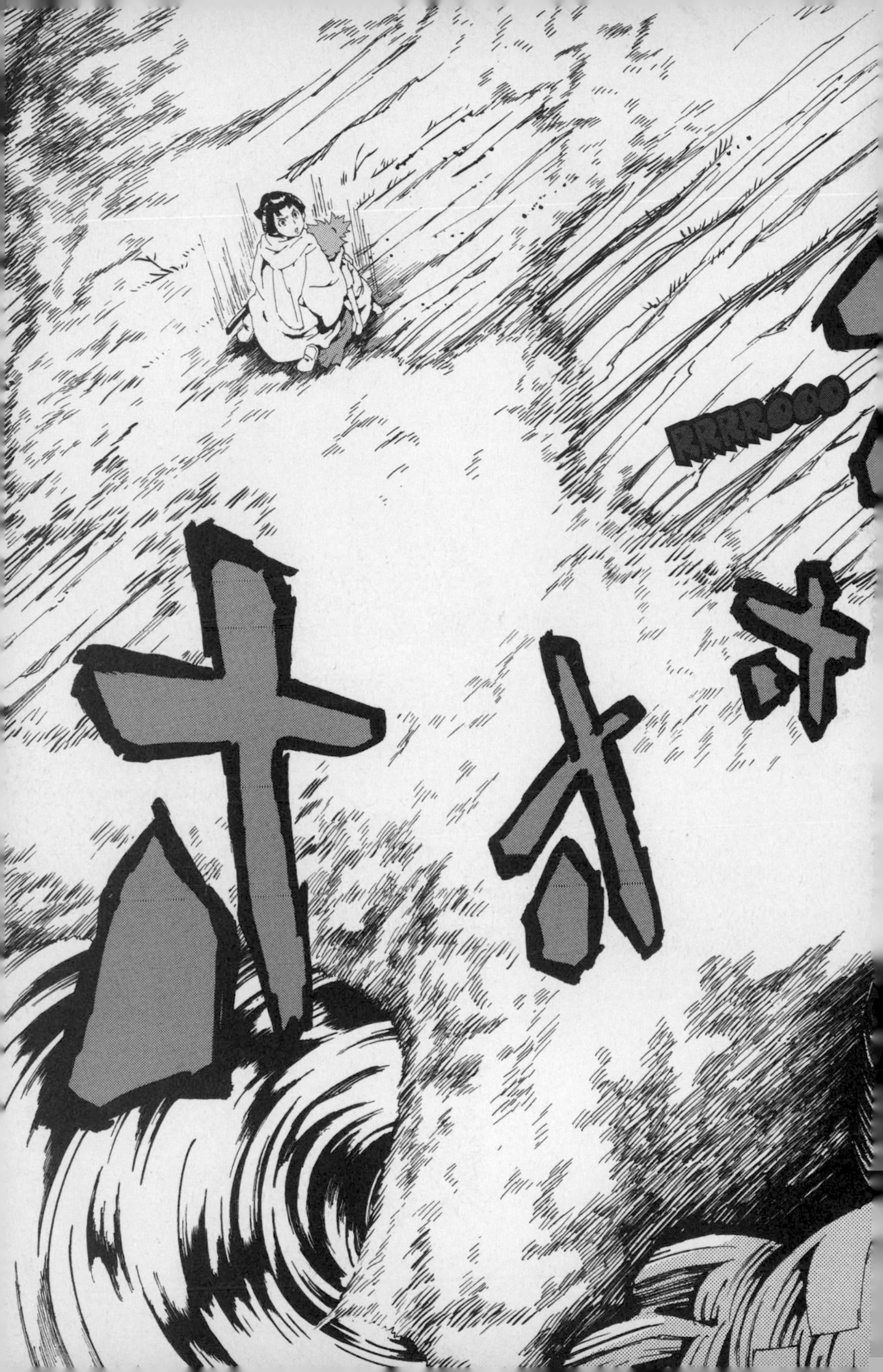
RRRROOO

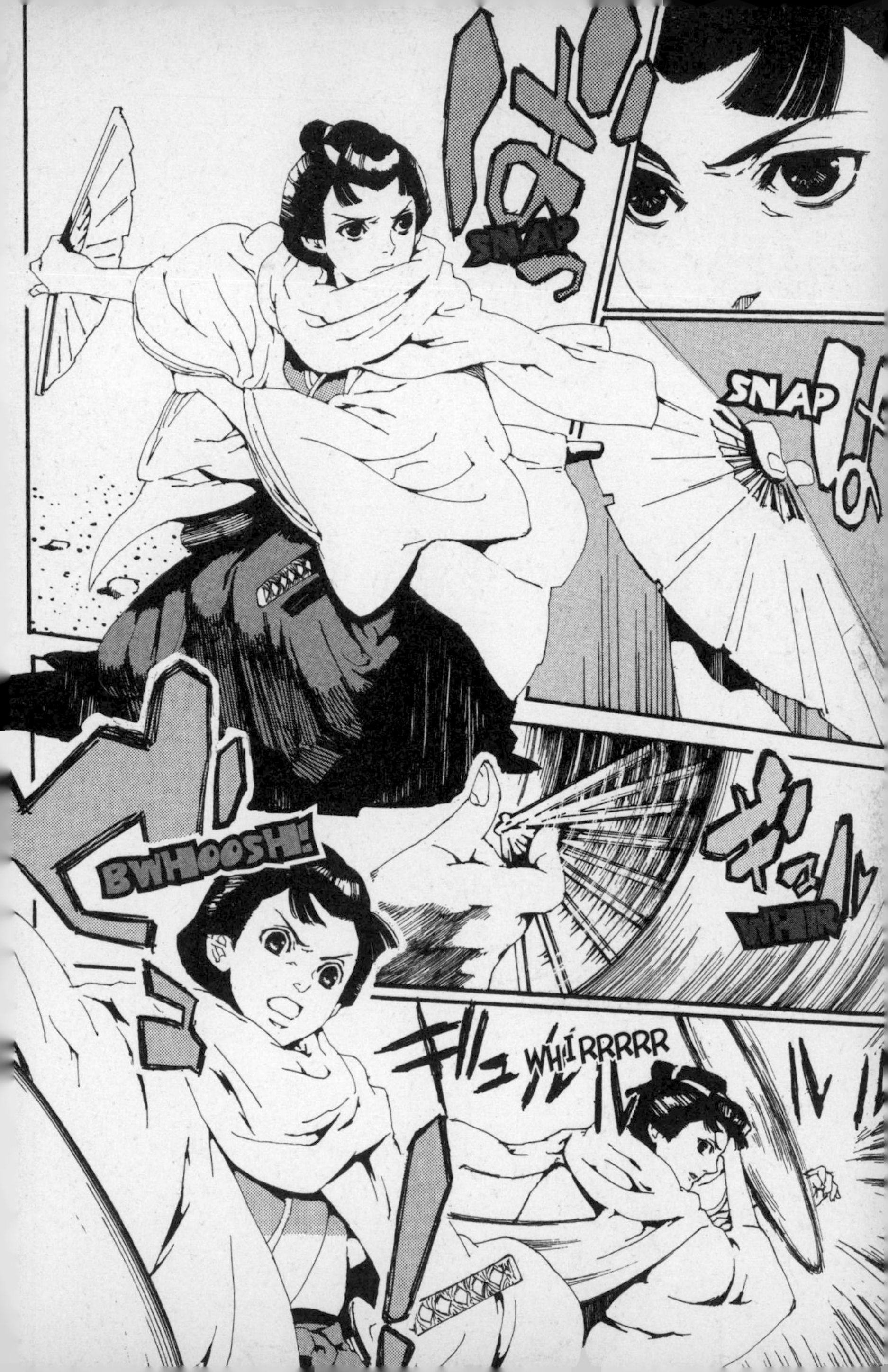
SNAP
SNAP
WHIR
BWHOOSH!
WHIRRRRR

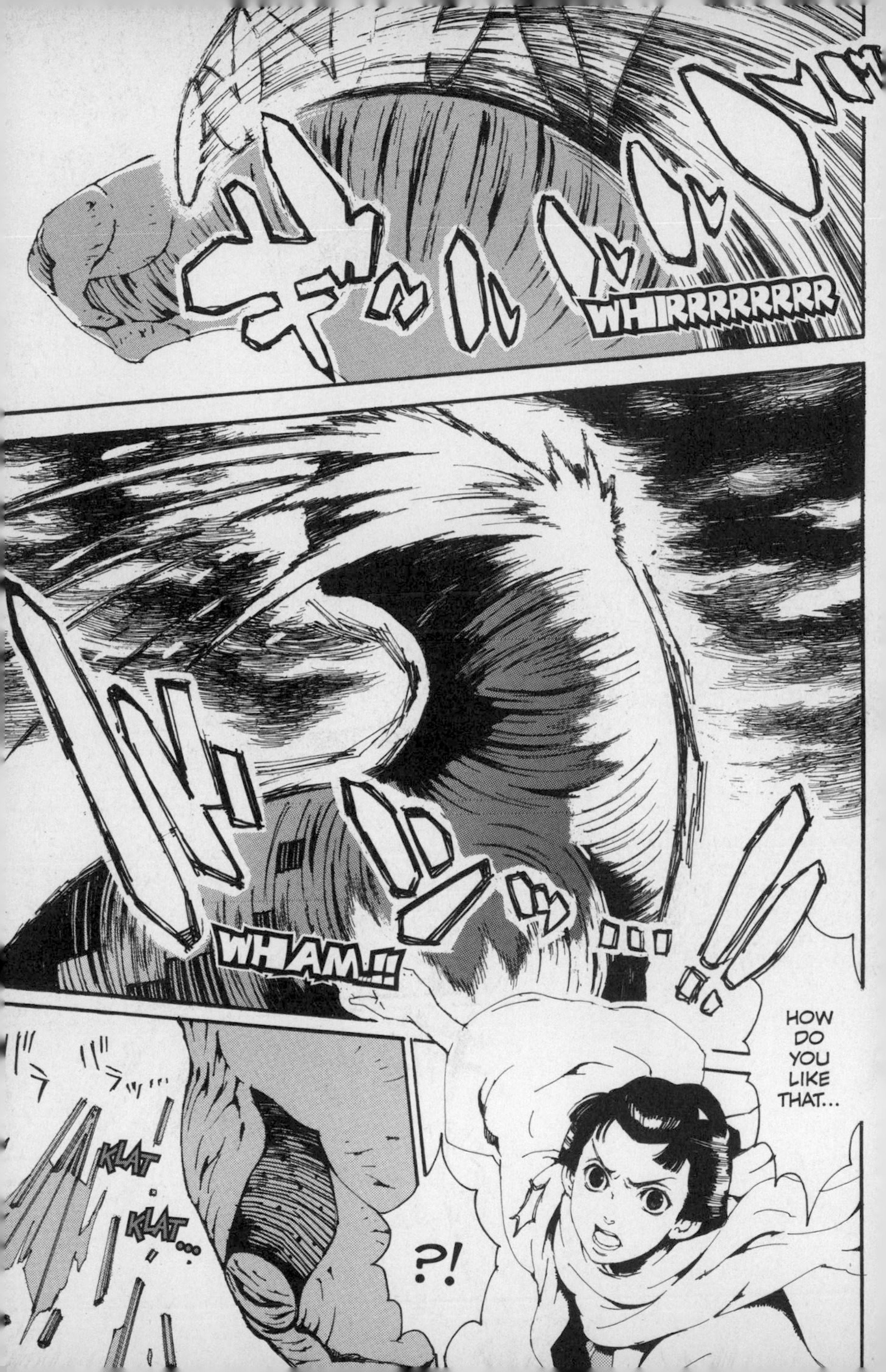
WHIRRRRRRRR
WHAM!!
HOW DO YOU LIKE THAT...
?!
KLAT
KLAT...

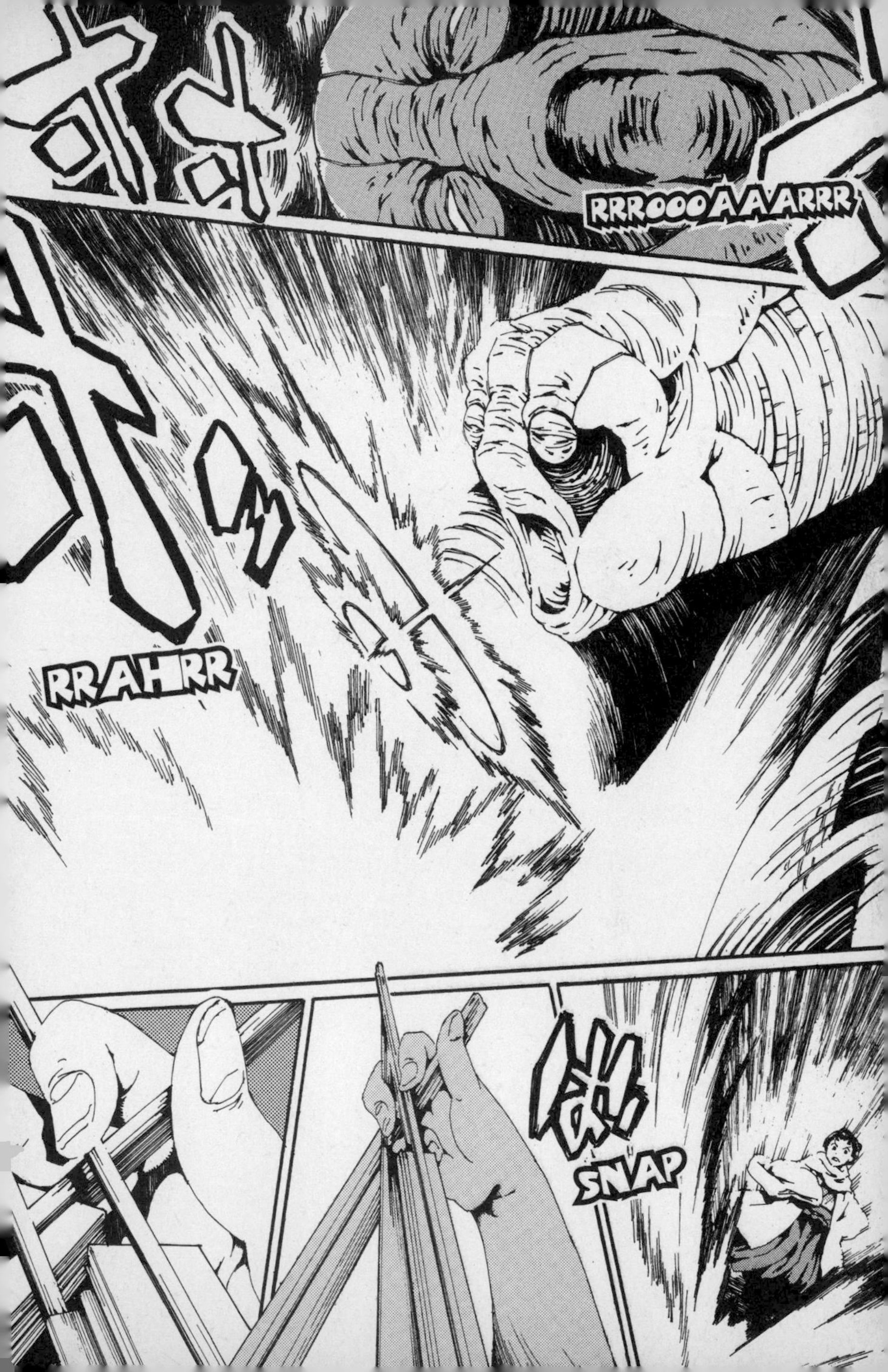
RRROOOAAARRR
RRAHRR
SNAP

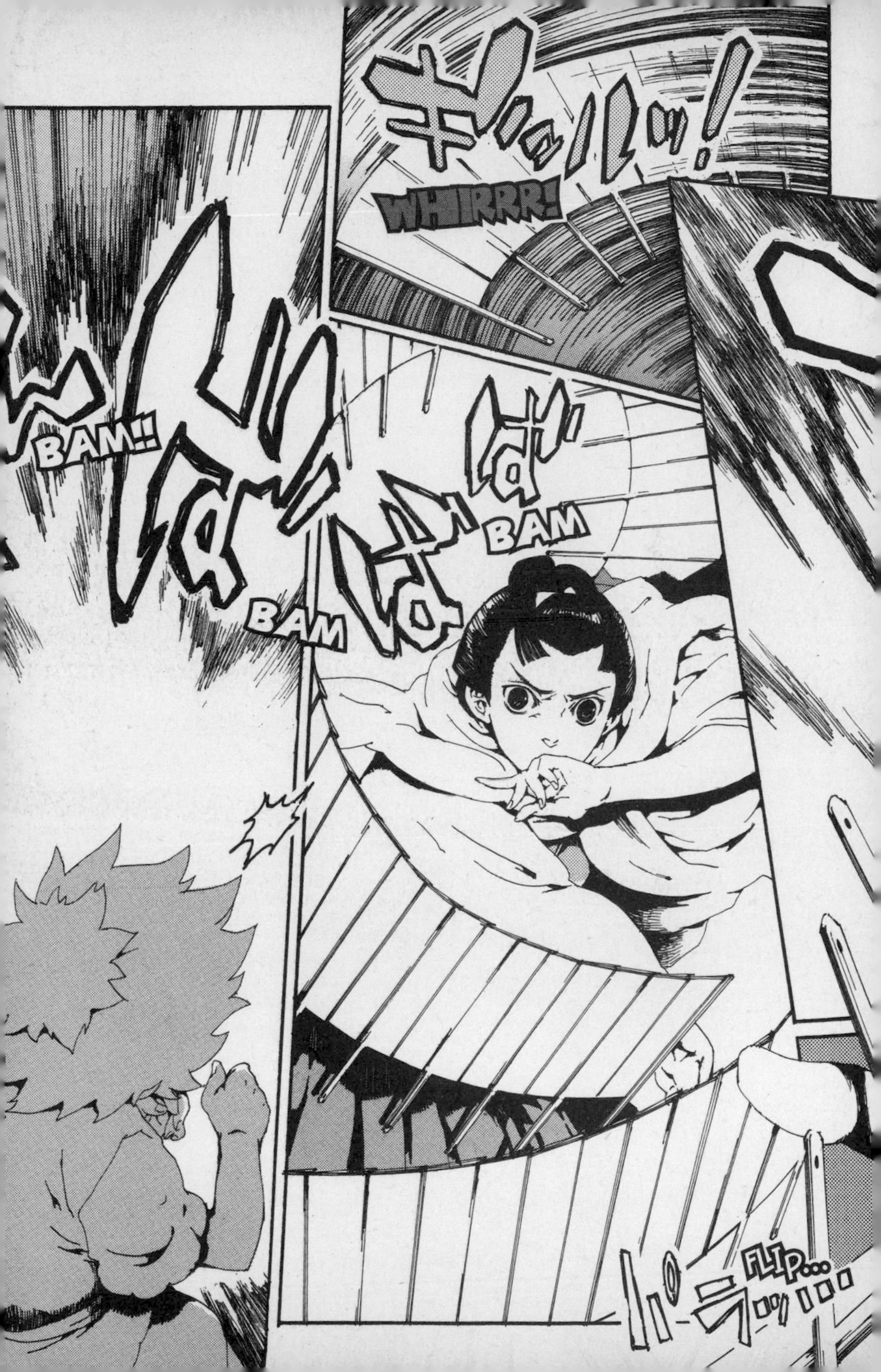
WHIRRR!
BAM!!
BAM
BAM
FLIP...

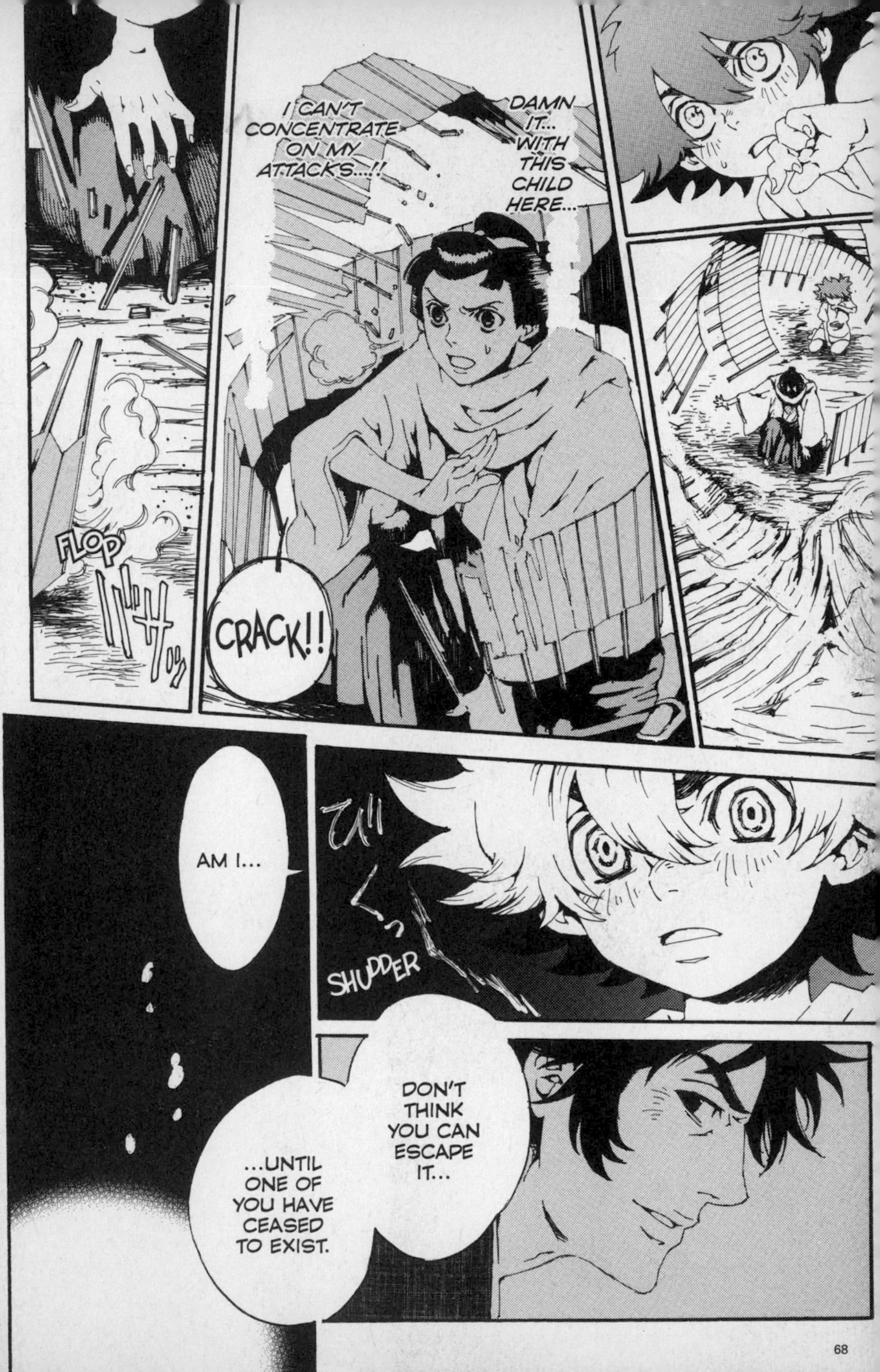
DAMN IT... WITH THIS CHILD HERE...
I CAN'T CONCENTRATE ON MY ATTACKS...!!
CRACK!!
FLOP
SHUDDER
DON'T THINK YOU CAN ESCAPE IT...
...UNTIL ONE OF YOU HAVE CEASED TO EXIST.
AM I...

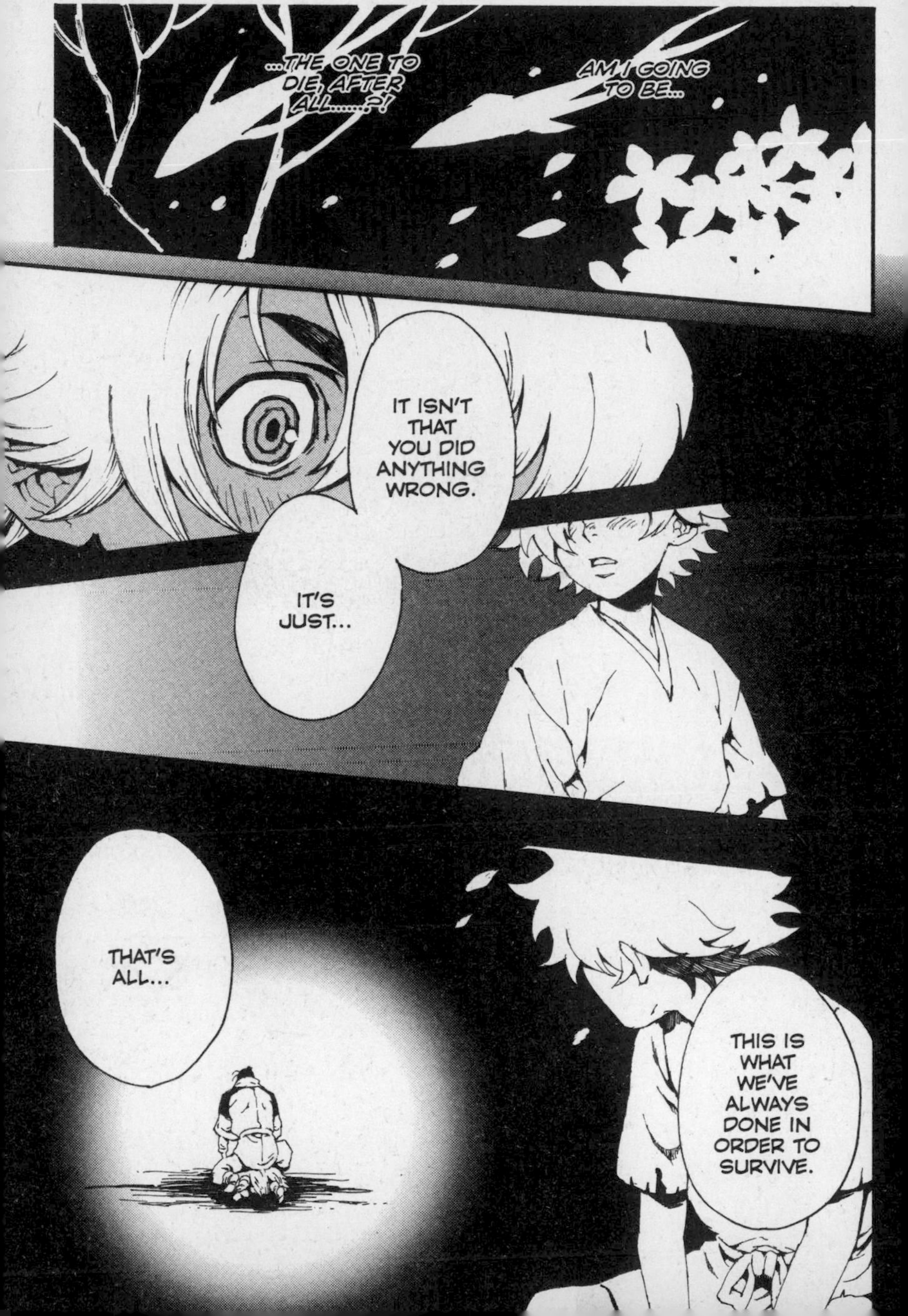
AM I GOING TO BE...
...THE ONE TO DIE, AFTER ALL......?!
IT ISN'T THAT YOU DID ANYTHING WRONG.
IT'S JUST...
THIS IS WHAT WE'VE ALWAYS DONE IN ORDER TO SURVIVE.
THAT'S ALL...

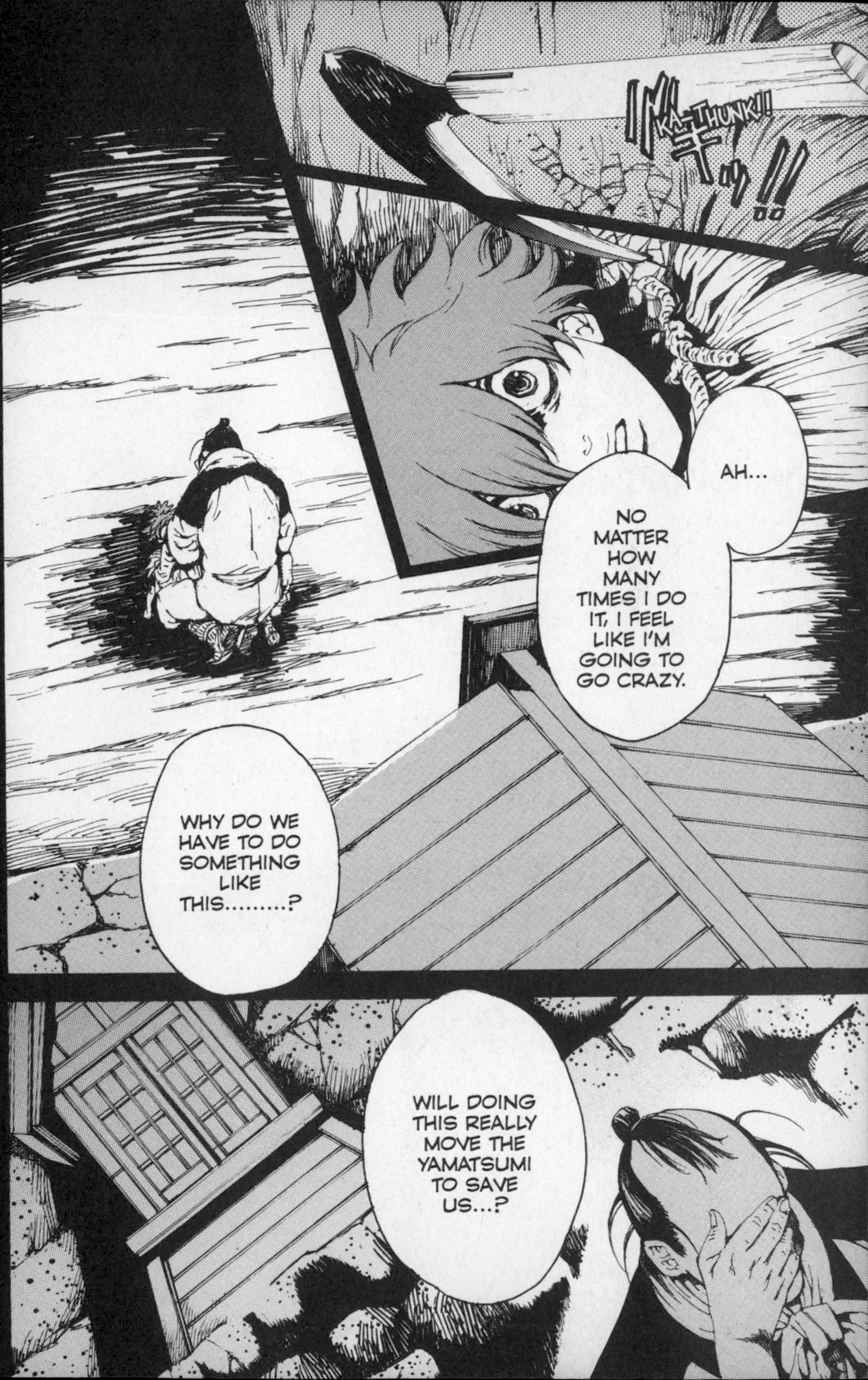
KA-THUNK!!
AH...
NO MATTER HOW MANY TIMES I DO IT, I FEEL LIKE I'M GOING TO GO CRAZY.
WHY DO WE HAVE TO DO SOMETHING LIKE THIS.........?
WILL DOING THIS REALLY MOVE THE YAMATSUMI TO SAVE US...?

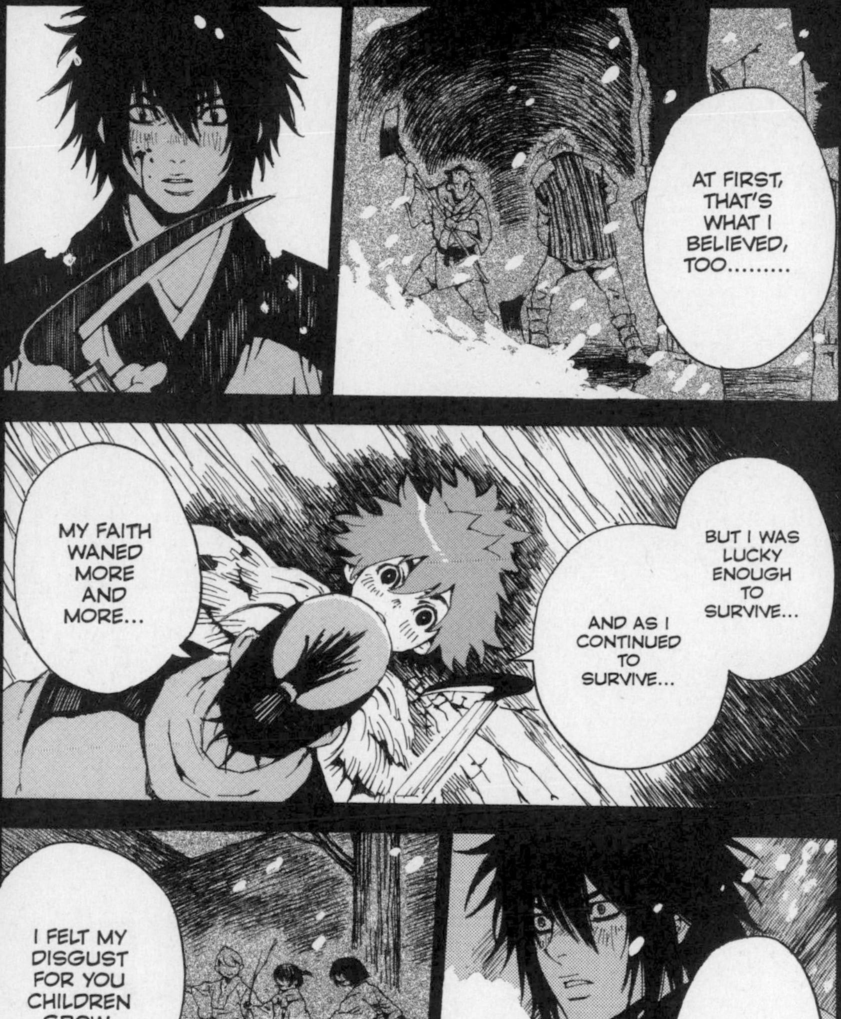
AT FIRST, THAT'S WHAT I BELIEVED, TOO.........
BUT I WAS LUCKY ENOUGH TO SURVIVE...
AND AS I CONTINUED TO SURVIVE...
MY FAITH WANED MORE AND MORE...
AND AS IF TO FILL THOSE CRACKS...
I FELT MY DISGUST FOR YOU CHILDREN GROW.

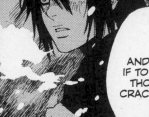

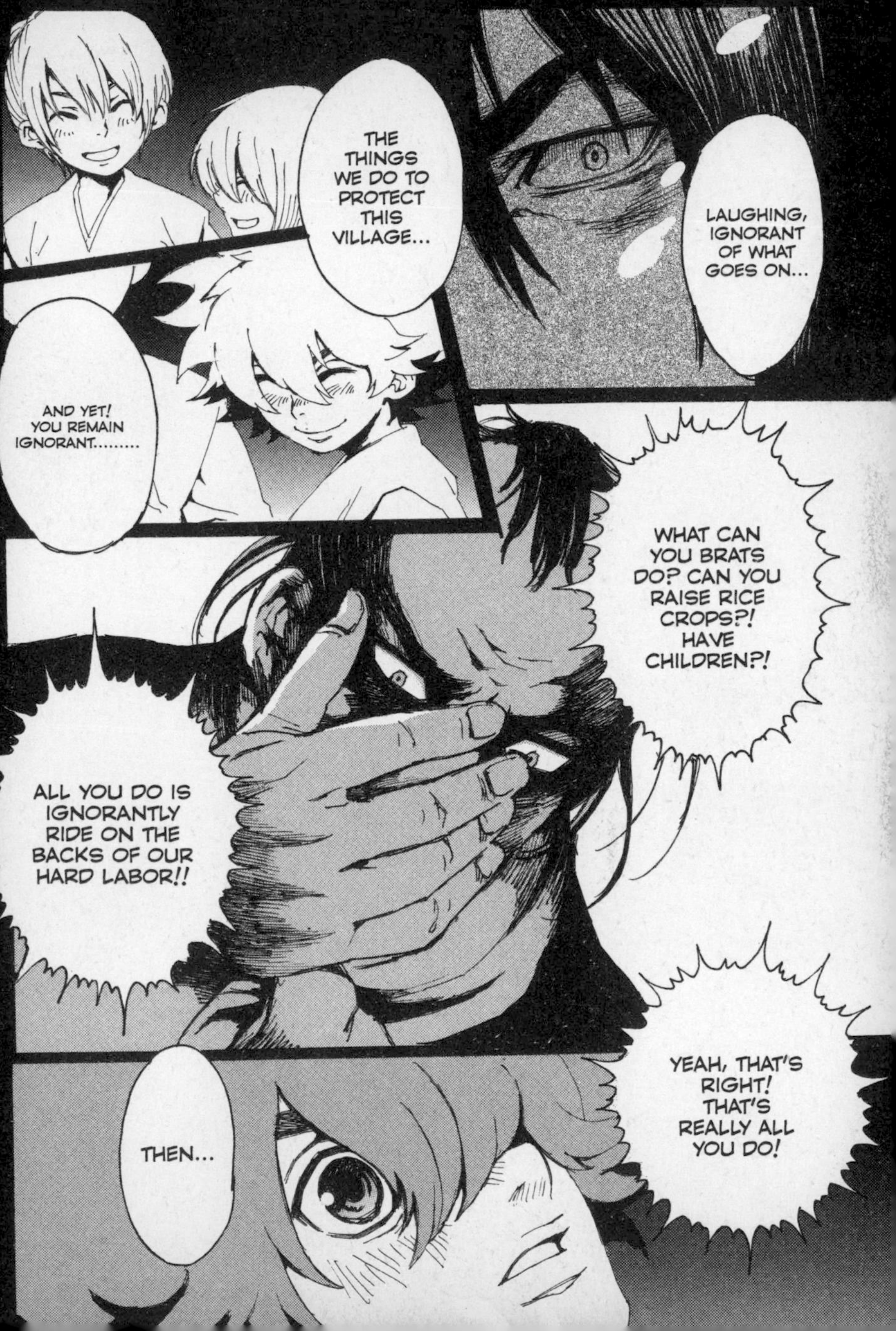
LAUGHING, IGNORANT OF WHAT GOES ON...
THE THINGS WE DO TO PROTECT THIS VILLAGE...
AND YET! YOU REMAIN IGNORANT.........
WHAT CAN YOU BRATS DO? CAN YOU RAISE RICE CROPS?! HAVE CHILDREN?!
ALL YOU DO IS IGNORANTLY RIDE ON THE BACKS OF OUR HARD LABOR!!
YEAH, THAT'S RIGHT! THAT'S REALLY ALL YOU DO!
THEN...

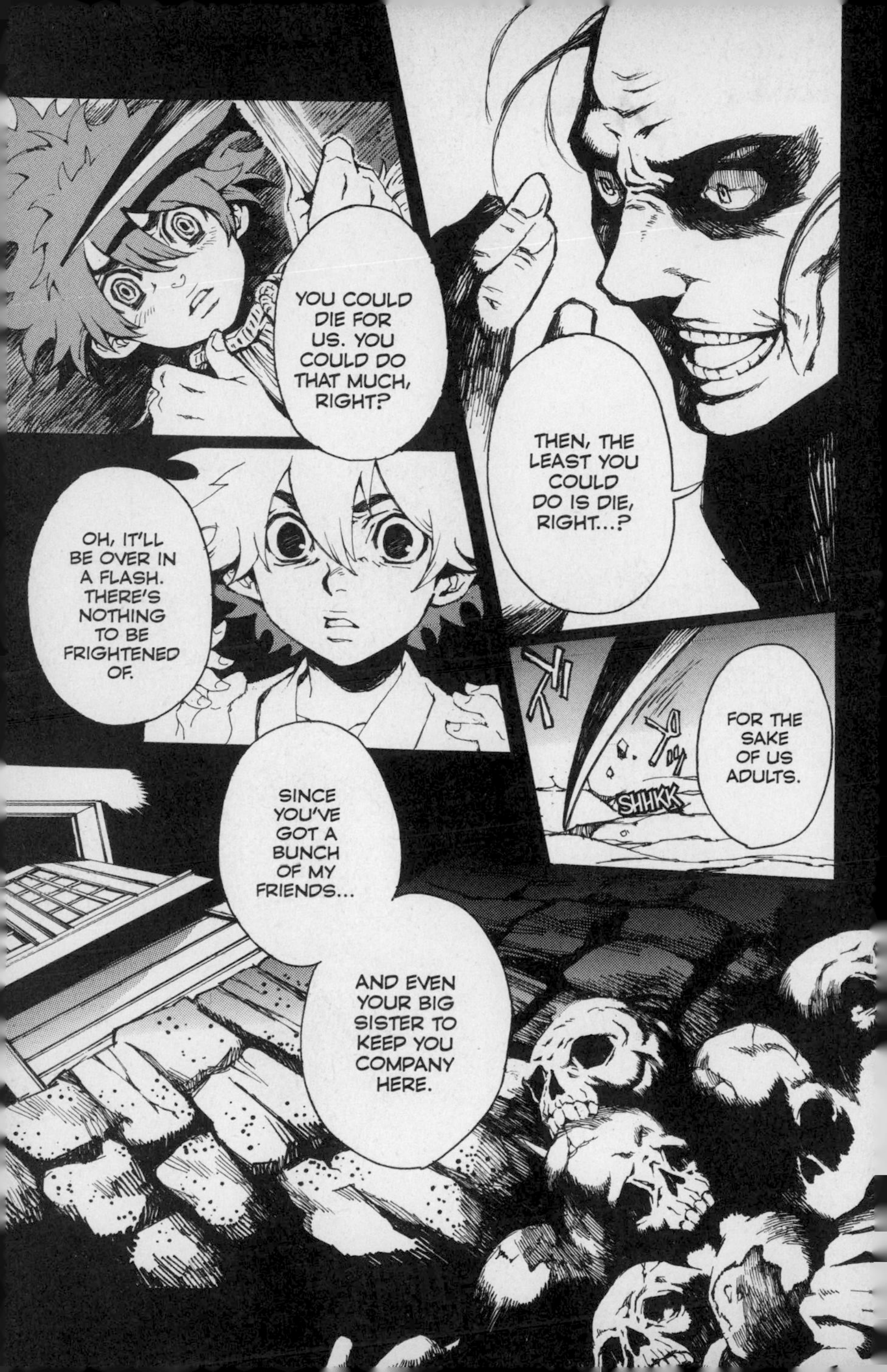
THEN, THE LEAST YOU COULD DO IS DIE, RIGHT...?
YOU COULD DIE FOR US. YOU COULD DO THAT MUCH, RIGHT?
OH, IT'LL BE OVER IN A FLASH. THERE'S NOTHING TO BE FRIGHTENED OF.
FOR THE SAKE OF US ADULTS.
SHHKK
SINCE YOU'VE GOT A BUNCH OF MY FRIENDS...
AND EVEN YOUR BIG SISTER TO KEEP YOU COMPANY HERE.

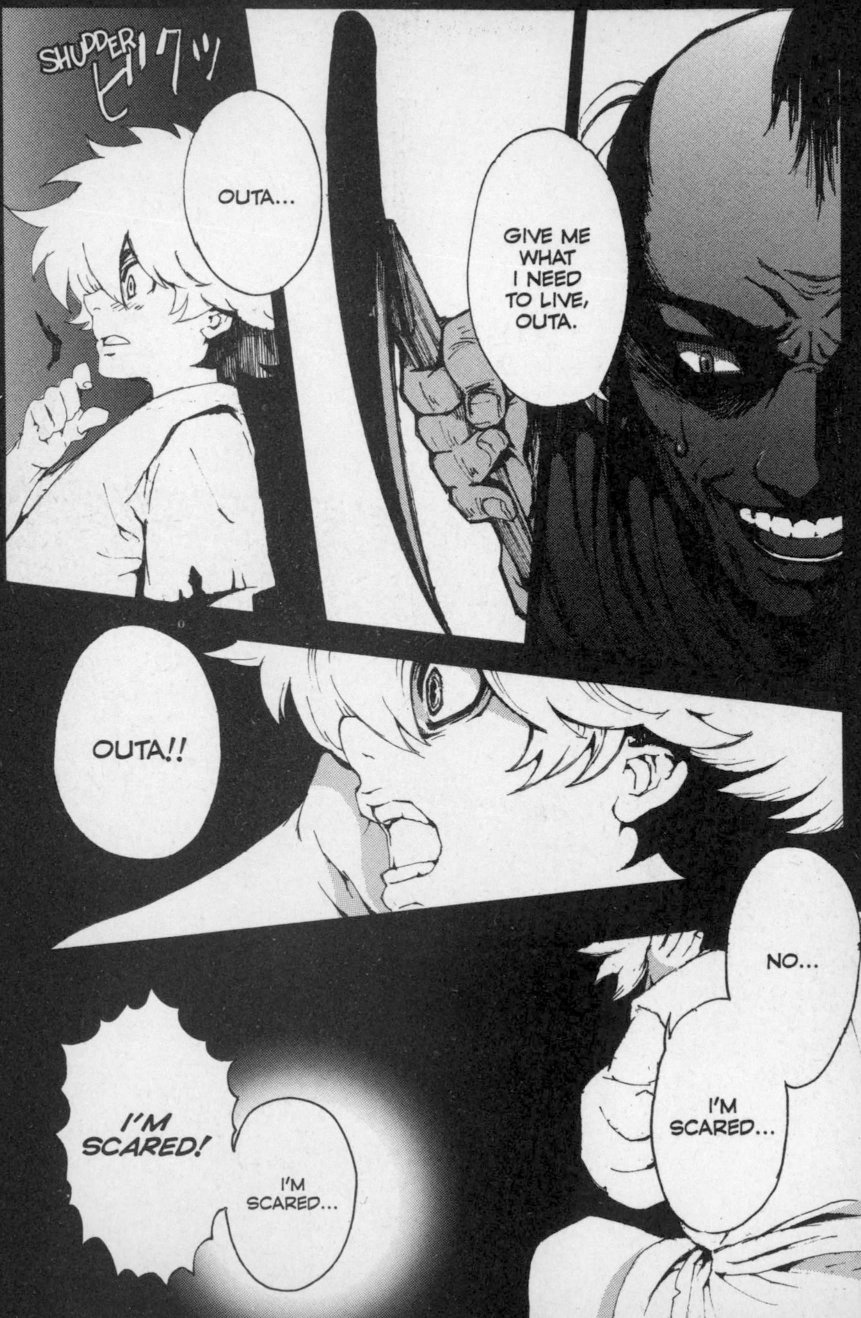
GIVE ME WHAT I NEED TO LIVE, OUTA.
SHUDDER ビクッ
OUTA...
OUTA!!
NO...
I'M SCARED...
I'M SCARED!
I'M SCARED...

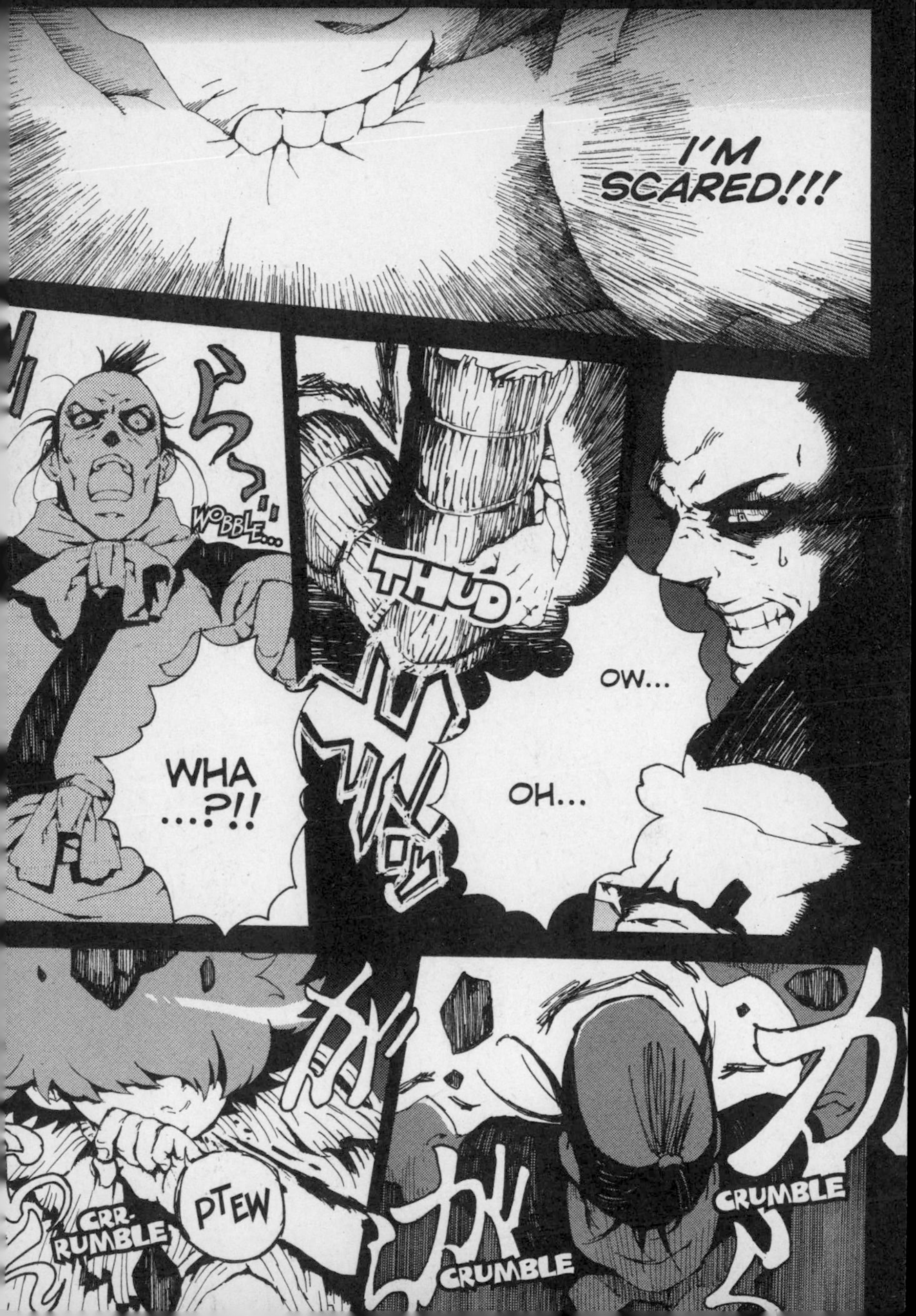
I'M SCARED!!!
OW...
OH...
THUD
WOBBLE...
WHA ...?!!
CRUMBLE
CRUMBLE
PTEW
CRR-RUMBLE

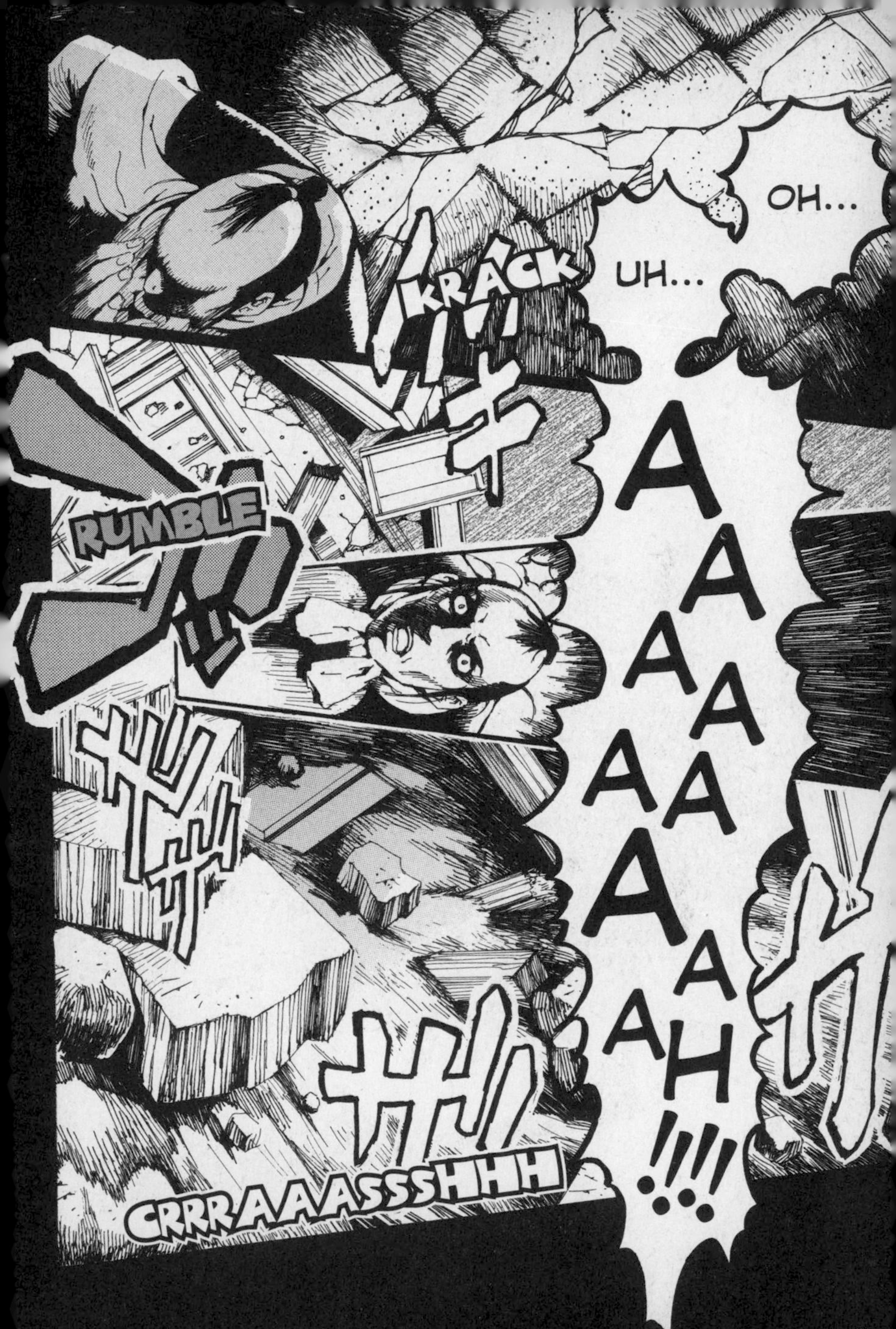
OH...
UH...
KRACK
RUMBLE
AAAAAAAAAH!!!!
CRRRAAAASSSHHH

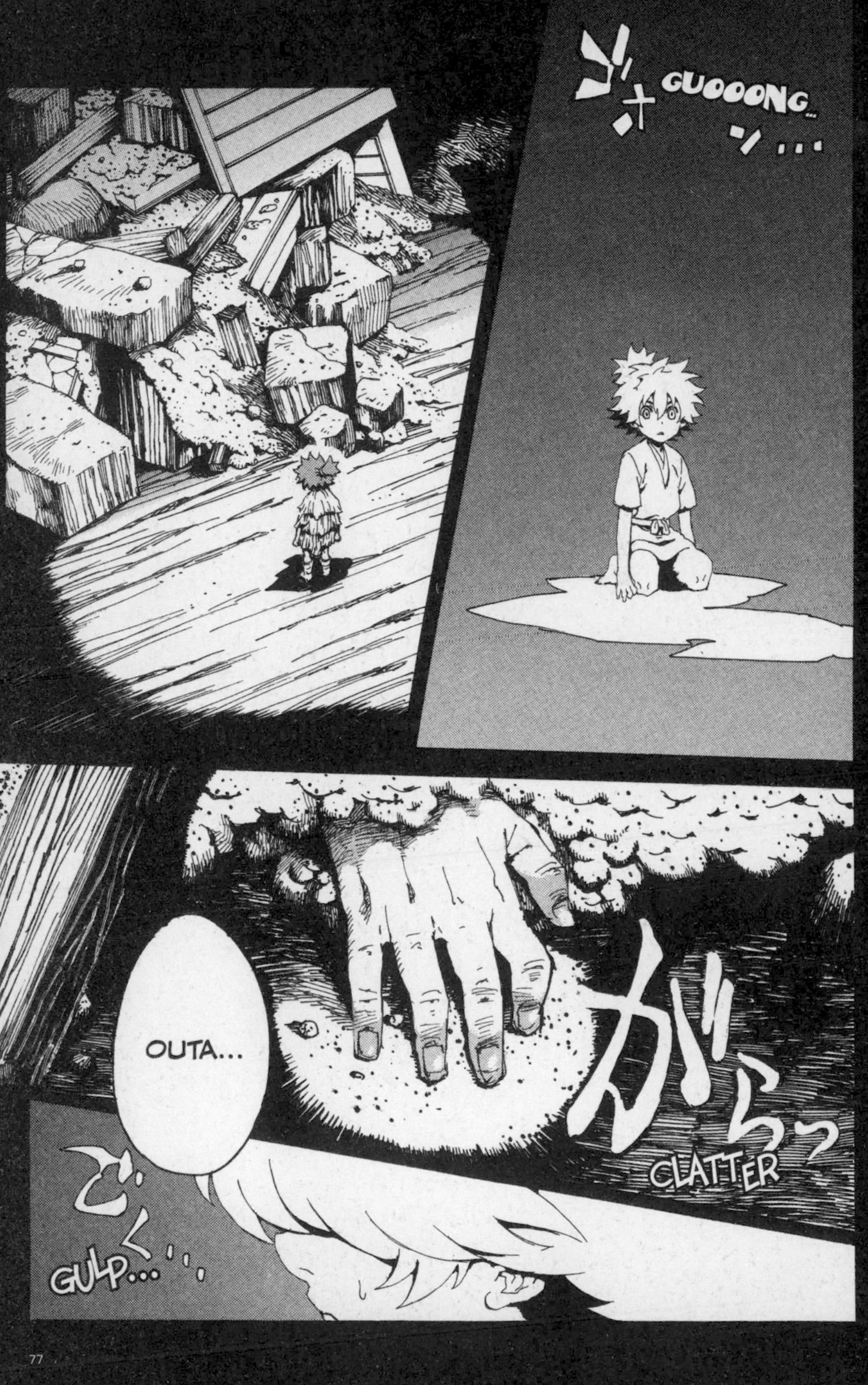
GUOOONG...
がらっ
CLATTER
OUTA...
GULP...

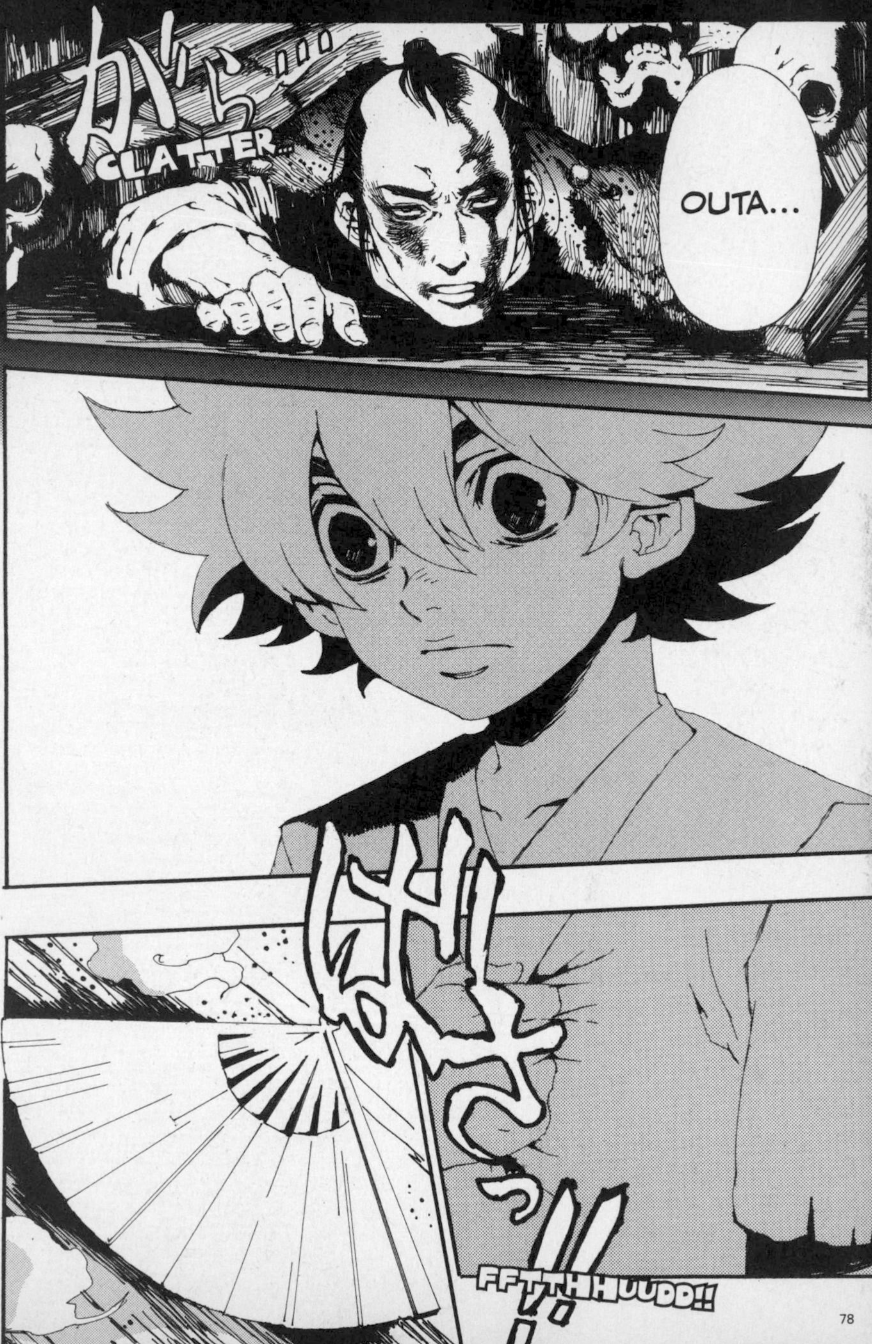
OUTA...
からら...
CLATTER...
ばさっ!!
FFTTHHUUDD!!

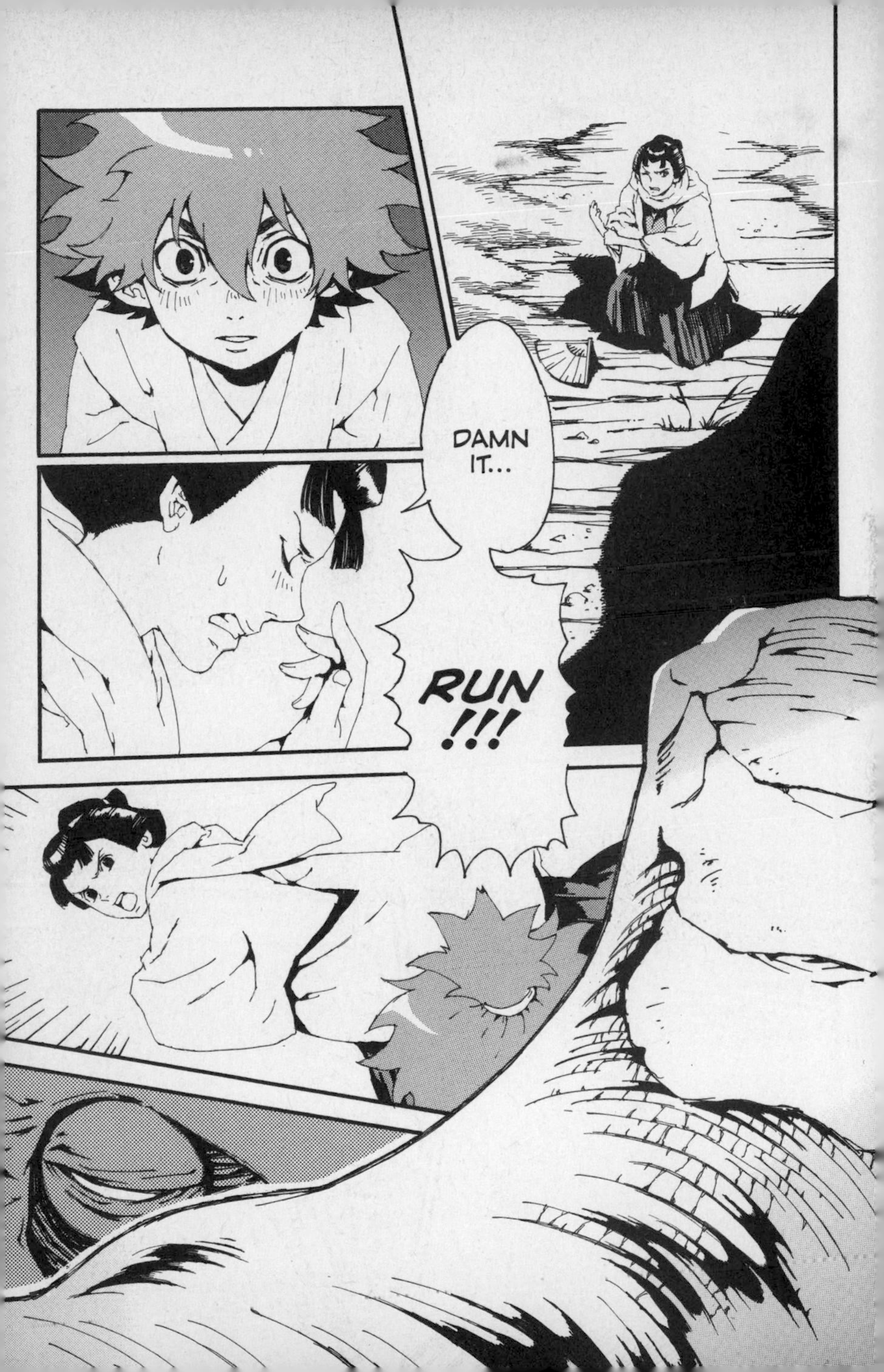
DAMN IT...
RUN !!!

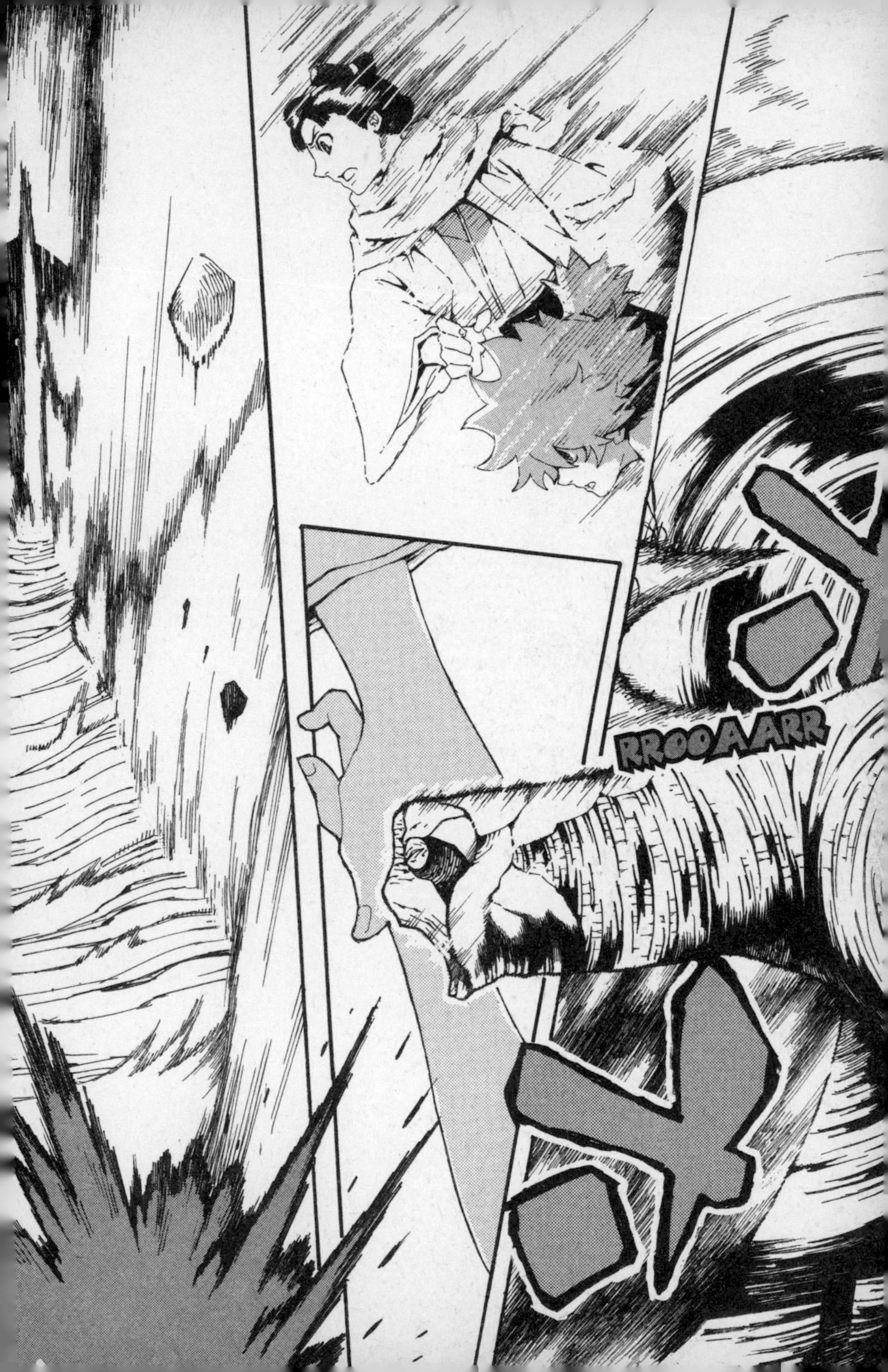
RROOAARR

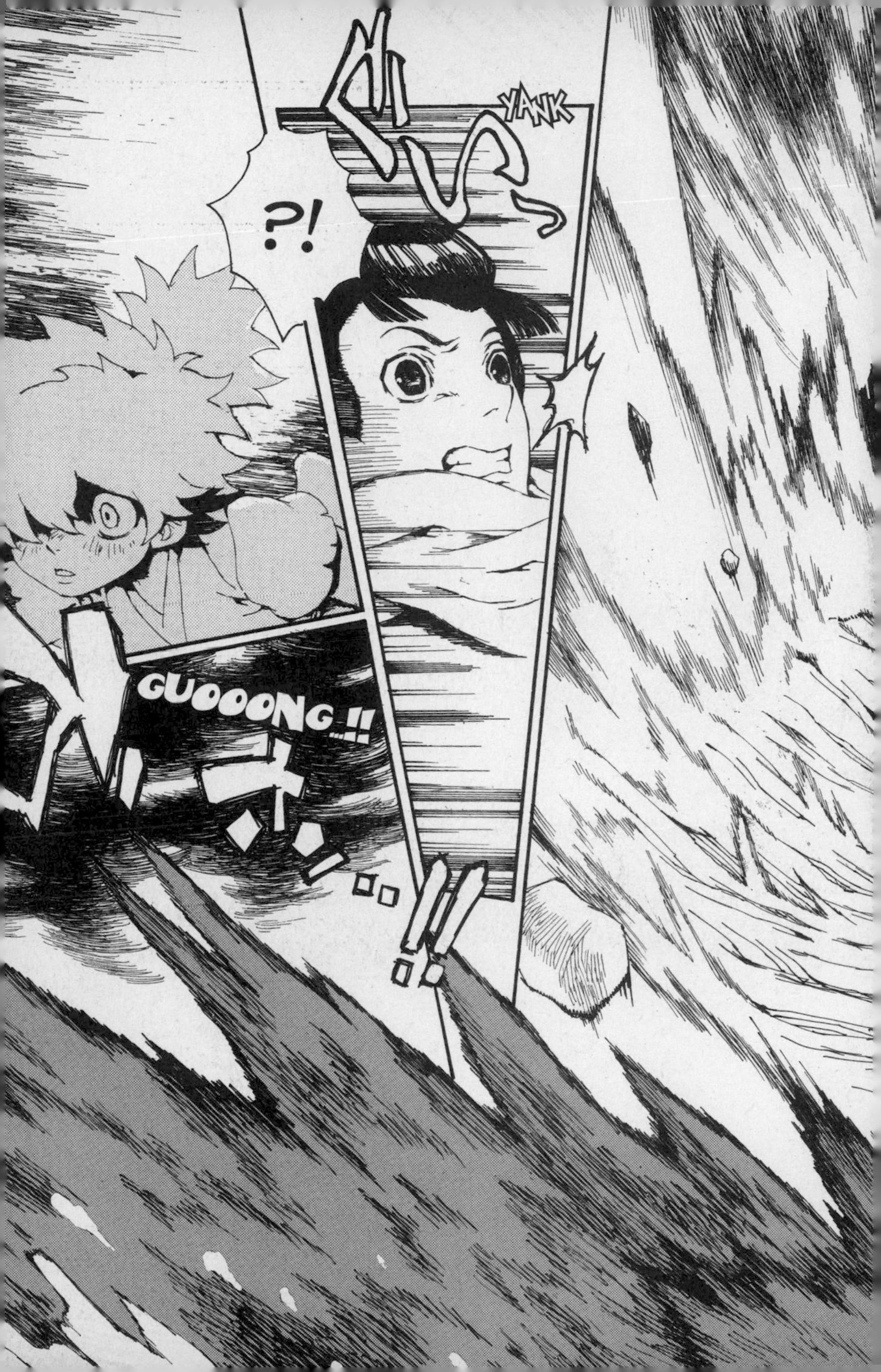
YANK
?!
GUOOONG..!!

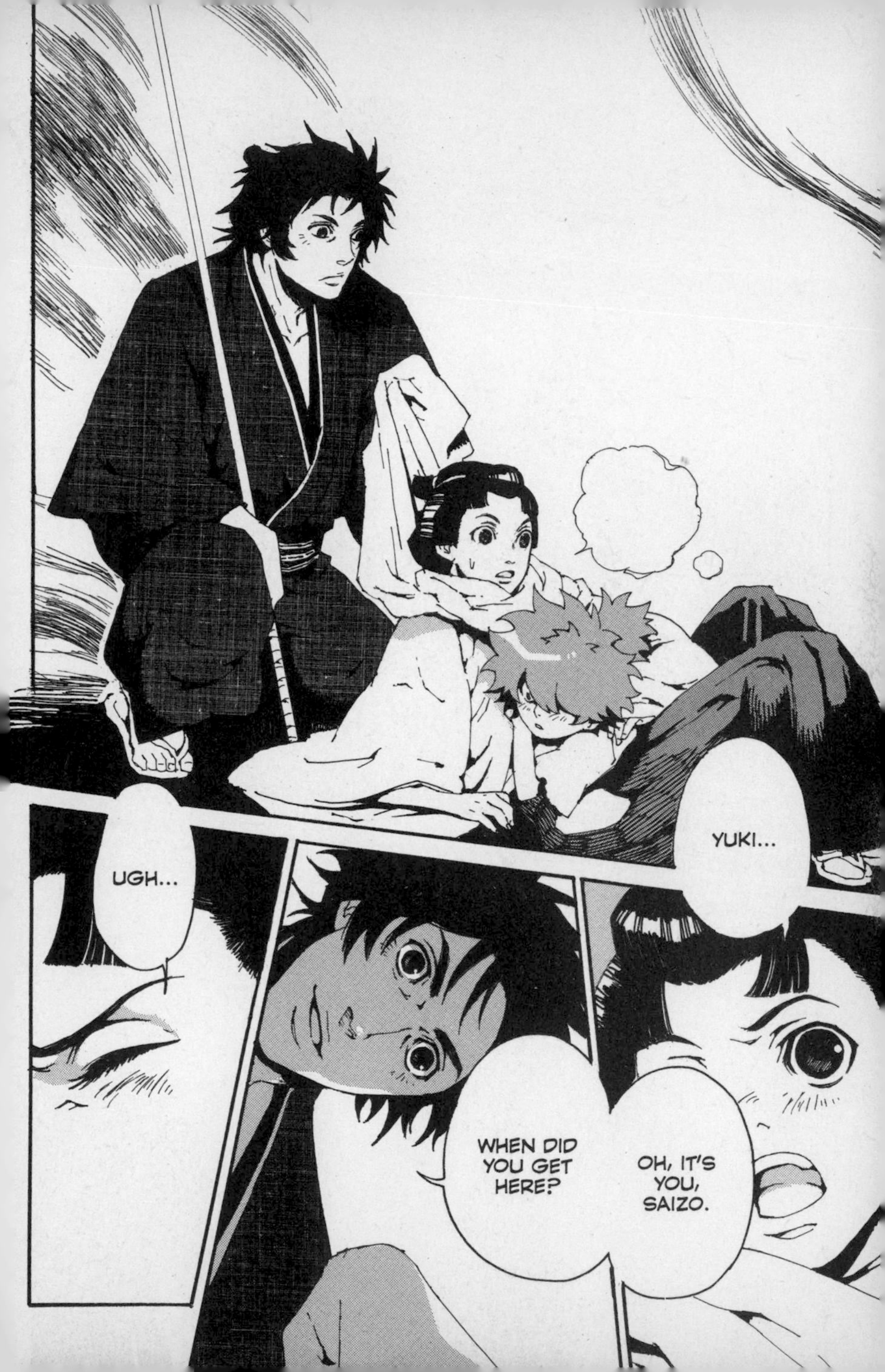
YUKI...
OH, IT'S YOU, SAIZO.
WHEN DID YOU GET HERE?
UGH...

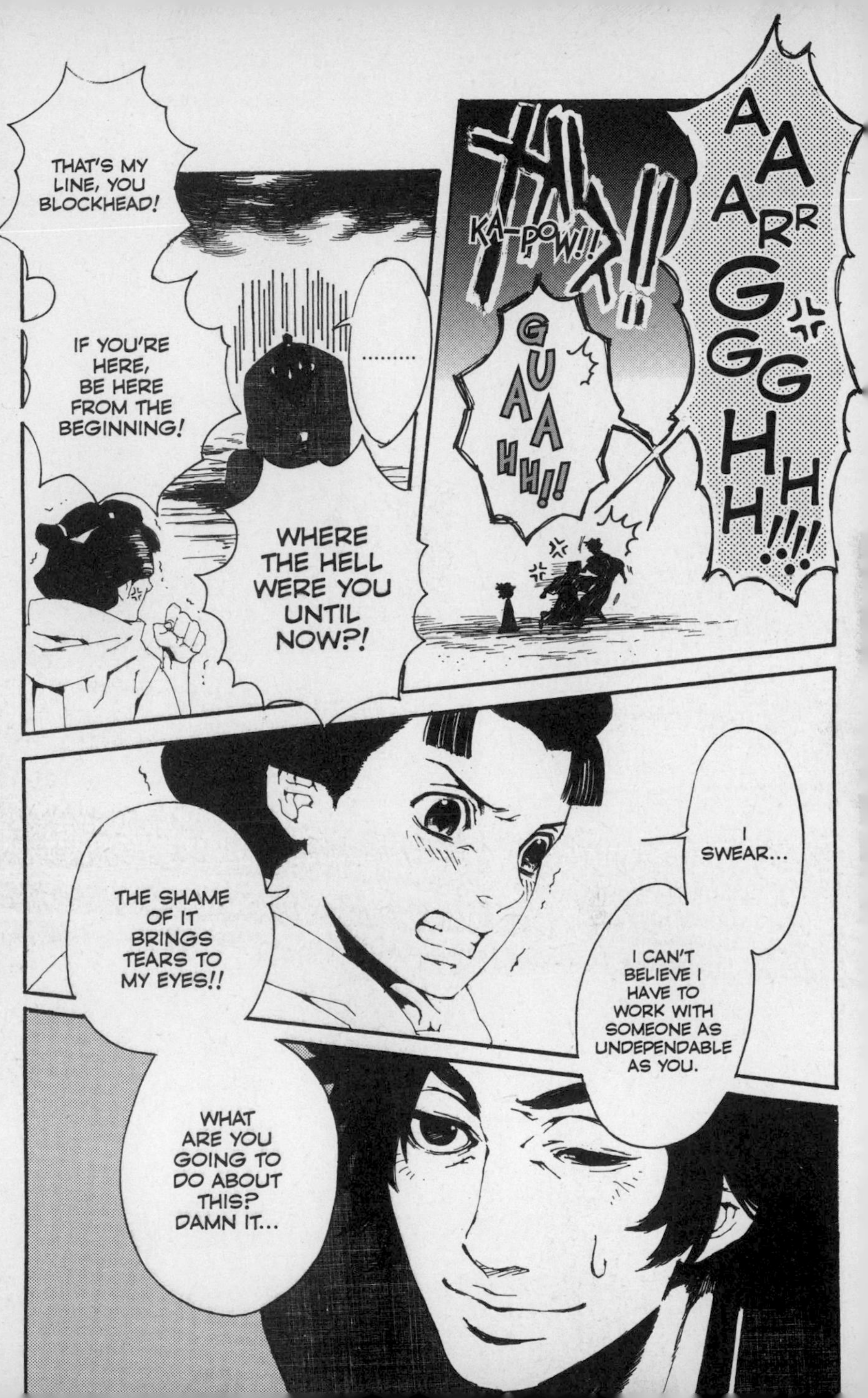
AAARRGGHHH!!!!
KA-POW!!
GUAAHH!!
WHERE THE HELL WERE YOU UNTIL NOW?!
....
THAT'S MY LINE, YOU BLOCKHEAD!
IF YOU'RE HERE, BE HERE FROM THE BEGINNING!
I SWEAR...
THE SHAME OF IT BRINGS TEARS TO MY EYES!!
I CAN'T BELIEVE I HAVE TO WORK WITH SOMEONE AS UNDEPENDABLE AS YOU.
WHAT ARE YOU GOING TO DO ABOUT THIS? DAMN IT...

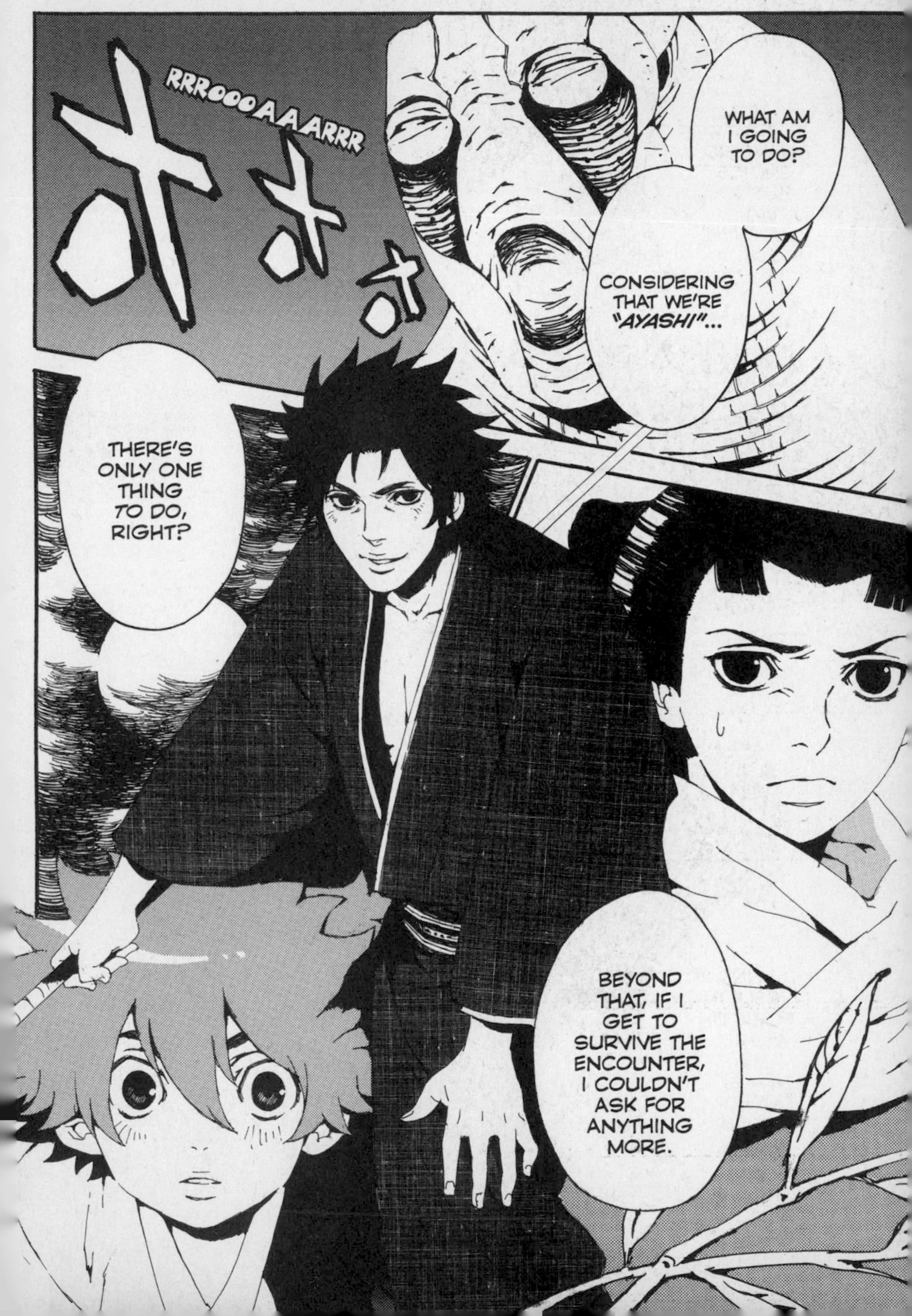

WHAT AM I GOING TO DO?
CONSIDERING THAT WE'RE "AYASHI"...
RRROOOAAARRR
THERE'S ONLY ONE THING TO DO, RIGHT?
BEYOND THAT, IF I GET TO SURVIVE THE ENCOUNTER, I COULDN'T ASK FOR ANYTHING MORE.

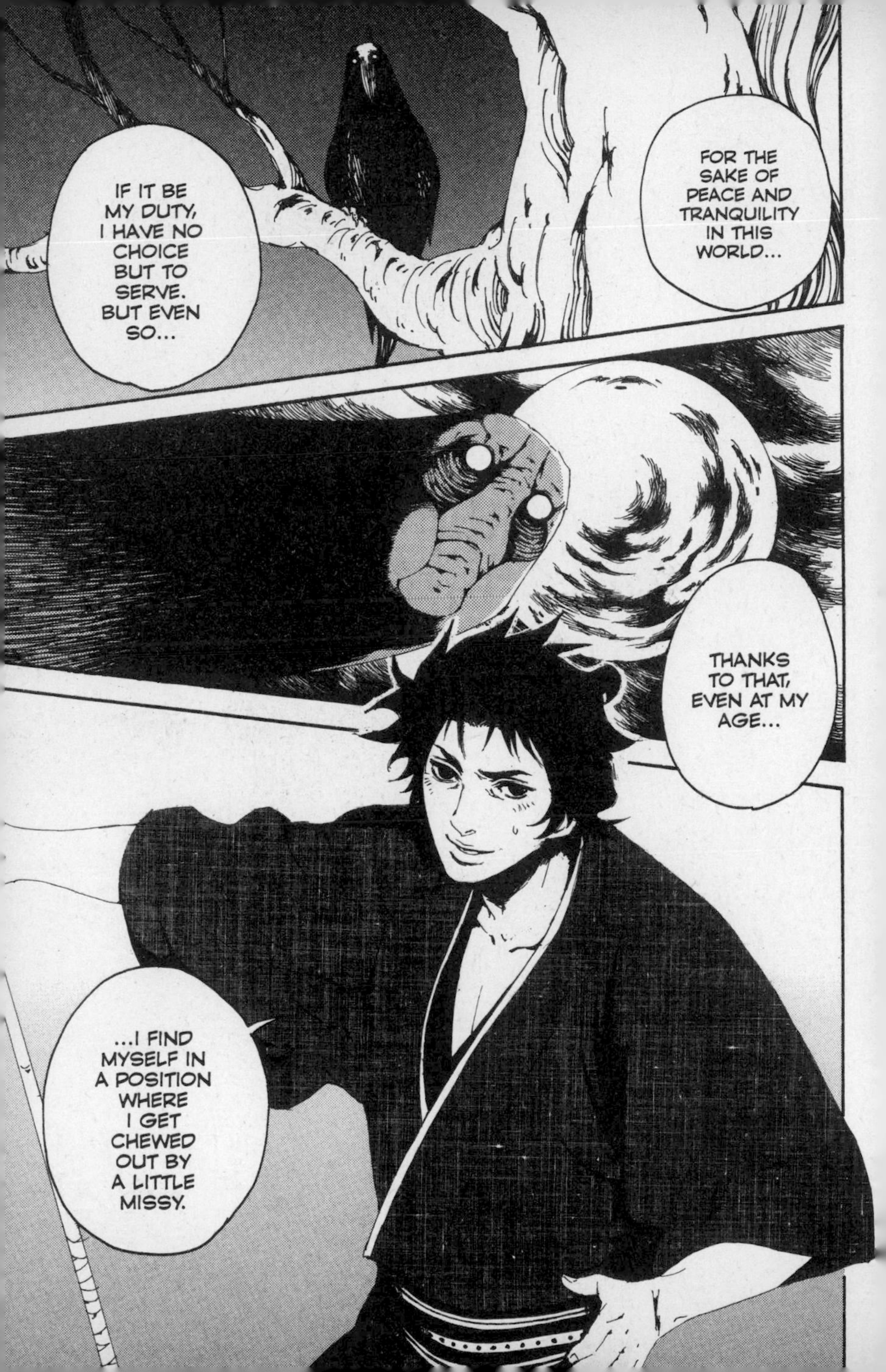
FOR THE SAKE OF PEACE AND TRANQUILITY IN THIS WORLD...
IF IT BE MY DUTY, I HAVE NO CHOICE BUT TO SERVE. BUT EVEN SO...
THANKS TO THAT, EVEN AT MY AGE...
...I FIND MYSELF IN A POSITION WHERE I GET CHEWED OUT BY A LITTLE MISSY.

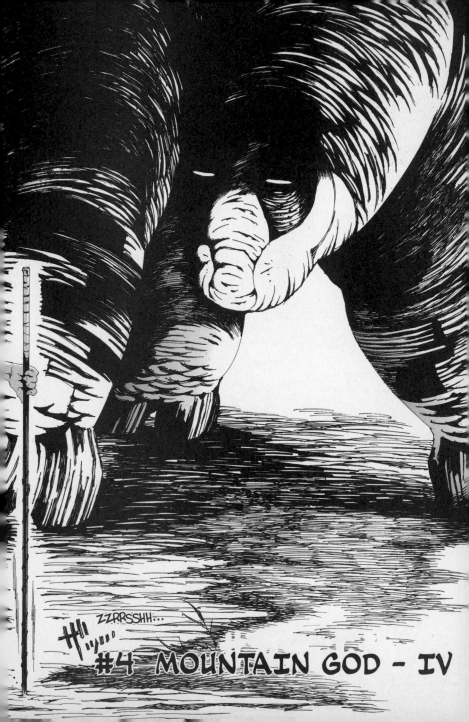

ZZRRSSHH...

#4 MOUNTAIN GOD - IV

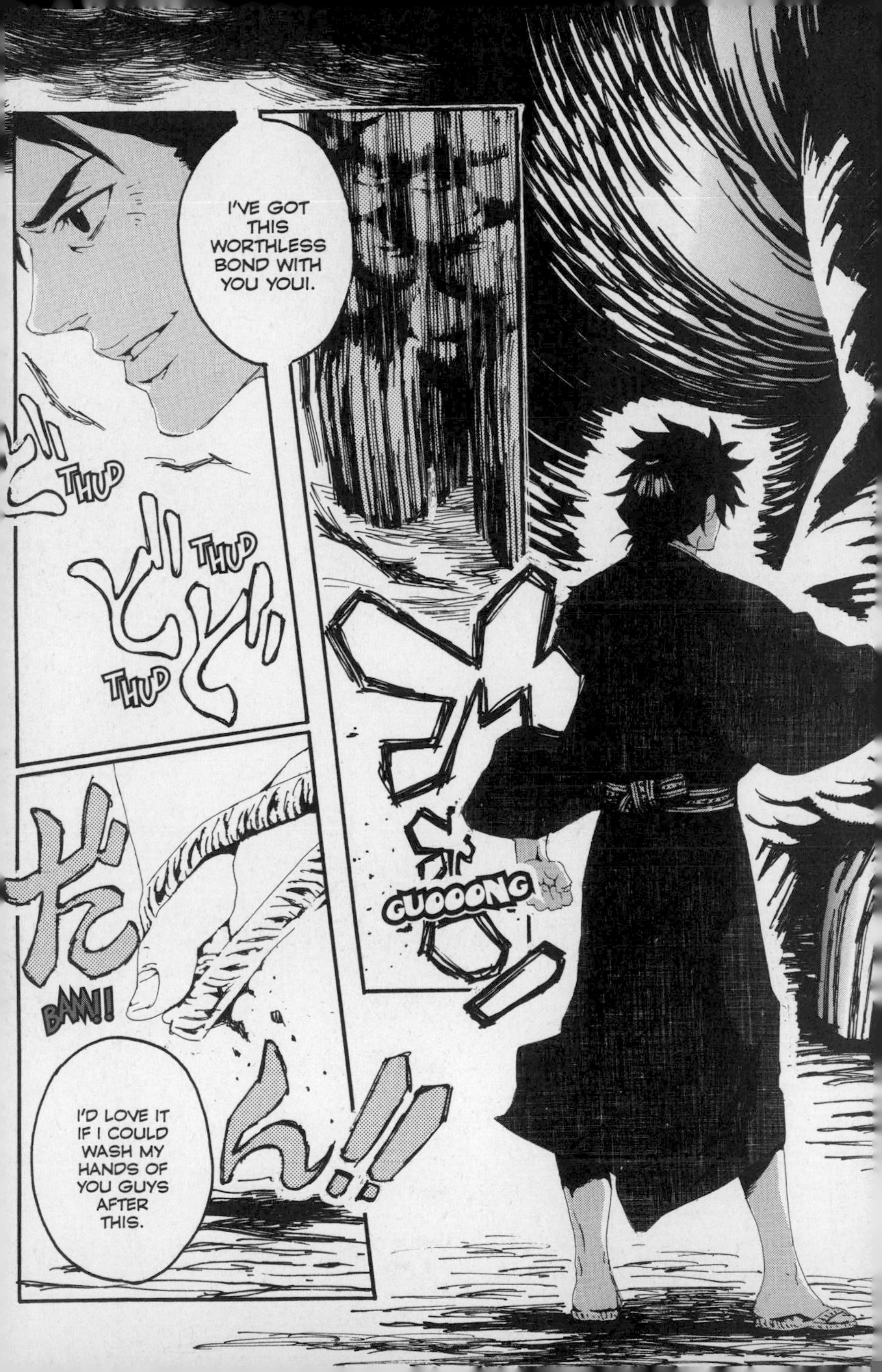

I'VE GOT THIS WORTHLESS BOND WITH YOU YOUI.
GUOOONG
THUD
THUD
THUD
BAM!
I'D LOVE IT IF I COULD WASH MY HANDS OF YOU GUYS AFTER THIS.

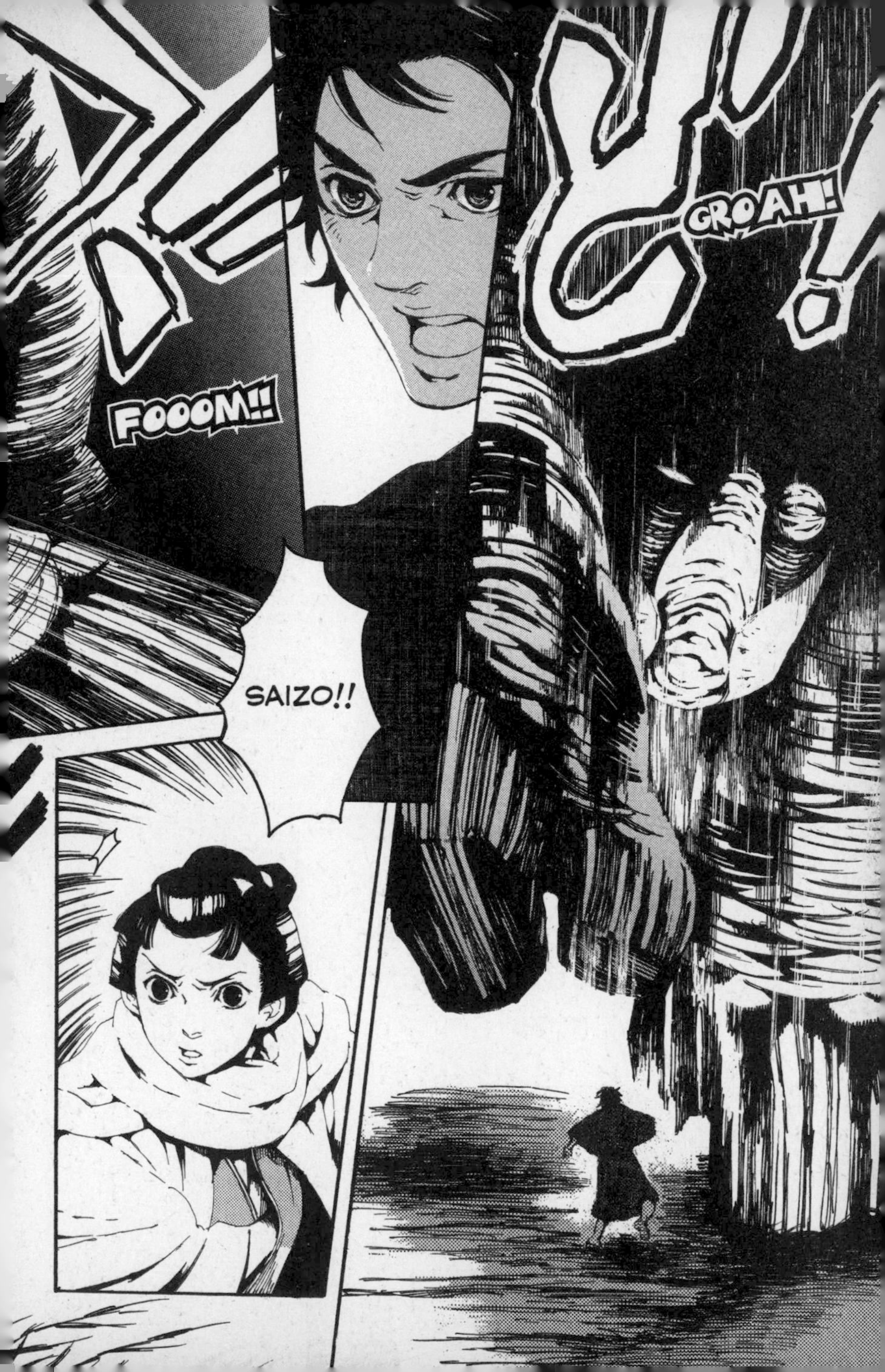
GROAH!
FOOOM!!
SAIZO!!

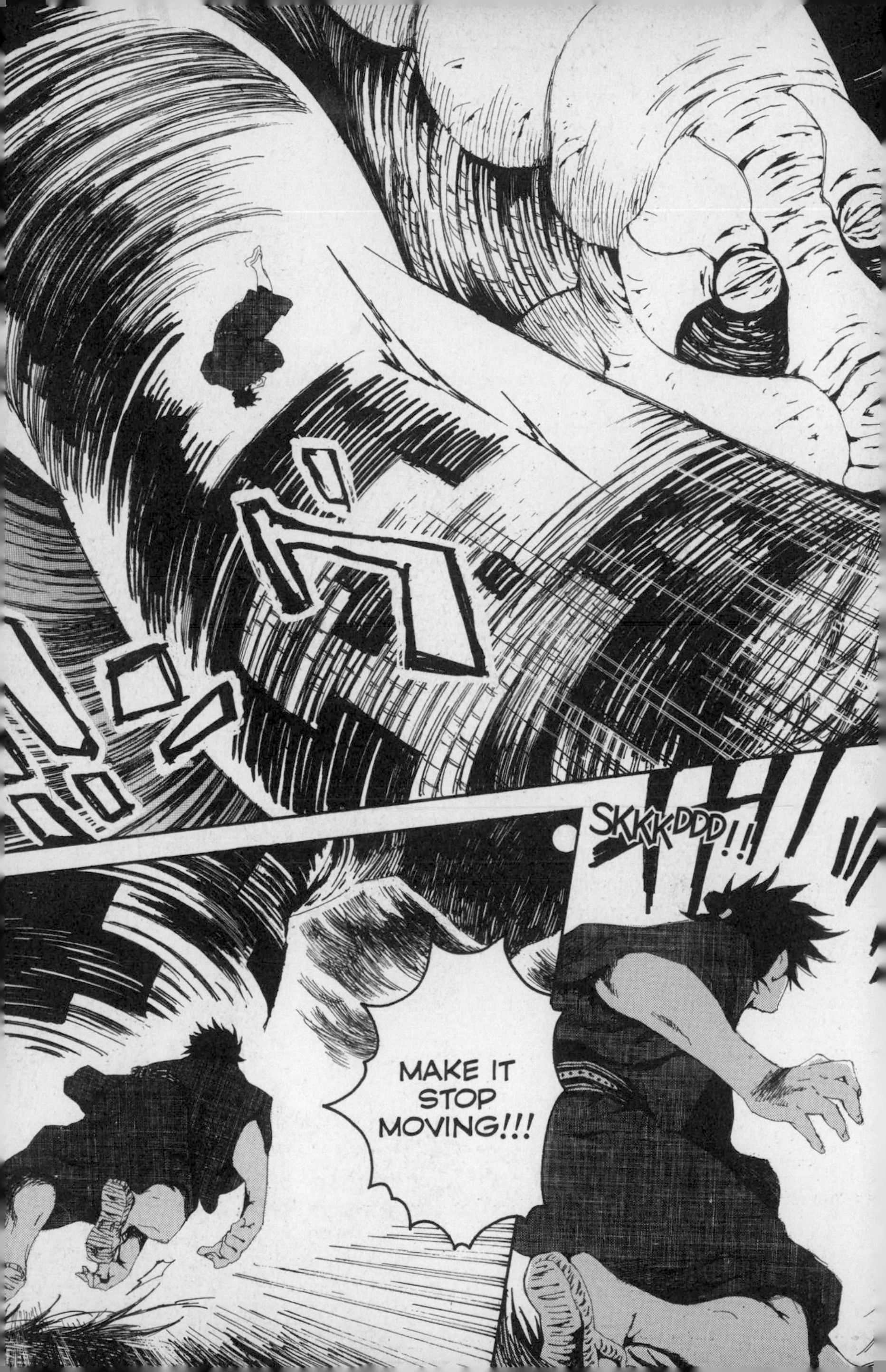
SKKKDDD!!
MAKE IT STOP MOVING!!!

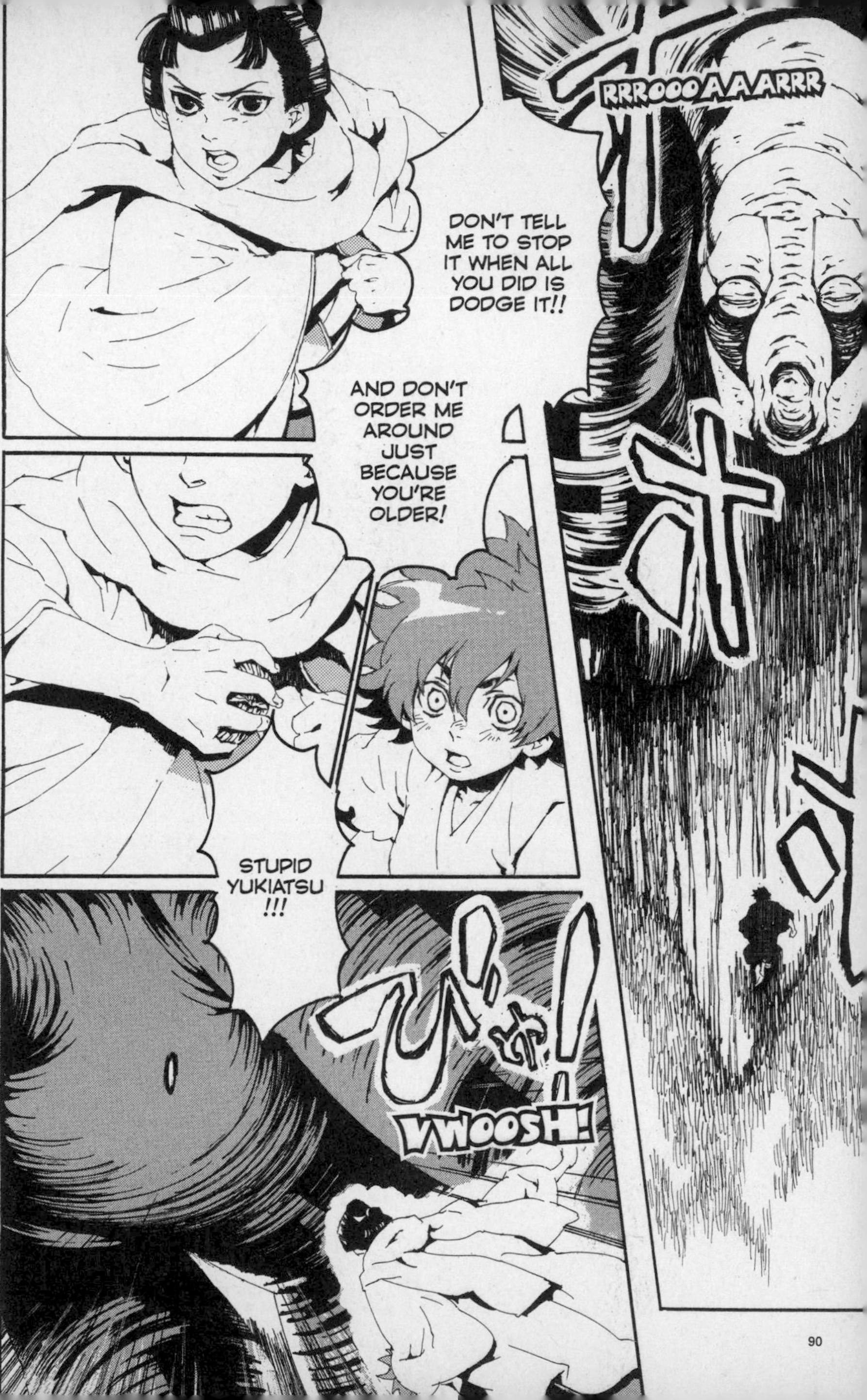
RRROOOAAARRR
DON'T TELL ME TO STOP IT WHEN ALL YOU DID IS DODGE IT!!
AND DON'T ORDER ME AROUND JUST BECAUSE YOU'RE OLDER!
STUPID YUKIATSU !!!
VWOOSH!

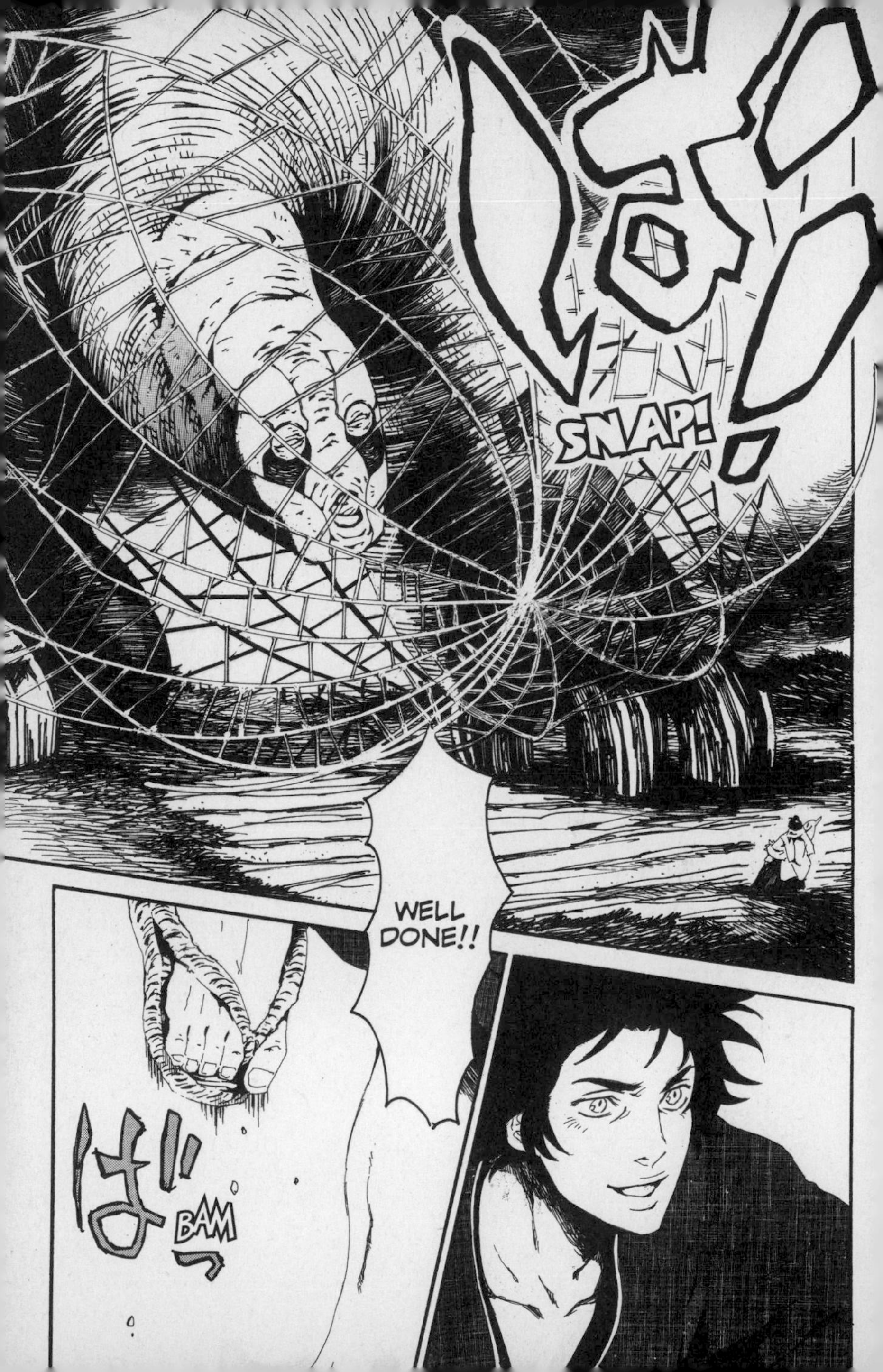
SNAP!
WELL DONE!!
BAM

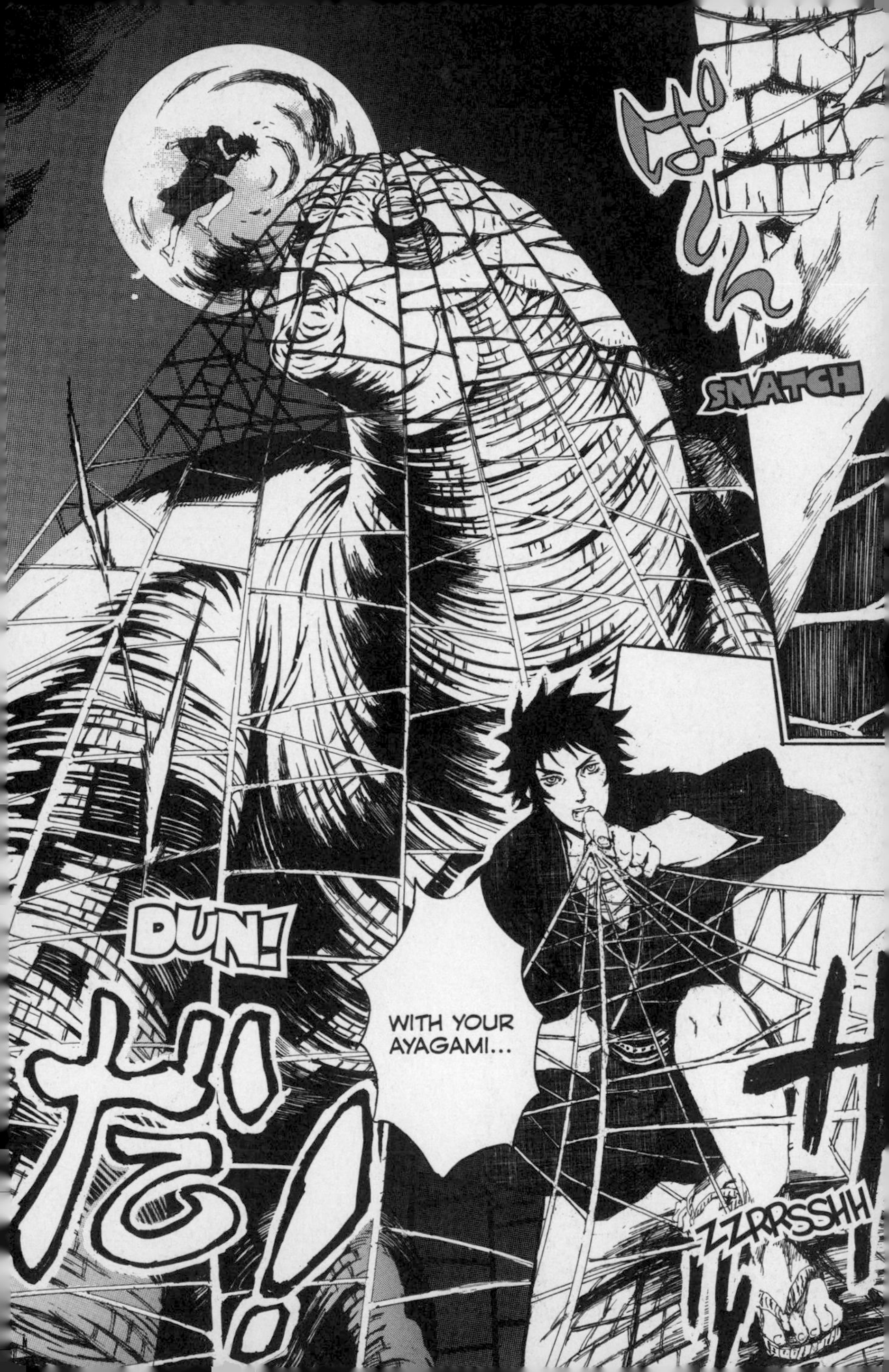
SNATCH
DUN!
WITH YOUR AYAGAMI...
ZZRRSSHH

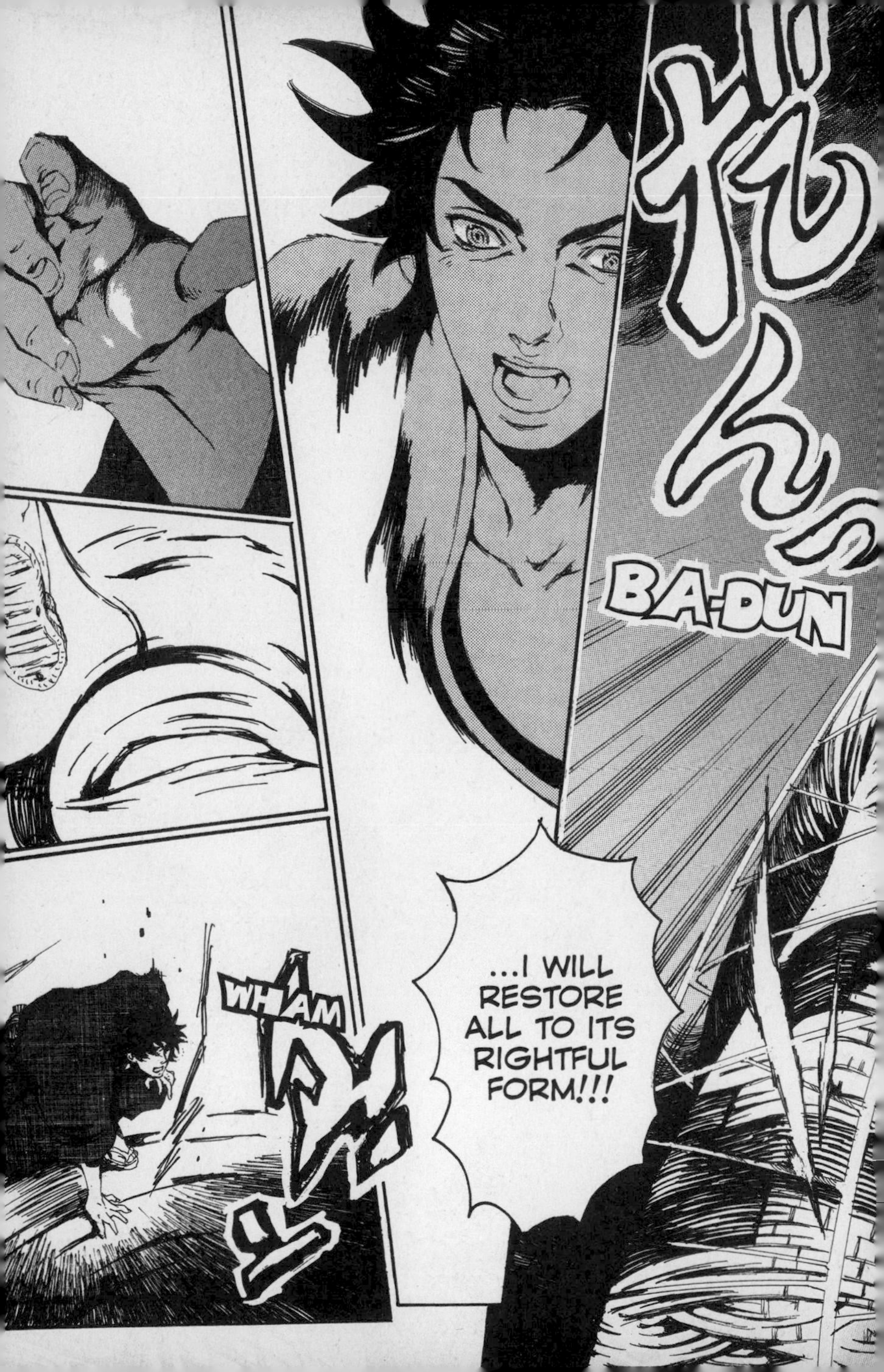
BA-DUN
...I WILL RESTORE ALL TO ITS RIGHTFUL FORM!!!
WHAM

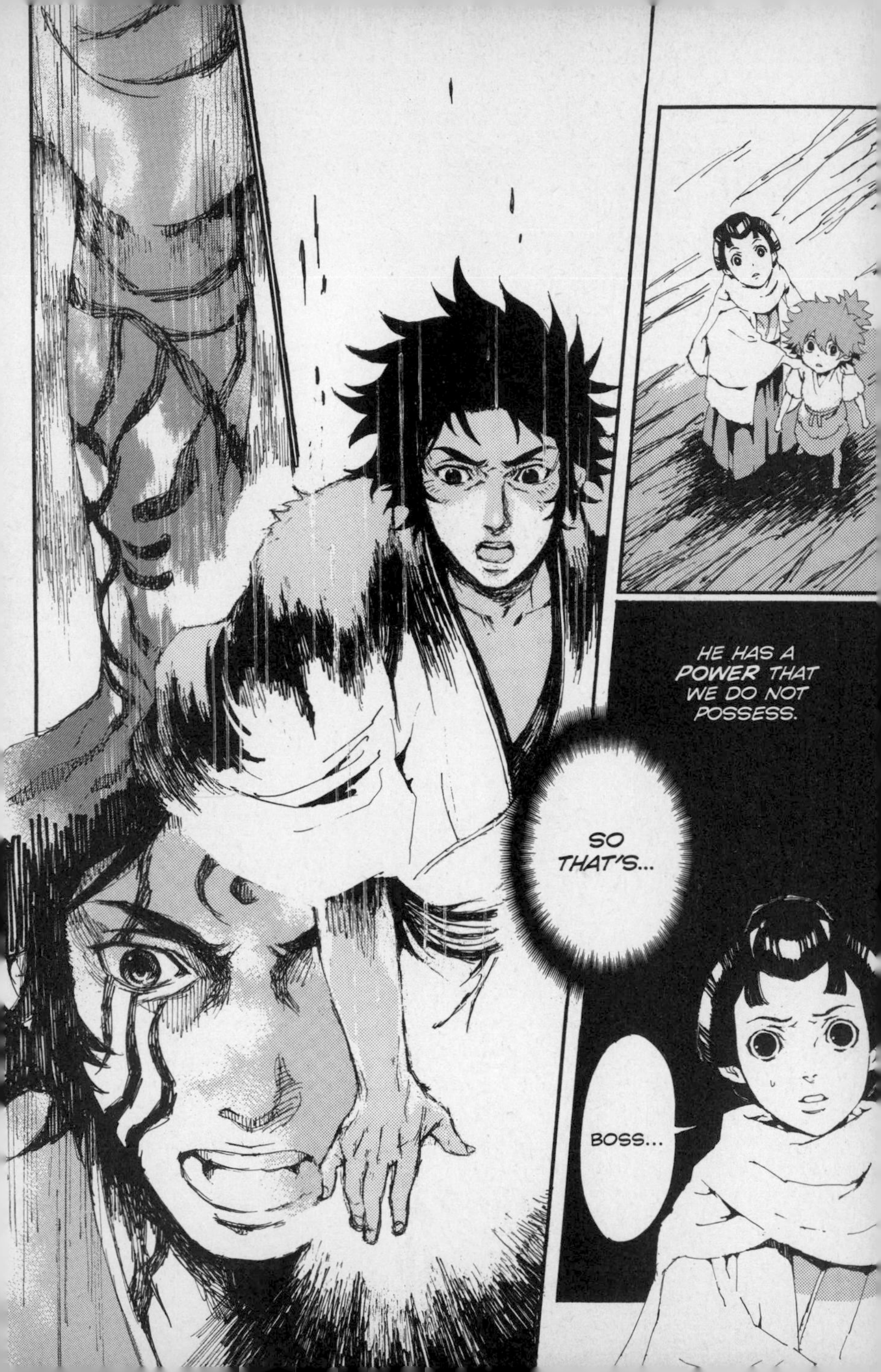
HE HAS A POWER THAT WE DO NOT POSSESS.
SO THAT'S...
BOSS...

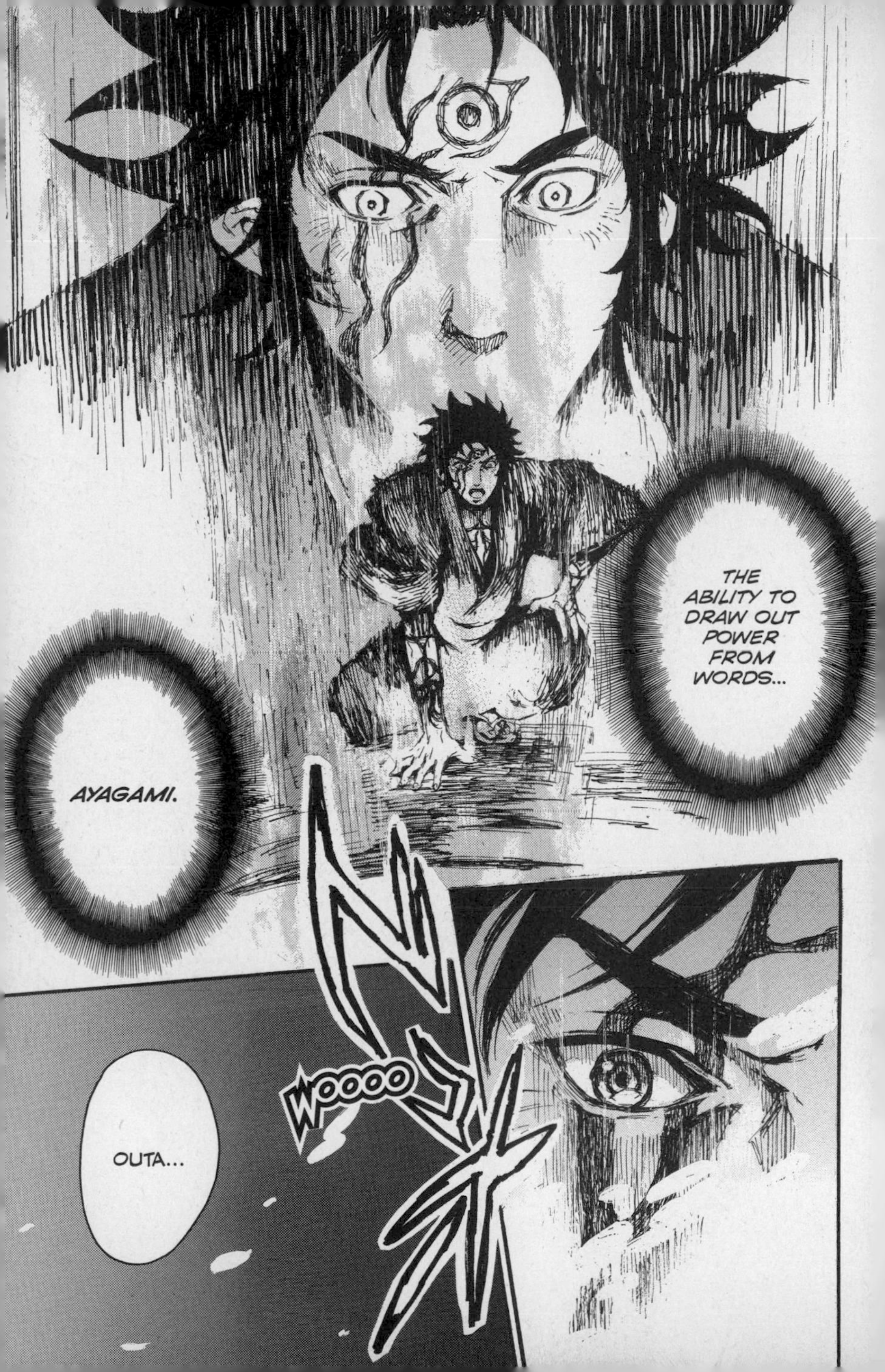
THE ABILITY TO DRAW OUT POWER FROM WORDS...
AYAGAMI.
WOOOO
OUTA...

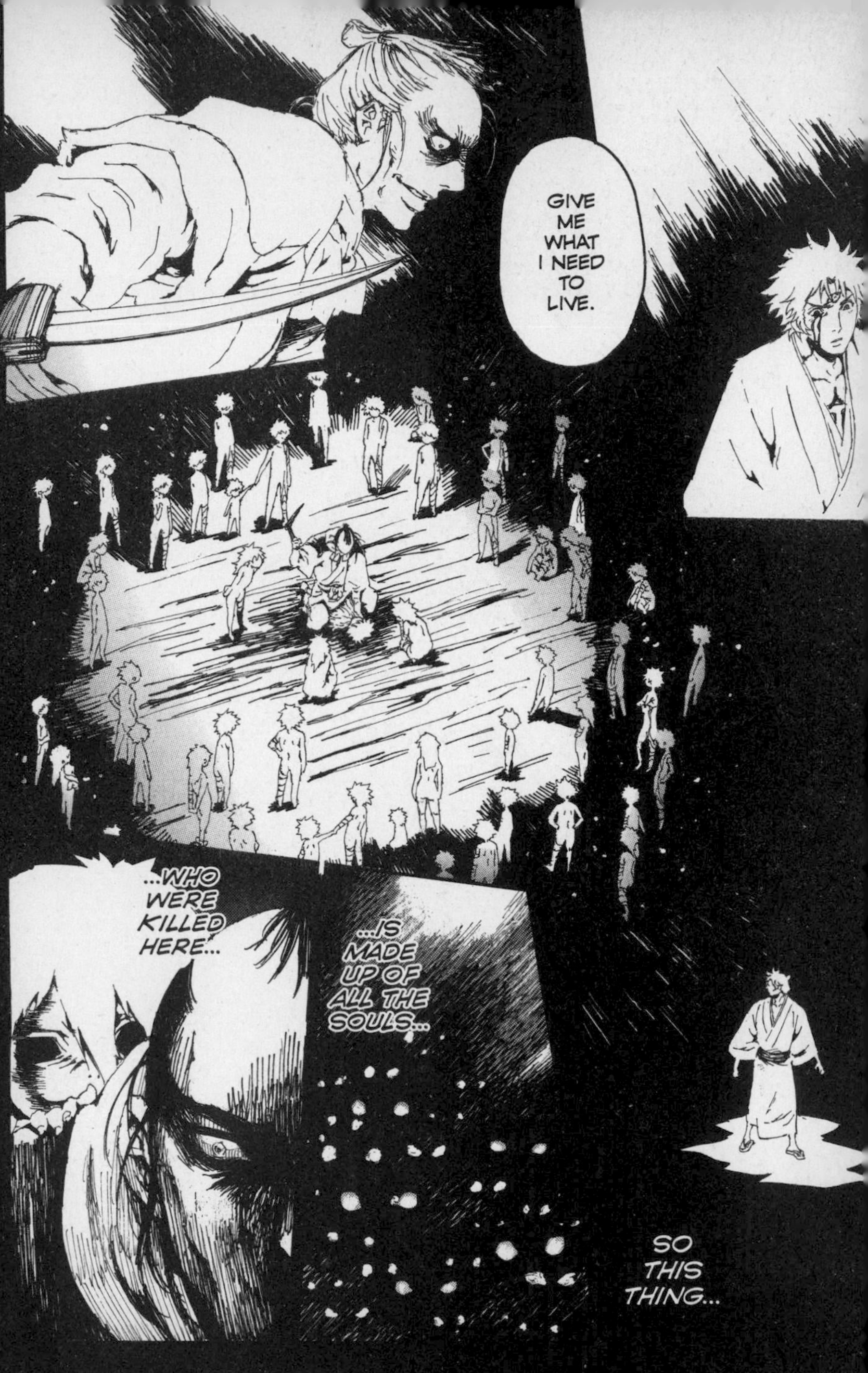
GIVE ME WHAT I NEED TO LIVE.
...WHO WERE KILLED HERE...
...IS MADE UP OF ALL THE SOULS...
SO THIS THING...

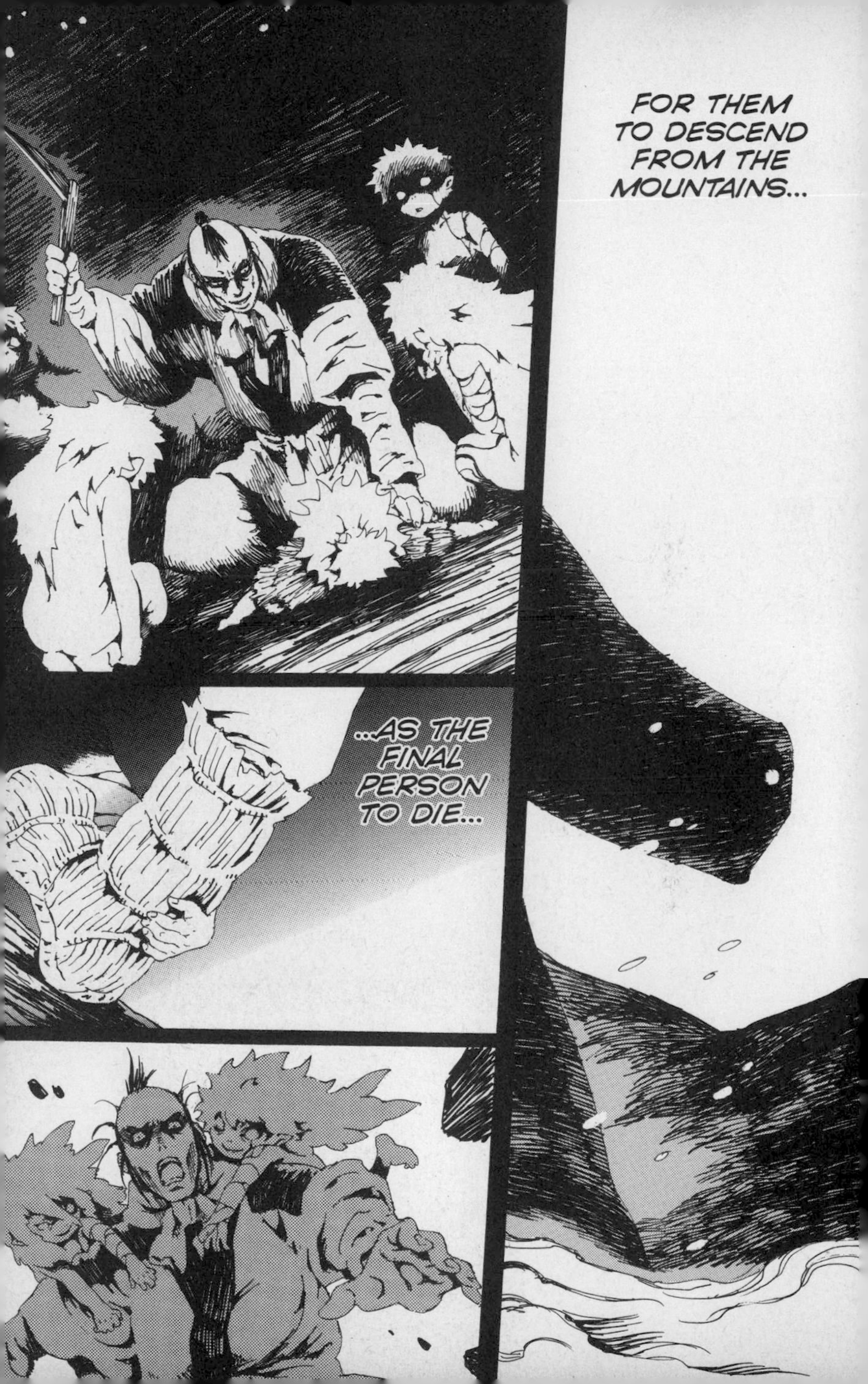
FOR THEM TO DESCEND FROM THE MOUNTAINS...
...AS THE FINAL PERSON TO DIE...

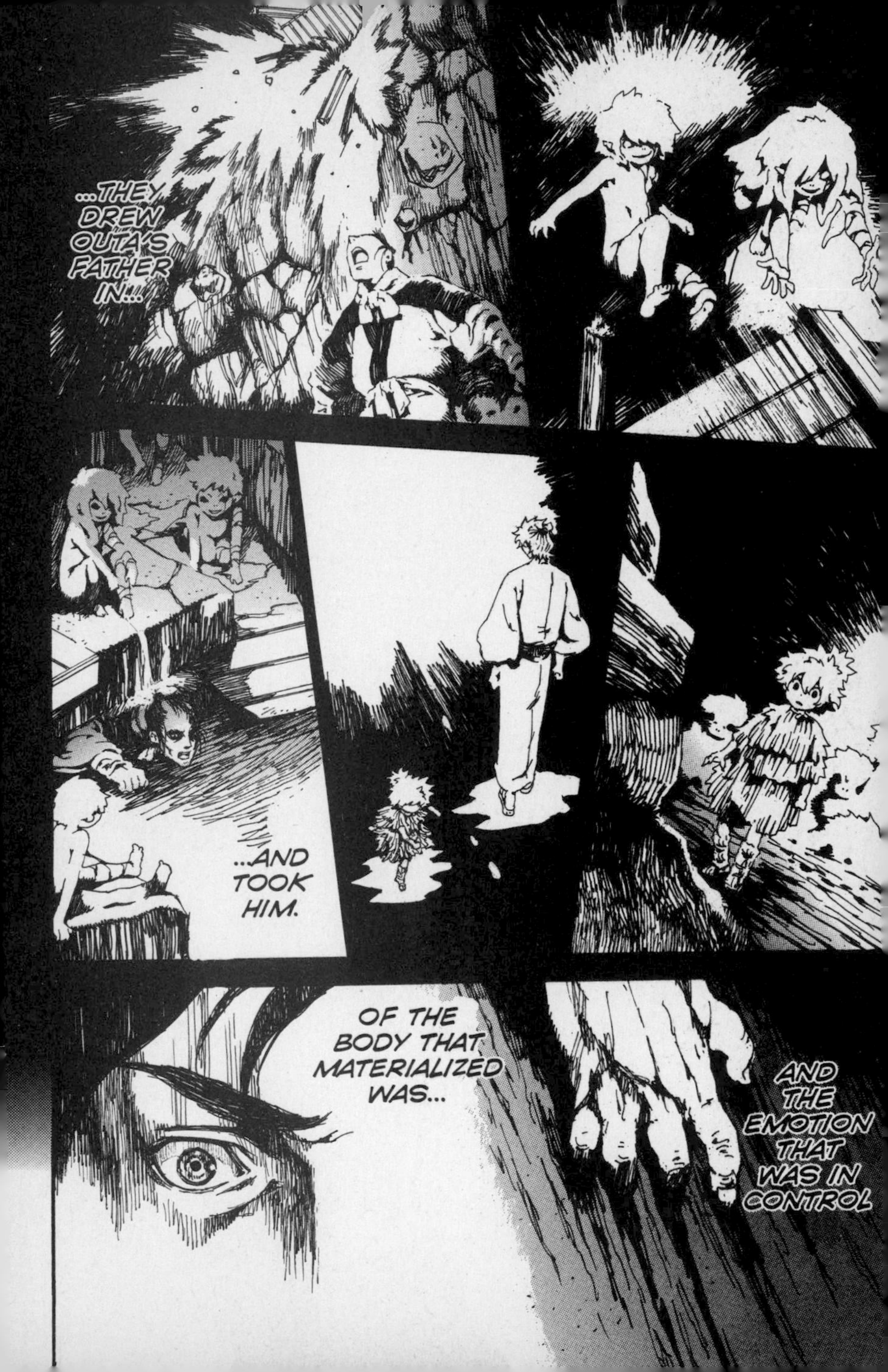
...THEY DREW OUTA'S FATHER IN...
...AND TOOK HIM.
AND THE EMOTION THAT WAS IN CONTROL
OF THE BODY THAT MATERIALIZED WAS...

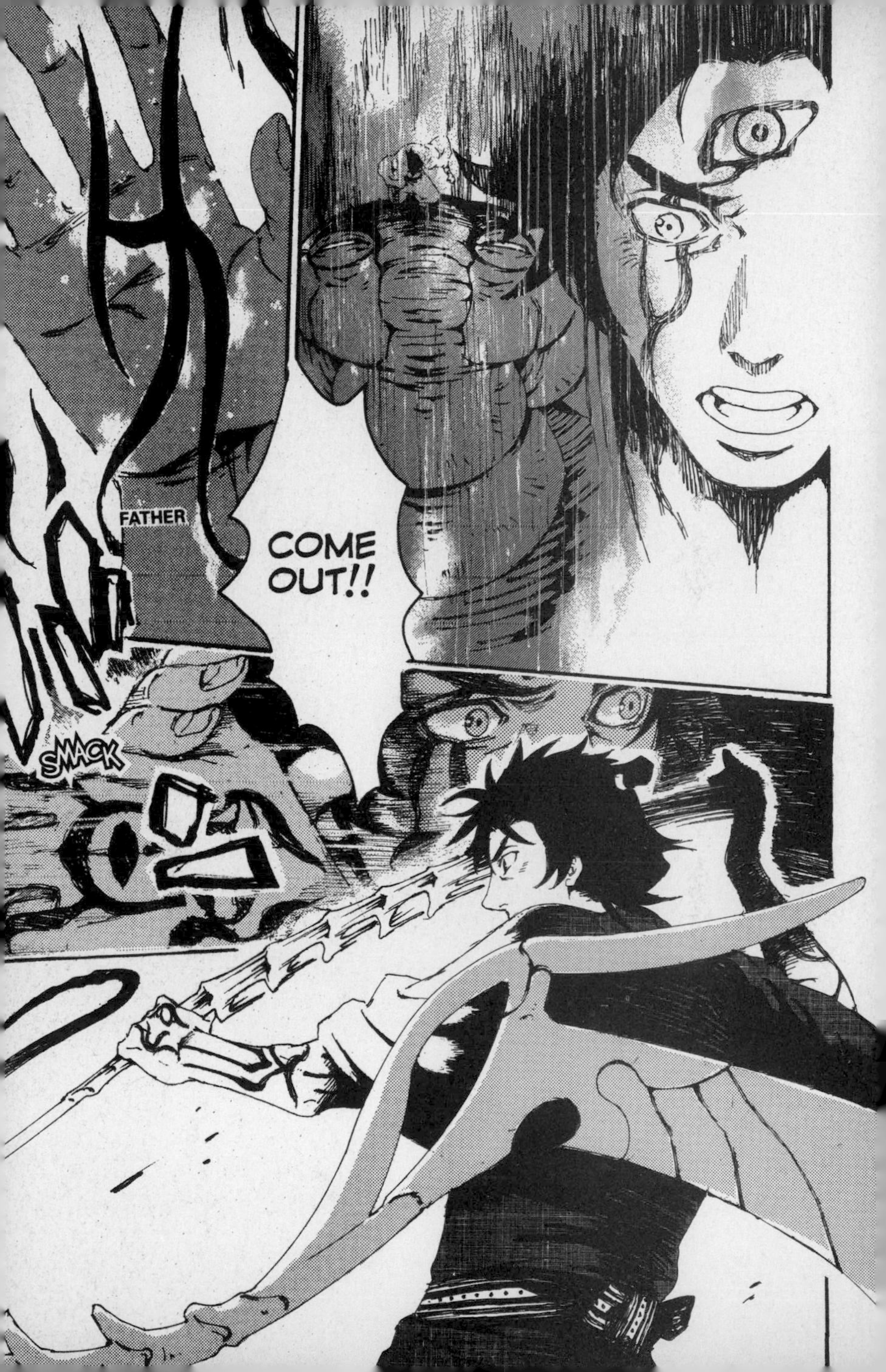
COME OUT!!
FATHER
SMACK

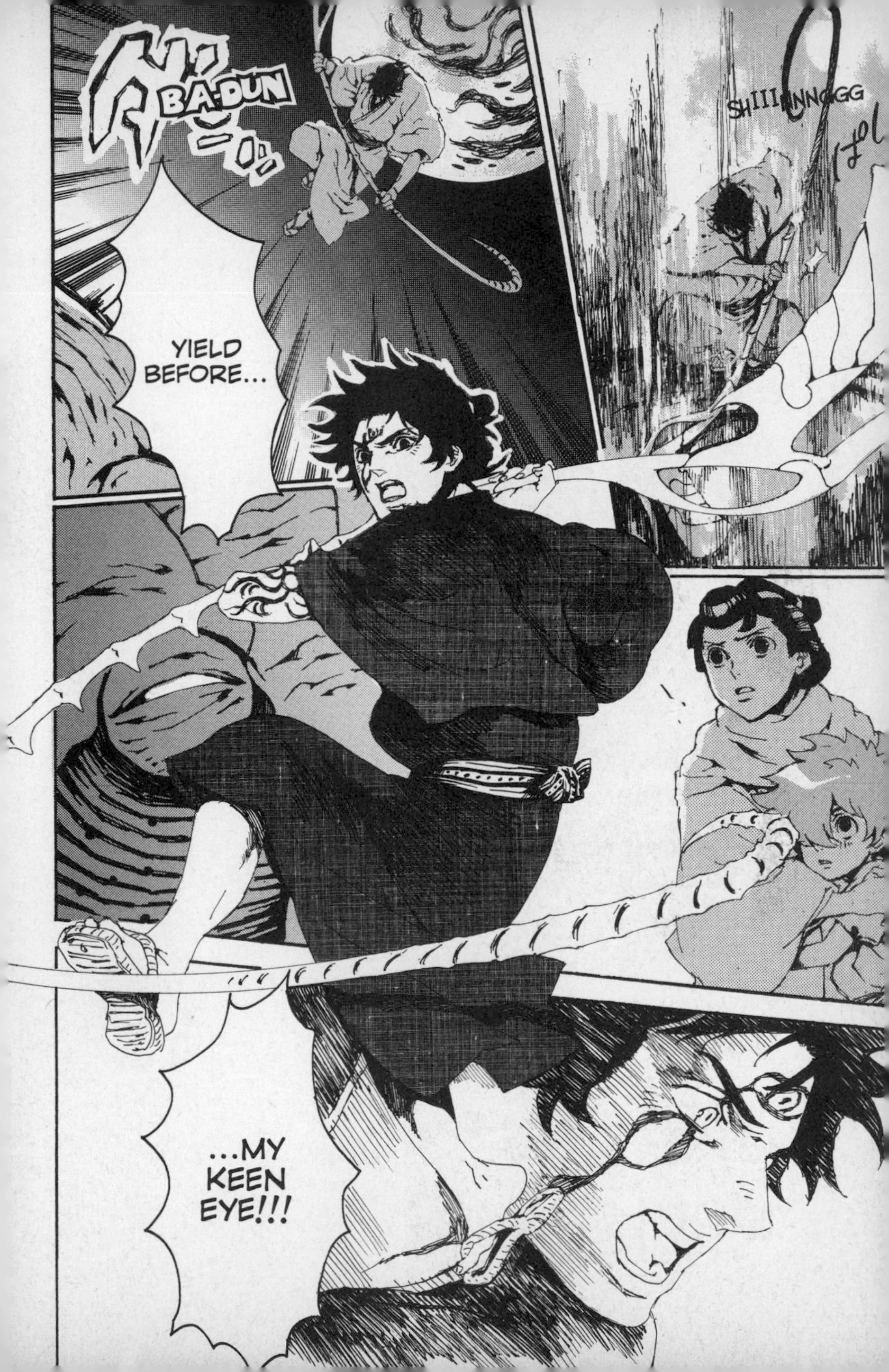
SHIIINNGG
ぱし
BA-DUN
YIELD BEFORE...
...MY KEEN EYE!!!

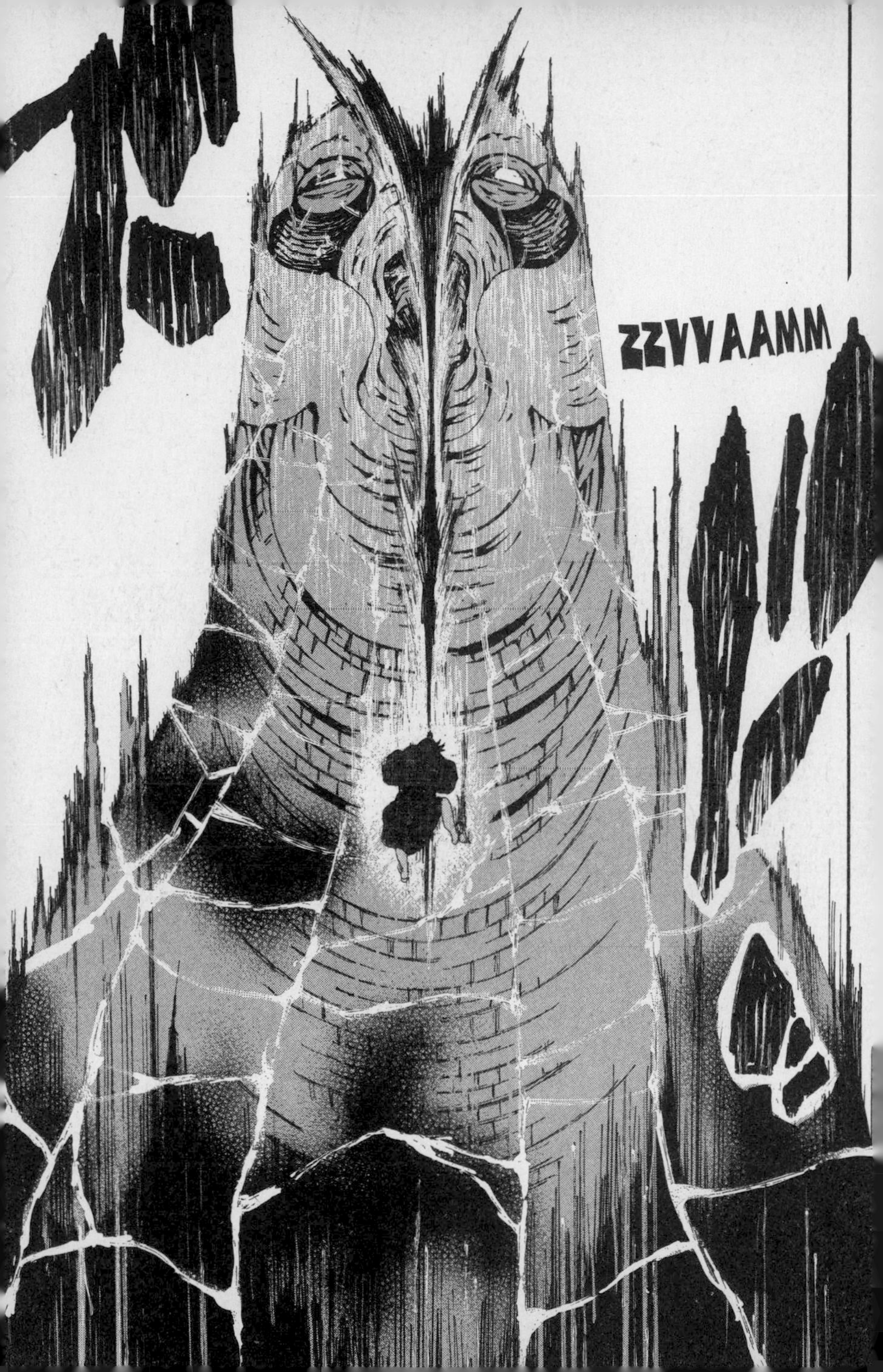
ZZVVAAMM

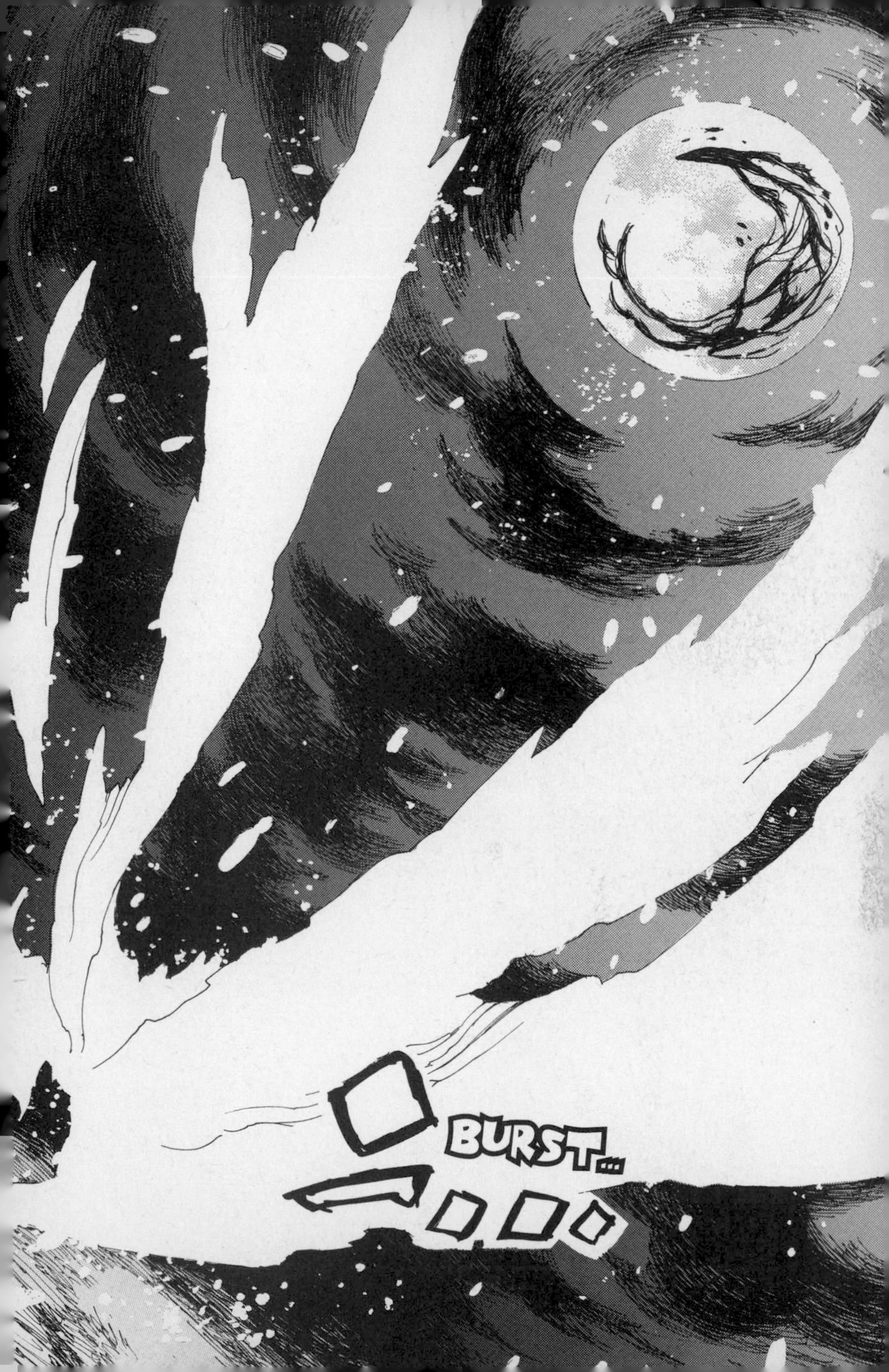
BURST...

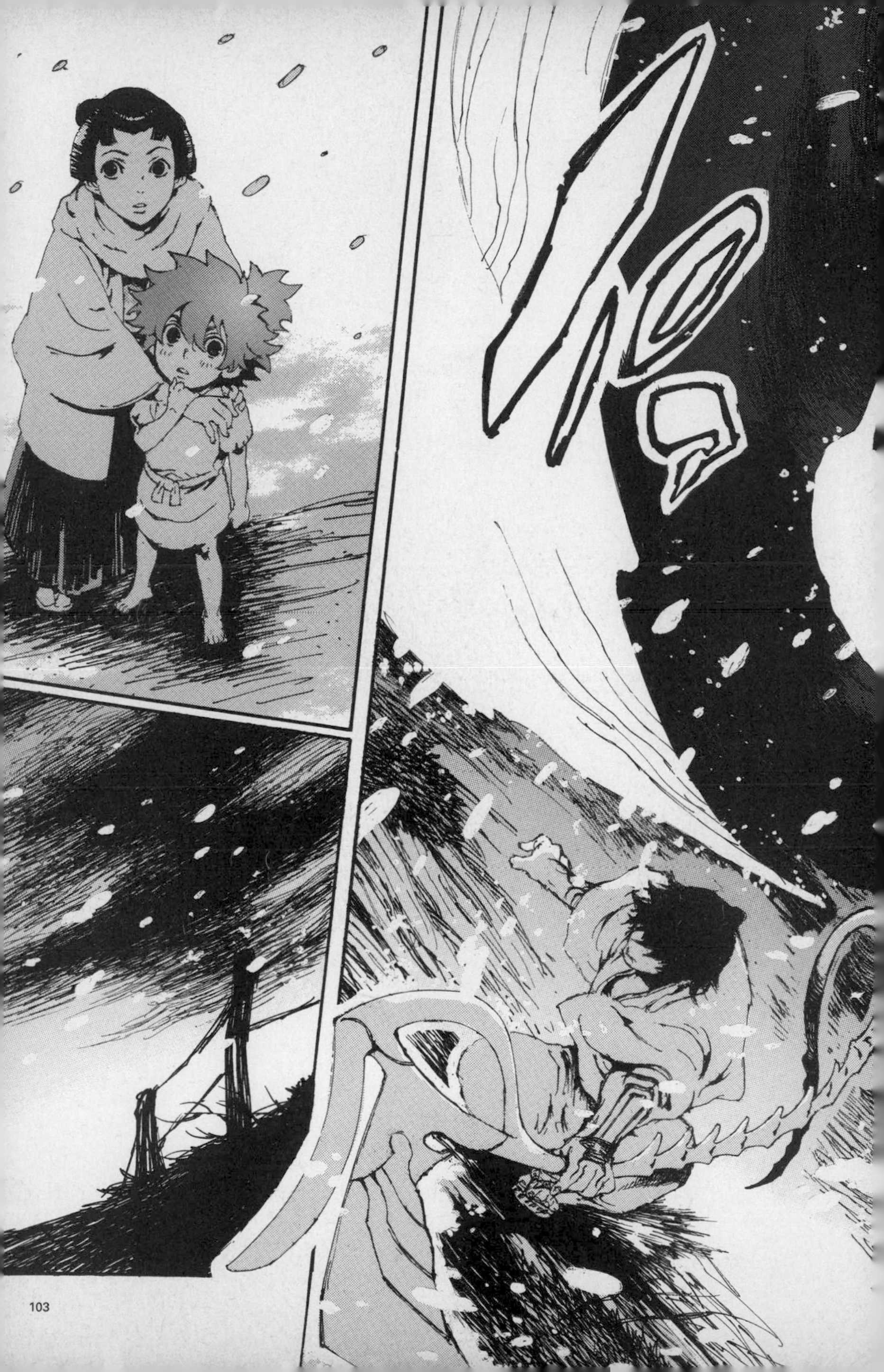

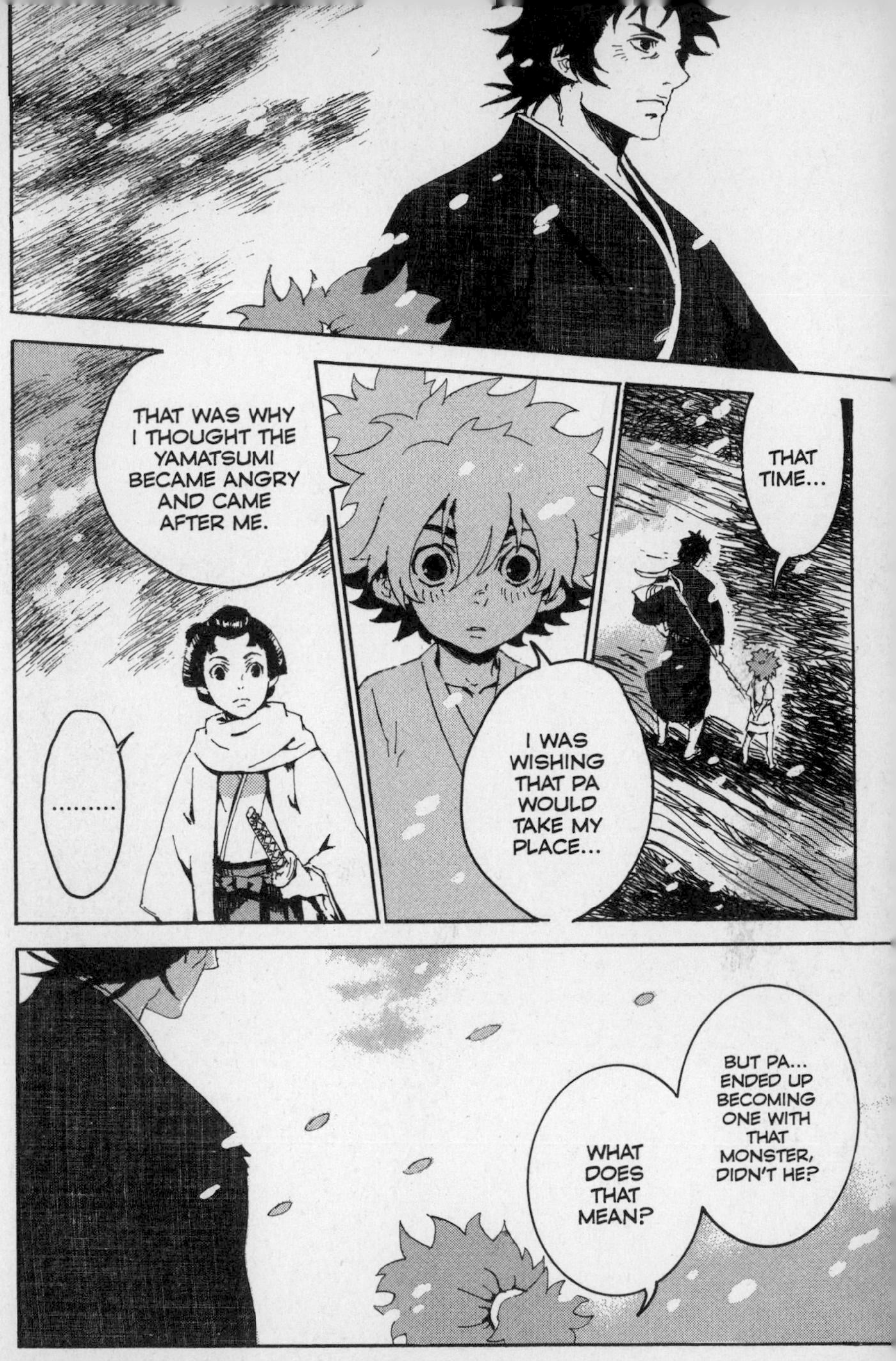
THAT TIME...
I WAS WISHING THAT PA WOULD TAKE MY PLACE...
THAT WAS WHY I THOUGHT THE YAMATSUMI BECAME ANGRY AND CAME AFTER ME.
....
BUT PA... ENDED UP BECOMING ONE WITH THAT MONSTER, DIDN'T HE?
WHAT DOES THAT MEAN?

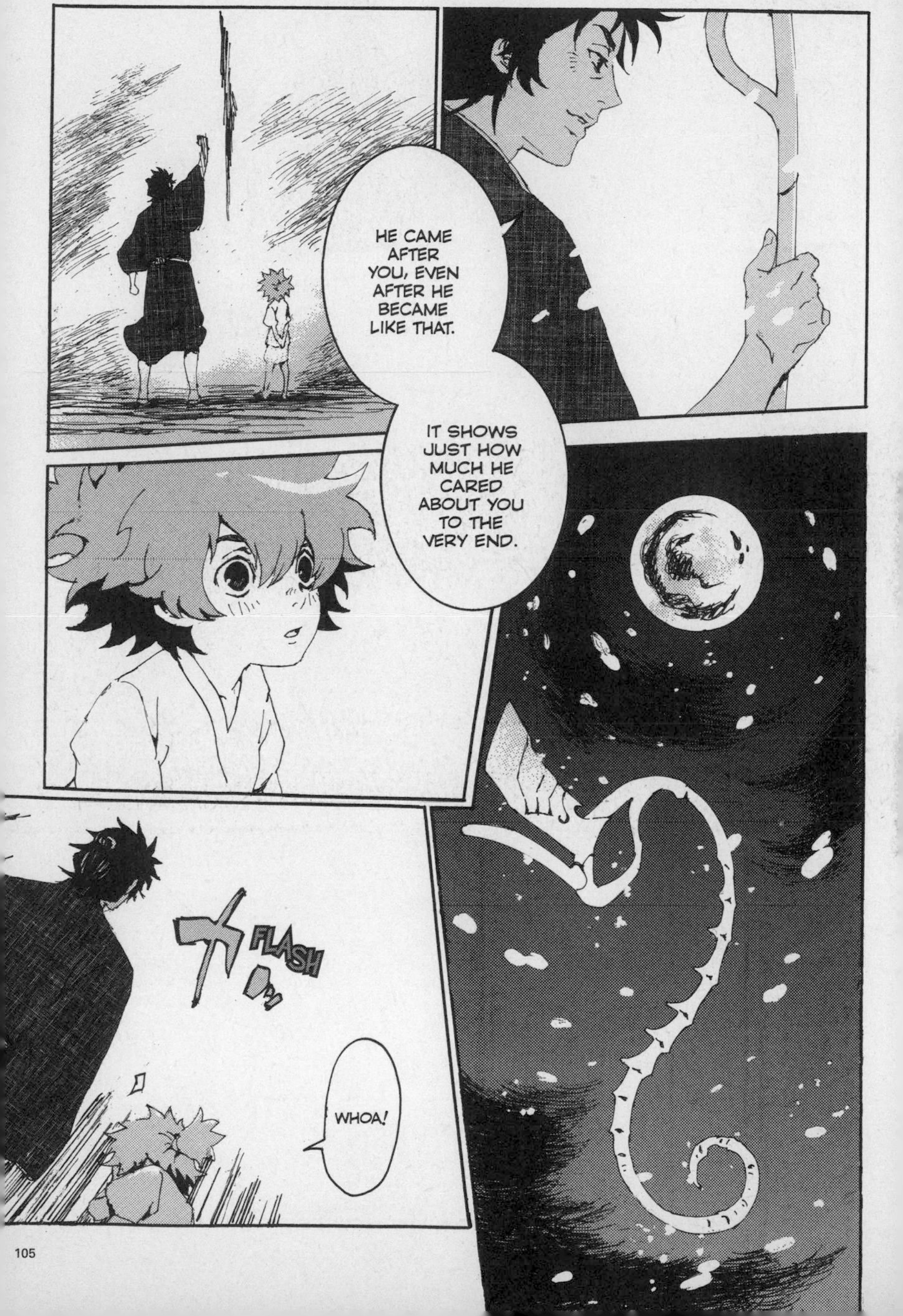
HE CAME AFTER YOU, EVEN AFTER HE BECAME LIKE THAT.
IT SHOWS JUST HOW MUCH HE CARED ABOUT YOU TO THE VERY END.
FLASH
WHOA!

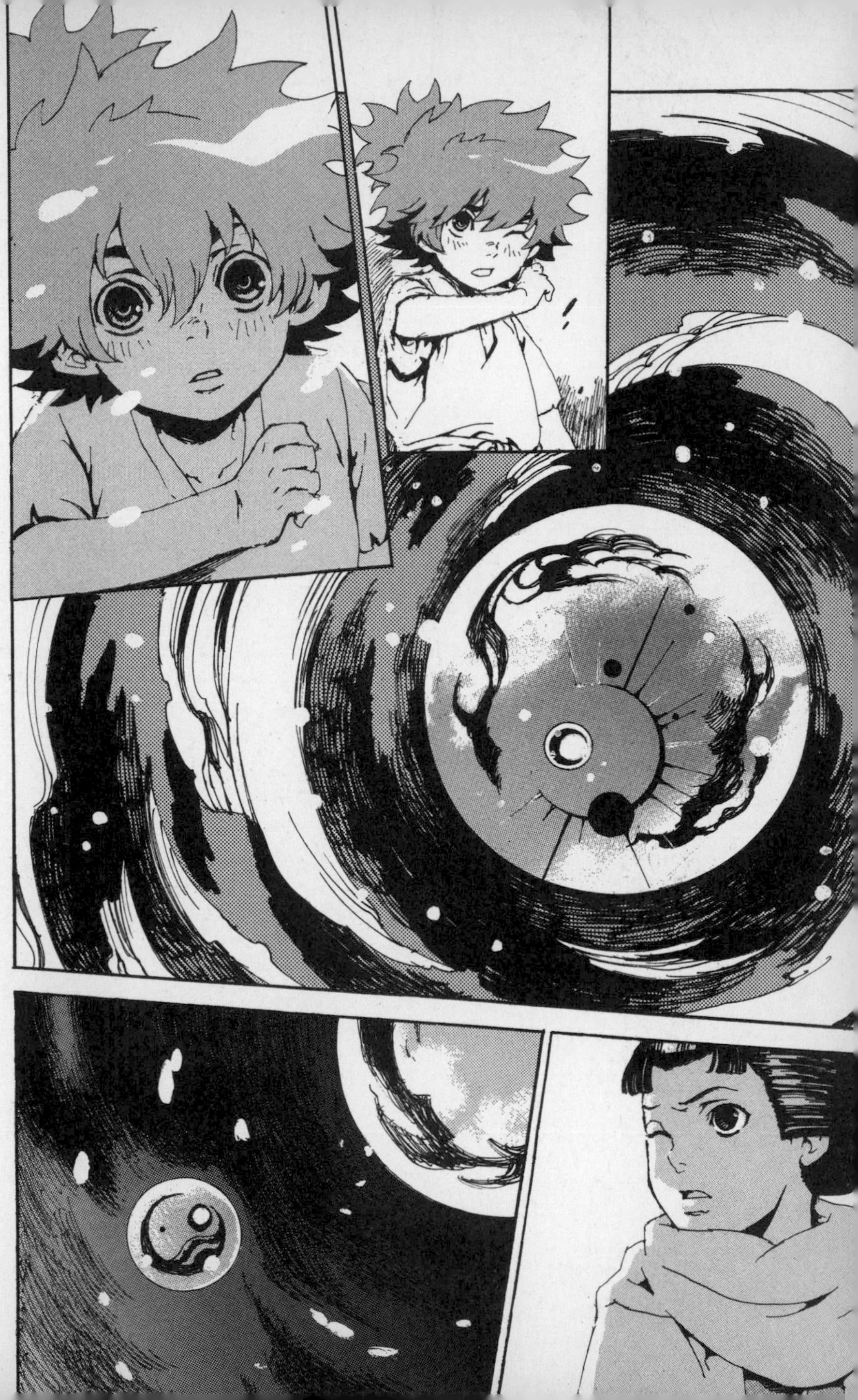

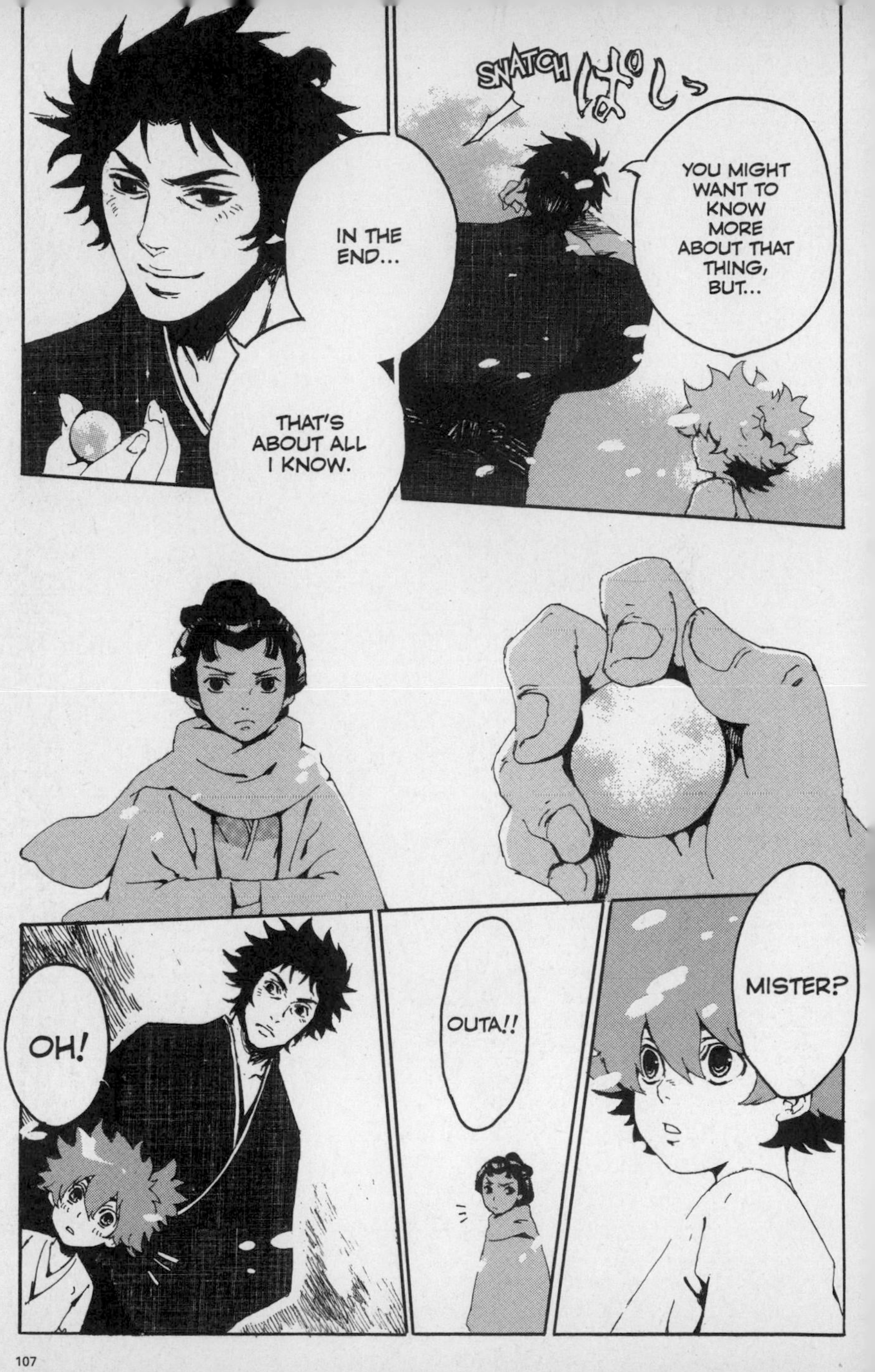
SNATCH
ぱしっ
YOU MIGHT WANT TO KNOW MORE ABOUT THAT THING, BUT...
IN THE END...
THAT'S ABOUT ALL I KNOW.
MISTER?
OUTA!!
OH!

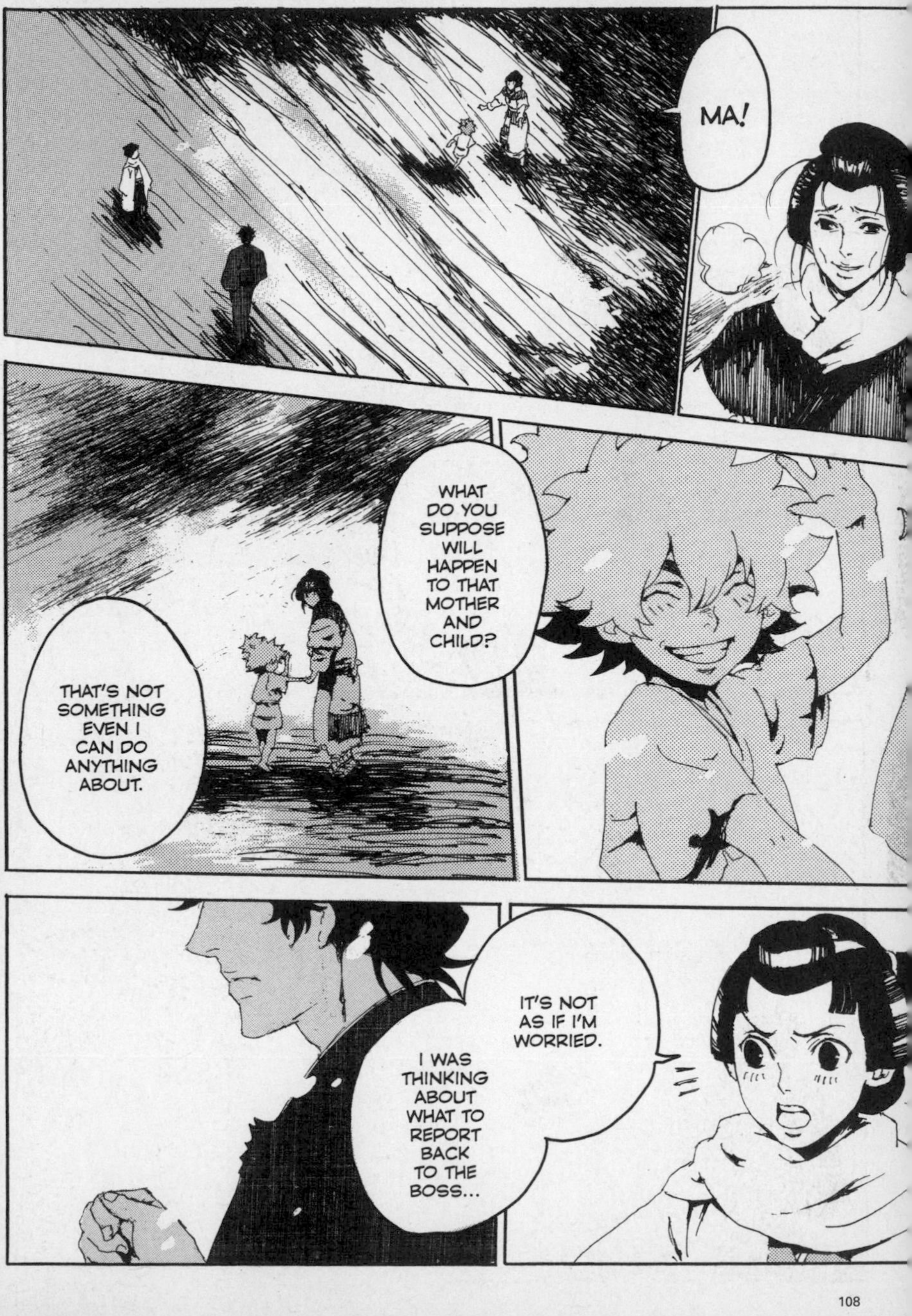
MA!
WHAT DO YOU SUPPOSE WILL HAPPEN TO THAT MOTHER AND CHILD?
THAT'S NOT SOMETHING EVEN I CAN DO ANYTHING ABOUT.
IT'S NOT AS IF I'M WORRIED.
I WAS THINKING ABOUT WHAT TO REPORT BACK TO THE BOSS...

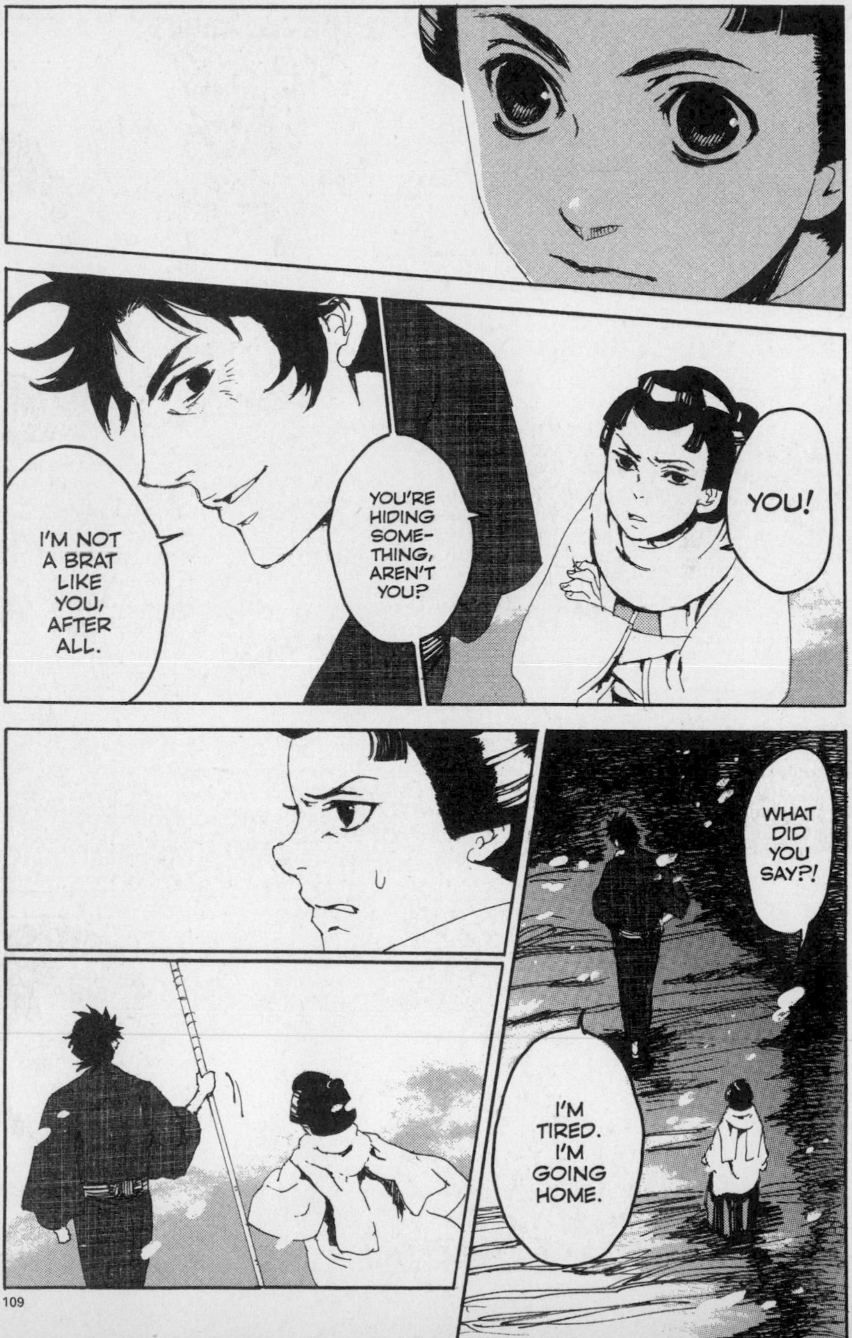
YOU!
YOU'RE HIDING SOME-THING, AREN'T YOU?
I'M NOT A BRAT LIKE YOU, AFTER ALL.
WHAT DID YOU SAY?!
I'M TIRED. I'M GOING HOME.

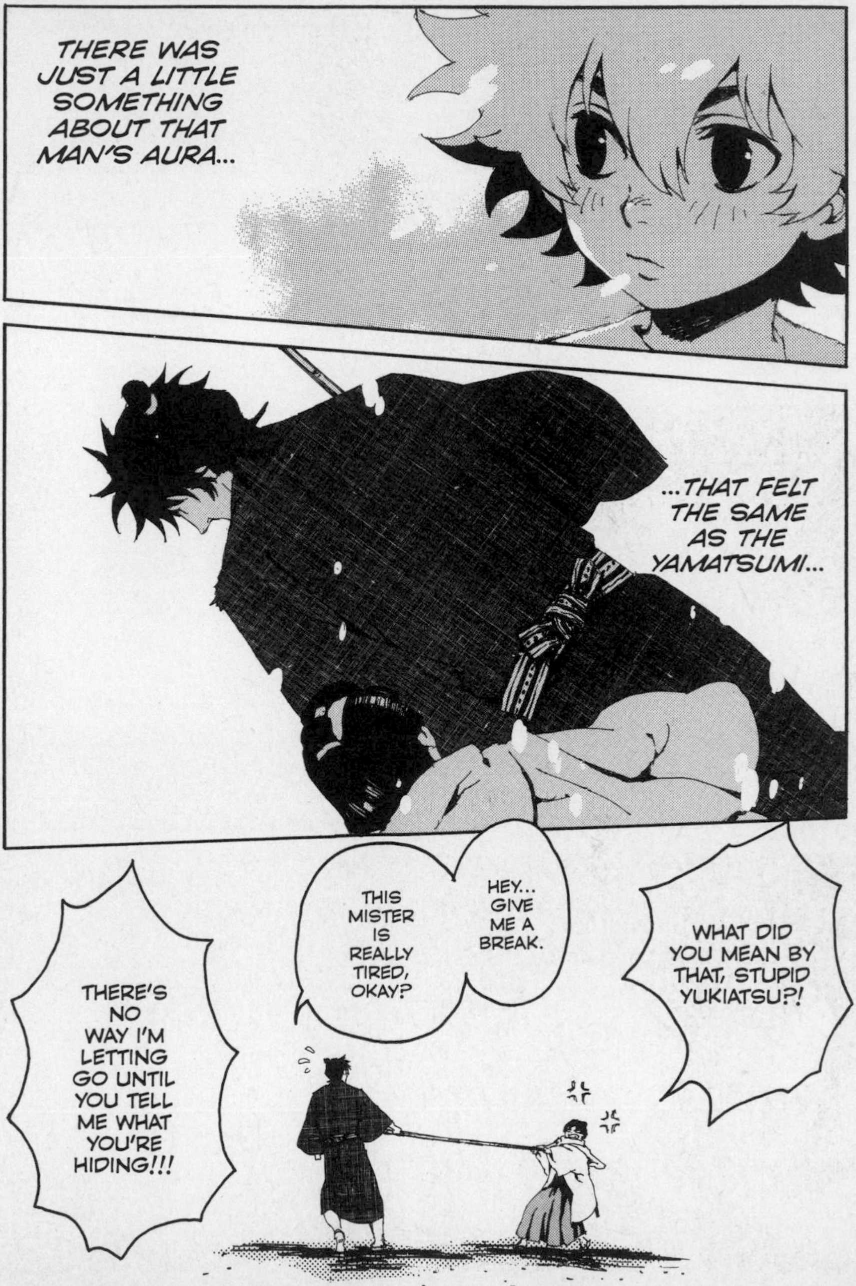
THERE WAS JUST A LITTLE SOMETHING ABOUT THAT MAN'S AURA...
...THAT FELT THE SAME AS THE YAMATSUMI...
WHAT DID YOU MEAN BY THAT, STUPID YUKIATSU?!
HEY... GIVE ME A BREAK.
THIS MISTER IS REALLY TIRED, OKAY?
THERE'S NO WAY I'M LETTING GO UNTIL YOU TELL ME WHAT YOU'RE HIDING!!!

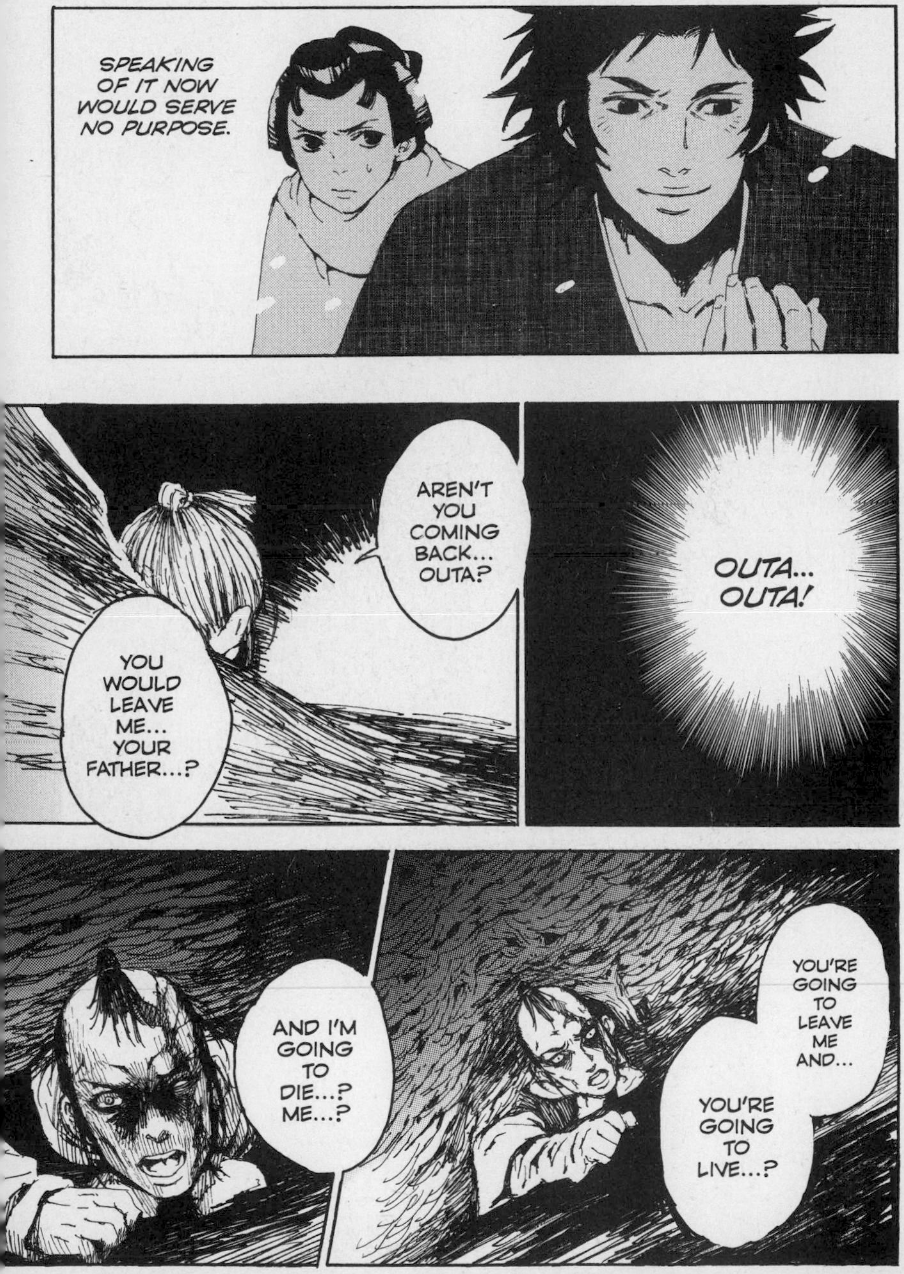
SPEAKING OF IT NOW WOULD SERVE NO PURPOSE.
OUTA... OUTA!
AREN'T YOU COMING BACK... OUTA?
YOU WOULD LEAVE ME... YOUR FATHER...?
YOU'RE GOING TO LEAVE ME AND...
YOU'RE GOING TO LIVE...?
AND I'M GOING TO DIE...? ME...?

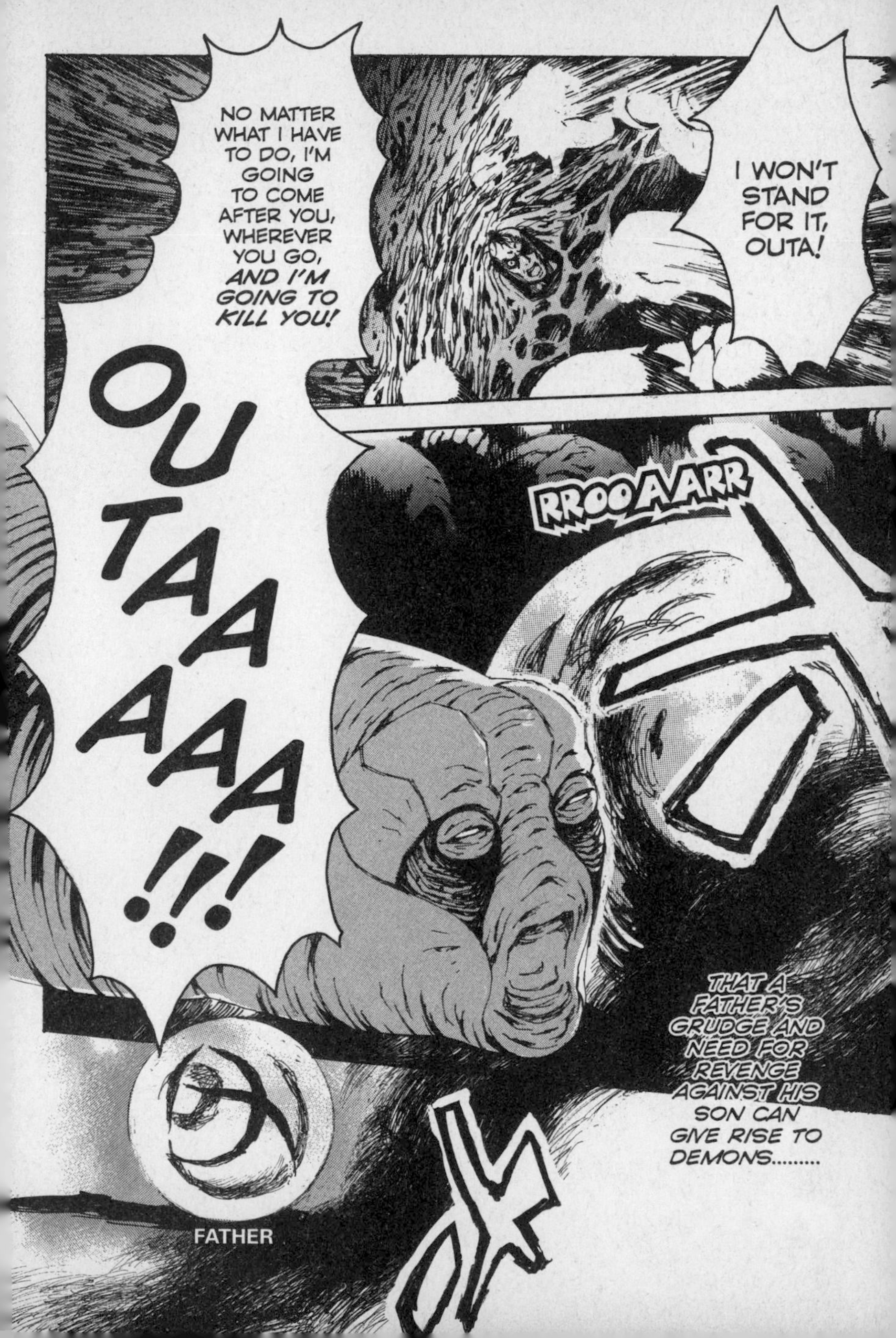
I WON'T STAND FOR IT, OUTA!
NO MATTER WHAT I HAVE TO DO, I'M GOING TO COME AFTER YOU, WHEREVER YOU GO, *AND I'M GOING TO KILL YOU!*
RROOAARR
OUTAAAAA!!!
THAT A FATHER'S GRUDGE AND NEED FOR REVENGE AGAINST HIS SON CAN GIVE RISE TO DEMONS.........
FATHER

天保異聞
妖奇士
あやかしあやし

GHOST SLAYERS
Ayashi

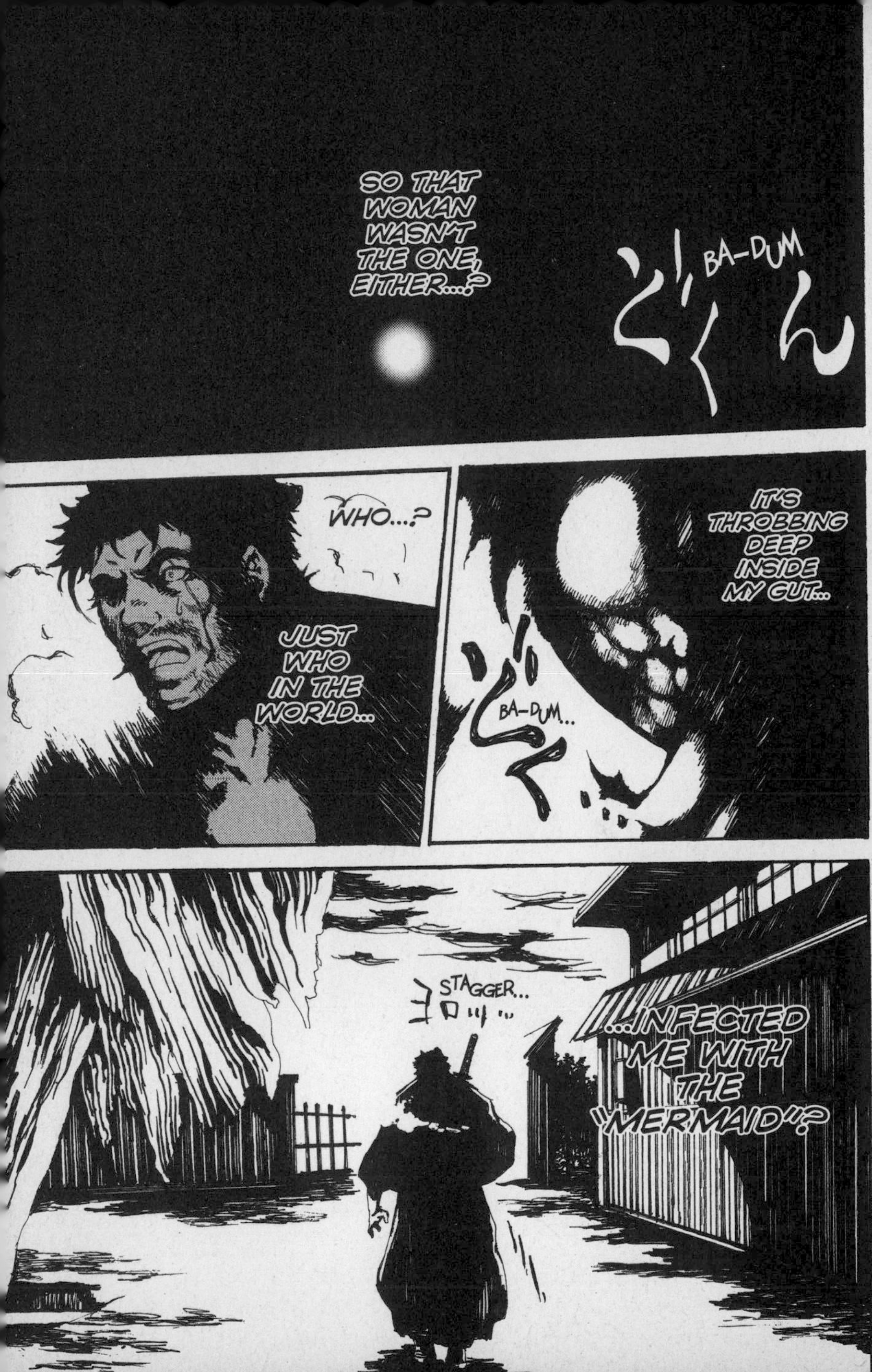

SO THAT WOMAN WASN'T THE ONE, EITHER...?
どくん
BA-DUM
IT'S THROBBING DEEP INSIDE MY GUT...
どく
BA-DUM...
WHO...?
JUST WHO IN THE WORLD...
...INFECTED ME WITH THE "MERMAID"?
ヨロッ
STAGGER...

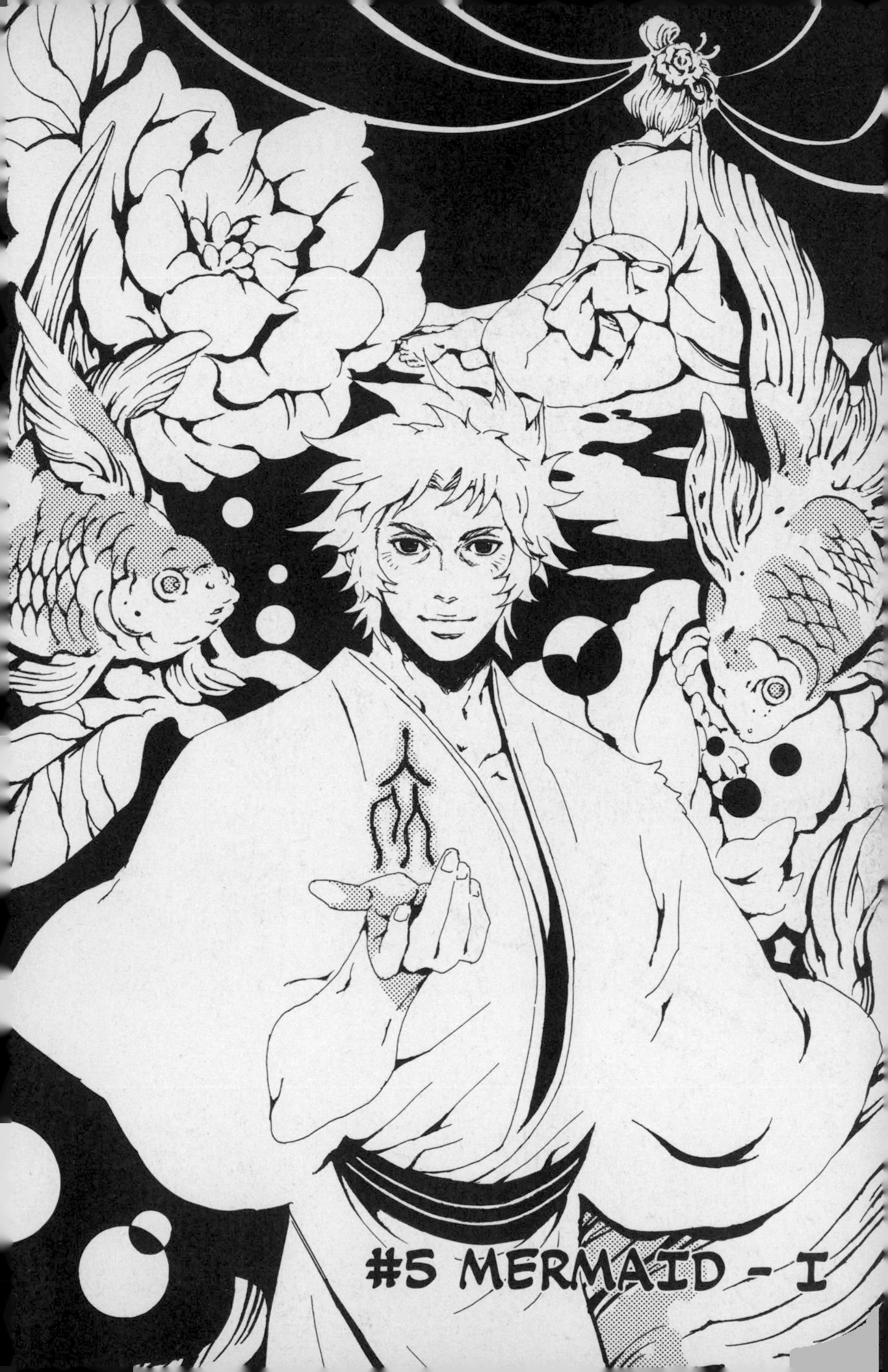
#5 MERMAID - I

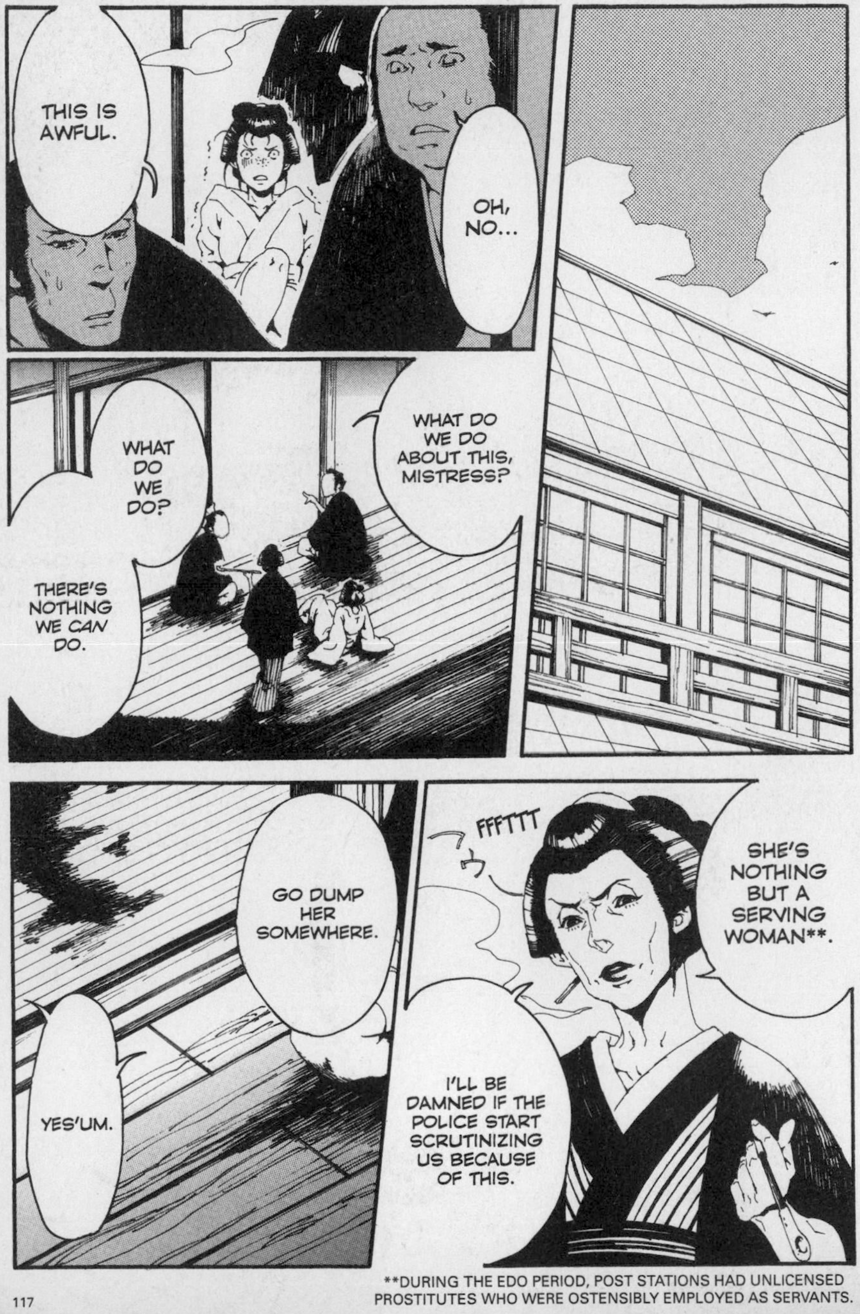
OH, NO...
THIS IS AWFUL.
WHAT DO WE DO ABOUT THIS, MISTRESS?
WHAT DO WE DO?
THERE'S NOTHING WE CAN DO.
FFFTTT
SHE'S NOTHING BUT A SERVING WOMAN**.
I'LL BE DAMNED IF THE POLICE START SCRUTINIZING US BECAUSE OF THIS.
GO DUMP HER SOMEWHERE.
YES'UM.

**DURING THE EDO PERIOD, POST STATIONS HAD UNLICENSED PROSTITUTES WHO WERE OSTENSIBLY EMPLOYED AS SERVANTS.

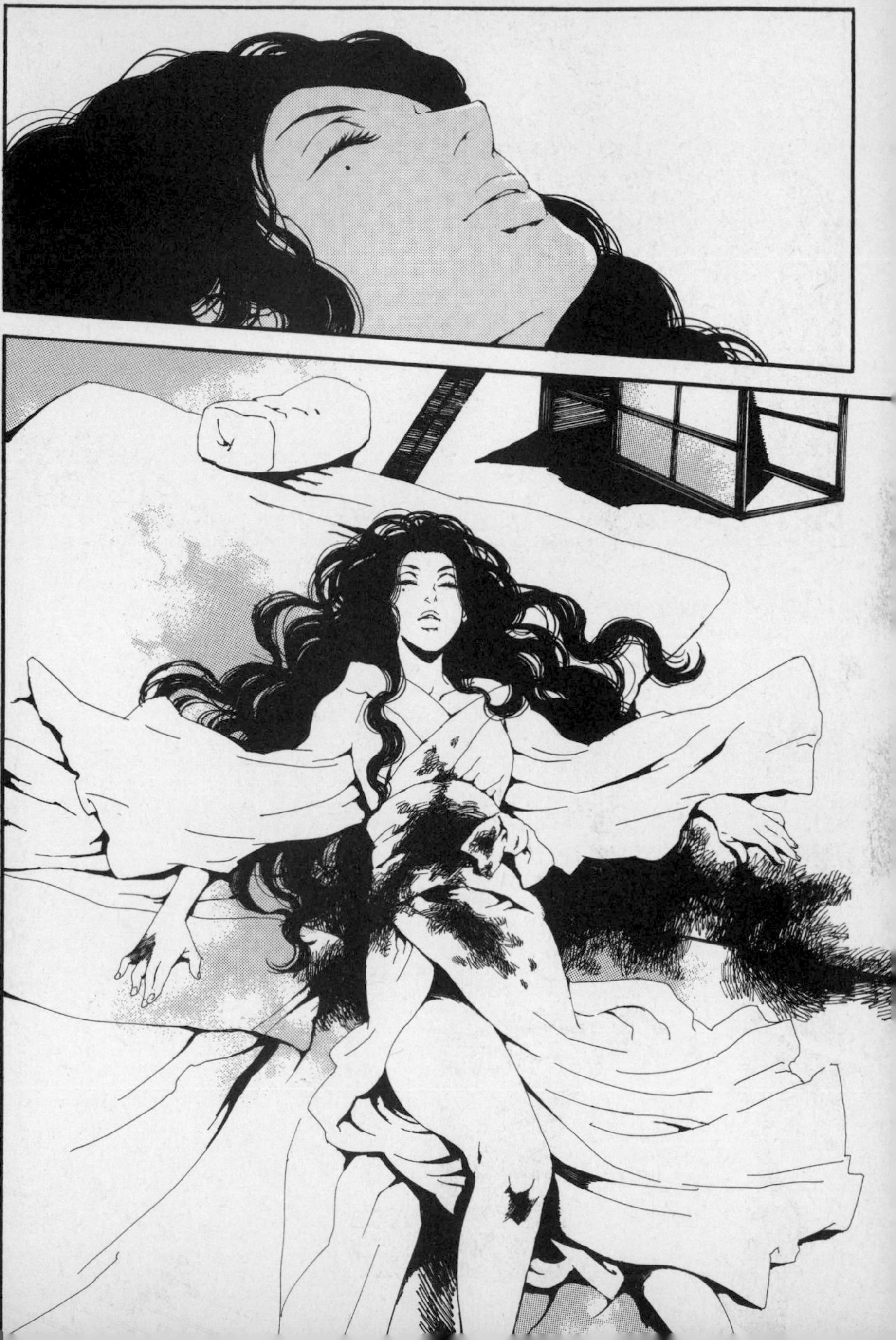

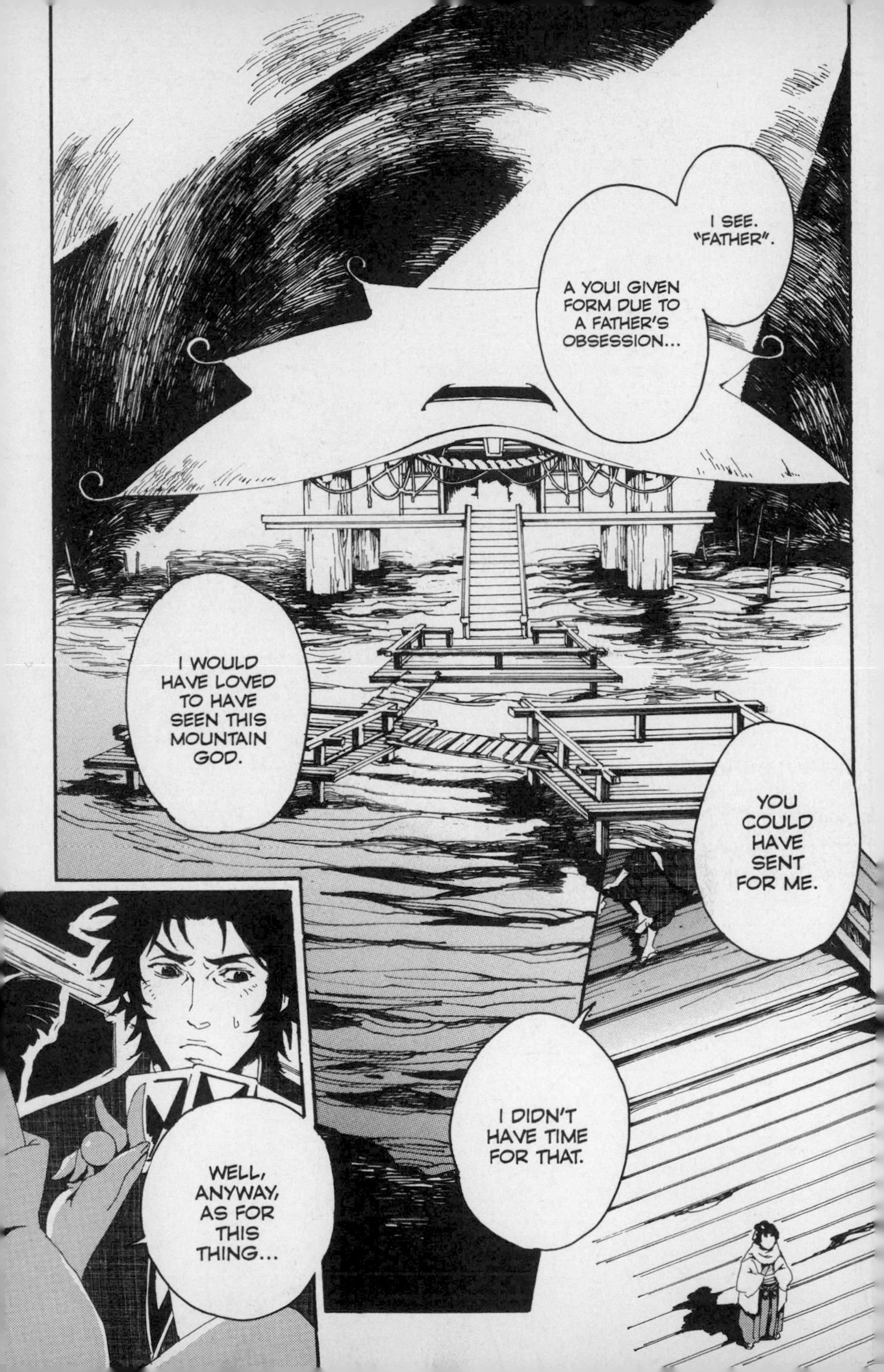
I SEE. "FATHER".
A YOUI GIVEN FORM DUE TO A FATHER'S OBSESSION...
I WOULD HAVE LOVED TO HAVE SEEN THIS MOUNTAIN GOD.
YOU COULD HAVE SENT FOR ME.
I DIDN'T HAVE TIME FOR THAT.
WELL, ANYWAY, AS FOR THIS THING...

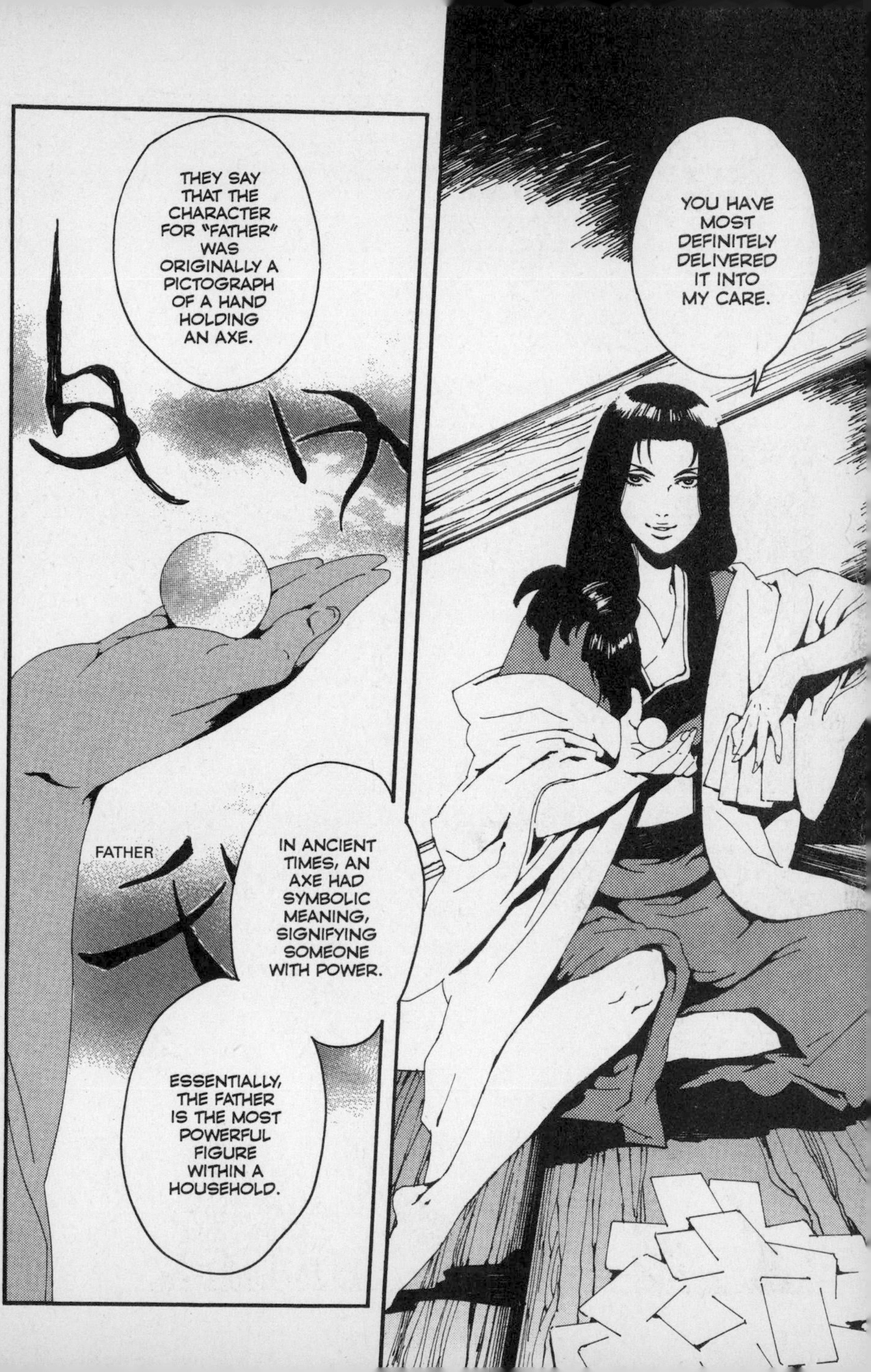

YOU HAVE MOST DEFINITELY DELIVERED IT INTO MY CARE.
THEY SAY THAT THE CHARACTER FOR "FATHER" WAS ORIGINALLY A PICTOGRAPH OF A HAND HOLDING AN AXE.
FATHER
IN ANCIENT TIMES, AN AXE HAD SYMBOLIC MEANING, SIGNIFYING SOMEONE WITH POWER.
ESSENTIALLY, THE FATHER IS THE MOST POWERFUL FIGURE WITHIN A HOUSEHOLD.

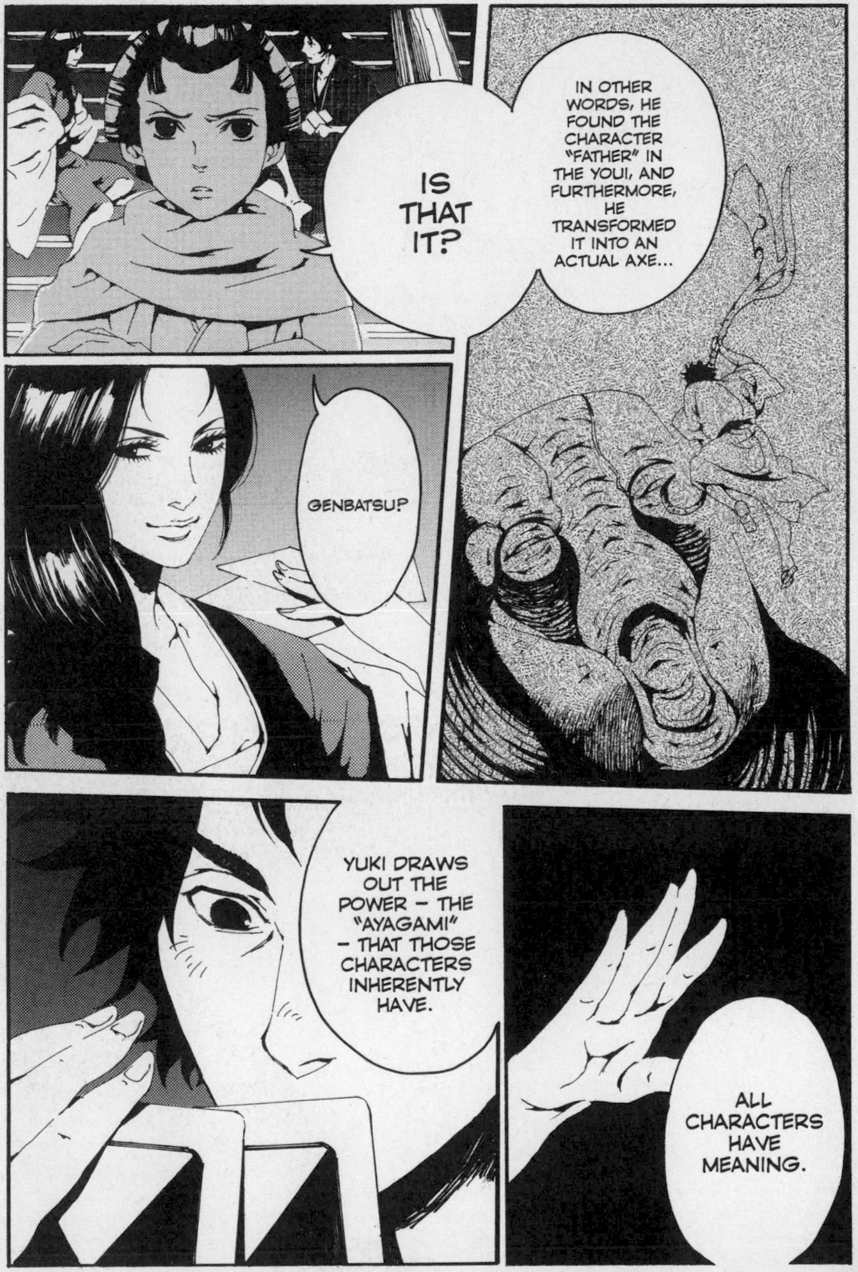
IN OTHER WORDS, HE FOUND THE CHARACTER "FATHER" IN THE YOUI, AND FURTHERMORE, HE TRANSFORMED IT INTO AN ACTUAL AXE...
IS THAT IT?
GENBATSU?
ALL CHARACTERS HAVE MEANING.
YUKI DRAWS OUT THE POWER - THE "AYAGAMI" - THAT THOSE CHARACTERS INHERENTLY HAVE.

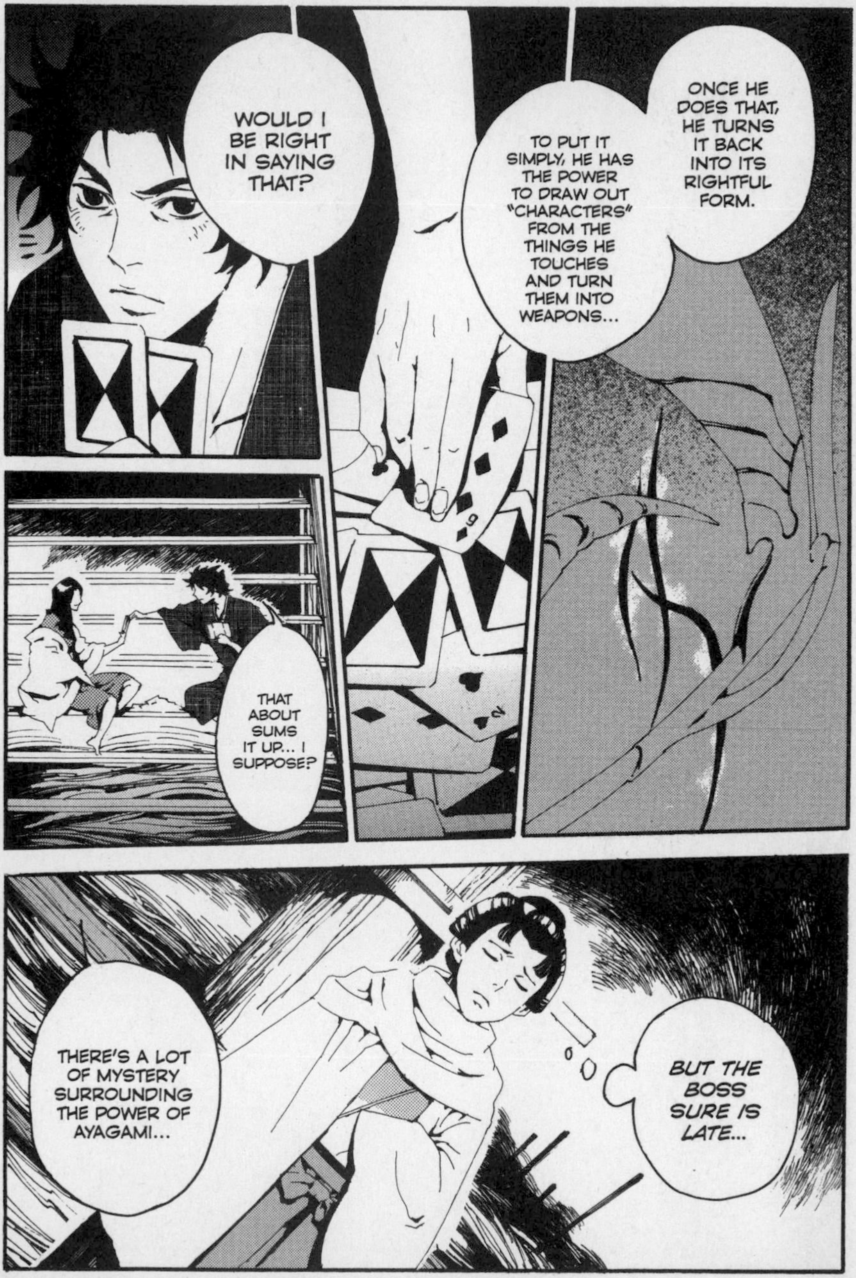
ONCE HE DOES THAT, HE TURNS IT BACK INTO ITS RIGHTFUL FORM.
TO PUT IT SIMPLY, HE HAS THE POWER TO DRAW OUT "CHARACTERS" FROM THE THINGS HE TOUCHES AND TURN THEM INTO WEAPONS...
WOULD I BE RIGHT IN SAYING THAT?
THAT ABOUT SUMS IT UP... I SUPPOSE?
BUT THE BOSS SURE IS LATE...
THERE'S A LOT OF MYSTERY SURROUNDING THE POWER OF AYAGAMI...

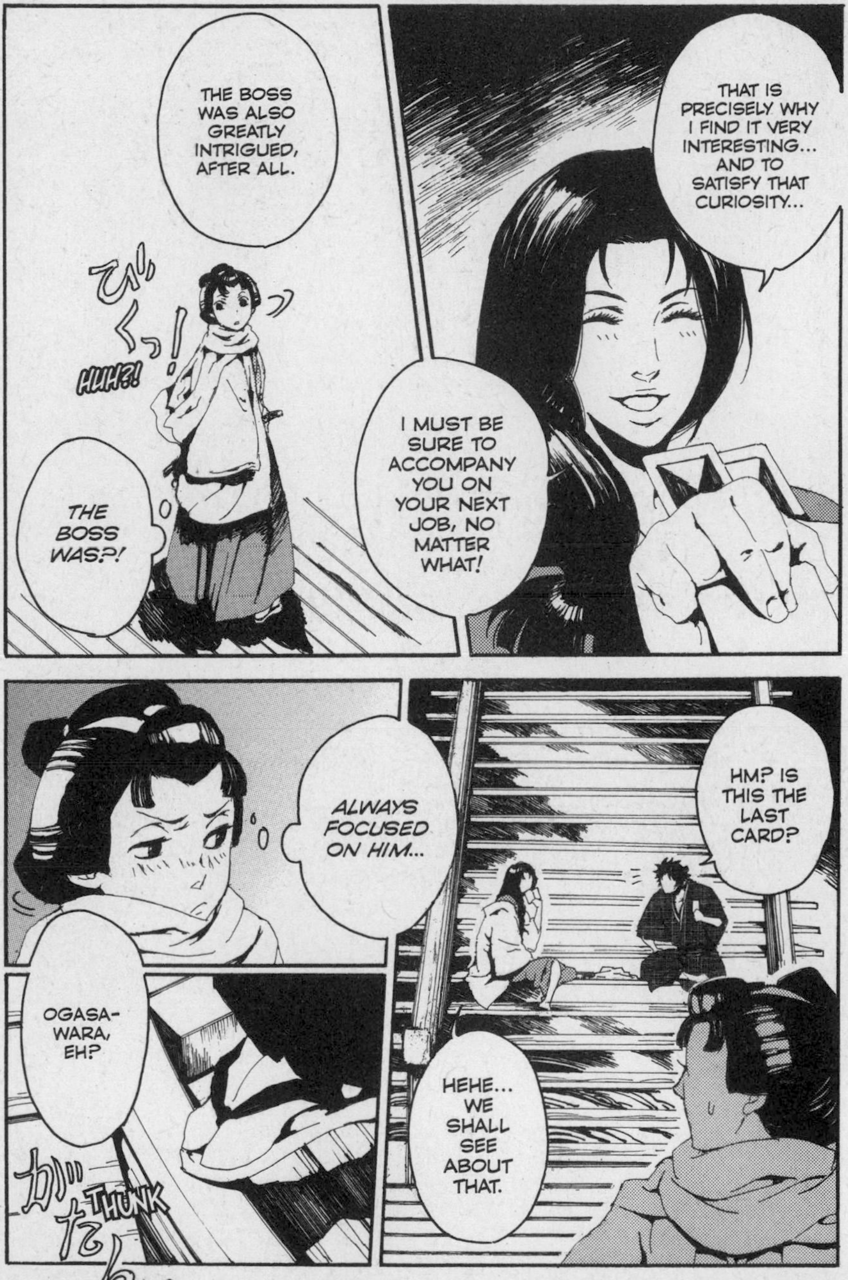
THAT IS PRECISELY WHY I FIND IT VERY INTERESTING... AND TO SATISFY THAT CURIOSITY...
I MUST BE SURE TO ACCOMPANY YOU ON YOUR NEXT JOB, NO MATTER WHAT!
THE BOSS WAS ALSO GREATLY INTRIGUED, AFTER ALL.
HUH?!
THE BOSS WAS?!
HM? IS THIS THE LAST CARD?
HEHE... WE SHALL SEE ABOUT THAT.
ALWAYS FOCUSED ON HIM...
OGASAWARA, EH?
THUNK

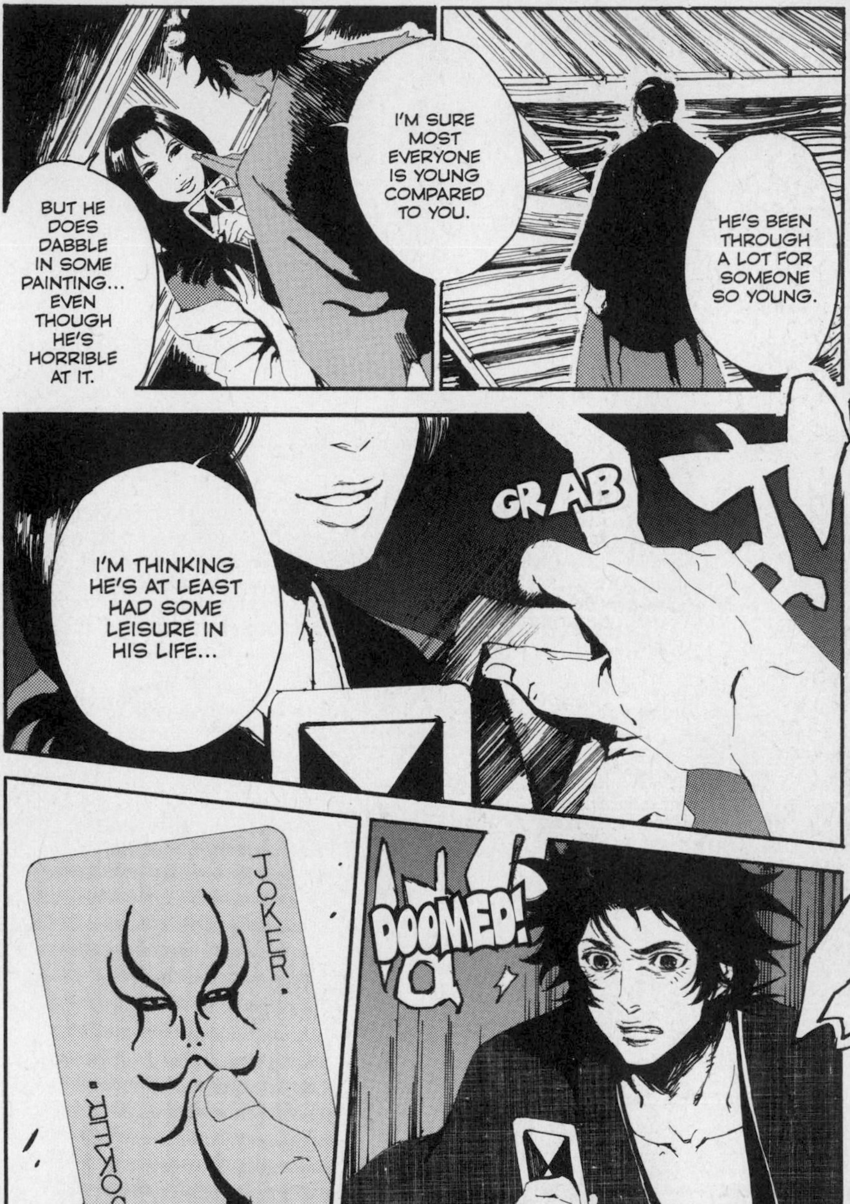
HE'S BEEN THROUGH A LOT FOR SOMEONE SO YOUNG.
I'M SURE MOST EVERYONE IS YOUNG COMPARED TO YOU.
BUT HE DOES DABBLE IN SOME PAINTING... EVEN THOUGH HE'S HORRIBLE AT IT.
GRAB
I'M THINKING HE'S AT LEAST HAD SOME LEISURE IN HIS LIFE...
DOOMED!
JOKER

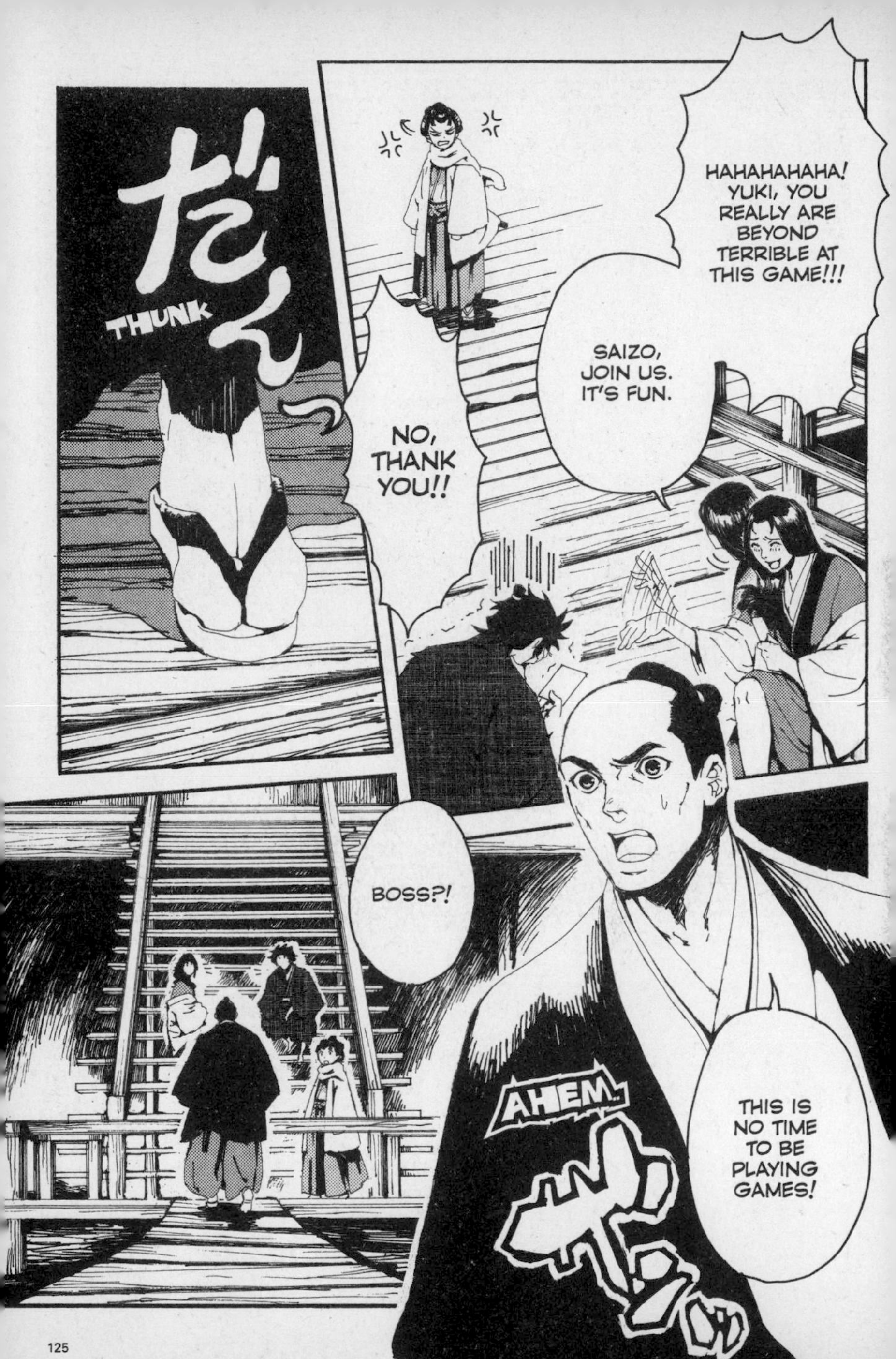
HAHAHAHAHA! YUKI, YOU REALLY ARE BEYOND TERRIBLE AT THIS GAME!!!
SAIZO, JOIN US. IT'S FUN.
NO, THANK YOU!!
だん
THUNK
BOSS?!
AHEM.
THIS IS NO TIME TO BE PLAYING GAMES!

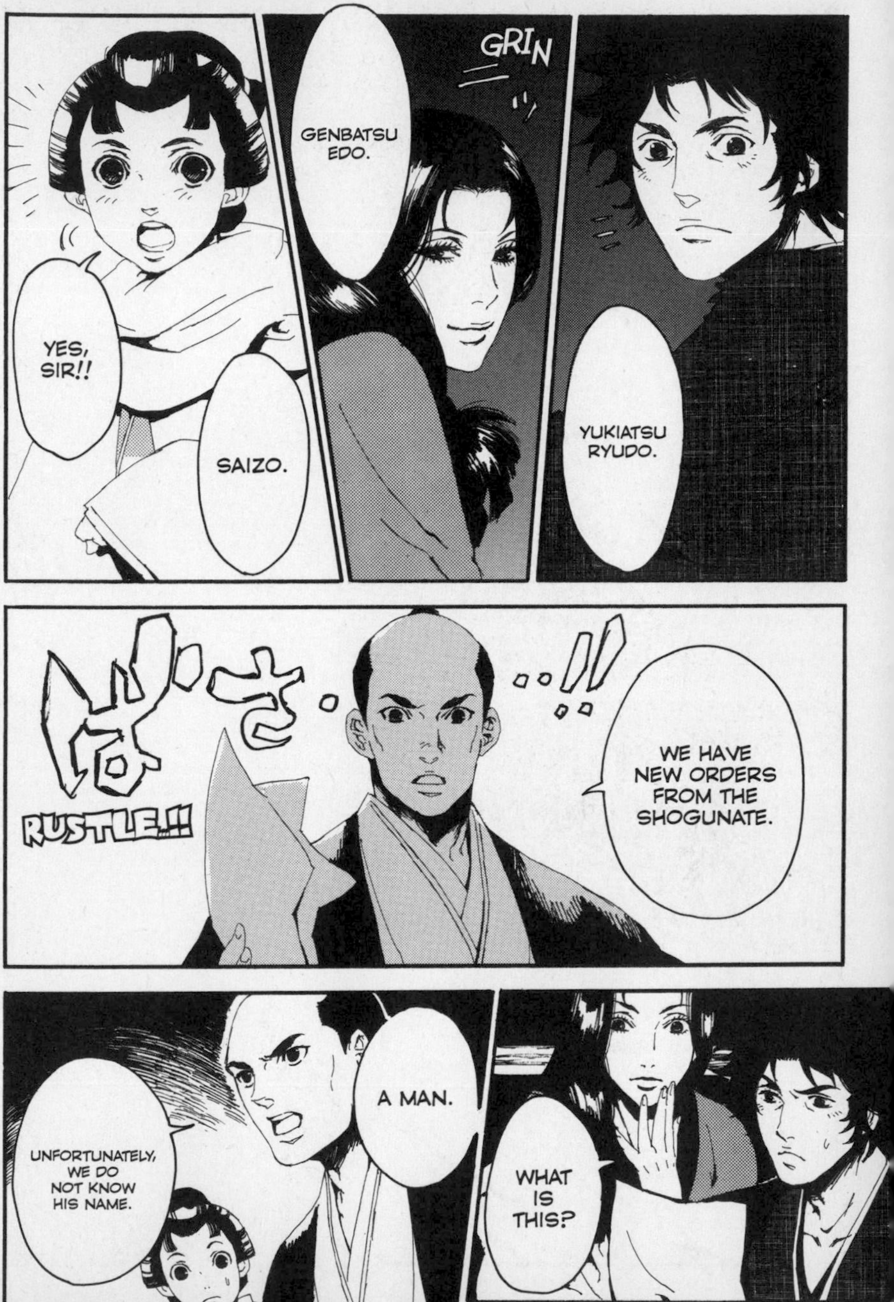
YUKIATSU RYUDO.
GRIN
GENBATSU EDO.
SAIZO.
YES, SIR!!
WE HAVE NEW ORDERS FROM THE SHOGUNATE.
..!!
ぱさ。
RUSTLE...!!
WHAT IS THIS?
A MAN.
UNFORTUNATELY, WE DO NOT KNOW HIS NAME.

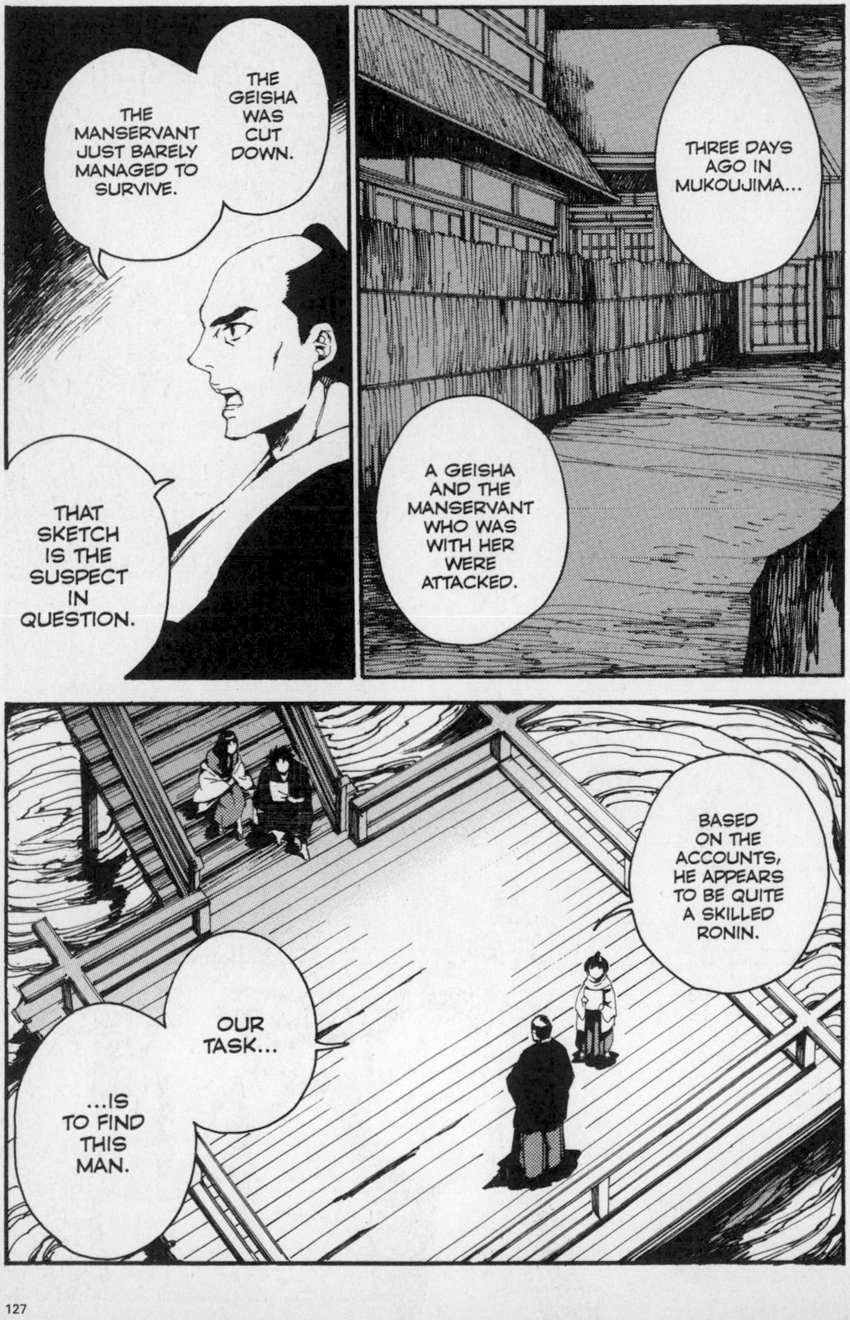
THREE DAYS AGO IN MUKOUJIMA...
A GEISHA AND THE MANSERVANT WHO WAS WITH HER WERE ATTACKED.
THE GEISHA WAS CUT DOWN.
THE MANSERVANT JUST BARELY MANAGED TO SURVIVE.
THAT SKETCH IS THE SUSPECT IN QUESTION.
BASED ON THE ACCOUNTS, HE APPEARS TO BE QUITE A SKILLED RONIN.
OUR TASK...
...IS TO FIND THIS MAN.

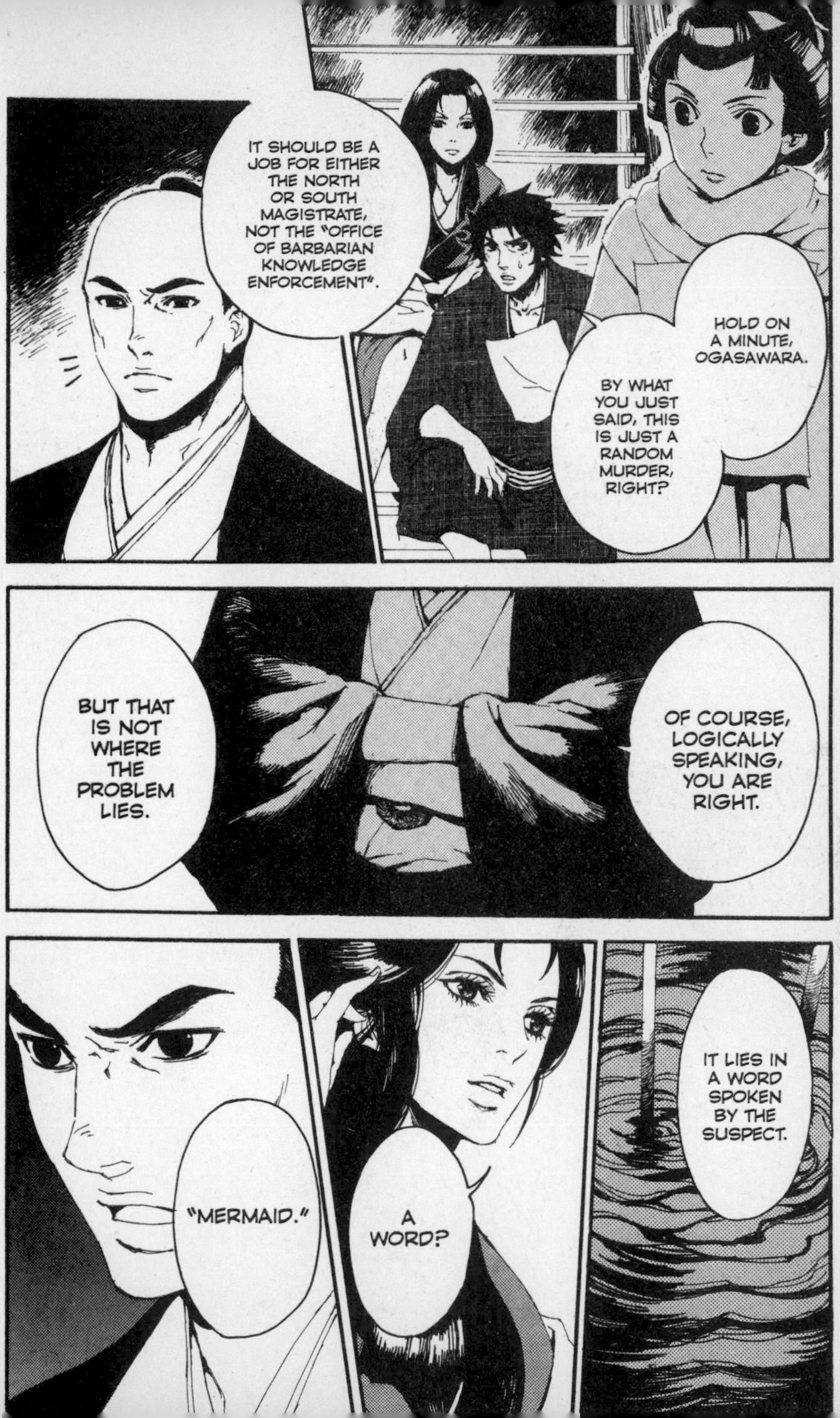
IT SHOULD BE A JOB FOR EITHER THE NORTH OR SOUTH MAGISTRATE, NOT THE "OFFICE OF BARBARIAN KNOWLEDGE ENFORCEMENT".
HOLD ON A MINUTE, OGASAWARA.
BY WHAT YOU JUST SAID, THIS IS JUST A RANDOM MURDER, RIGHT?
OF COURSE, LOGICALLY SPEAKING, YOU ARE RIGHT.
BUT THAT IS NOT WHERE THE PROBLEM LIES.
IT LIES IN A WORD SPOKEN BY THE SUSPECT.
A WORD?
"MERMAID."

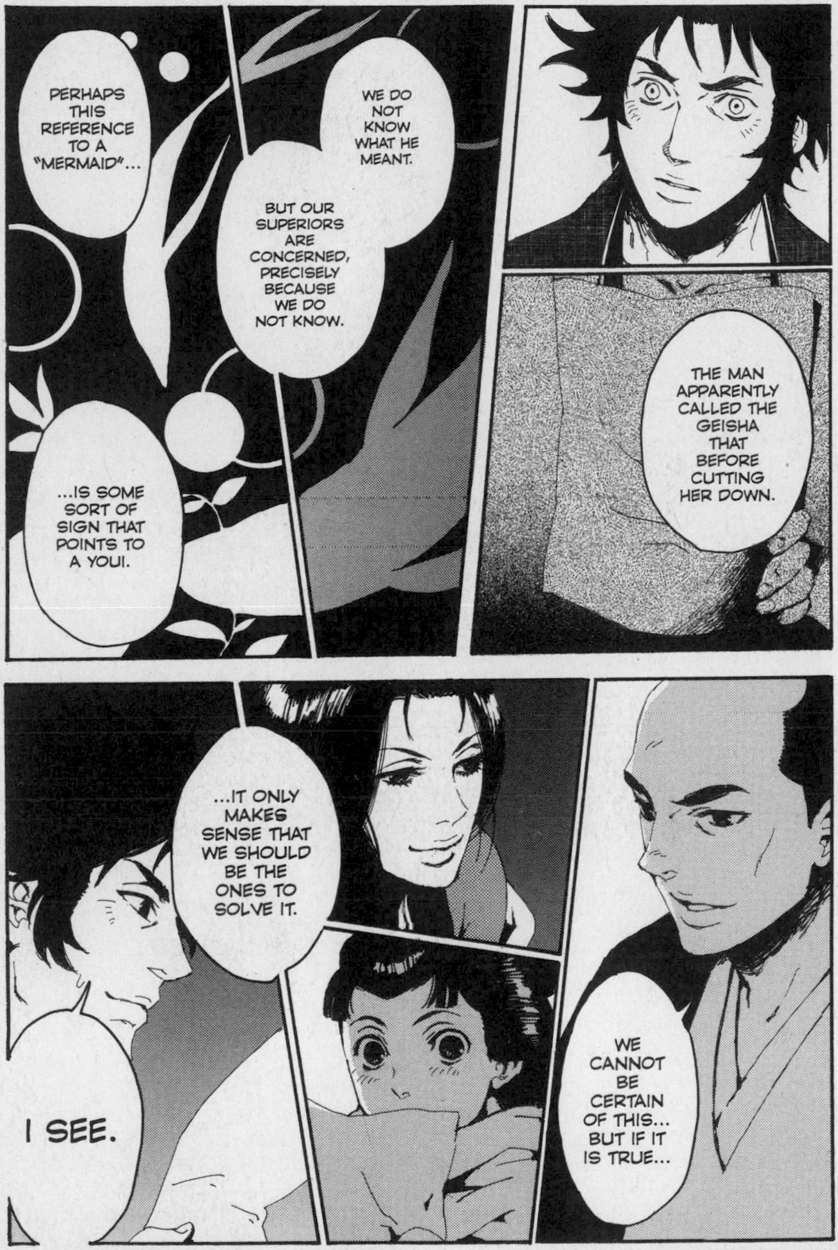
THE MAN APPARENTLY CALLED THE GEISHA THAT BEFORE CUTTING HER DOWN.
WE DO NOT KNOW WHAT HE MEANT.
BUT OUR SUPERIORS ARE CONCERNED, PRECISELY BECAUSE WE DO NOT KNOW.
PERHAPS THIS REFERENCE TO A "MERMAID"...
...IS SOME SORT OF SIGN THAT POINTS TO A YOUI.
WE CANNOT BE CERTAIN OF THIS... BUT IF IT IS TRUE...
...IT ONLY MAKES SENSE THAT WE SHOULD BE THE ONES TO SOLVE IT.
I SEE.

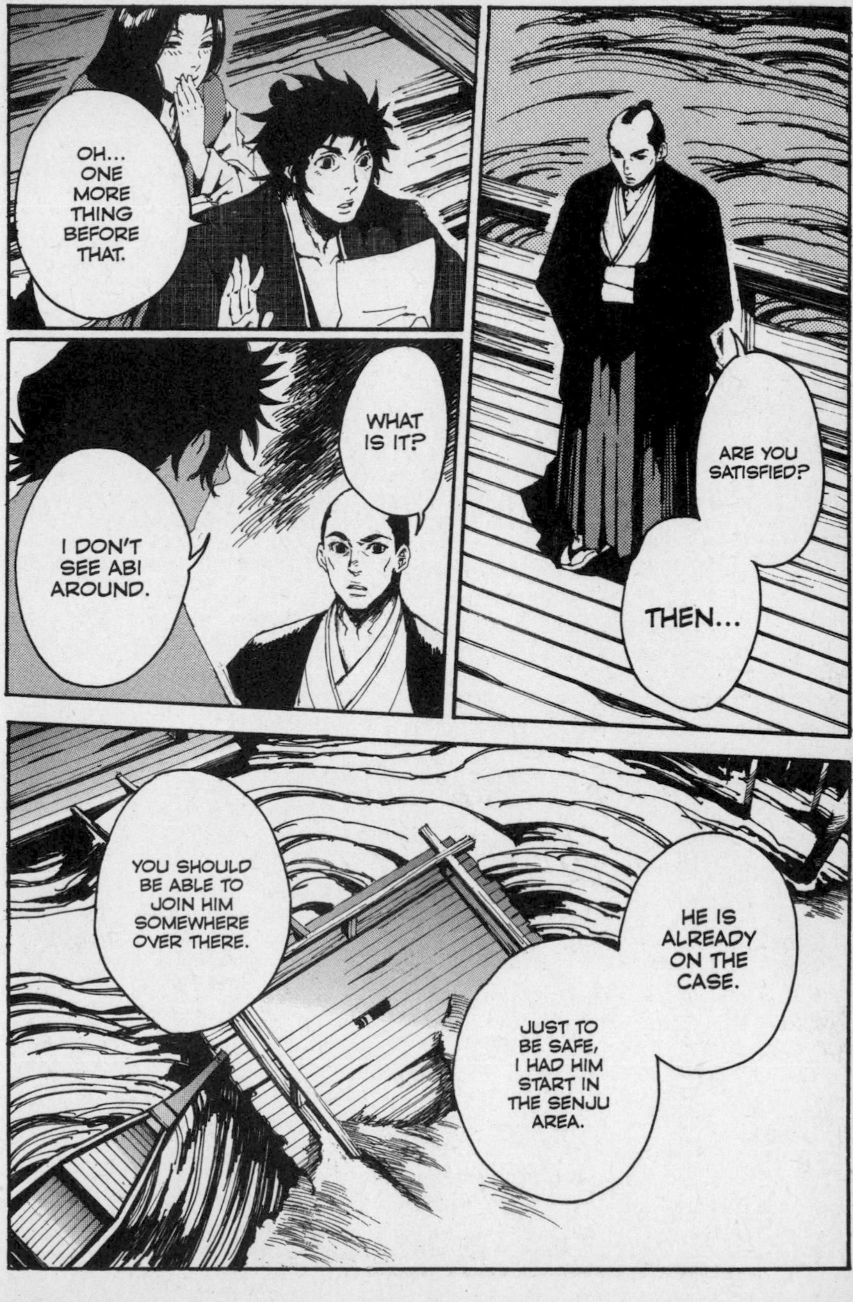

ARE YOU SATISFIED?
THEN...
OH... ONE MORE THING BEFORE THAT.
WHAT IS IT?
I DON'T SEE ABI AROUND.
HE IS ALREADY ON THE CASE.
JUST TO BE SAFE, I HAD HIM START IN THE SENJU AREA.
YOU SHOULD BE ABLE TO JOIN HIM SOMEWHERE OVER THERE.

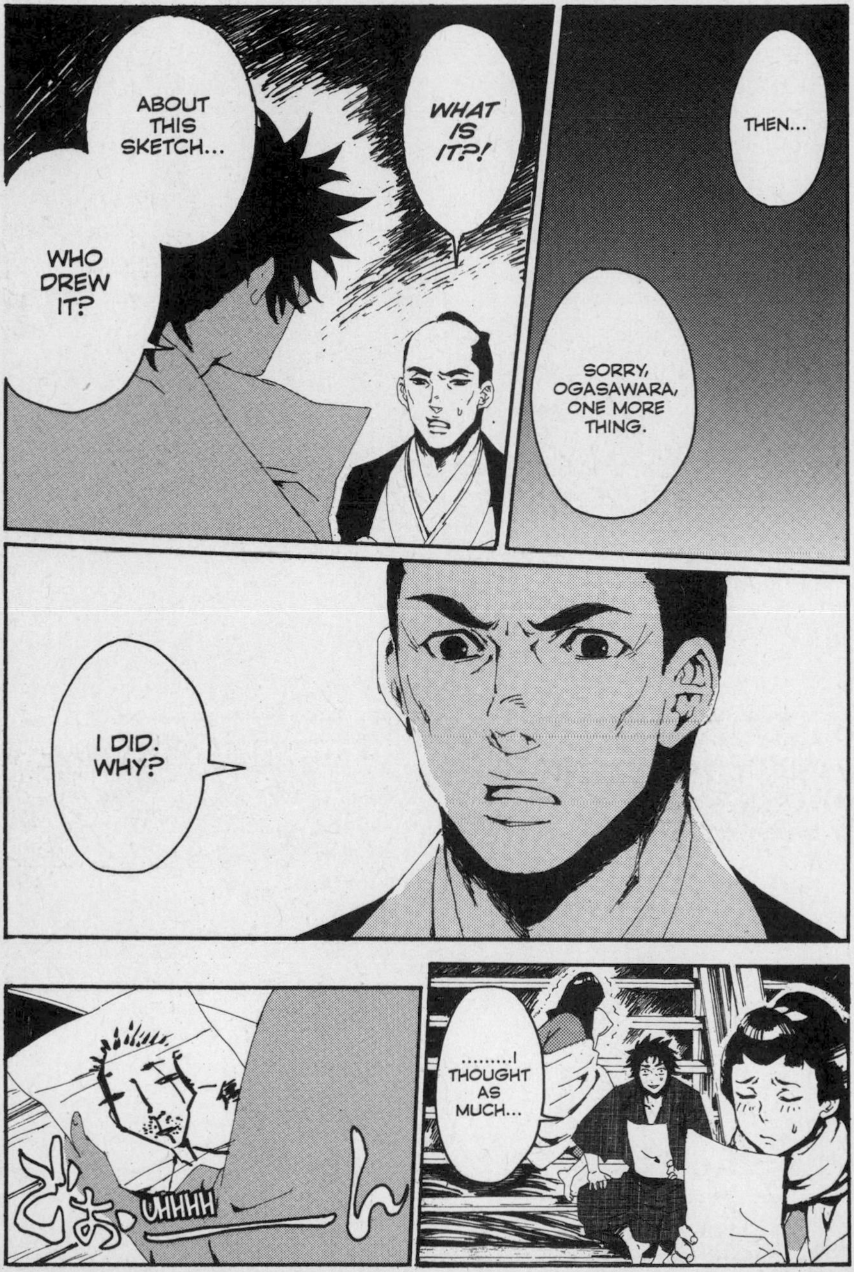
THEN...
SORRY, OGASAWARA, ONE MORE THING.
WHAT IS IT?!
ABOUT THIS SKETCH...
WHO DREW IT?
I DID. WHY?
..........I THOUGHT AS MUCH...
どお
UHHHH
ん

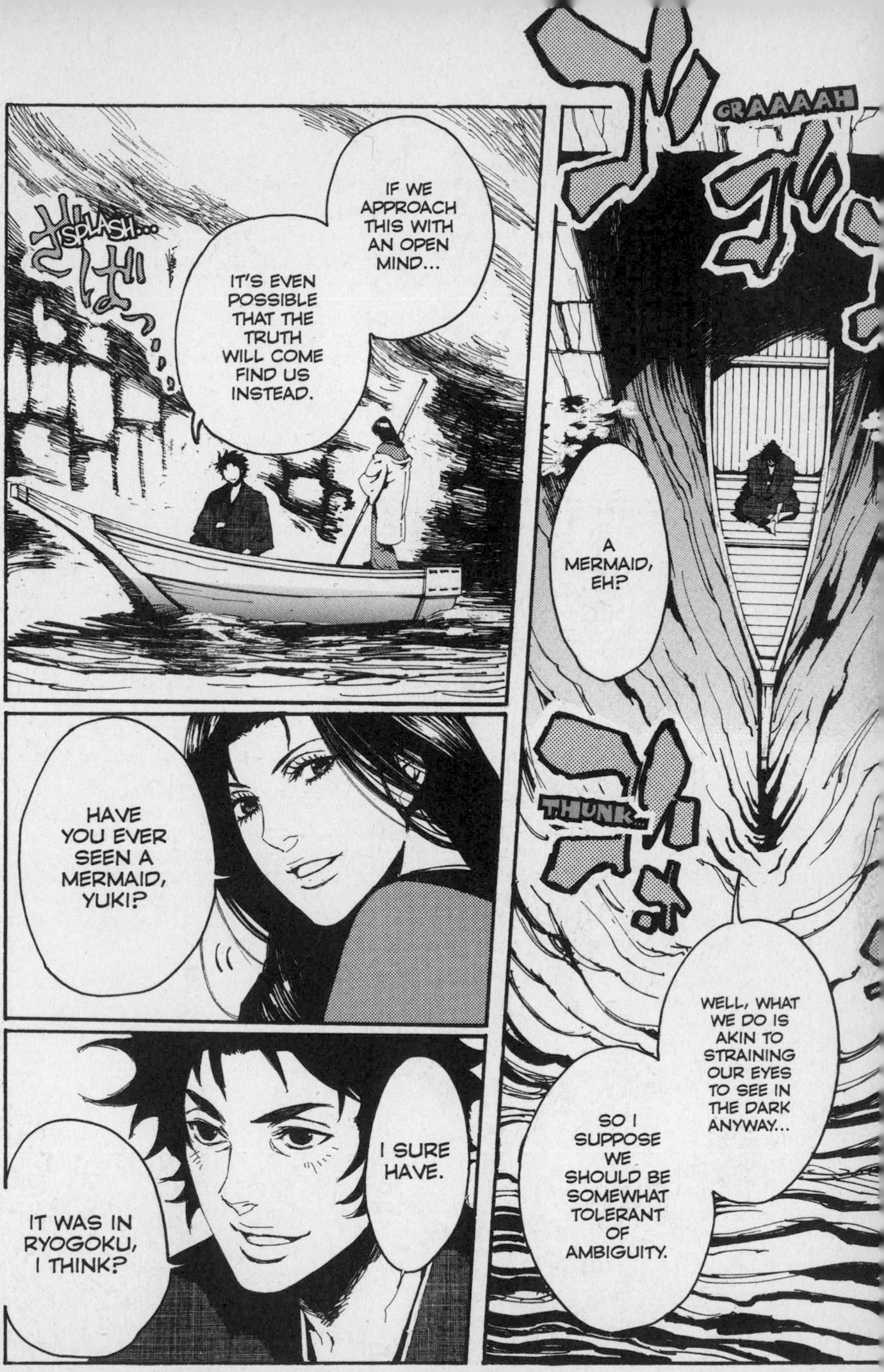
GRAAAAH
A MERMAID, EH?
THUNK...
WELL, WHAT WE DO IS AKIN TO STRAINING OUR EYES TO SEE IN THE DARK ANYWAY...
SO I SUPPOSE WE SHOULD BE SOMEWHAT TOLERANT OF AMBIGUITY.
SPLASH...
IF WE APPROACH THIS WITH AN OPEN MIND...
IT'S EVEN POSSIBLE THAT THE TRUTH WILL COME FIND US INSTEAD.
HAVE YOU EVER SEEN A MERMAID, YUKI?
I SURE HAVE.
IT WAS IN RYOGOKU, I THINK?

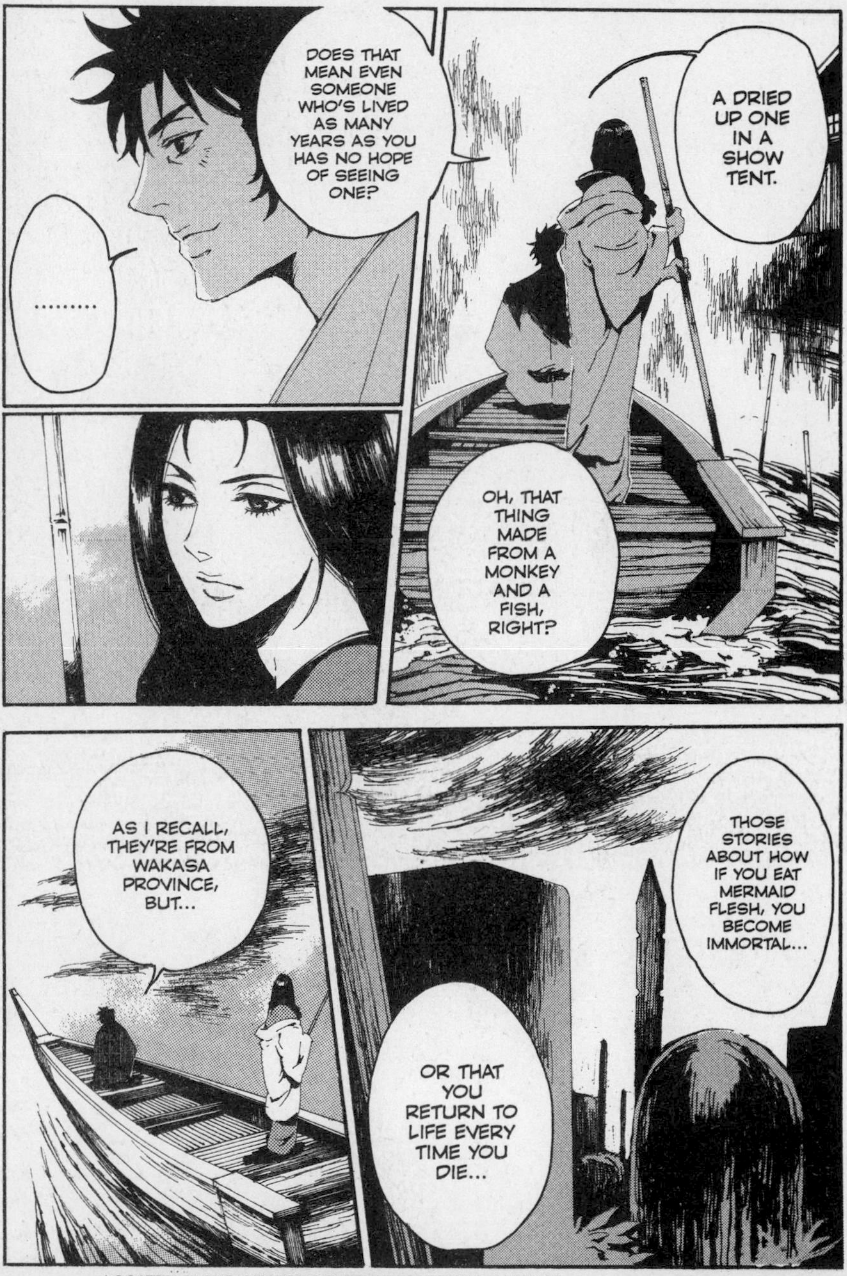
A DRIED UP ONE IN A SHOW TENT.
OH, THAT THING MADE FROM A MONKEY AND A FISH, RIGHT?
DOES THAT MEAN EVEN SOMEONE WHO'S LIVED AS MANY YEARS AS YOU HAS NO HOPE OF SEEING ONE?
....
THOSE STORIES ABOUT HOW IF YOU EAT MERMAID FLESH, YOU BECOME IMMORTAL...
OR THAT YOU RETURN TO LIFE EVERY TIME YOU DIE...
AS I RECALL, THEY'RE FROM WAKASA PROVINCE, BUT...

LOCATED IN THE WESTERN PART OF PRESENT DAY FUKUI PREFECTURE, ALONG THE SHORES OF WAKASA BAY.

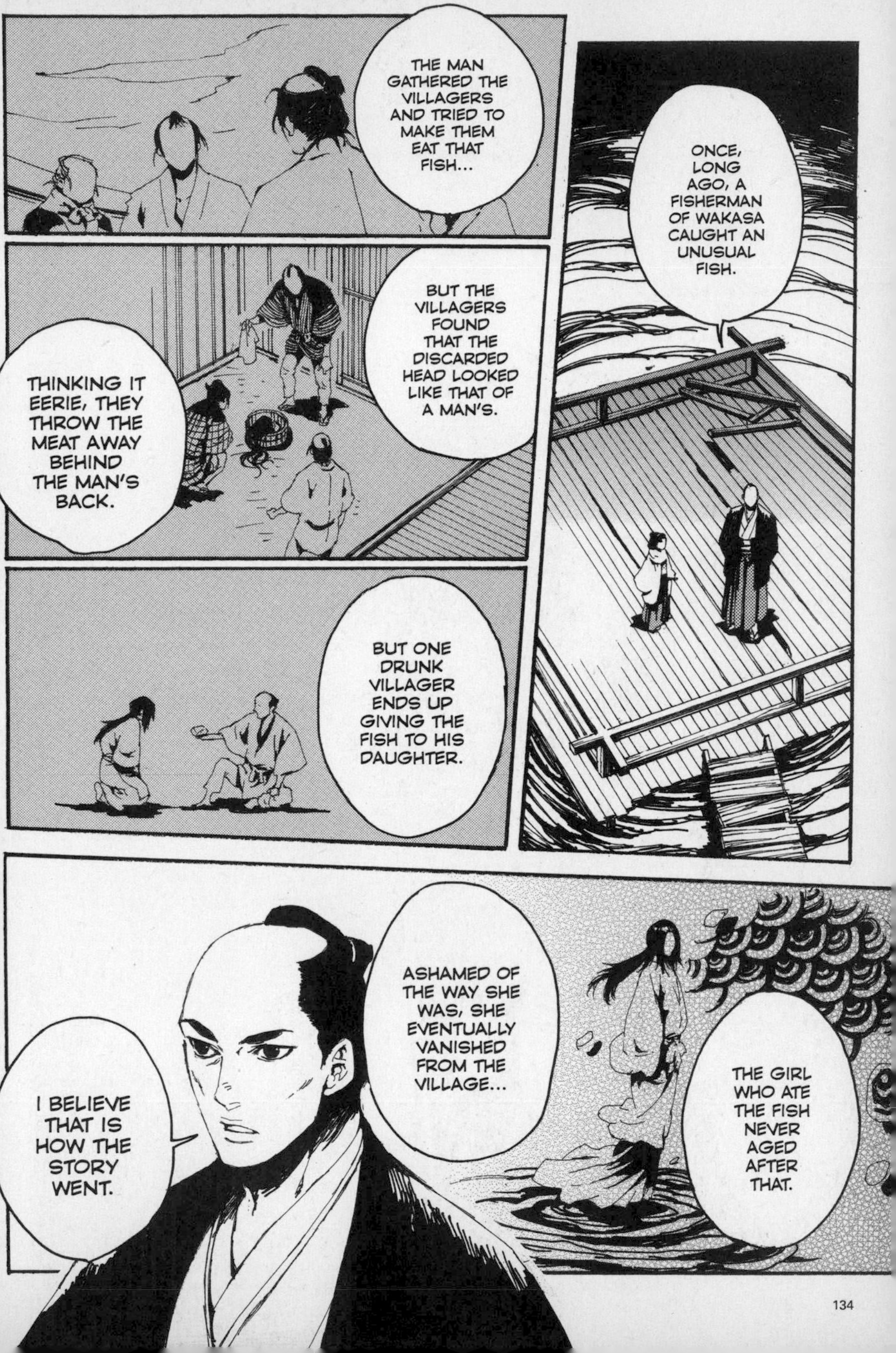
ONCE, LONG AGO, A FISHERMAN OF WAKASA CAUGHT AN UNUSUAL FISH.
THE MAN GATHERED THE VILLAGERS AND TRIED TO MAKE THEM EAT THAT FISH...
BUT THE VILLAGERS FOUND THAT THE DISCARDED HEAD LOOKED LIKE THAT OF A MAN'S.
THINKING IT EERIE, THEY THROW THE MEAT AWAY BEHIND THE MAN'S BACK.
BUT ONE DRUNK VILLAGER ENDS UP GIVING THE FISH TO HIS DAUGHTER.
THE GIRL WHO ATE THE FISH NEVER AGED AFTER THAT.
ASHAMED OF THE WAY SHE WAS, SHE EVENTUALLY VANISHED FROM THE VILLAGE...
I BELIEVE THAT IS HOW THE STORY WENT.

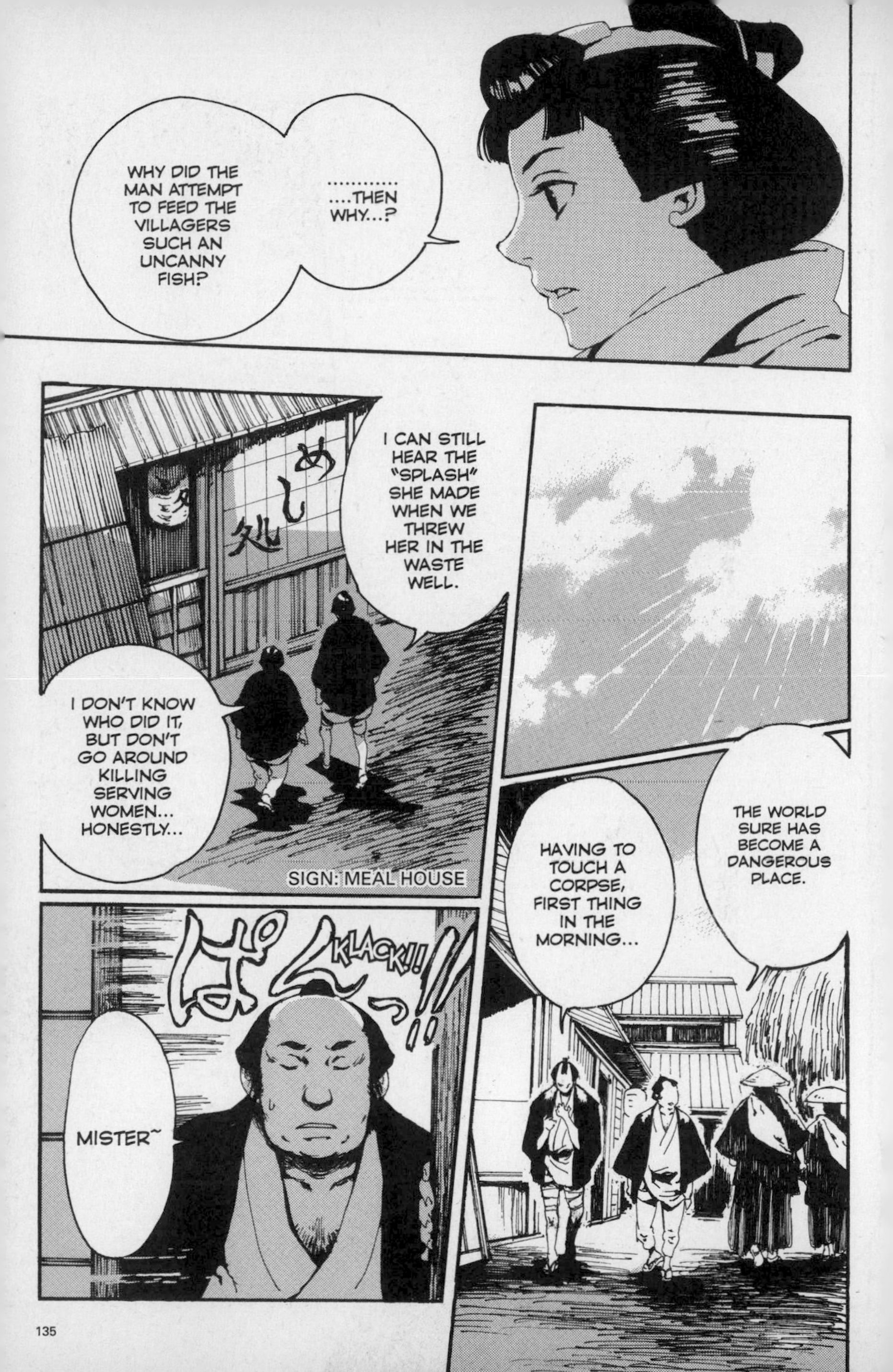
....THEN WHY...?
WHY DID THE MAN ATTEMPT TO FEED THE VILLAGERS SUCH AN UNCANNY FISH?
THE WORLD SURE HAS BECOME A DANGEROUS PLACE.
HAVING TO TOUCH A CORPSE, FIRST THING IN THE MORNING...
めし処
I CAN STILL HEAR THE "SPLASH" SHE MADE WHEN WE THREW HER IN THE WASTE WELL.
I DON'T KNOW WHO DID IT, BUT DON'T GO AROUND KILLING SERVING WOMEN... HONESTLY...
SIGN: MEAL HOUSE
ぱんっ!! KLACK!!
MISTER~

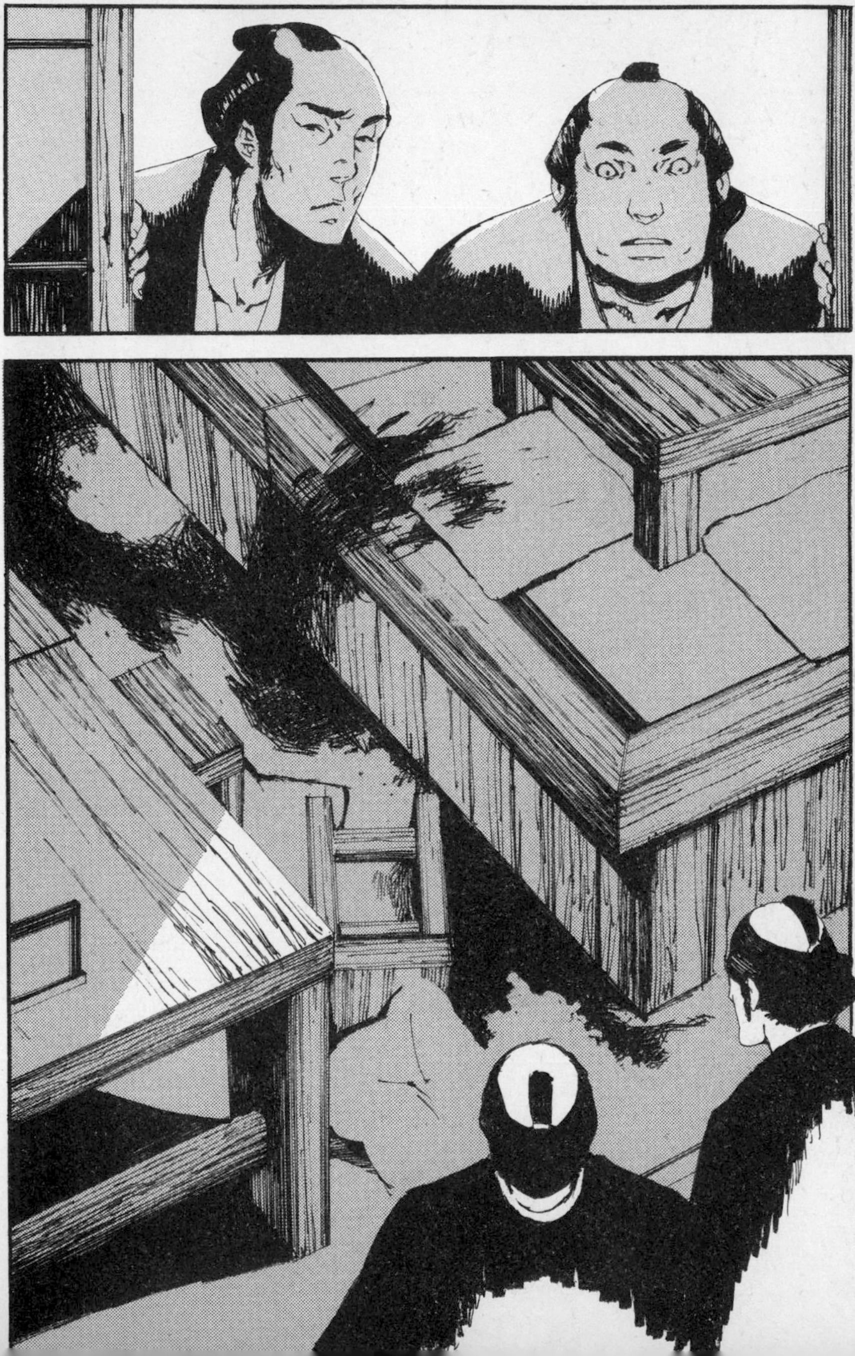

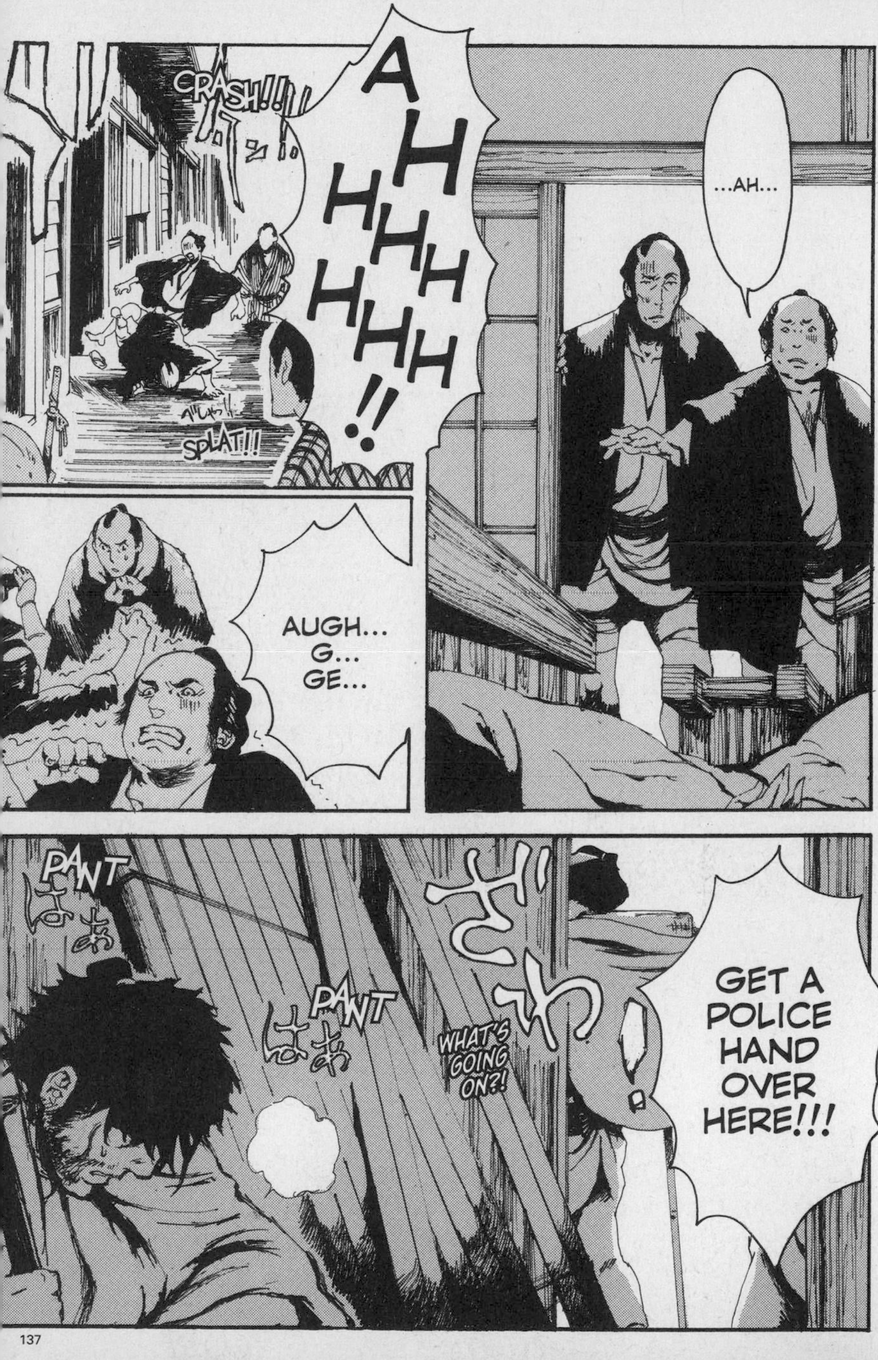
...AH...
AHHHHHHH!!
CRASH!!
SPLAT!!
AUGH... G... GE...
GET A POLICE HAND OVER HERE!!!
WHAT'S GOING ON?!
PANT
PANT

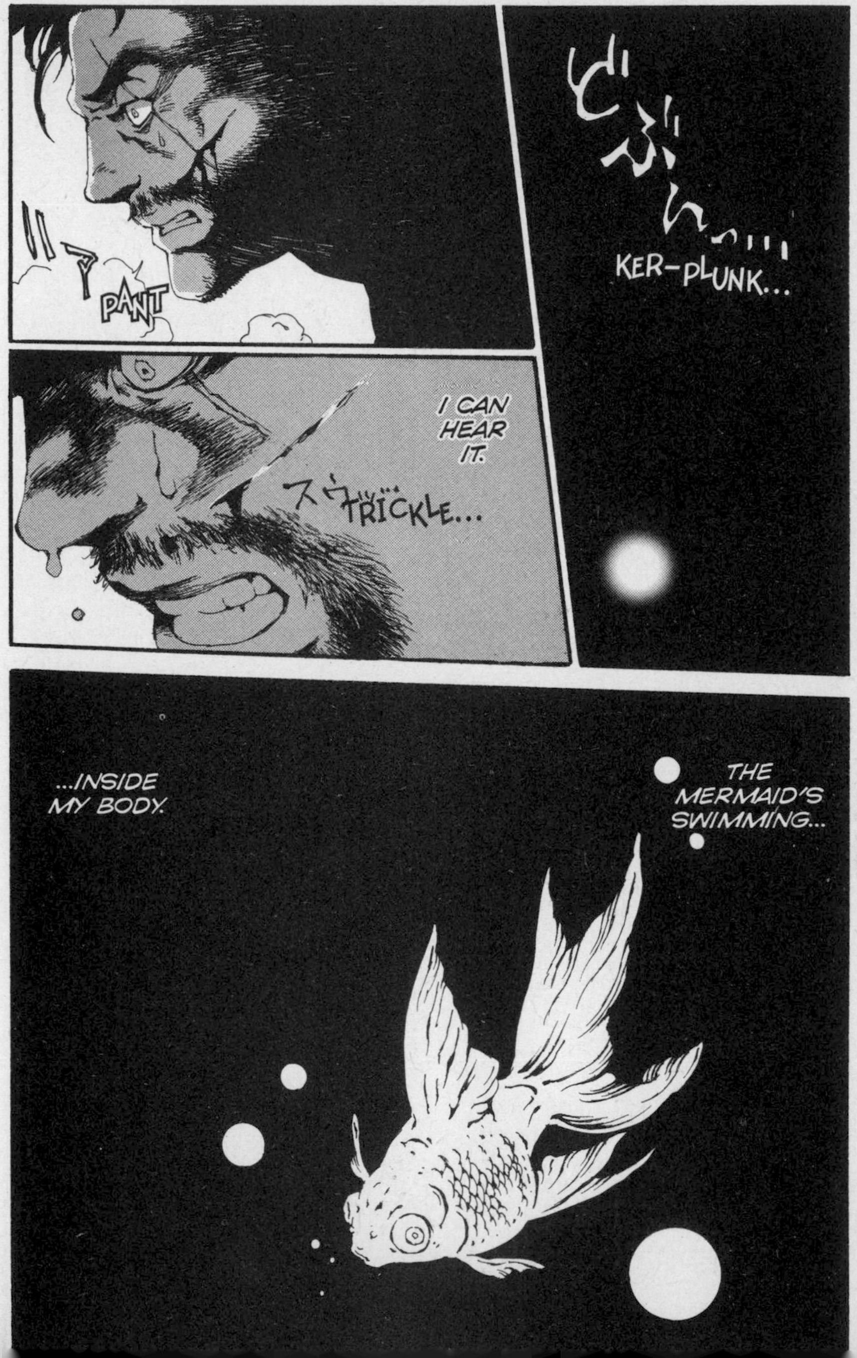
どぶん…
KER-PLUNK...
PANT
I CAN HEAR IT.
TRICKLE...
THE MERMAID'S SWIMMING...
...INSIDE MY BODY.

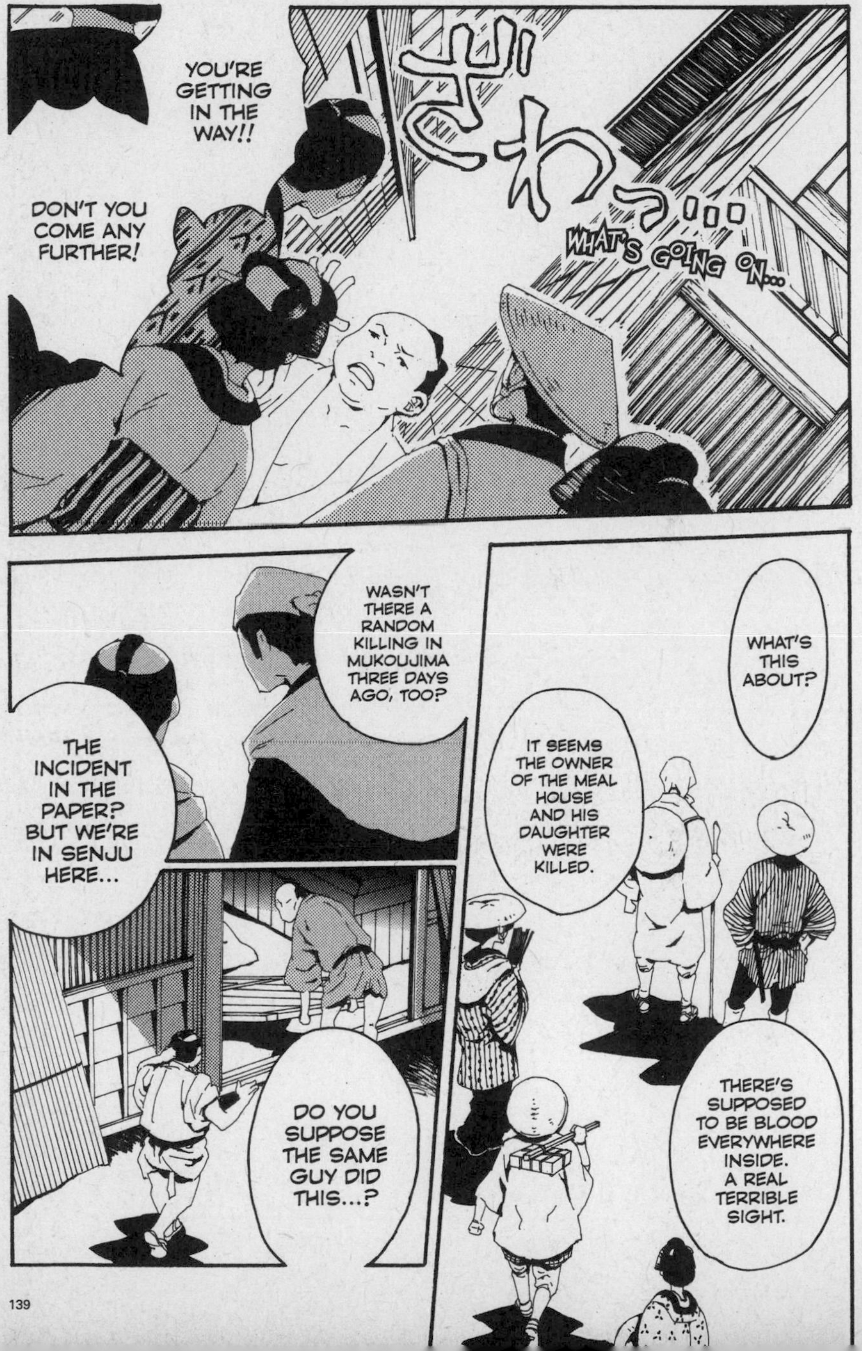
ざわっ...
WHAT'S GOING ON...
YOU'RE GETTING IN THE WAY!!
DON'T YOU COME ANY FURTHER!
WHAT'S THIS ABOUT?
IT SEEMS THE OWNER OF THE MEAL HOUSE AND HIS DAUGHTER WERE KILLED.
THERE'S SUPPOSED TO BE BLOOD EVERYWHERE INSIDE. A REAL TERRIBLE SIGHT.
WASN'T THERE A RANDOM KILLING IN MUKOUJIMA THREE DAYS AGO, TOO?
THE INCIDENT IN THE PAPER? BUT WE'RE IN SENJU HERE...
DO YOU SUPPOSE THE SAME GUY DID THIS...?

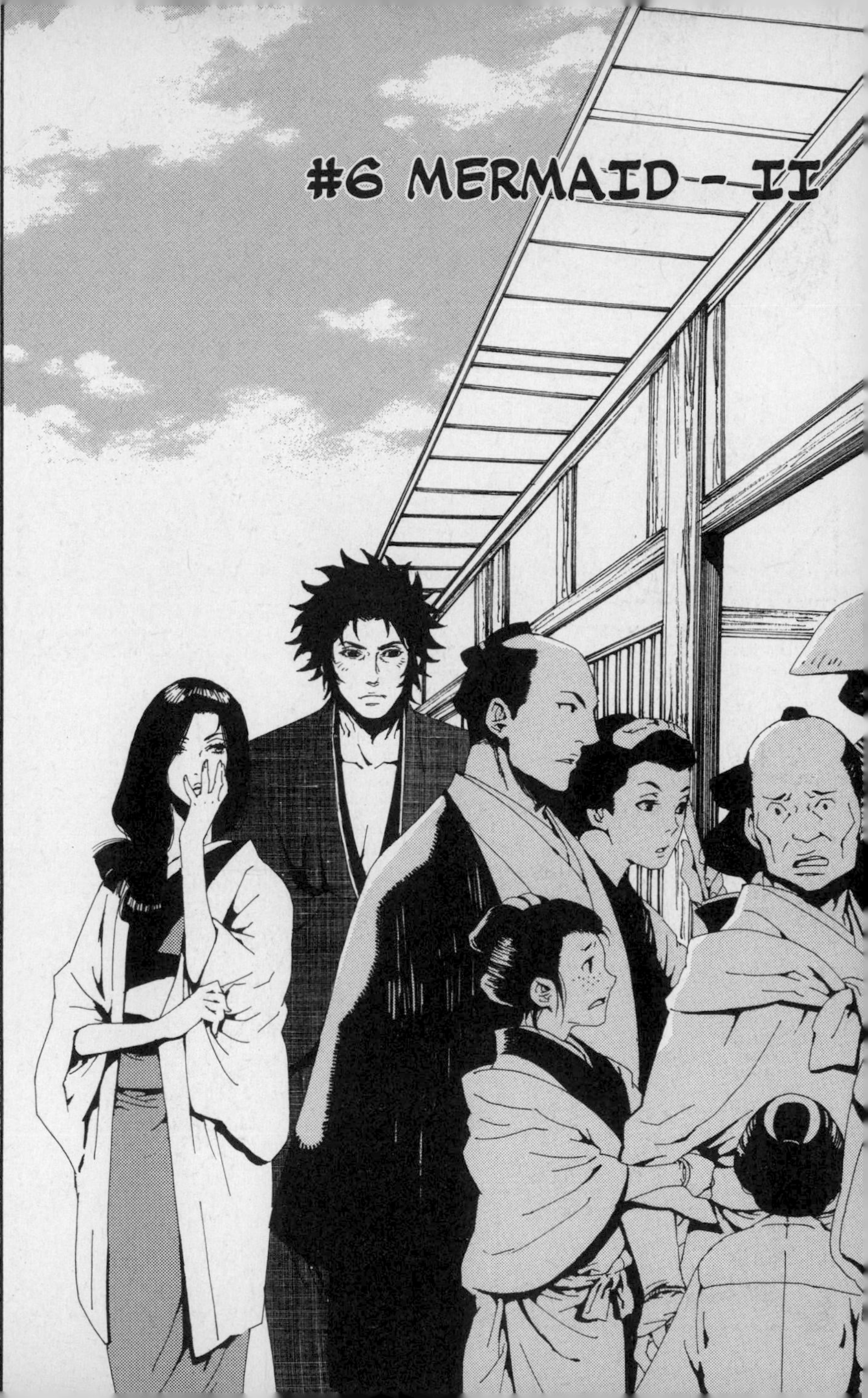
#6 MERMAID - II

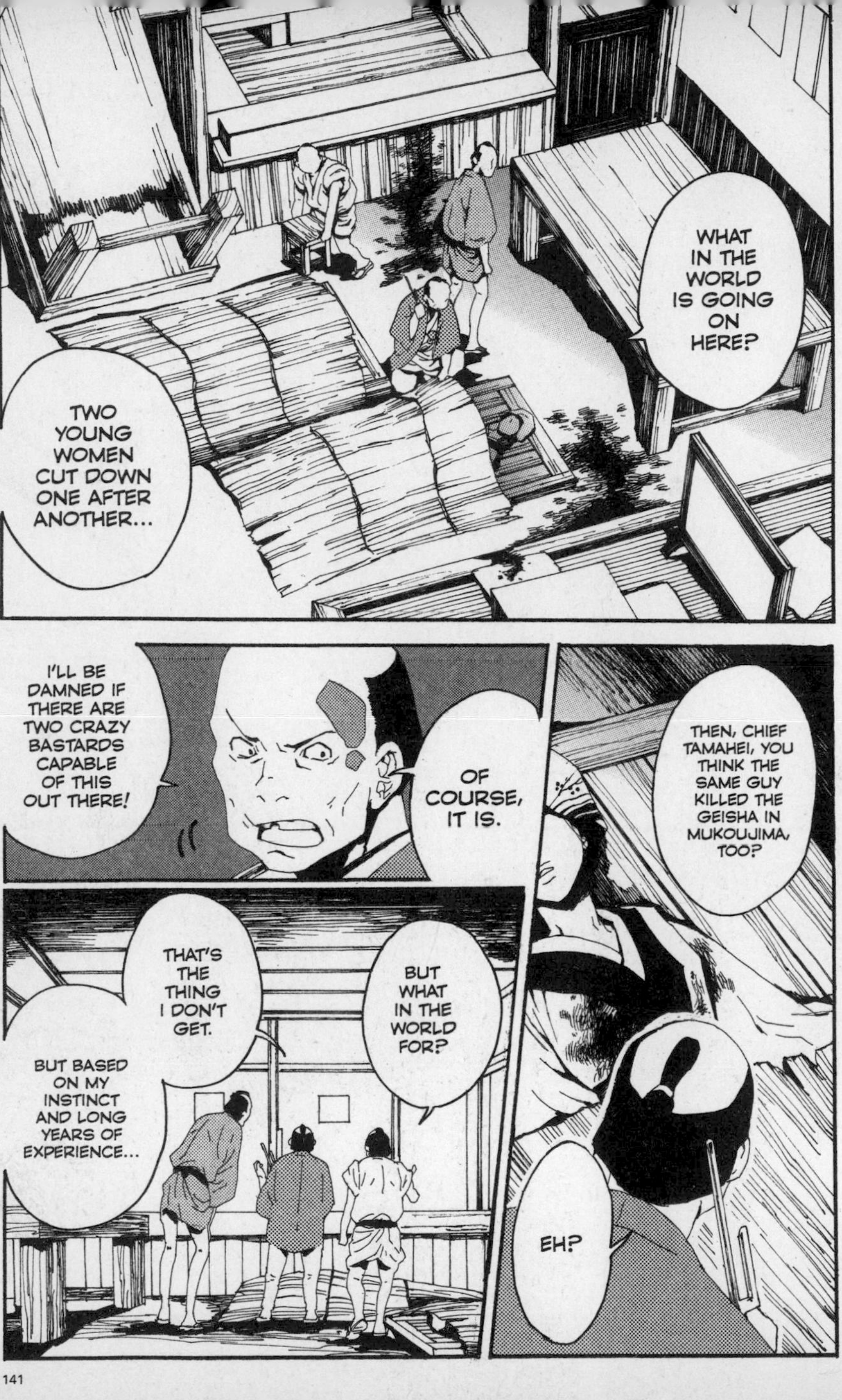
WHAT IN THE WORLD IS GOING ON HERE?
TWO YOUNG WOMEN CUT DOWN ONE AFTER ANOTHER...
THEN, CHIEF TAMAHEI, YOU THINK THE SAME GUY KILLED THE GEISHA IN MUKOUJIMA, TOO?
EH?
OF COURSE, IT IS.
I'LL BE DAMNED IF THERE ARE TWO CRAZY BASTARDS CAPABLE OF THIS OUT THERE!
BUT WHAT IN THE WORLD FOR?
THAT'S THE THING I DON'T GET.
BUT BASED ON MY INSTINCT AND LONG YEARS OF EXPERIENCE...

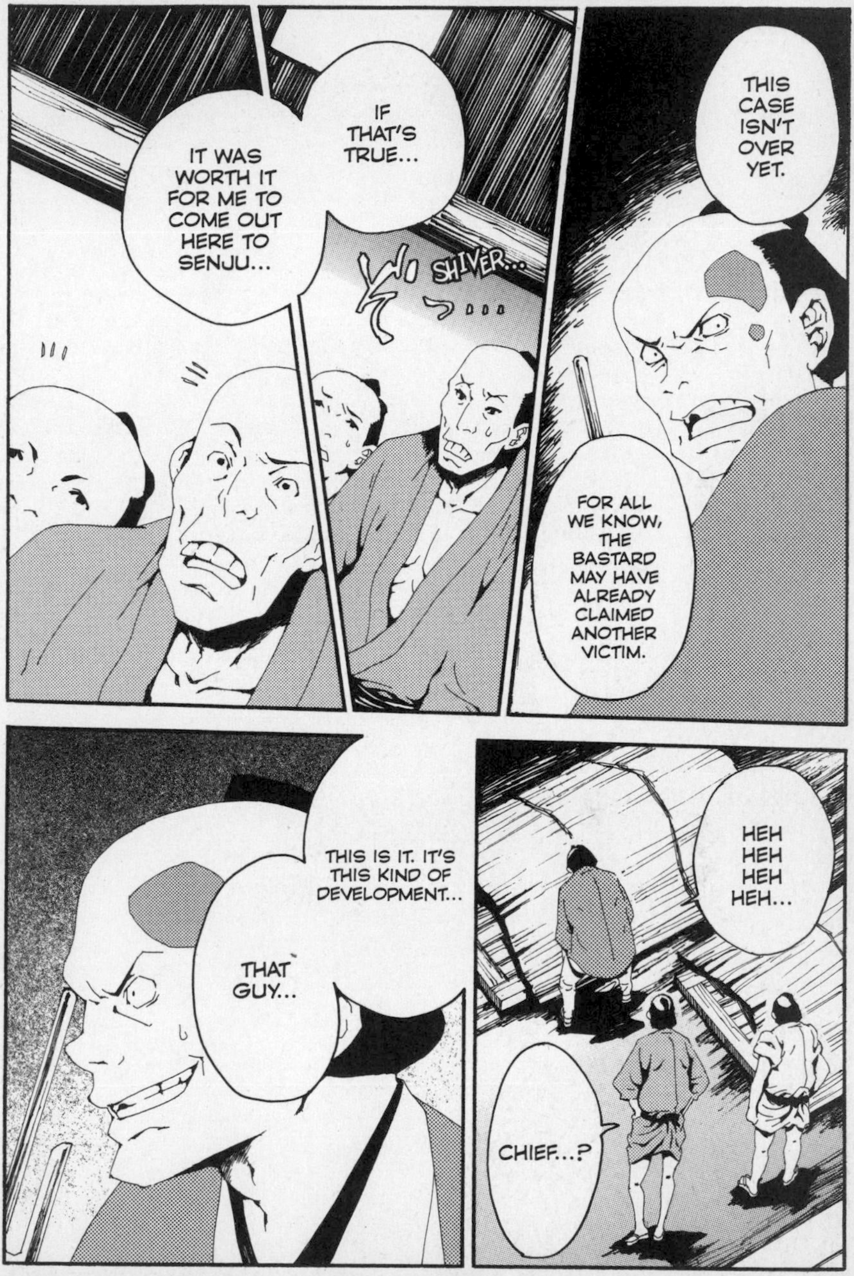
THIS CASE ISN'T OVER YET.
FOR ALL WE KNOW, THE BASTARD MAY HAVE ALREADY CLAIMED ANOTHER VICTIM.
IF THAT'S TRUE...
SHIVER...
IT WAS WORTH IT FOR ME TO COME OUT HERE TO SENJU...
HEH HEH HEH HEH...
CHIEF...?
THIS IS IT. IT'S THIS KIND OF DEVELOPMENT...
THAT GUY...

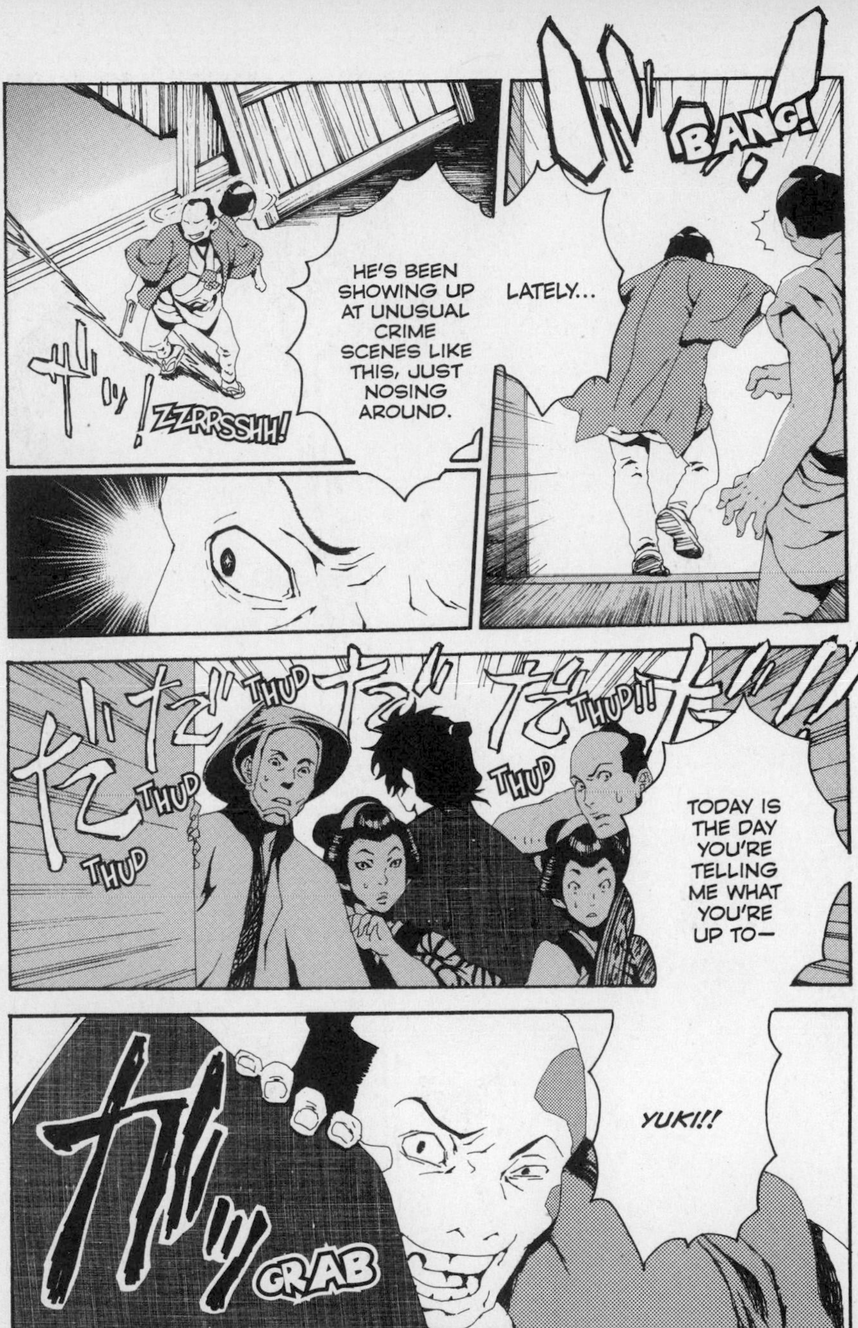

BANG!
LATELY...
HE'S BEEN SHOWING UP AT UNUSUAL CRIME SCENES LIKE THIS, JUST NOSING AROUND.
ZZRRSSHH!
THUD!!
THUD
THUD
THUD
THUD
TODAY IS THE DAY YOU'RE TELLING ME WHAT YOU'RE UP TO—
YUKI!!
GRAB

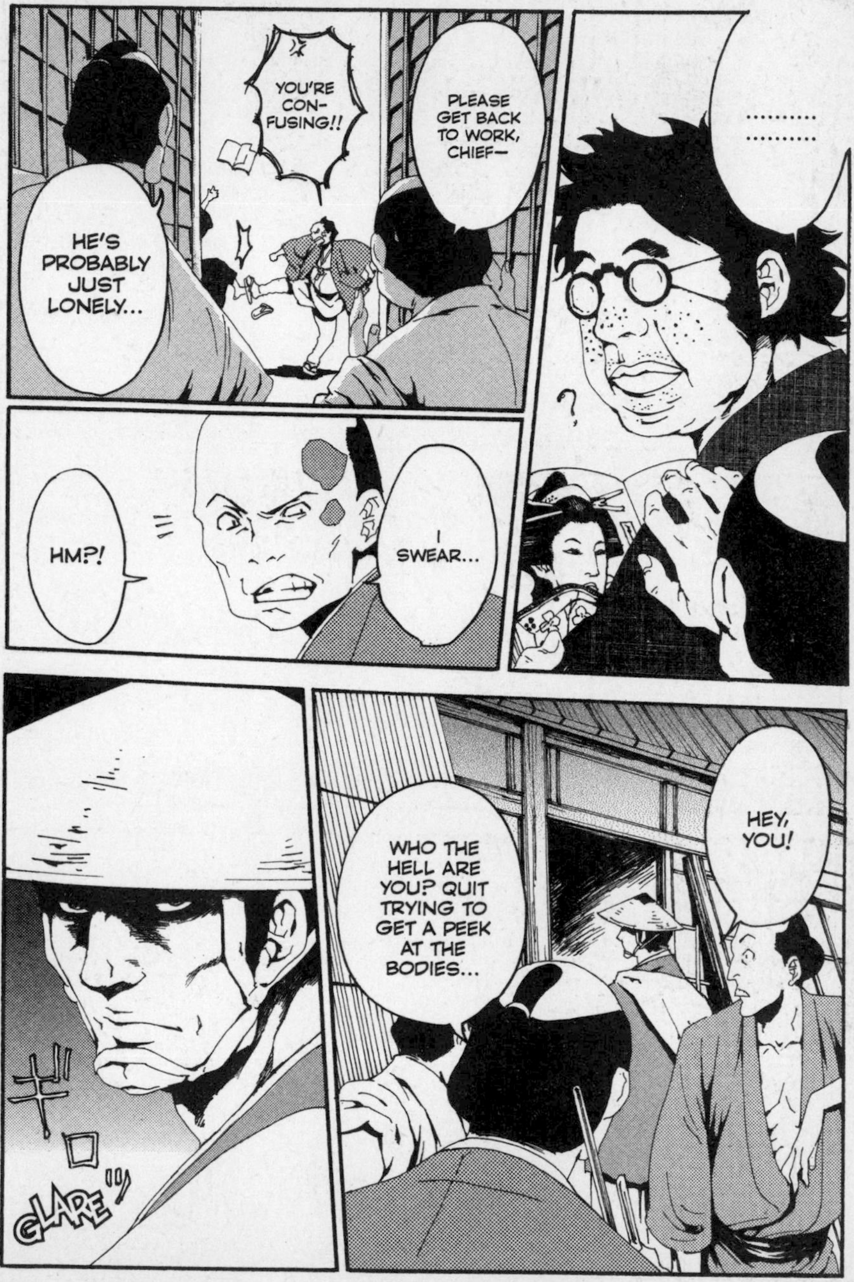
....
....
PLEASE GET BACK TO WORK, CHIEF—
YOU'RE CON-FUSING!!
HE'S PROBABLY JUST LONELY...
I SWEAR...
HM?!
HEY, YOU!
WHO THE HELL ARE YOU? QUIT TRYING TO GET A PEEK AT THE BODIES...
ギロ
GLARE

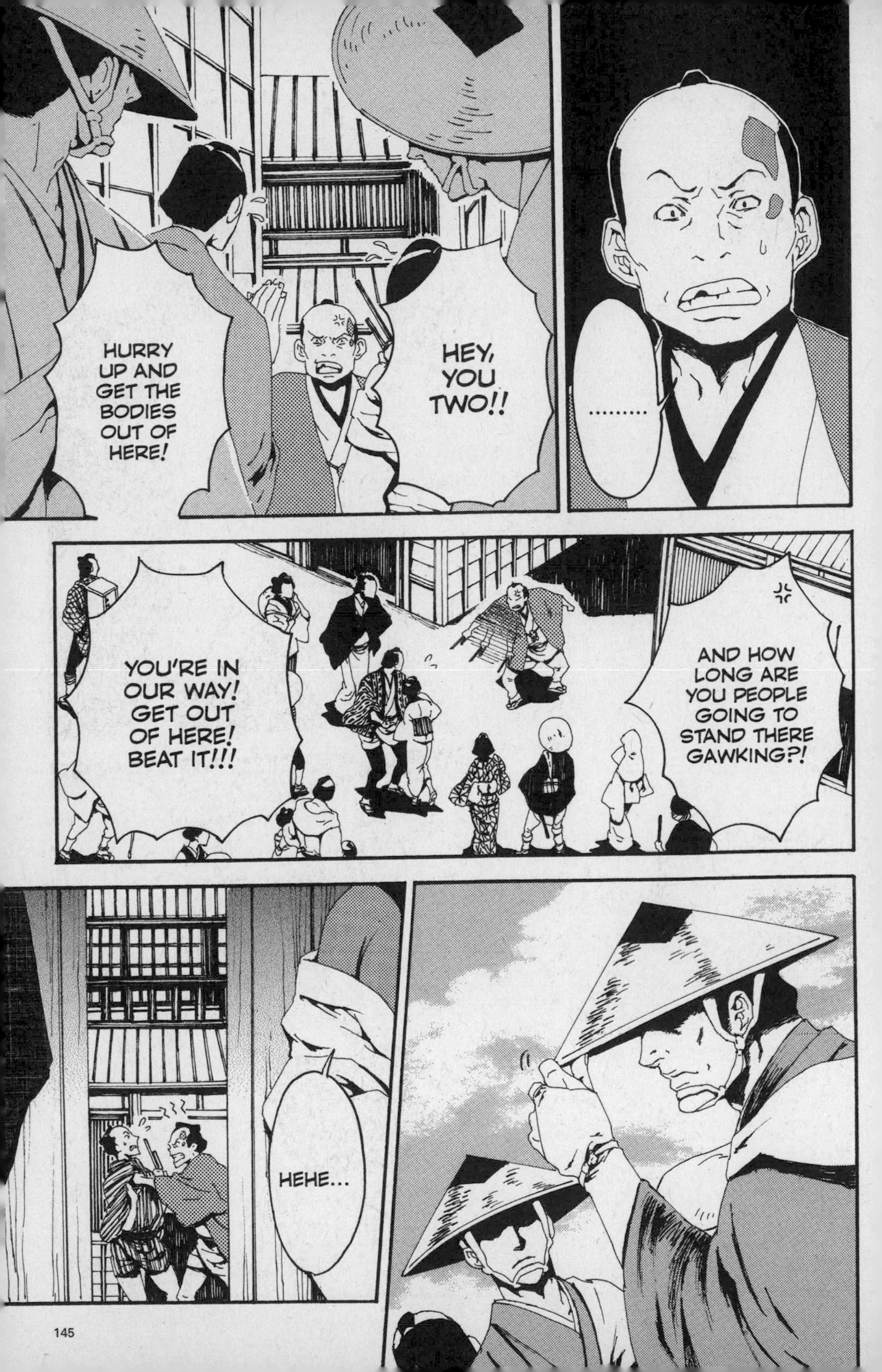
....
HEY, YOU TWO!!
HURRY UP AND GET THE BODIES OUT OF HERE!
AND HOW LONG ARE YOU PEOPLE GOING TO STAND THERE GAWKING?!
YOU'RE IN OUR WAY! GET OUT OF HERE! BEAT IT!!!
HEHE...

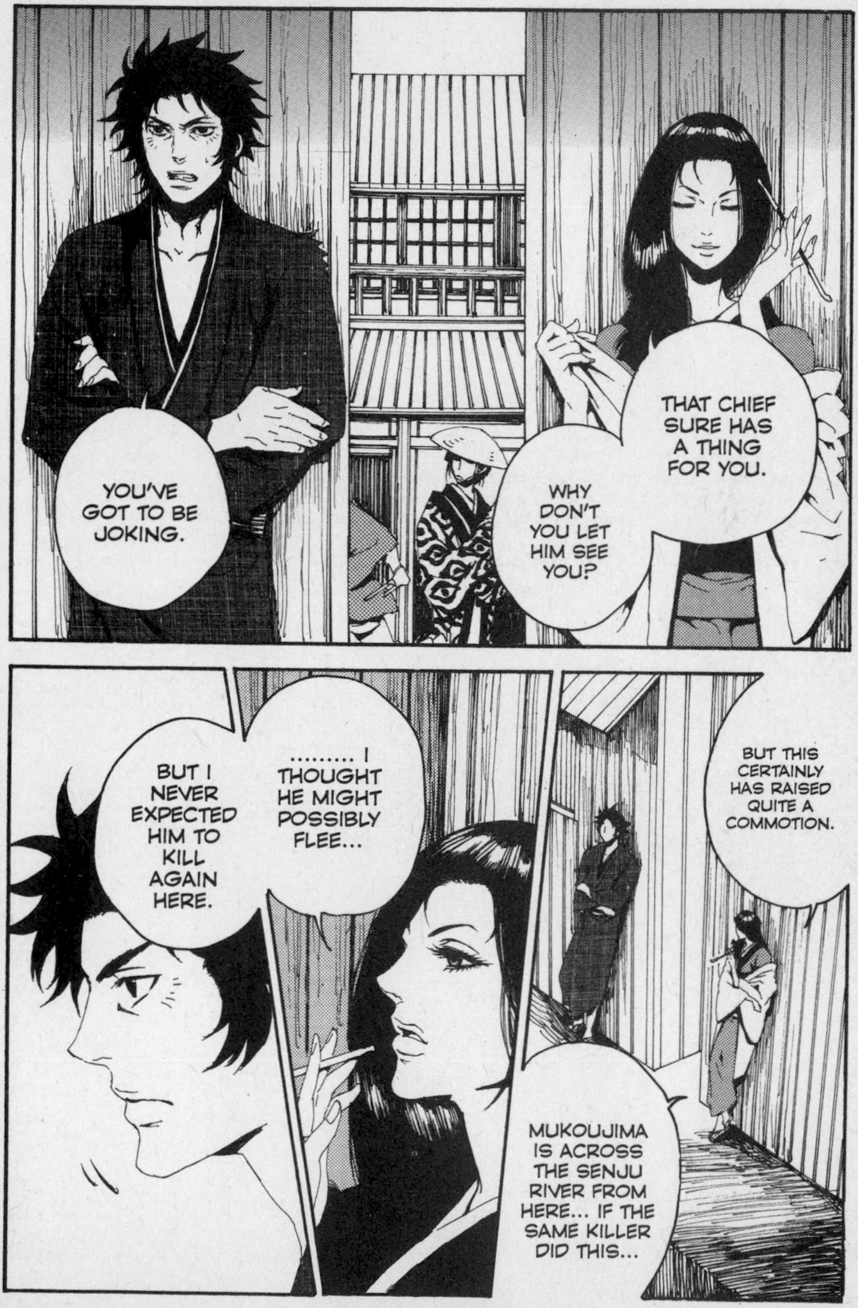
THAT CHIEF SURE HAS A THING FOR YOU.
WHY DON'T YOU LET HIM SEE YOU?
YOU'VE GOT TO BE JOKING.
BUT THIS CERTAINLY HAS RAISED QUITE A COMMOTION.
MUKOUJIMA IS ACROSS THE SENJU RIVER FROM HERE... IF THE SAME KILLER DID THIS...
.... I THOUGHT HE MIGHT POSSIBLY FLEE...
BUT I NEVER EXPECTED HIM TO KILL AGAIN HERE.

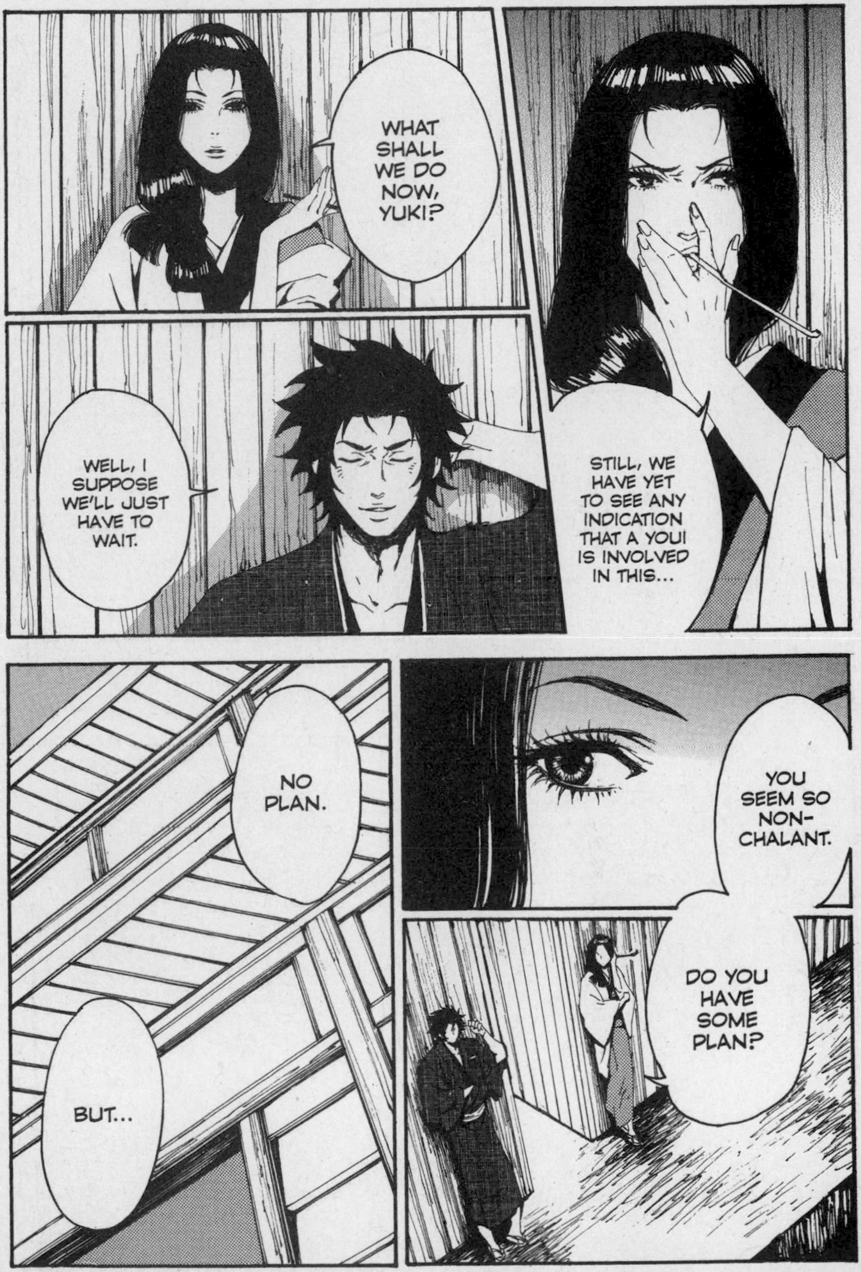
STILL, WE HAVE YET TO SEE ANY INDICATION THAT A YOUI IS INVOLVED IN THIS...
WHAT SHALL WE DO NOW, YUKI?
WELL, I SUPPOSE WE'LL JUST HAVE TO WAIT.
YOU SEEM SO NON-CHALANT.
DO YOU HAVE SOME PLAN?
NO PLAN.
BUT...

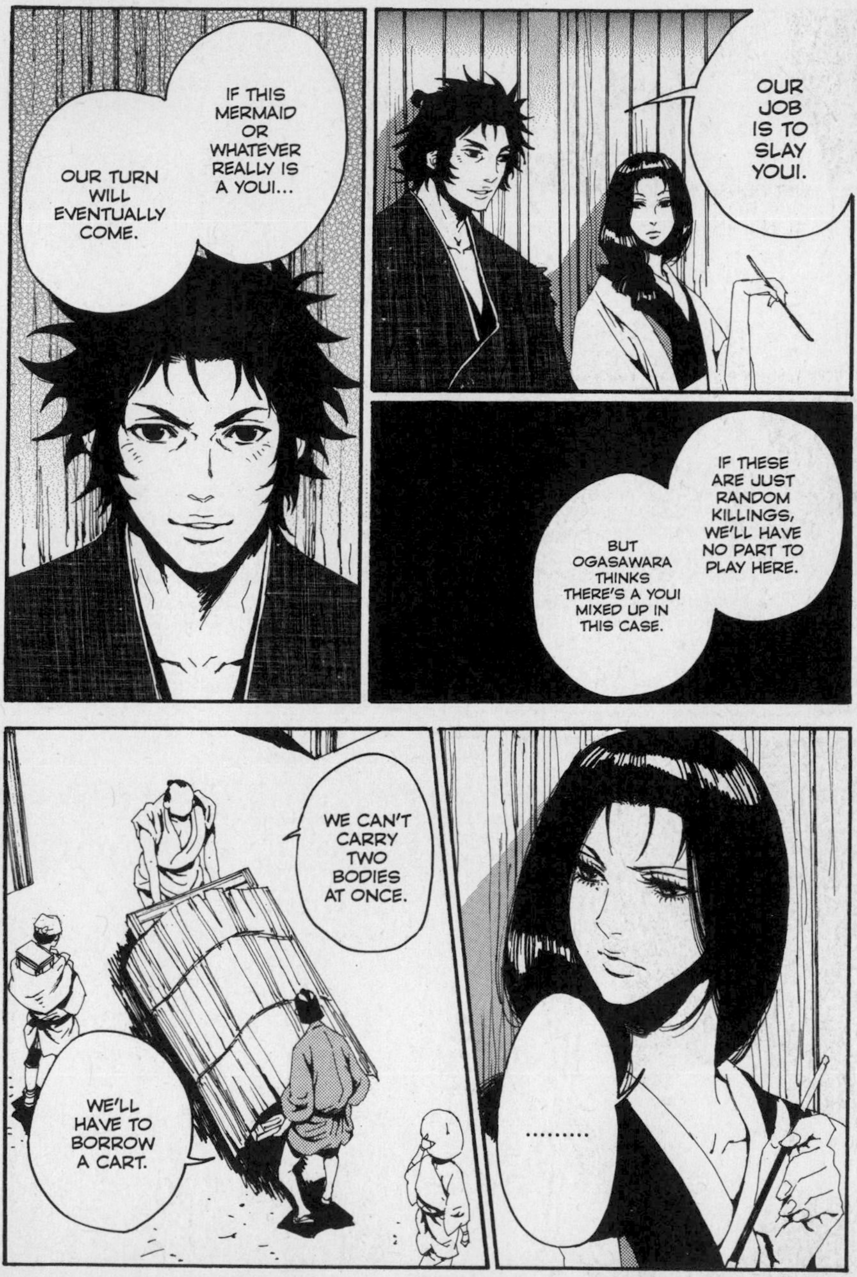
OUR JOB IS TO SLAY YOUI.
IF THESE ARE JUST RANDOM KILLINGS, WE'LL HAVE NO PART TO PLAY HERE.
BUT OGASAWARA THINKS THERE'S A YOUI MIXED UP IN THIS CASE.
IF THIS MERMAID OR WHATEVER REALLY IS A YOUI...
OUR TURN WILL EVENTUALLY COME.
....
WE CAN'T CARRY TWO BODIES AT ONCE.
WE'LL HAVE TO BORROW A CART.

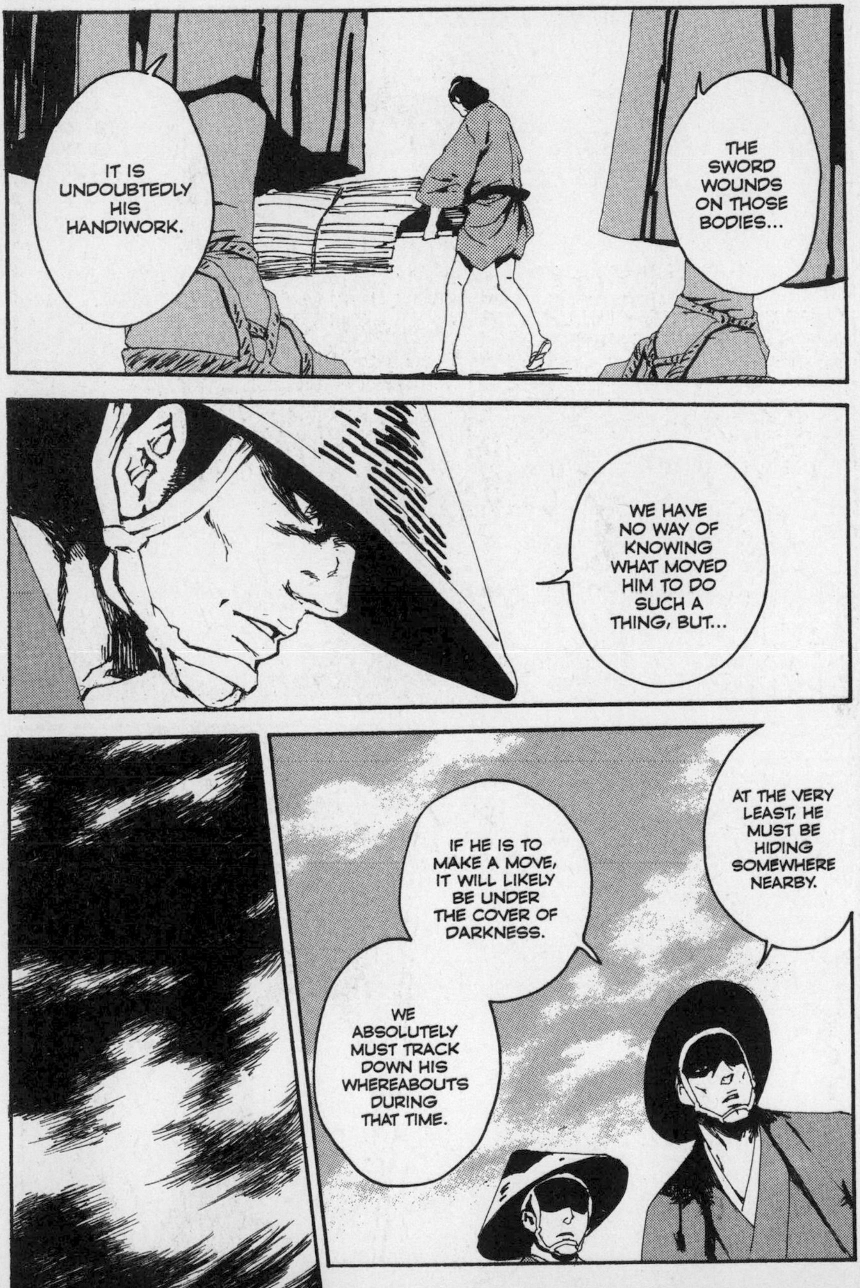
THE SWORD WOUNDS ON THOSE BODIES...
IT IS UNDOUBTEDLY HIS HANDIWORK.
WE HAVE NO WAY OF KNOWING WHAT MOVED HIM TO DO SUCH A THING, BUT...
AT THE VERY LEAST, HE MUST BE HIDING SOMEWHERE NEARBY.
IF HE IS TO MAKE A MOVE, IT WILL LIKELY BE UNDER THE COVER OF DARKNESS.
WE ABSOLUTELY MUST TRACK DOWN HIS WHEREABOUTS DURING THAT TIME.

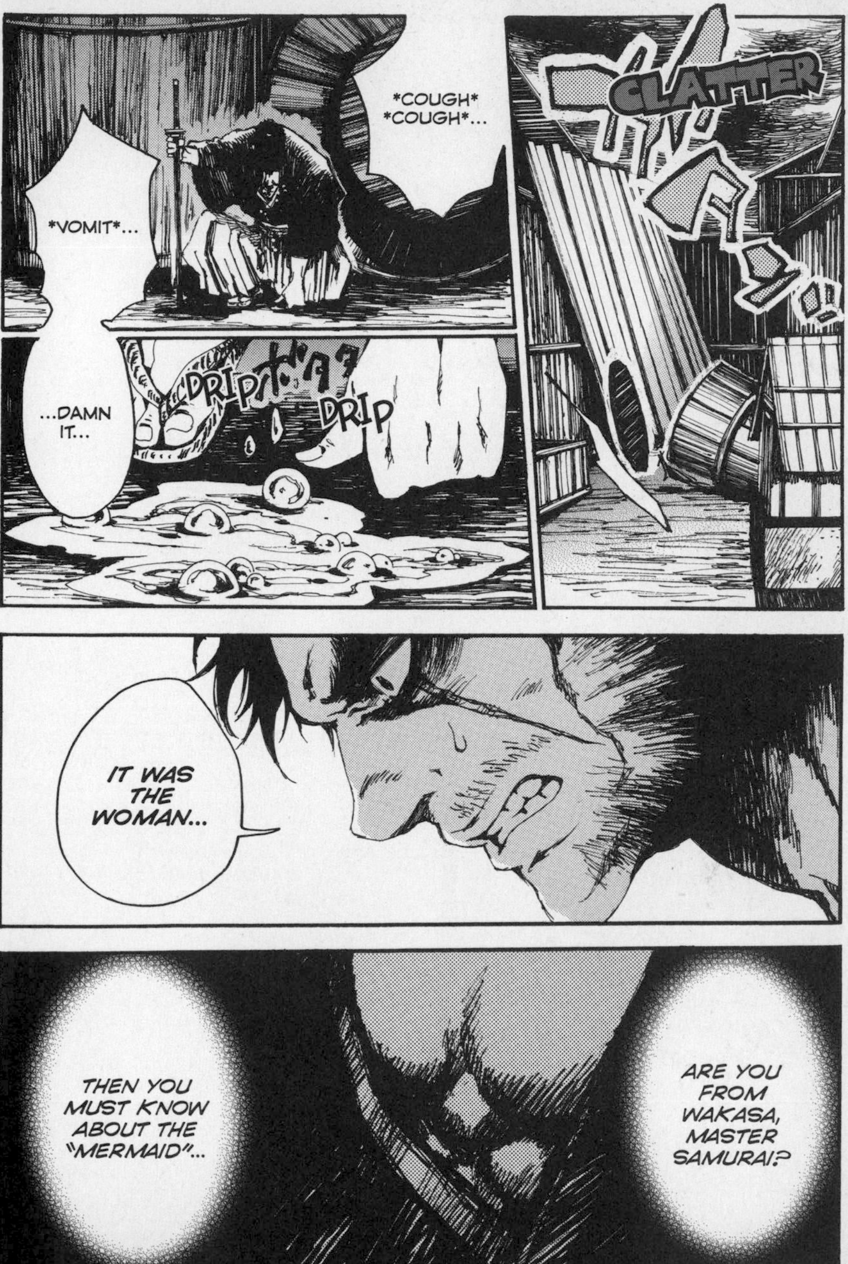
CLATTER
COUGH *COUGH*...
VOMIT...
DRIP
DRIP
...DAMN IT...
IT WAS THE WOMAN...
ARE YOU FROM WAKASA, MASTER SAMURAI?
THEN YOU MUST KNOW ABOUT THE "MERMAID"...

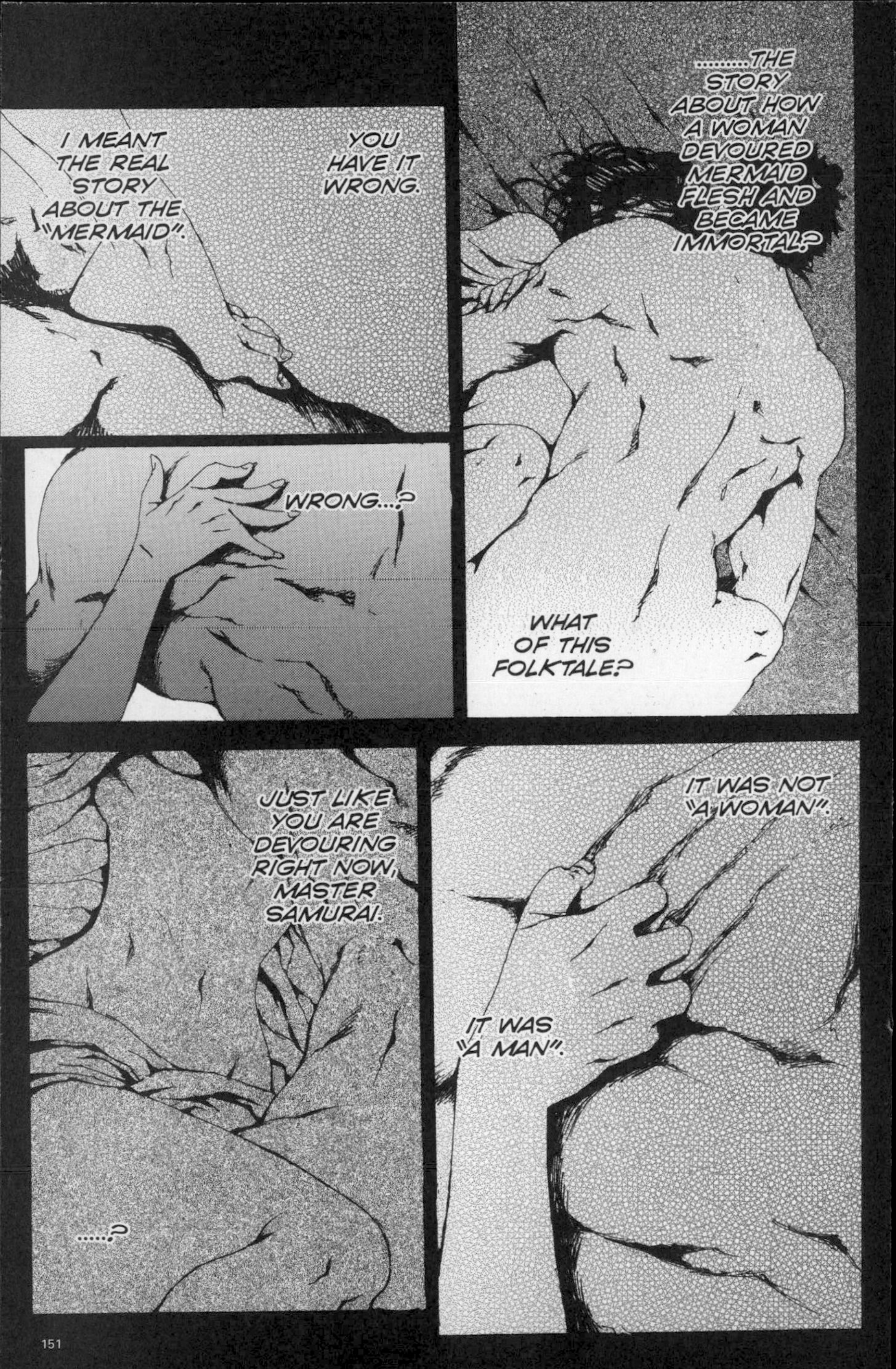
..........THE STORY ABOUT HOW A WOMAN DEVOURED MERMAID FLESH AND BECAME IMMORTAL?
WHAT OF THIS FOLKTALE?
YOU HAVE IT WRONG.
I MEANT THE REAL STORY ABOUT THE "MERMAID".
WRONG...?
IT WAS NOT "A WOMAN".
IT WAS "A MAN".
JUST LIKE YOU ARE DEVOURING RIGHT NOW, MASTER SAMURAI.
.....?

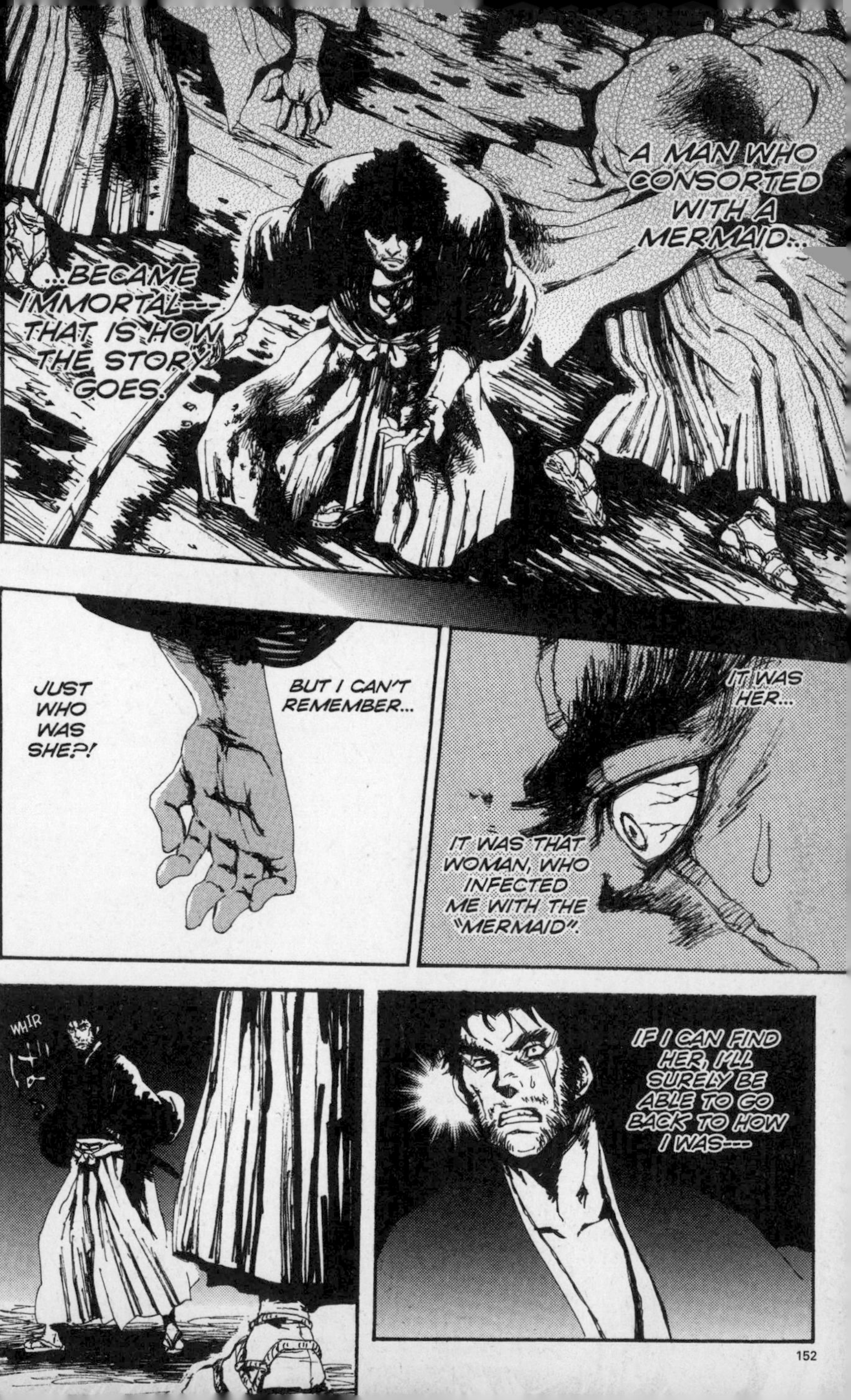
A MAN WHO CONSORTED WITH A MERMAID...
...BECAME IMMORTAL--- THAT IS HOW THE STORY GOES.
IT WAS HER...
IT WAS THAT WOMAN, WHO INFECTED ME WITH THE "MERMAID".
BUT I CAN'T REMEMBER...
JUST WHO WAS SHE?!
IF I CAN FIND HER, I'LL SURELY BE ABLE TO GO BACK TO HOW I WAS---
WHIR

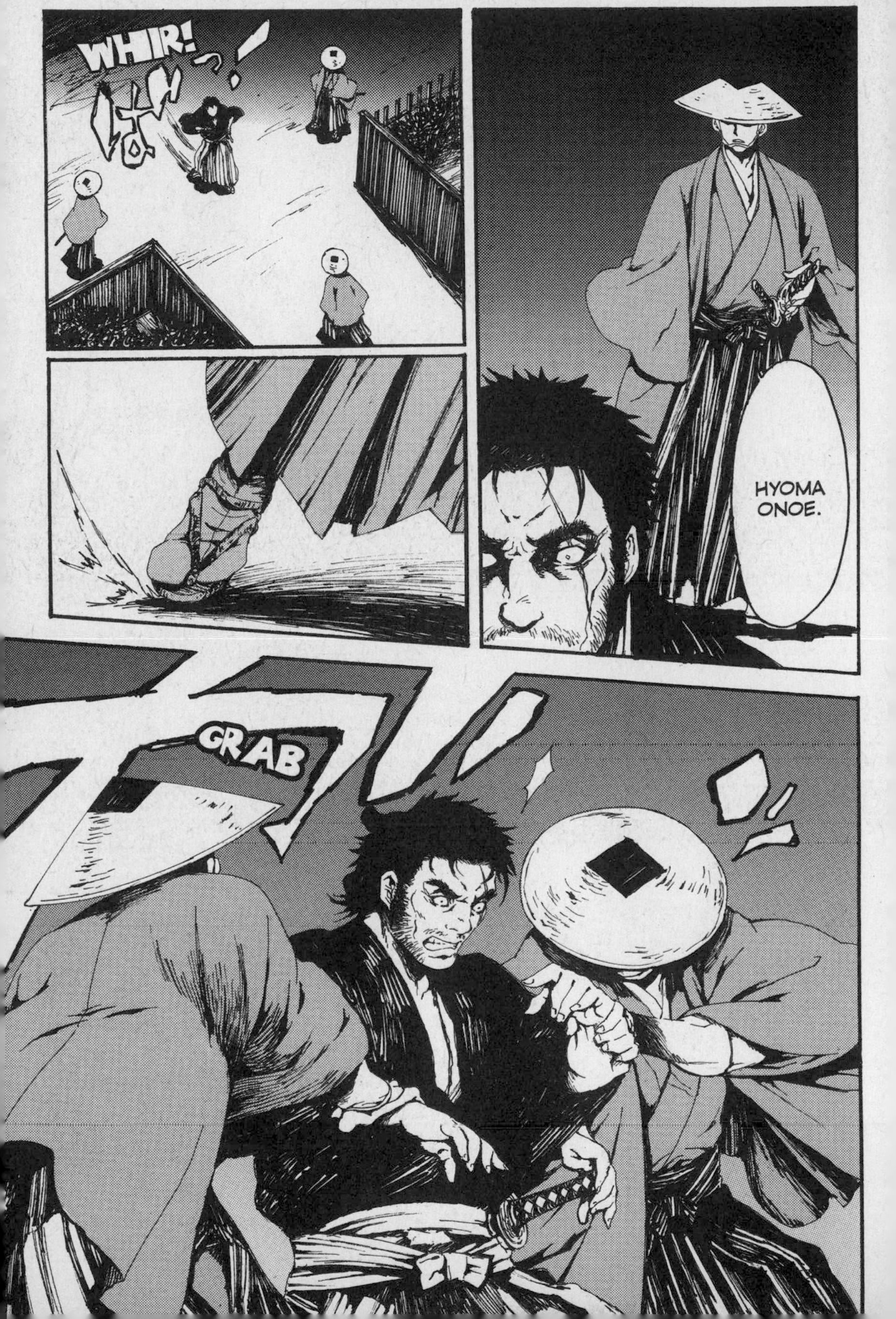
HYOMA ONOE.
WHIR!
GRAB

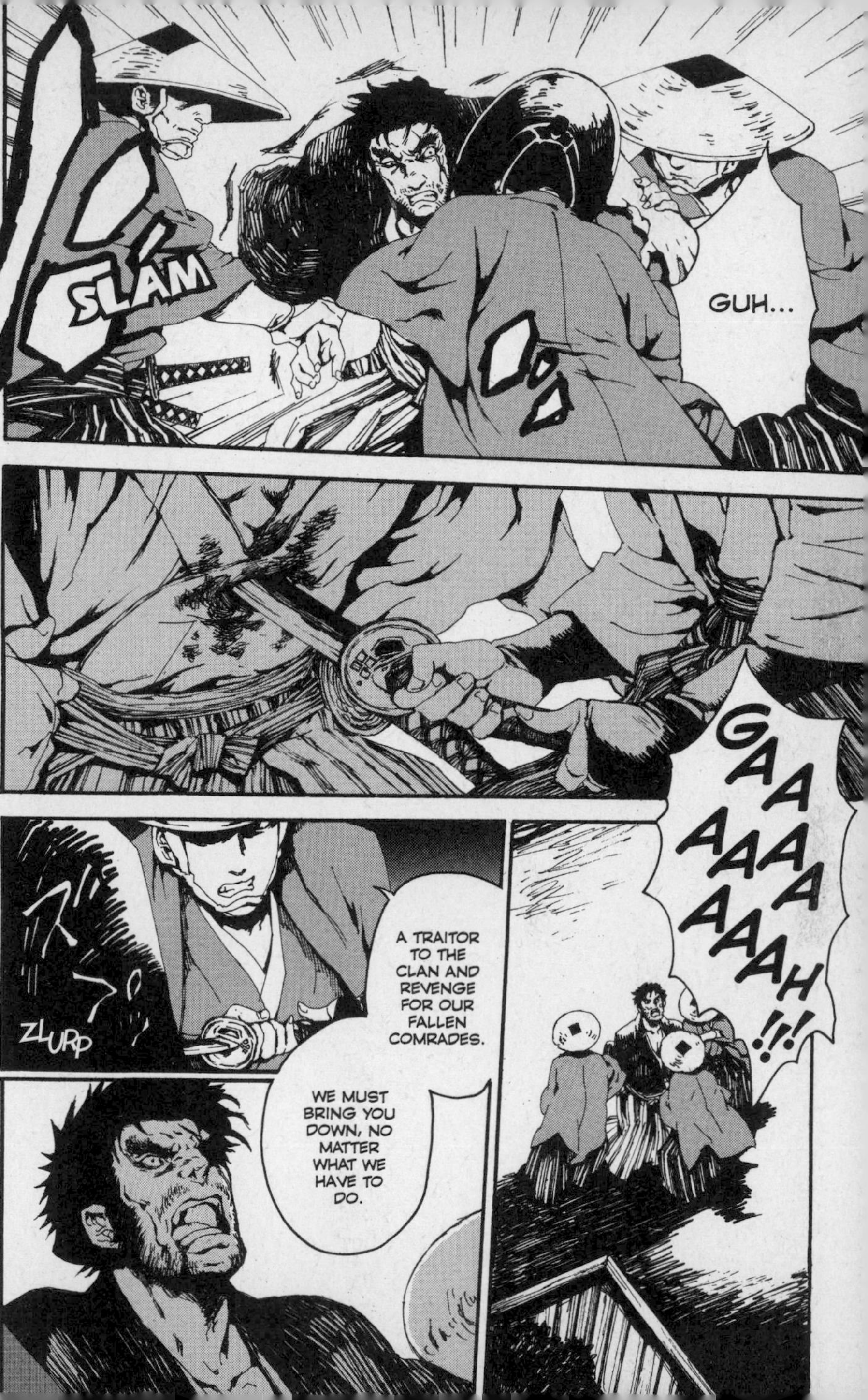
GUH...
SLAM
GAAAAAAAAAAH!!!
A TRAITOR TO THE CLAN AND REVENGE FOR OUR FALLEN COMRADES.
ZLURP
WE MUST BRING YOU DOWN, NO MATTER WHAT WE HAVE TO DO.

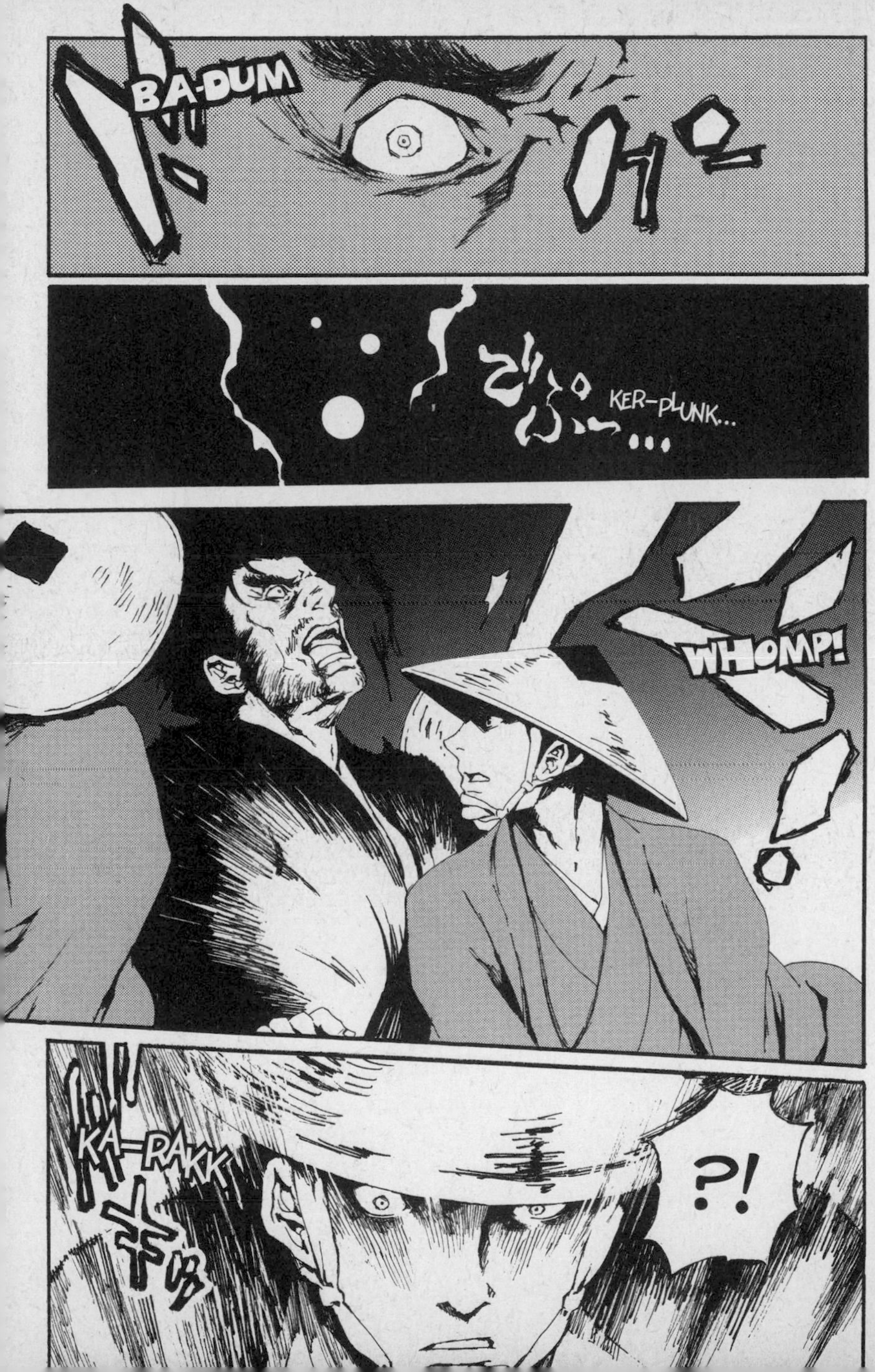
BA-DUM
KER-PLUNK...
WHOMP!
KA-RAKK
?!

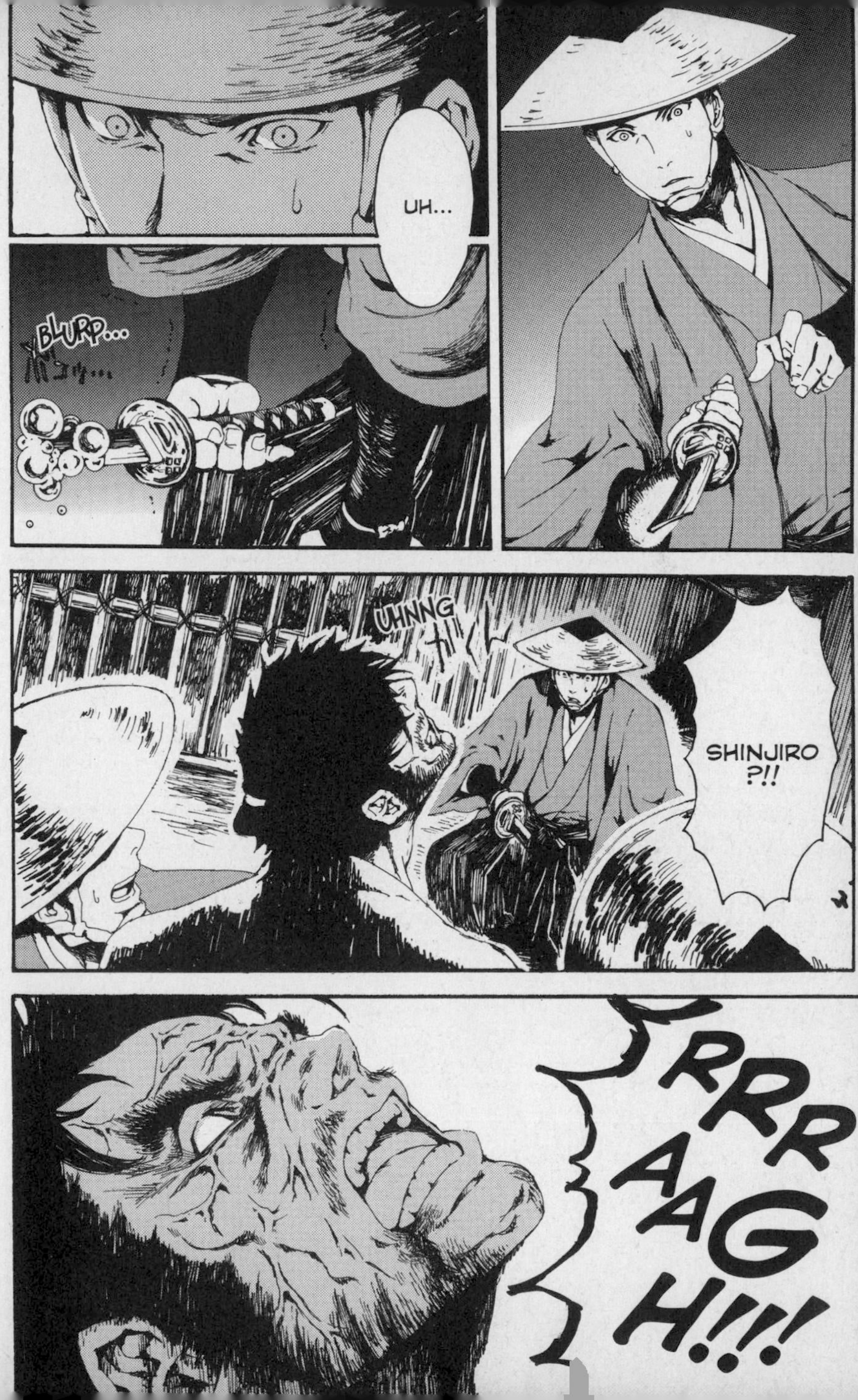
UH...
BLURP...
UHNNG
SHINJIRO ?!!
RRRAAGH!!!

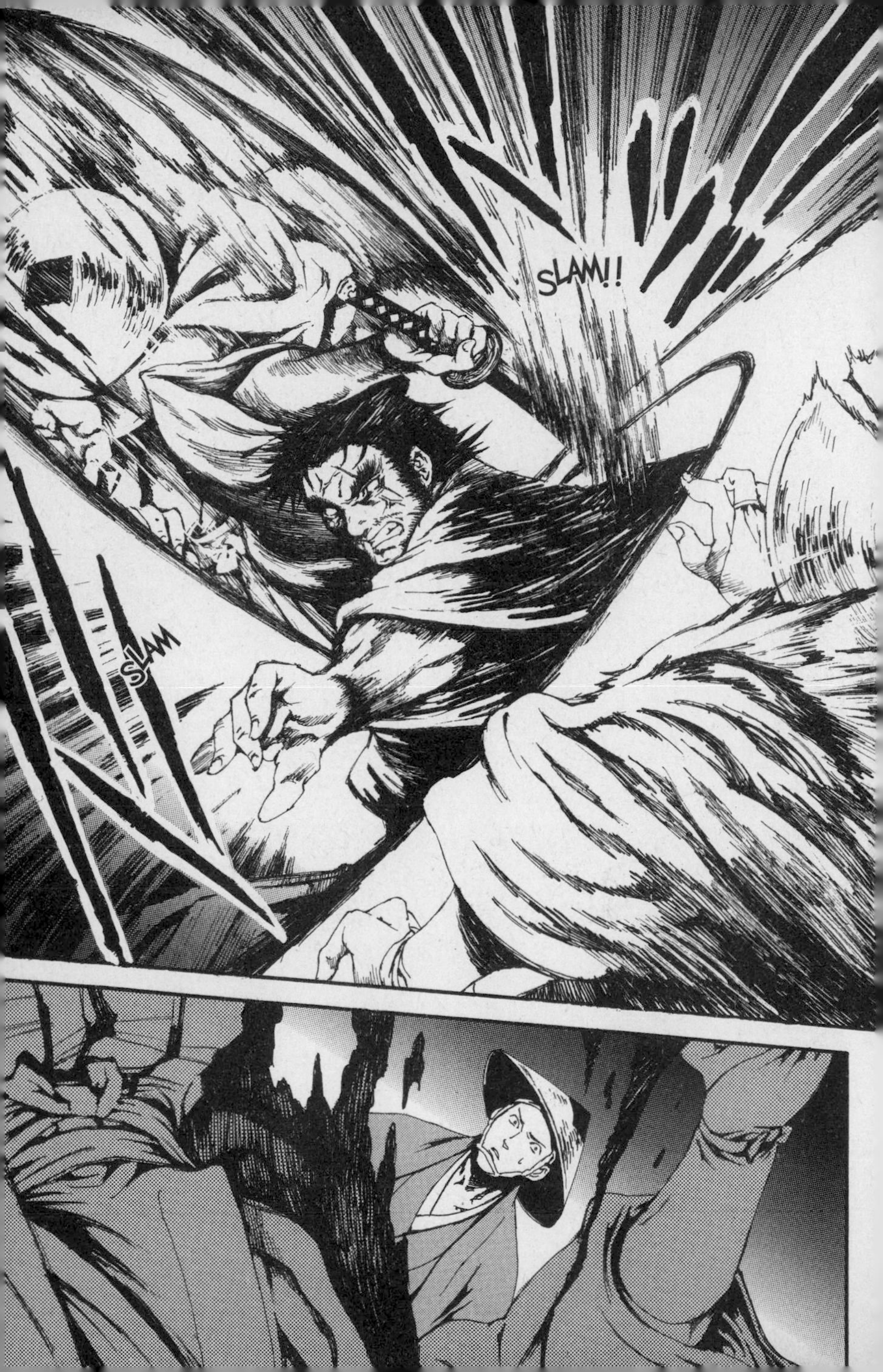
SLAM!!
SLAM

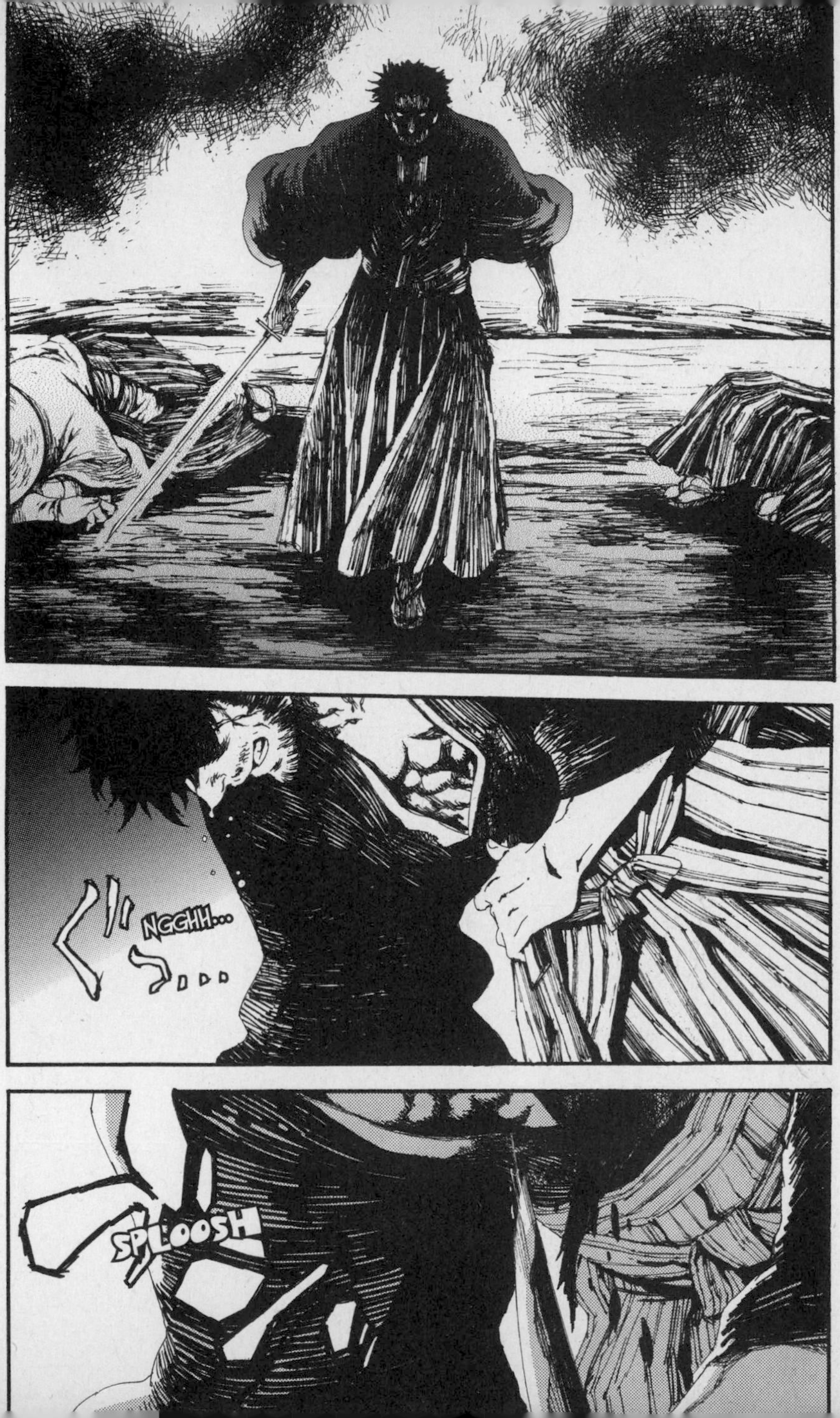
NGGHH...
SPLOOSH

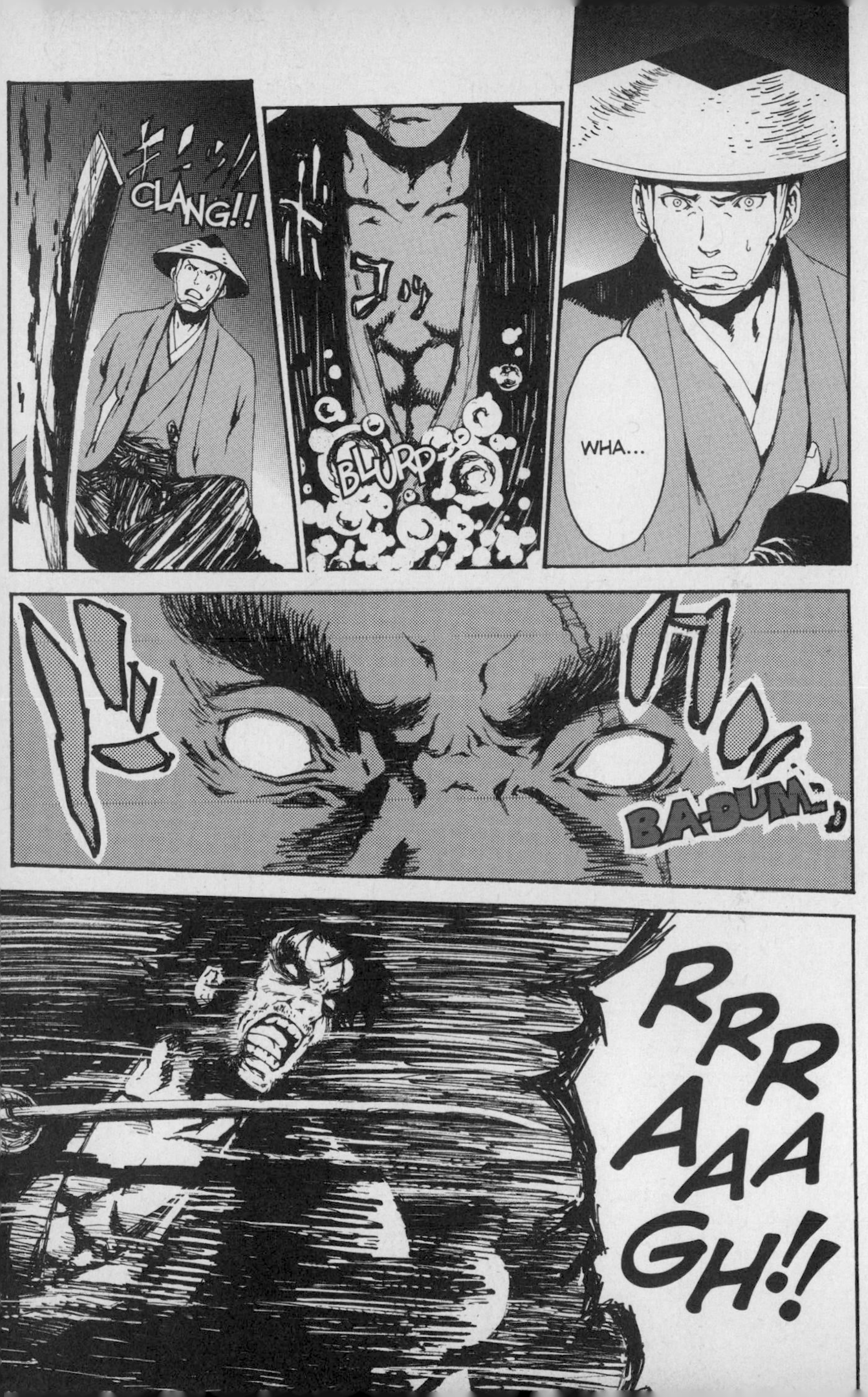
WHA...
BLURP
CLANG!!
BA-DUM
RRRAAAGH!!

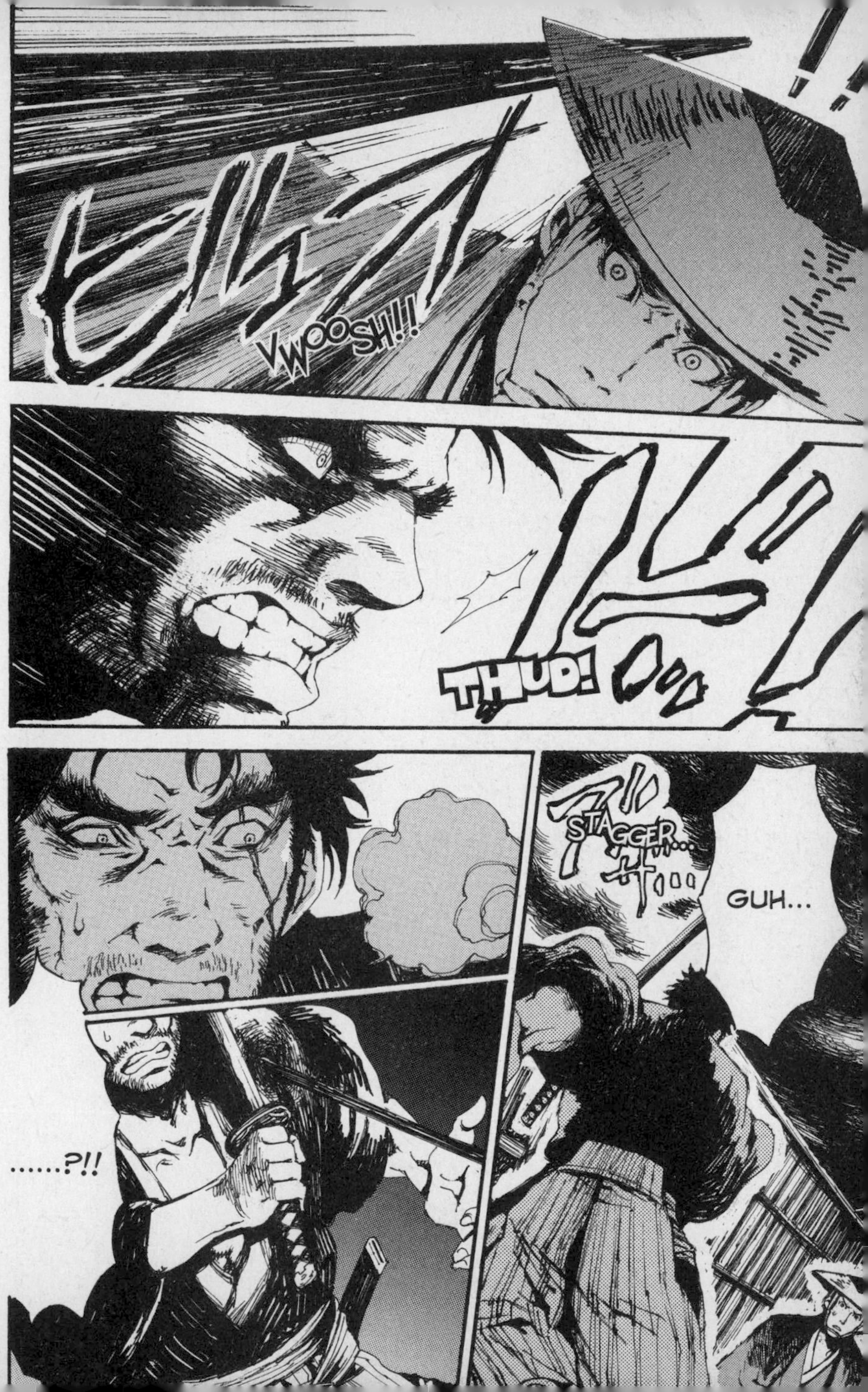

VWOOSH!!
THUD!
STAGGER...
GUH...
......?!!

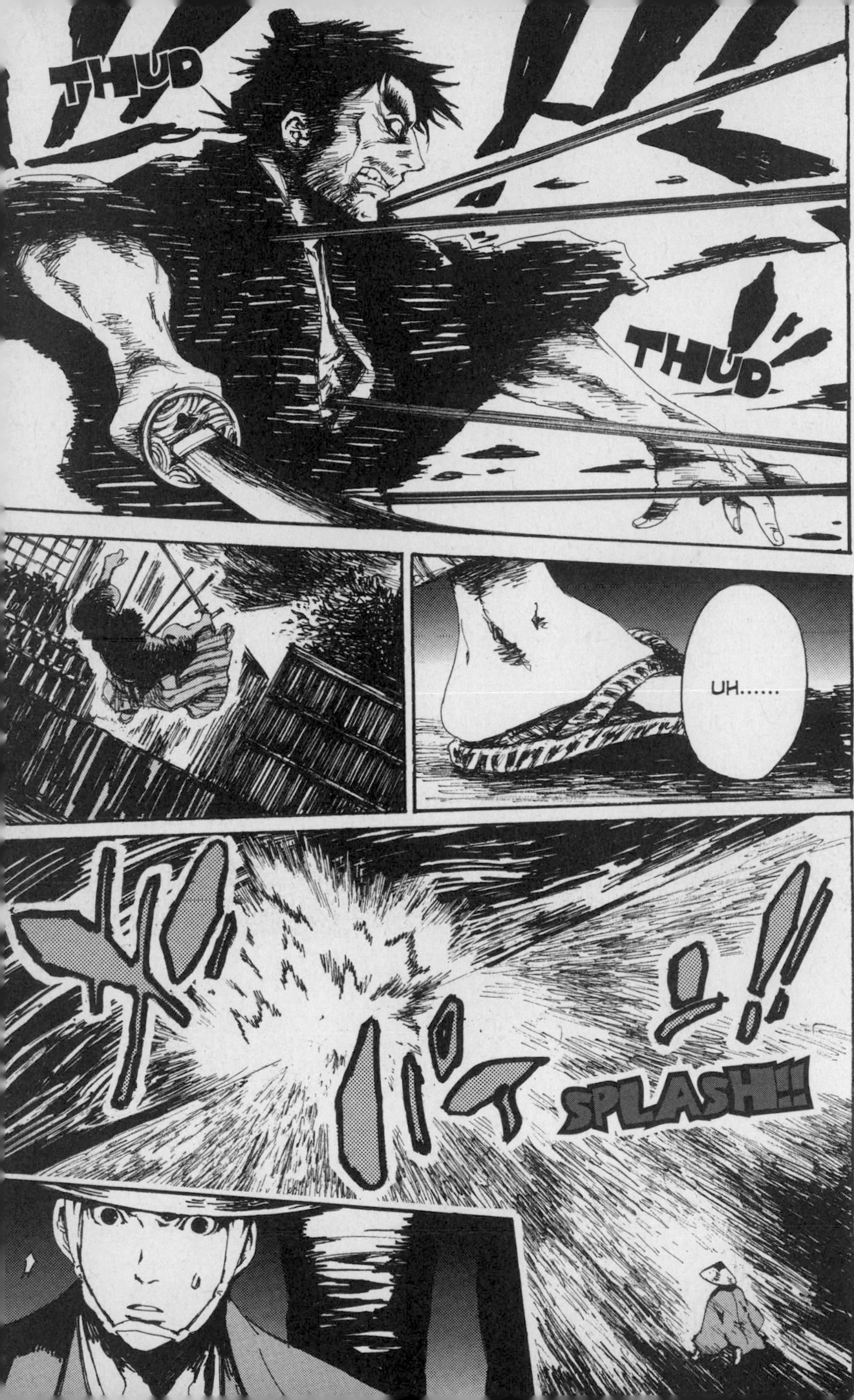
THUD
THUD
UH......
SPLASH!!

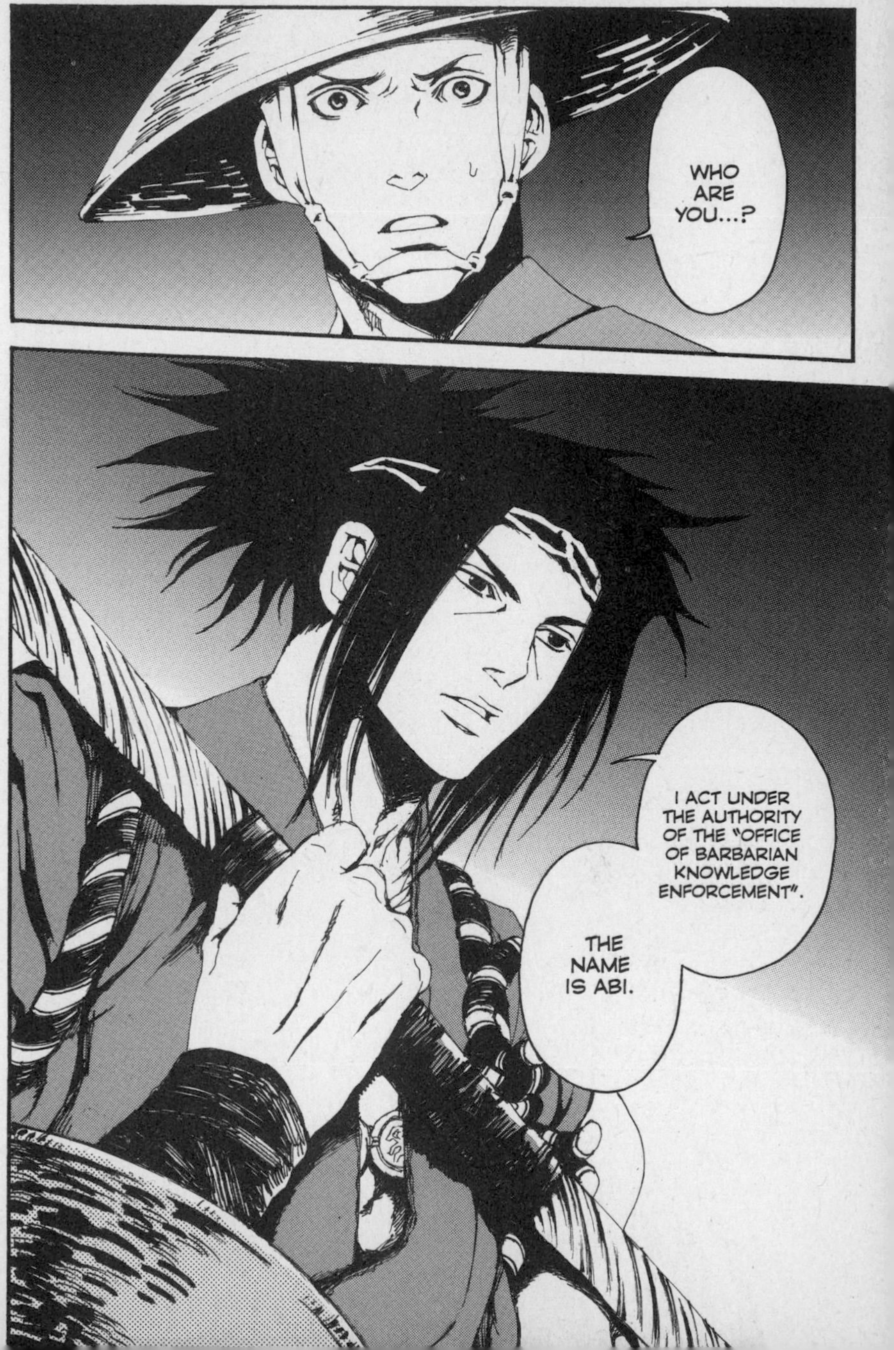
WHO ARE YOU...?
I ACT UNDER THE AUTHORITY OF THE "OFFICE OF BARBARIAN KNOWLEDGE ENFORCEMENT".
THE NAME IS ABI.

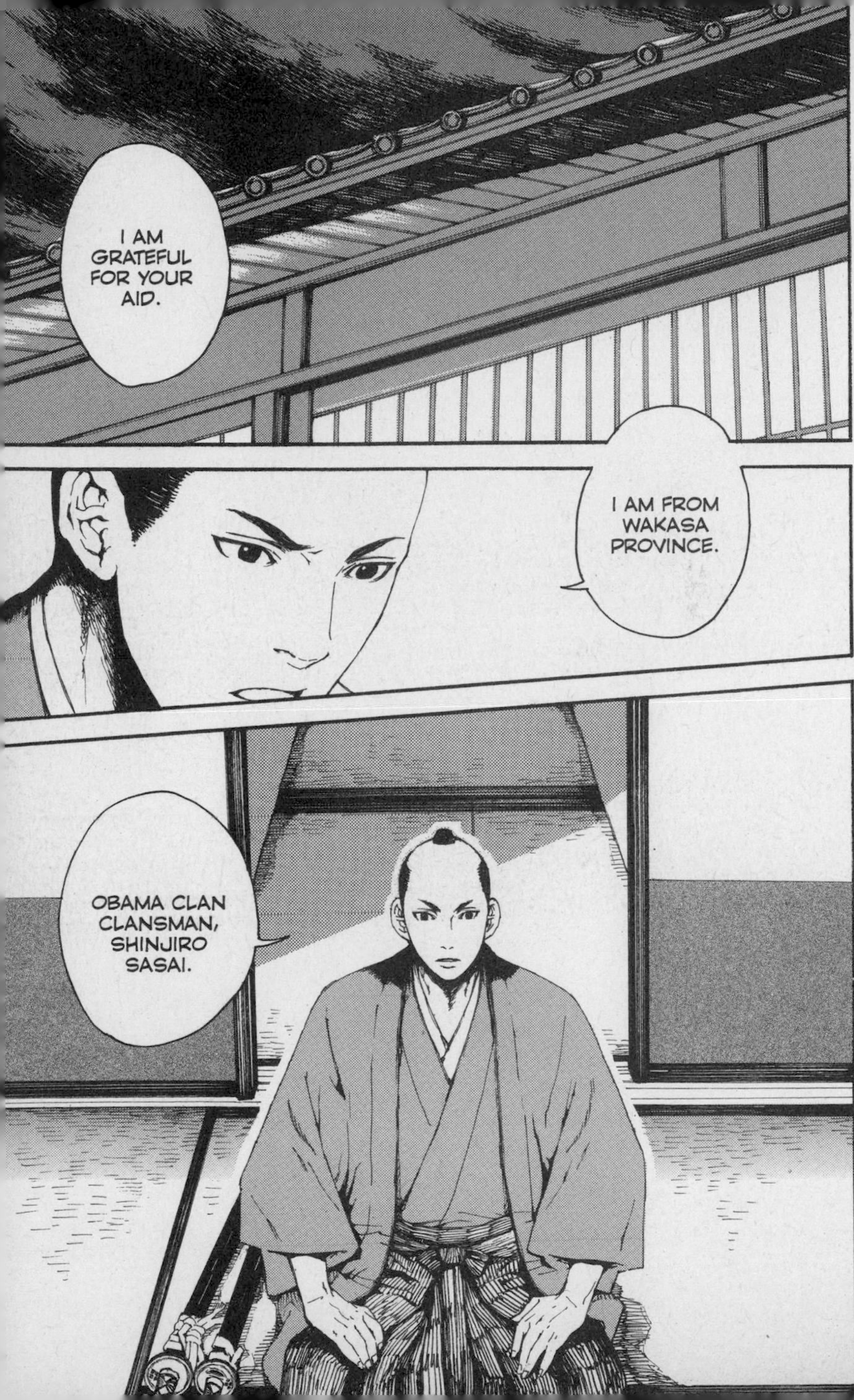
I AM GRATEFUL FOR YOUR AID.
I AM FROM WAKASA PROVINCE.
OBAMA CLAN CLANSMAN, SHINJIRO SASAI.

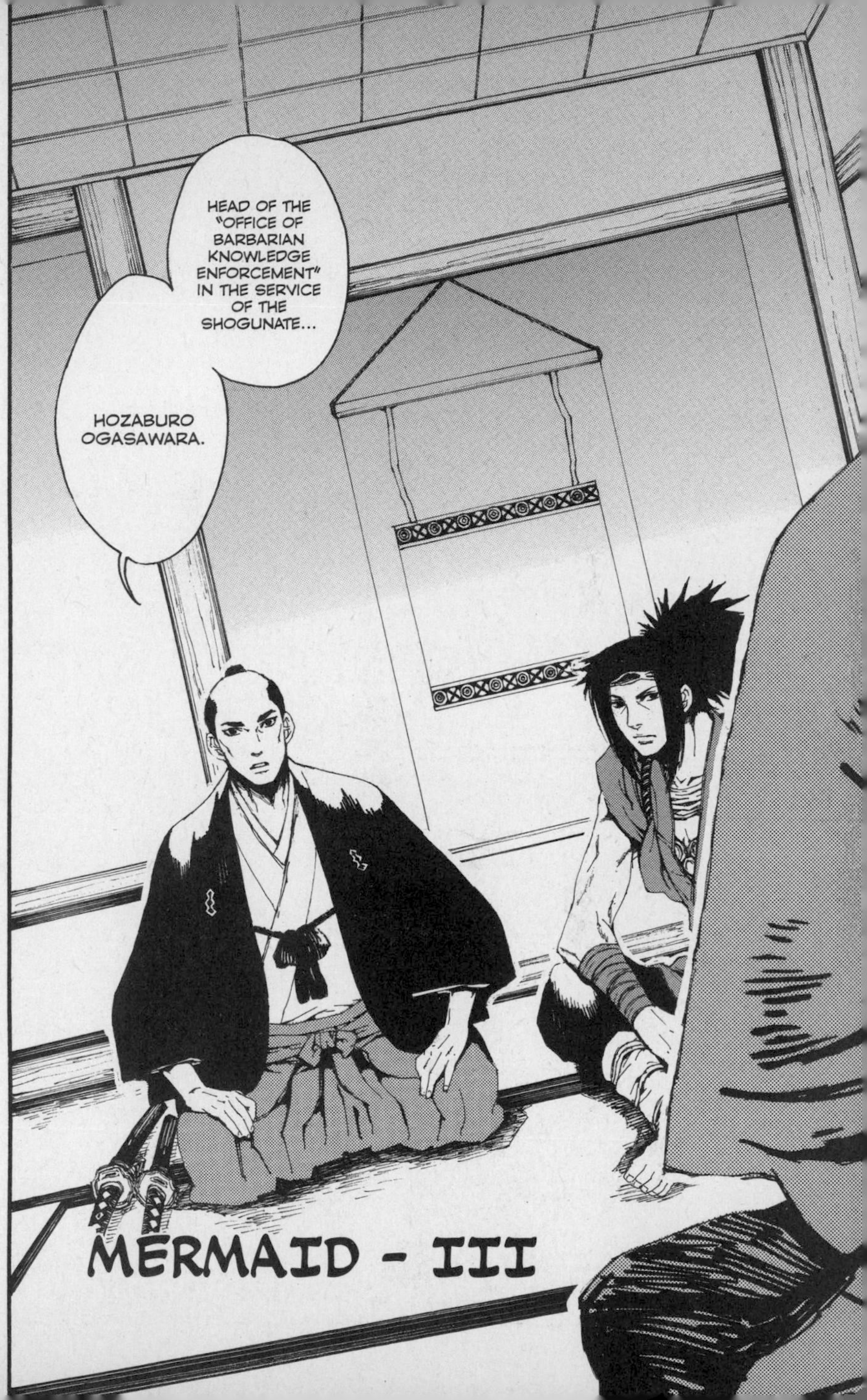
HEAD OF THE "OFFICE OF BARBARIAN KNOWLEDGE ENFORCEMENT" IN THE SERVICE OF THE SHOGUNATE...
HOZABURO OGASAWARA.
MERMAID - III

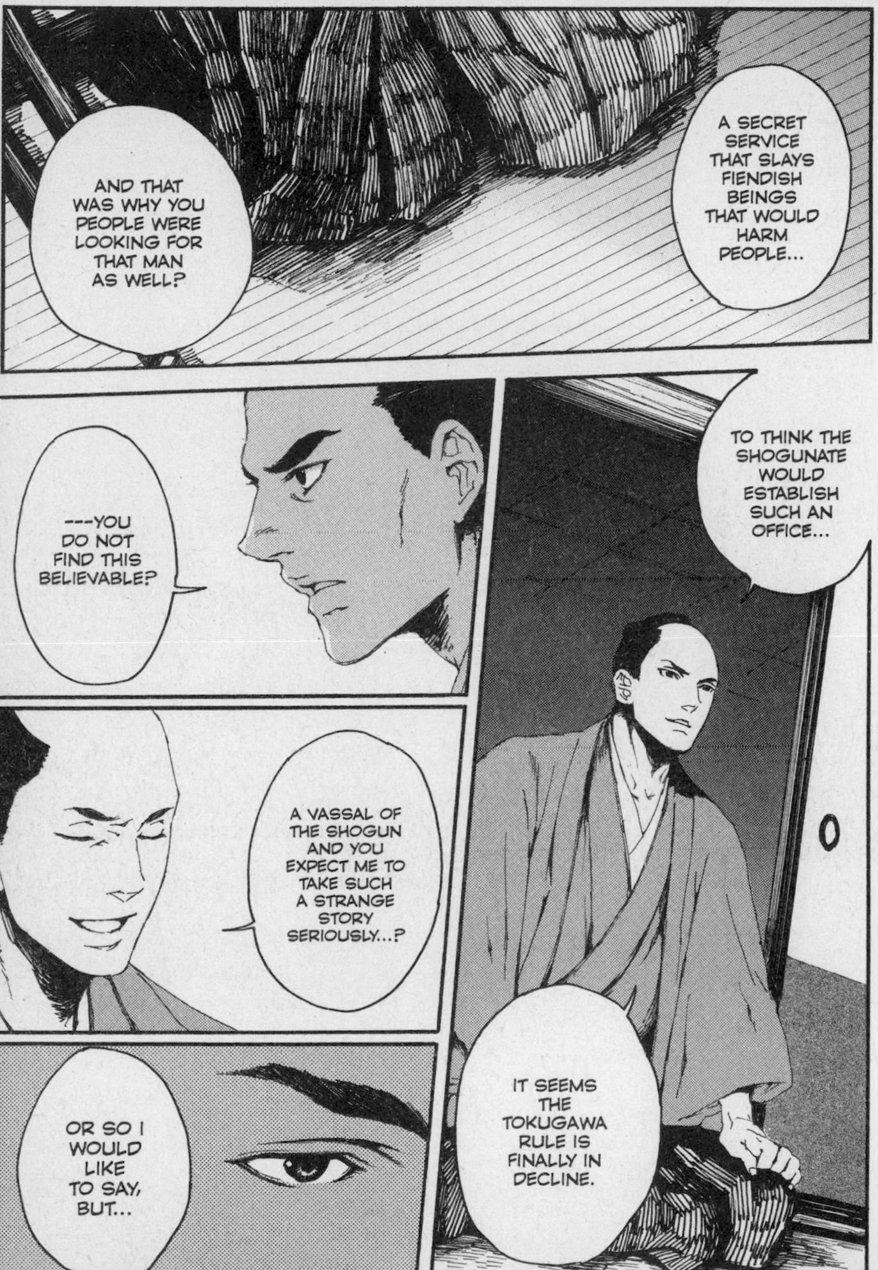
A SECRET SERVICE THAT SLAYS FIENDISH BEINGS THAT WOULD HARM PEOPLE...
AND THAT WAS WHY YOU PEOPLE WERE LOOKING FOR THAT MAN AS WELL?
TO THINK THE SHOGUNATE WOULD ESTABLISH SUCH AN OFFICE...
IT SEEMS THE TOKUGAWA RULE IS FINALLY IN DECLINE.
---YOU DO NOT FIND THIS BELIEVABLE?
A VASSAL OF THE SHOGUN AND YOU EXPECT ME TO TAKE SUCH A STRANGE STORY SERIOUSLY...?
OR SO I WOULD LIKE TO SAY, BUT...

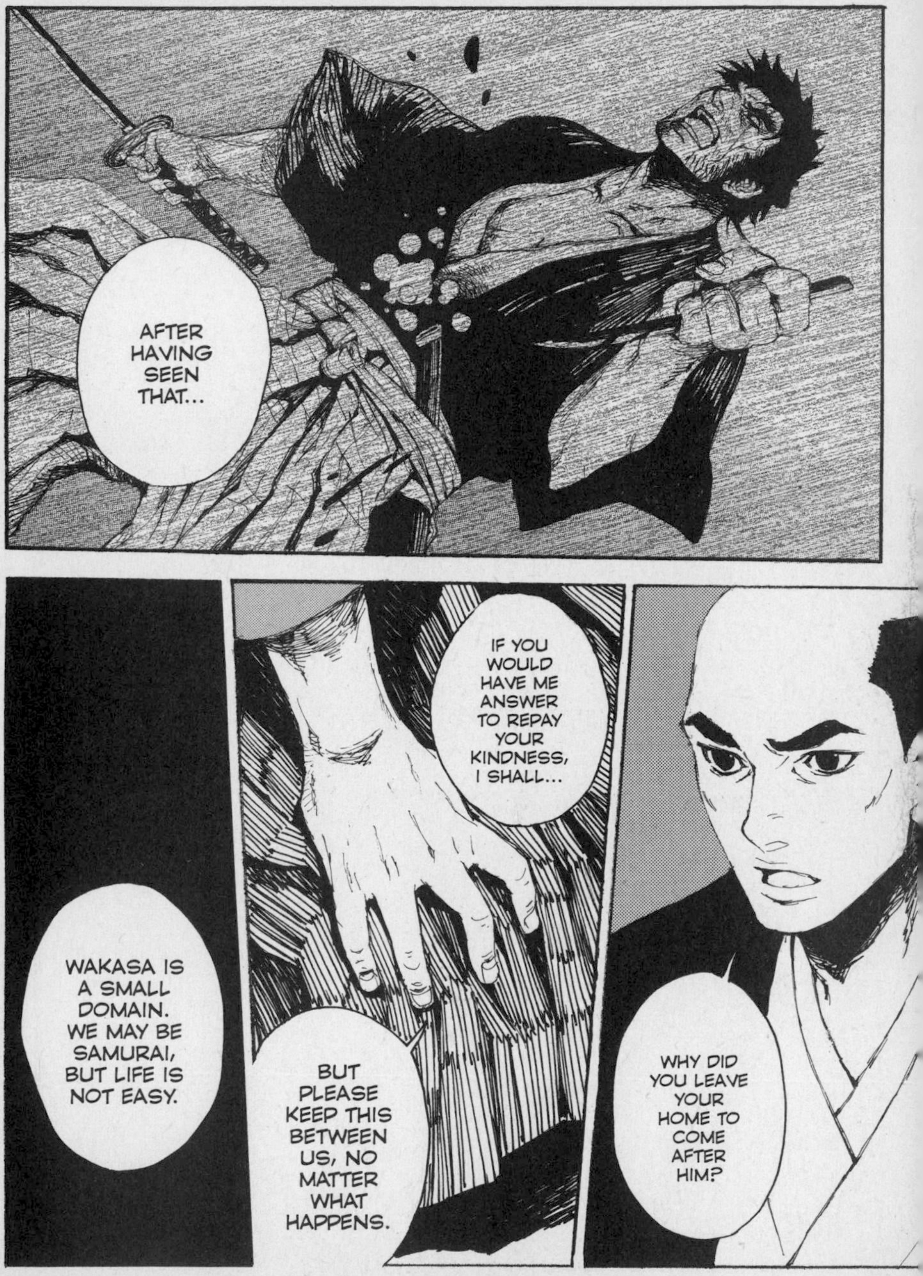
AFTER HAVING SEEN THAT...
WHY DID YOU LEAVE YOUR HOME TO COME AFTER HIM?
IF YOU WOULD HAVE ME ANSWER TO REPAY YOUR KINDNESS, I SHALL...
BUT PLEASE KEEP THIS BETWEEN US, NO MATTER WHAT HAPPENS.
WAKASA IS A SMALL DOMAIN. WE MAY BE SAMURAI, BUT LIFE IS NOT EASY.

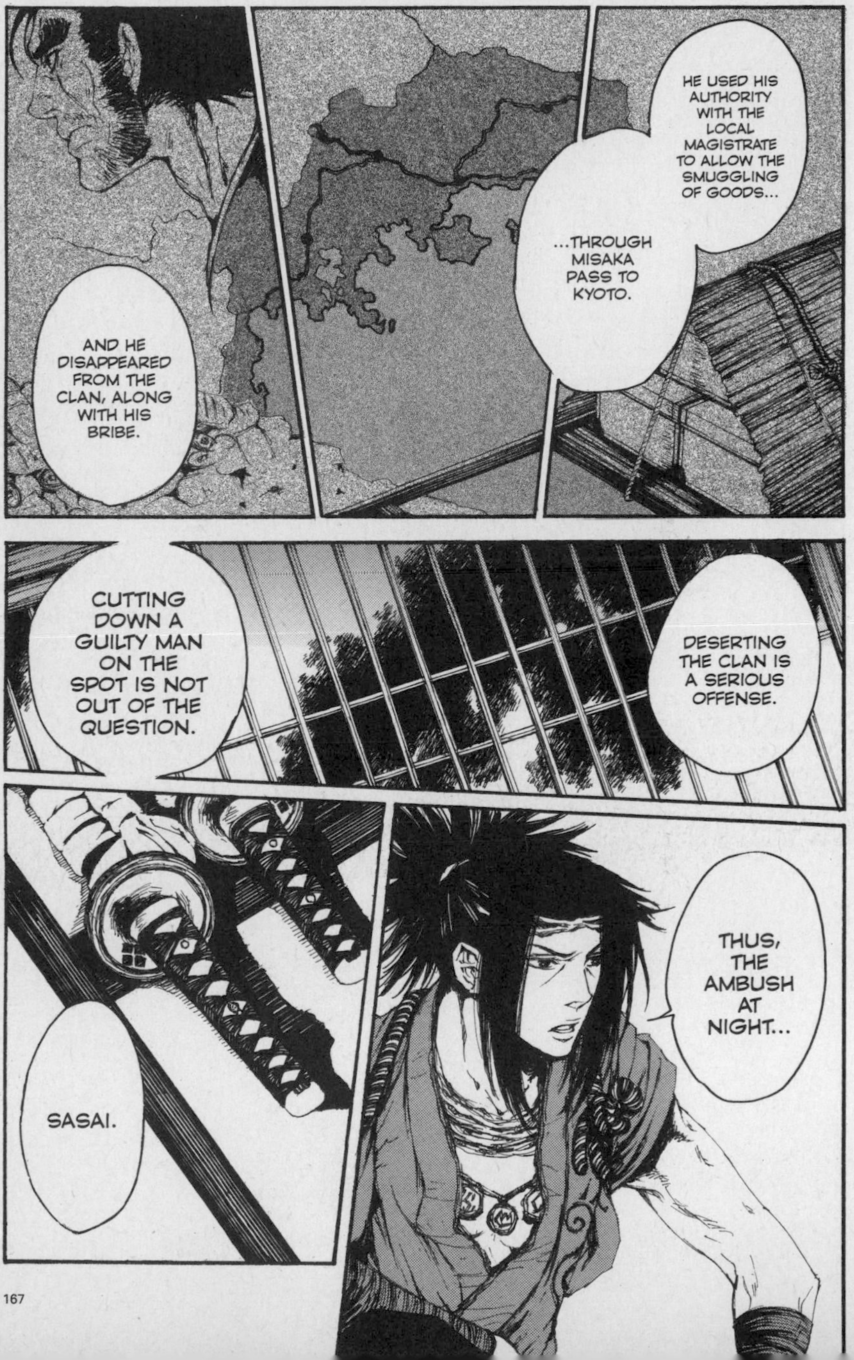
HE USED HIS AUTHORITY WITH THE LOCAL MAGISTRATE TO ALLOW THE SMUGGLING OF GOODS...
...THROUGH MISAKA PASS TO KYOTO.
AND HE DISAPPEARED FROM THE CLAN, ALONG WITH HIS BRIBE.
DESERTING THE CLAN IS A SERIOUS OFFENSE.
CUTTING DOWN A GUILTY MAN ON THE SPOT IS NOT OUT OF THE QUESTION.
THUS, THE AMBUSH AT NIGHT...
SASAI.

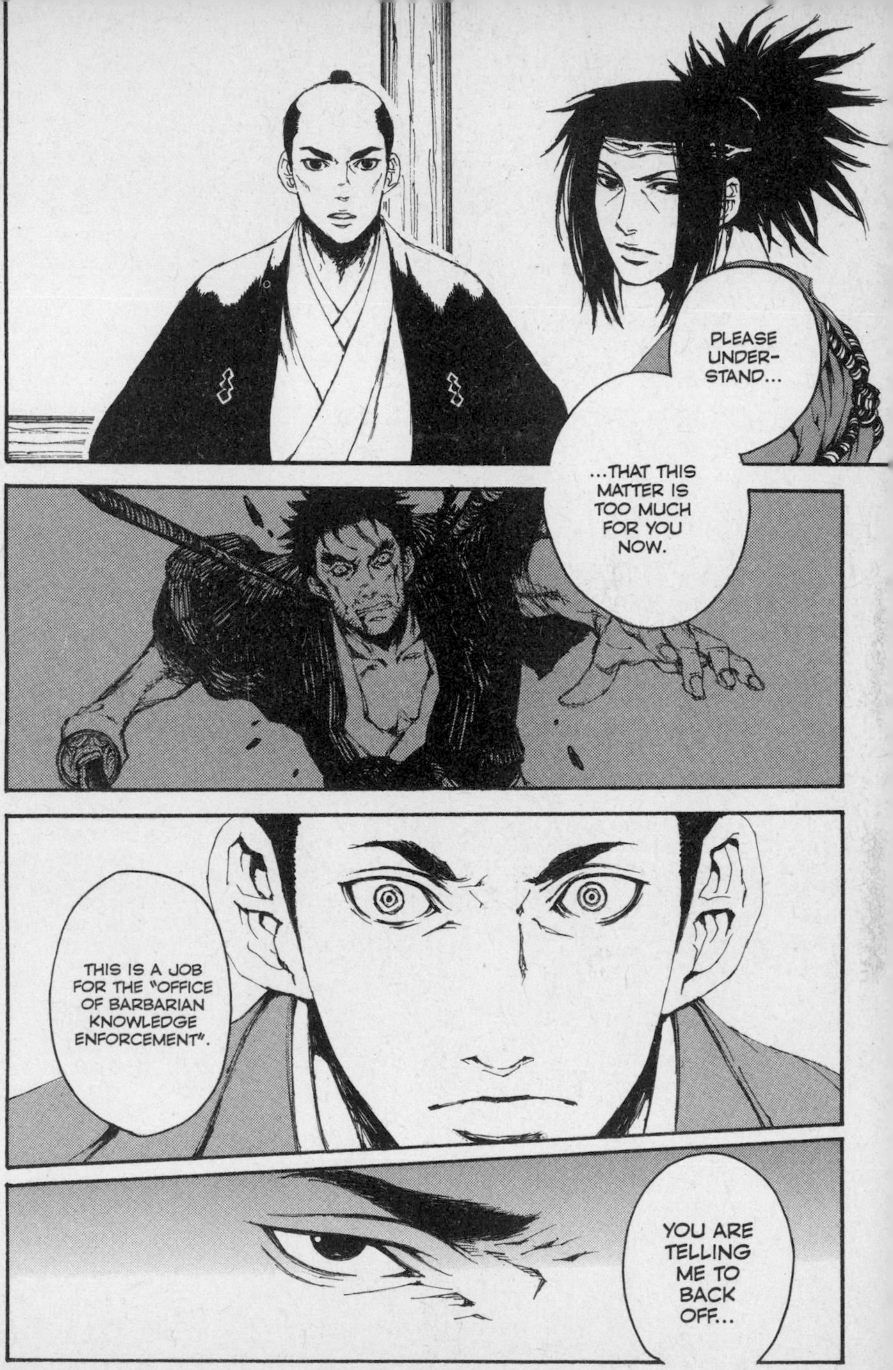
PLEASE UNDER-STAND...
...THAT THIS MATTER IS TOO MUCH FOR YOU NOW.
THIS IS A JOB FOR THE "OFFICE OF BARBARIAN KNOWLEDGE ENFORCEMENT".
YOU ARE TELLING ME TO BACK OFF...

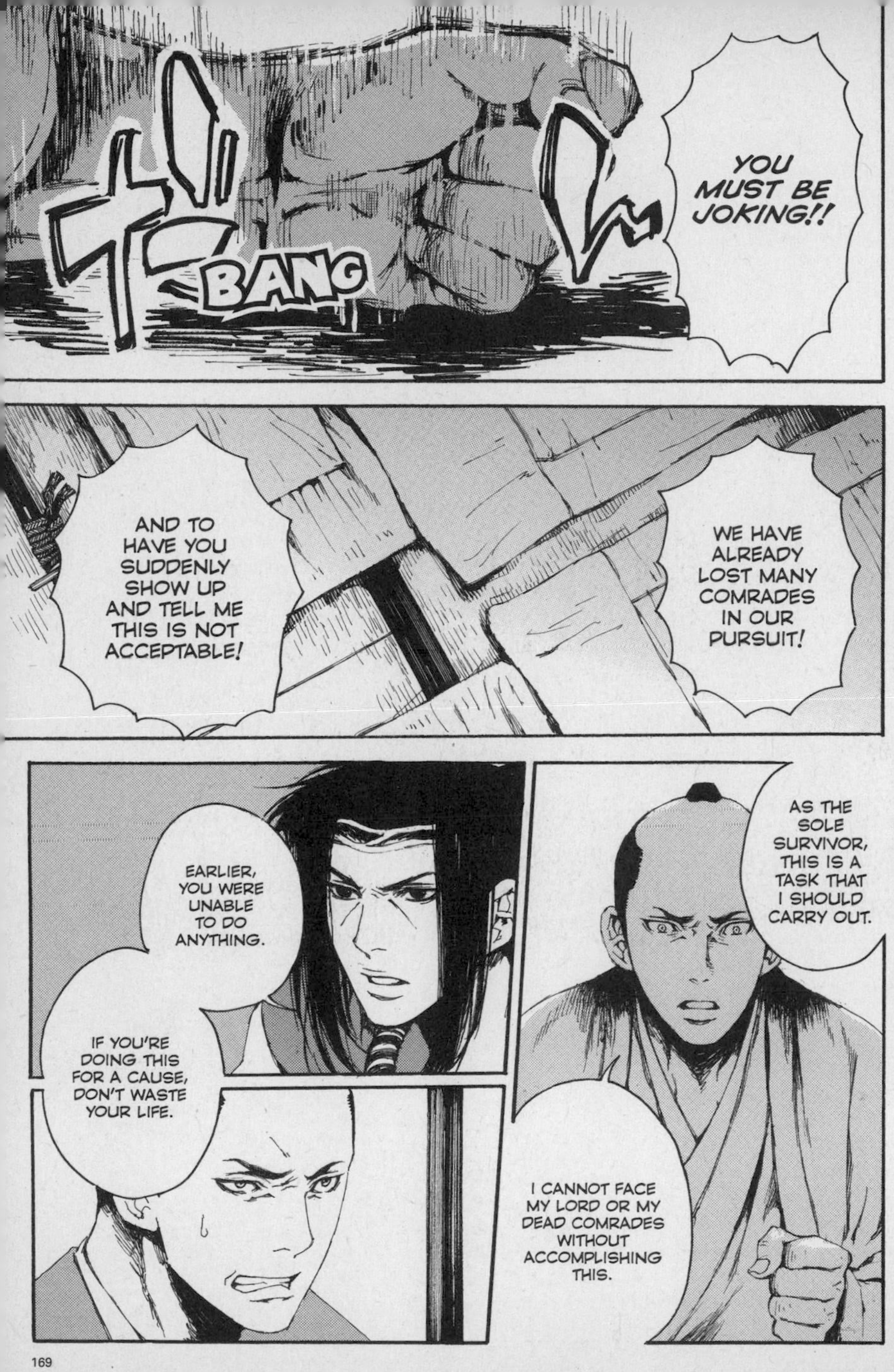
YOU MUST BE JOKING!!
BANG
WE HAVE ALREADY LOST MANY COMRADES IN OUR PURSUIT!
AND TO HAVE YOU SUDDENLY SHOW UP AND TELL ME THIS IS NOT ACCEPTABLE!
AS THE SOLE SURVIVOR, THIS IS A TASK THAT I SHOULD CARRY OUT.
I CANNOT FACE MY LORD OR MY DEAD COMRADES WITHOUT ACCOMPLISHING THIS.
EARLIER, YOU WERE UNABLE TO DO ANYTHING.
IF YOU'RE DOING THIS FOR A CAUSE, DON'T WASTE YOUR LIFE.

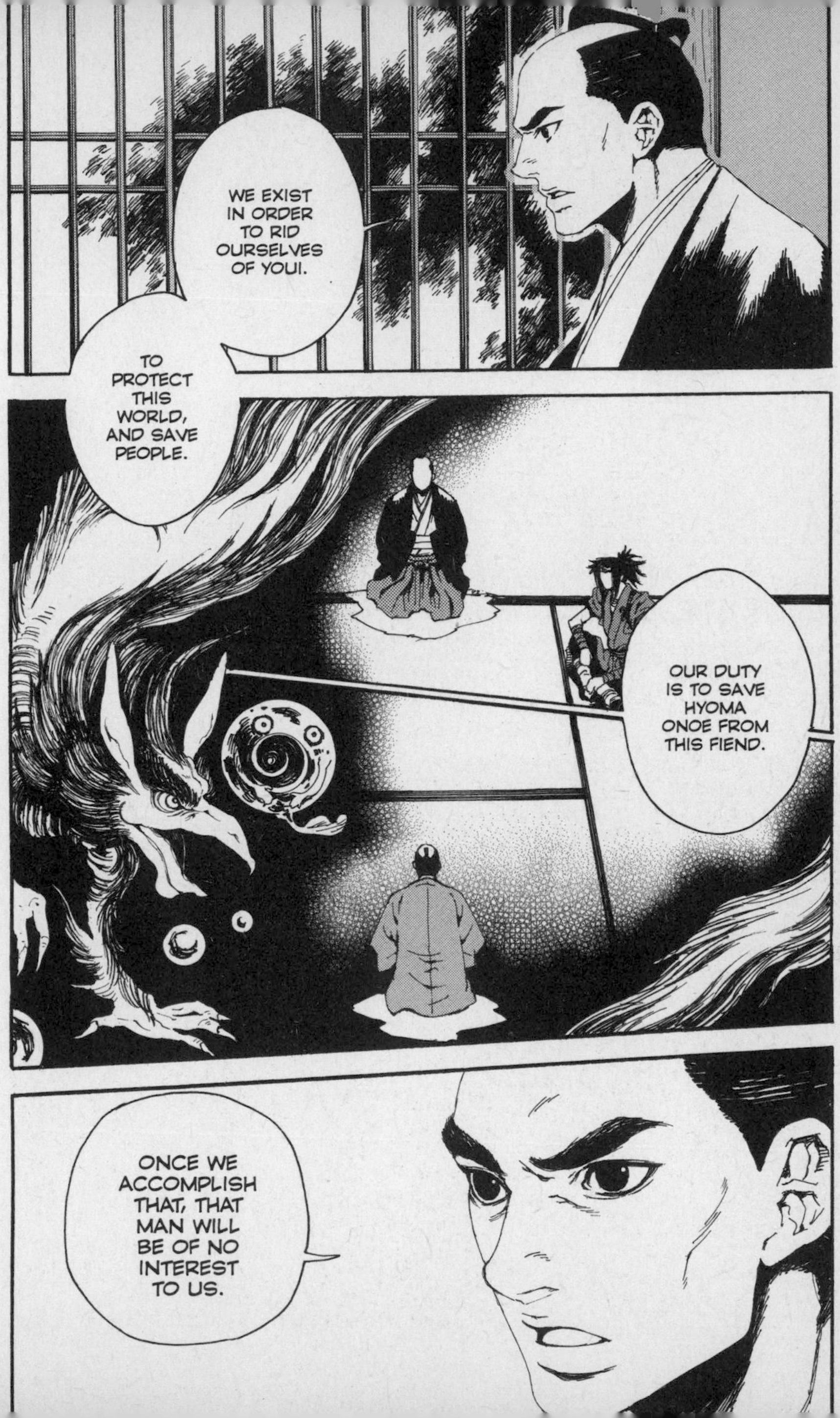
WE EXIST IN ORDER TO RID OURSELVES OF YOUI.
TO PROTECT THIS WORLD, AND SAVE PEOPLE.
OUR DUTY IS TO SAVE HYOMA ONOE FROM THIS FIEND.
ONCE WE ACCOMPLISH THAT, THAT MAN WILL BE OF NO INTEREST TO US.

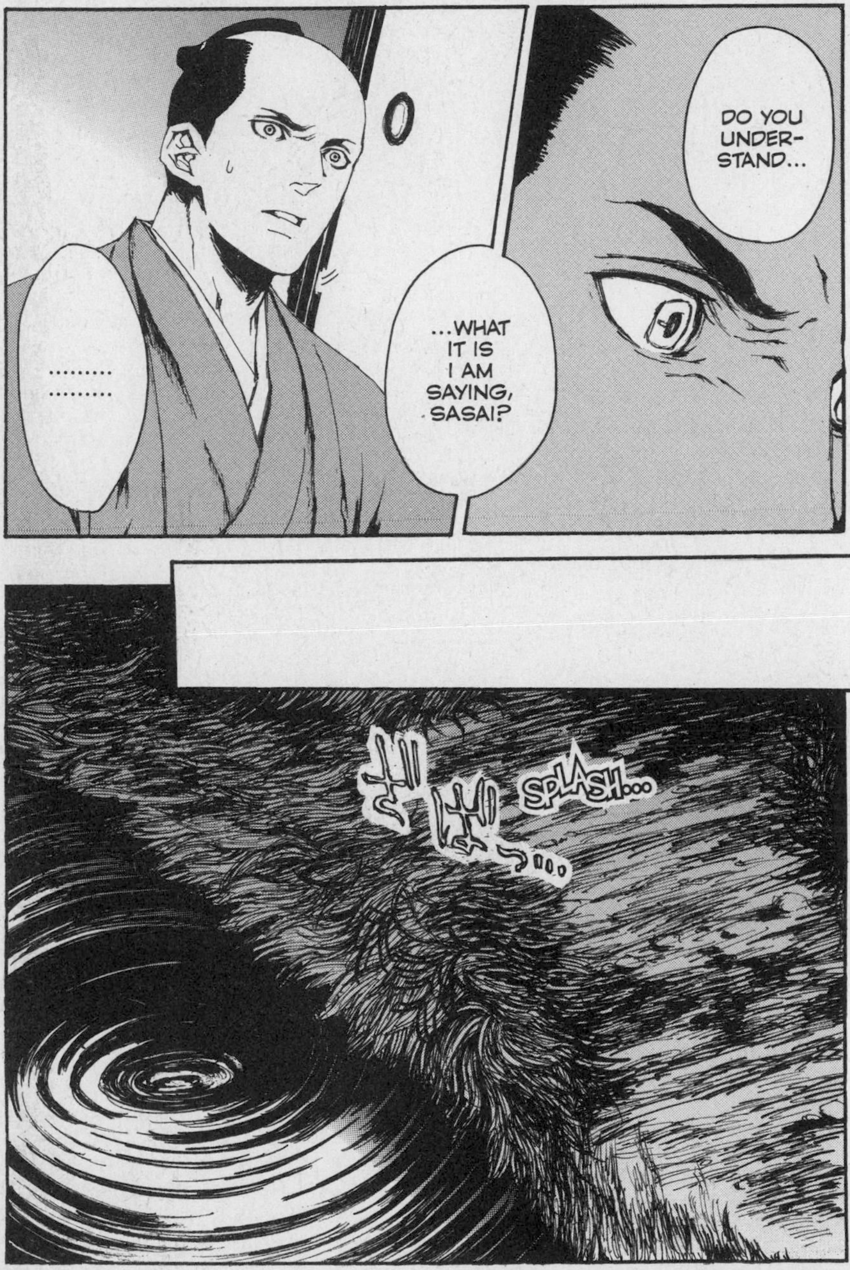
DO YOU UNDERSTAND...
...WHAT IT IS I AM SAYING, SASAI?
....
....
SPLASH...

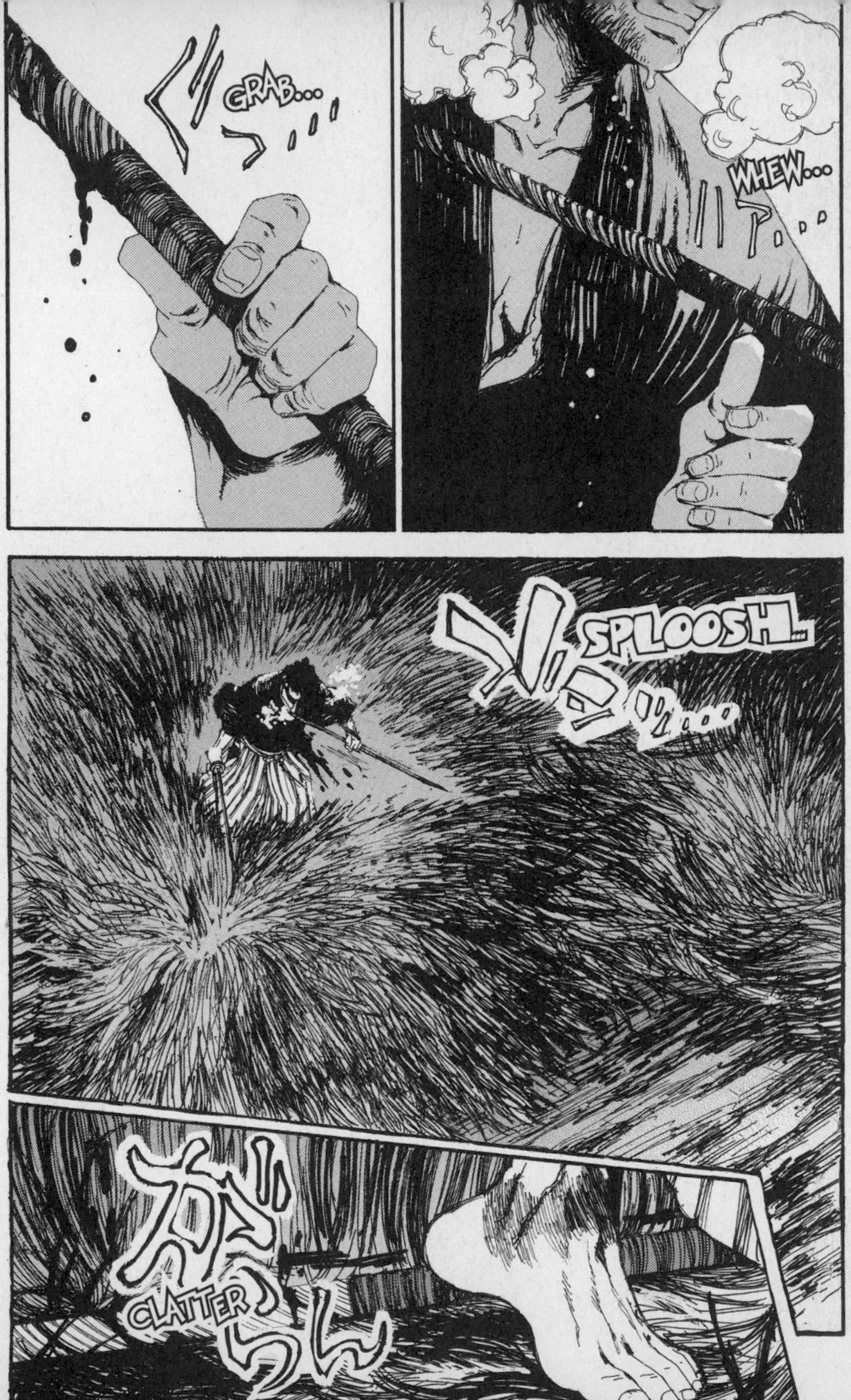
WHEW...
GRAB...
SPLOOSH
CLATTER

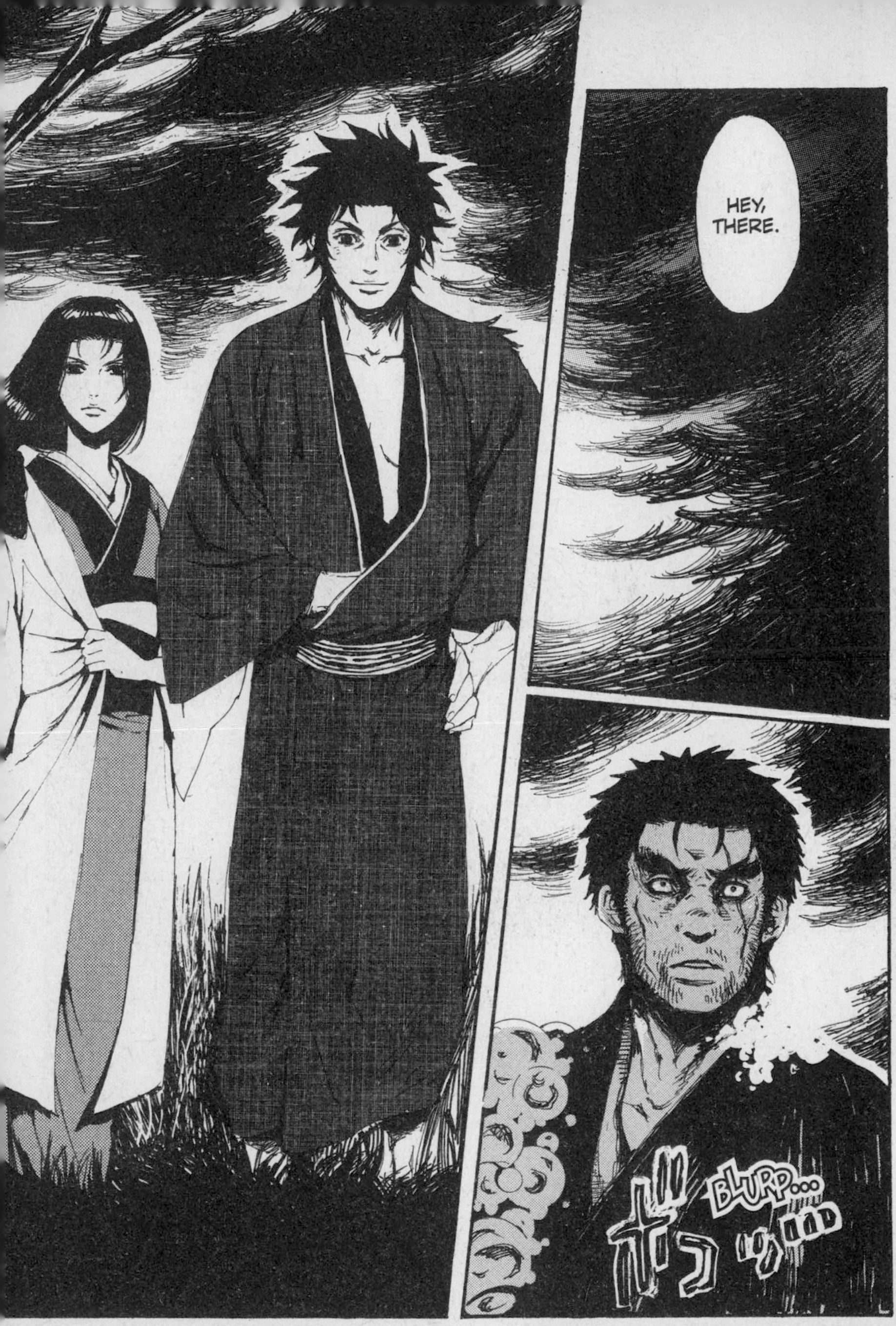
HEY, THERE.
BLURP...

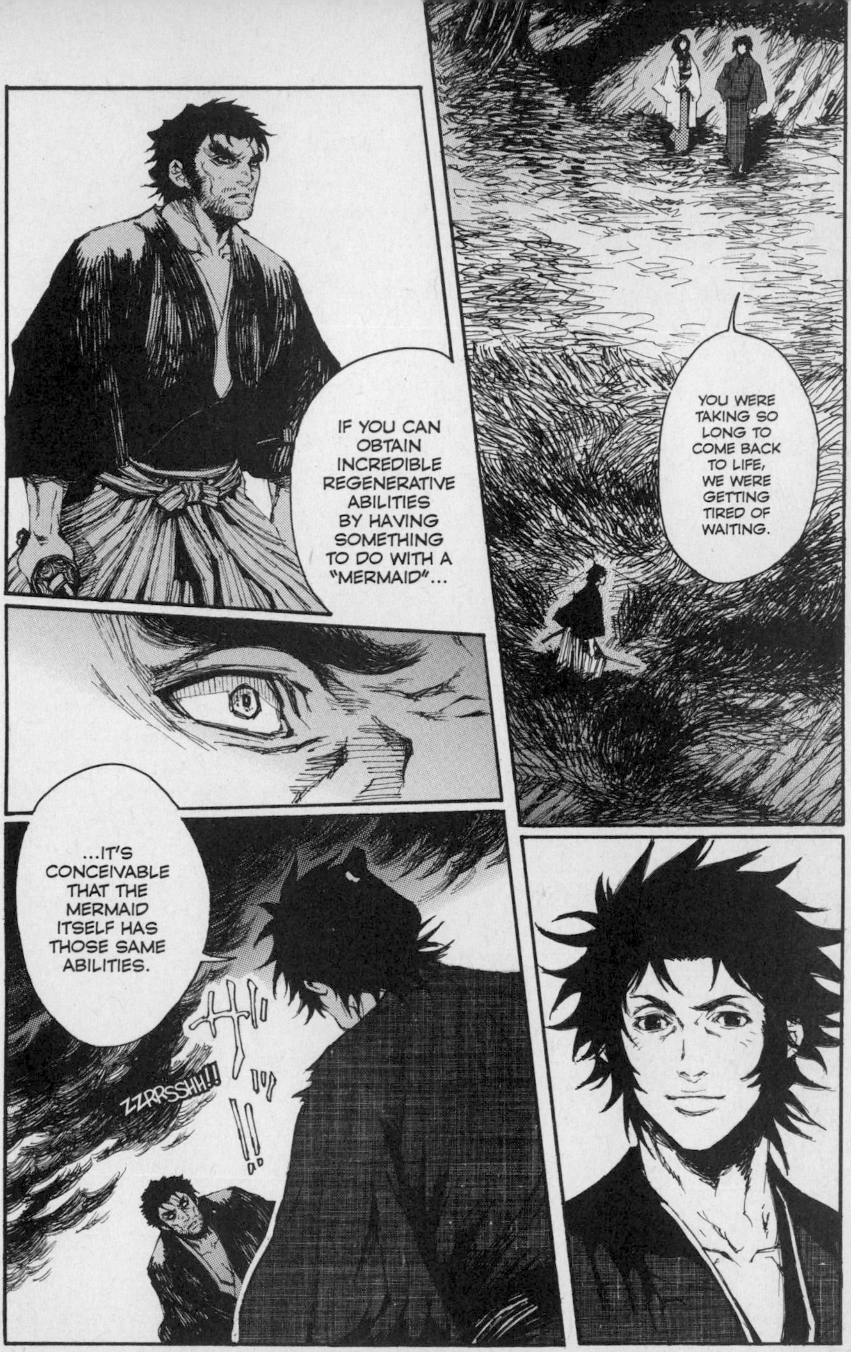
YOU WERE TAKING SO LONG TO COME BACK TO LIFE, WE WERE GETTING TIRED OF WAITING.
IF YOU CAN OBTAIN INCREDIBLE REGENERATIVE ABILITIES BY HAVING SOMETHING TO DO WITH A "MERMAID"...
...IT'S CONCEIVABLE THAT THE MERMAID ITSELF HAS THOSE SAME ABILITIES.
ZZRRSSHH!!

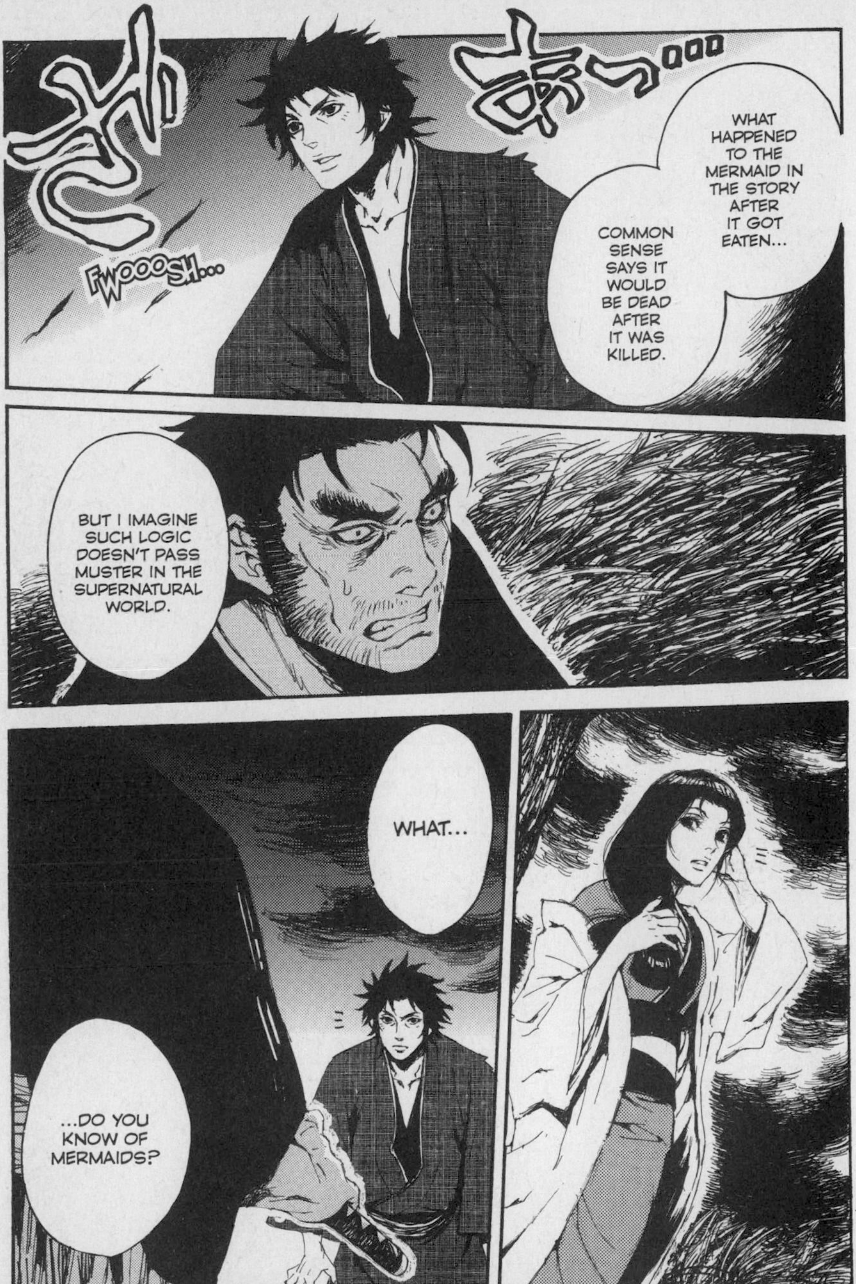
WHAT HAPPENED TO THE MERMAID IN THE STORY AFTER IT GOT EATEN...
COMMON SENSE SAYS IT WOULD BE DEAD AFTER IT WAS KILLED.
FWOOOSH...
BUT I IMAGINE SUCH LOGIC DOESN'T PASS MUSTER IN THE SUPERNATURAL WORLD.
WHAT...
...DO YOU KNOW OF MERMAIDS?

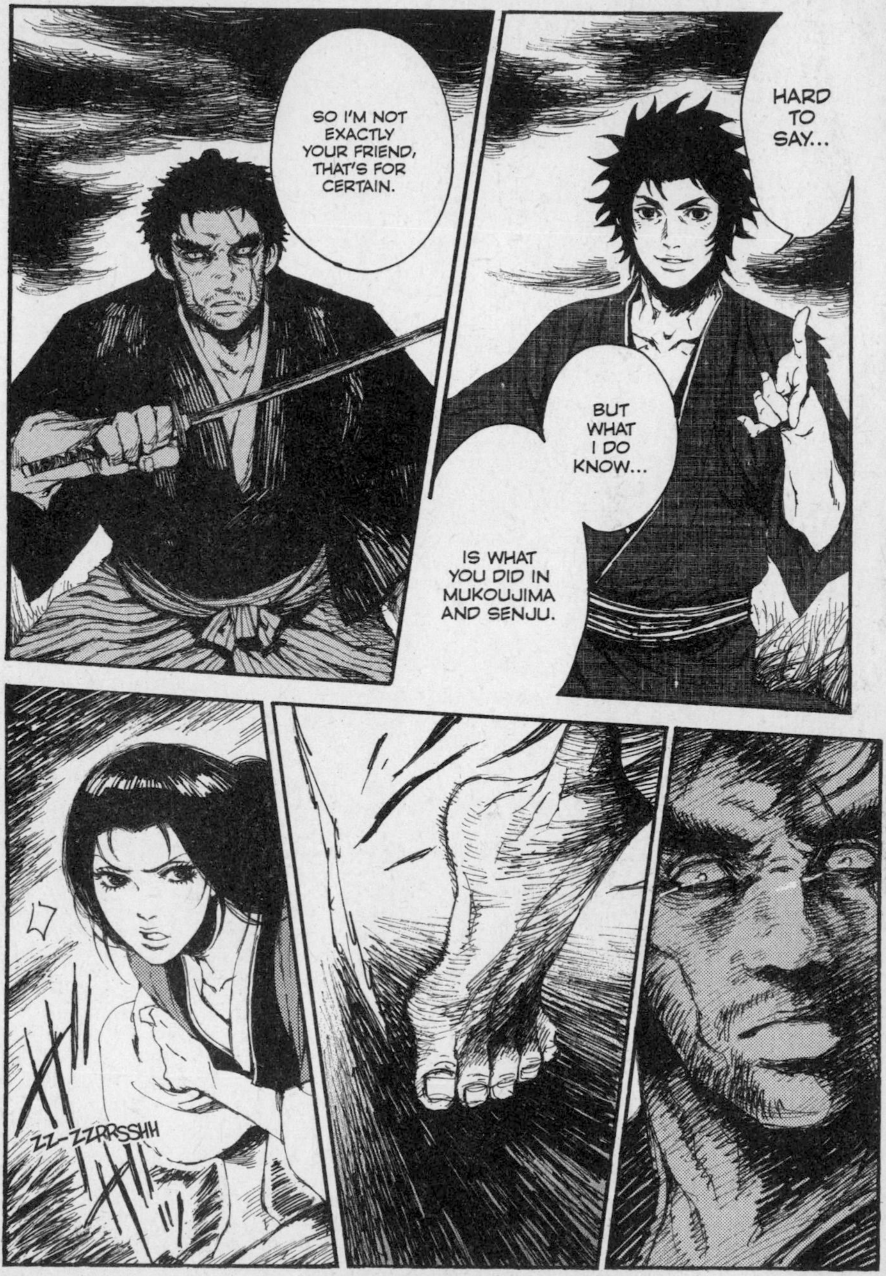
HARD TO SAY...
BUT WHAT I DO KNOW...
IS WHAT YOU DID IN MUKOUJIMA AND SENJU.
SO I'M NOT EXACTLY YOUR FRIEND, THAT'S FOR CERTAIN.
ZZ-ZZRRSSHH

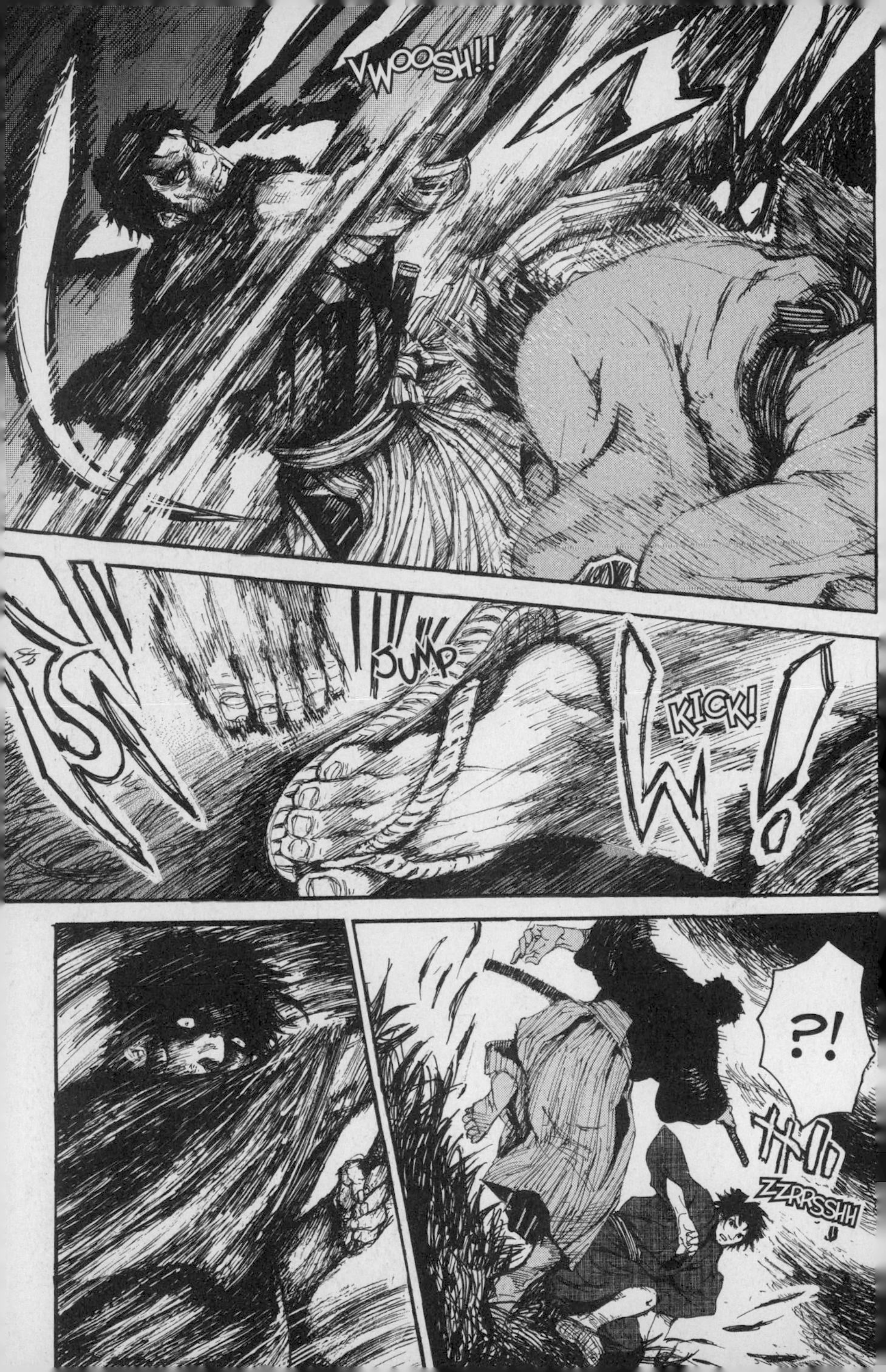
VWOOSH!!
KICK!
JUMP
?!
ZZRRSSHH

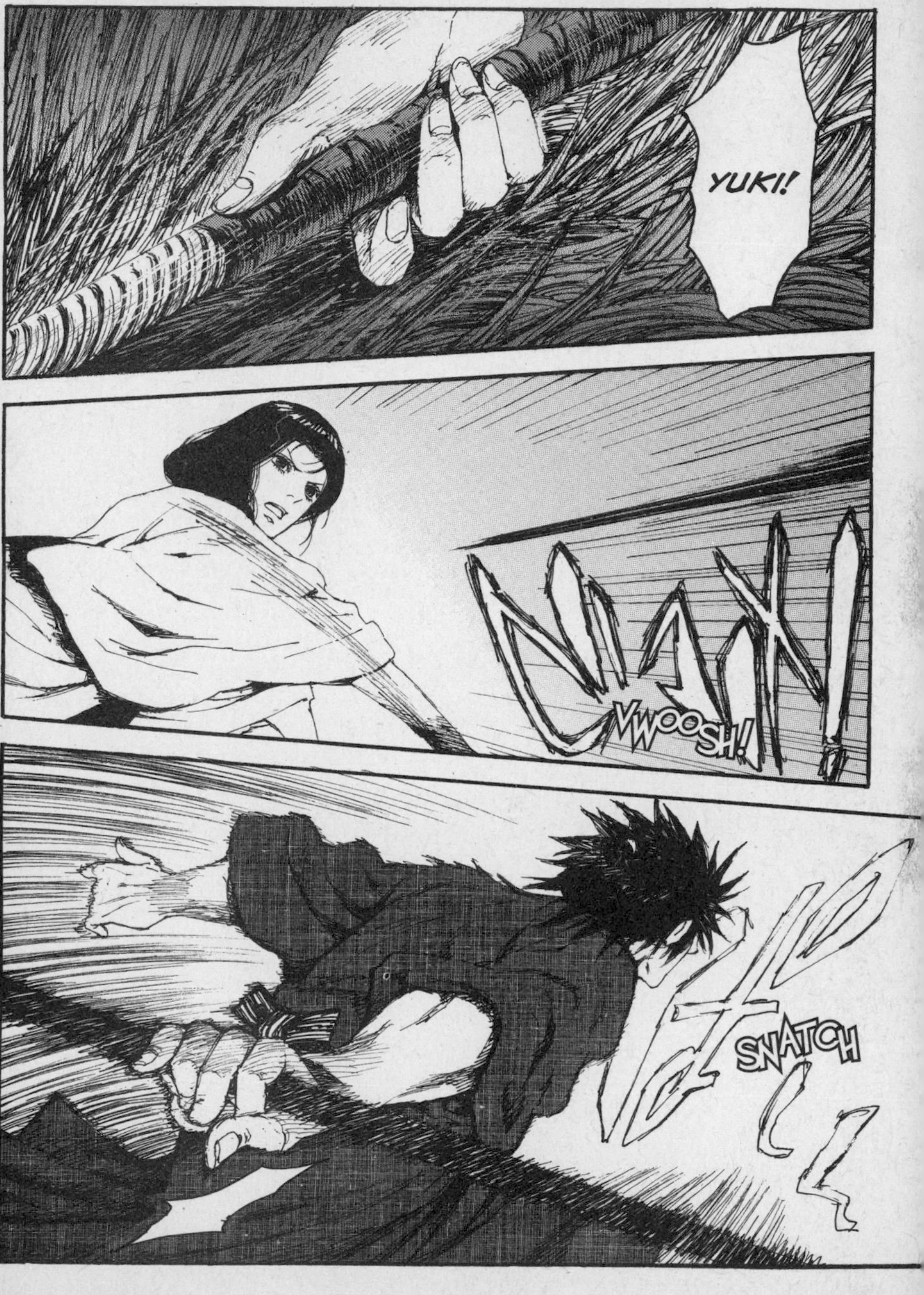
YUKI!
VWOOSH!
SNATCH

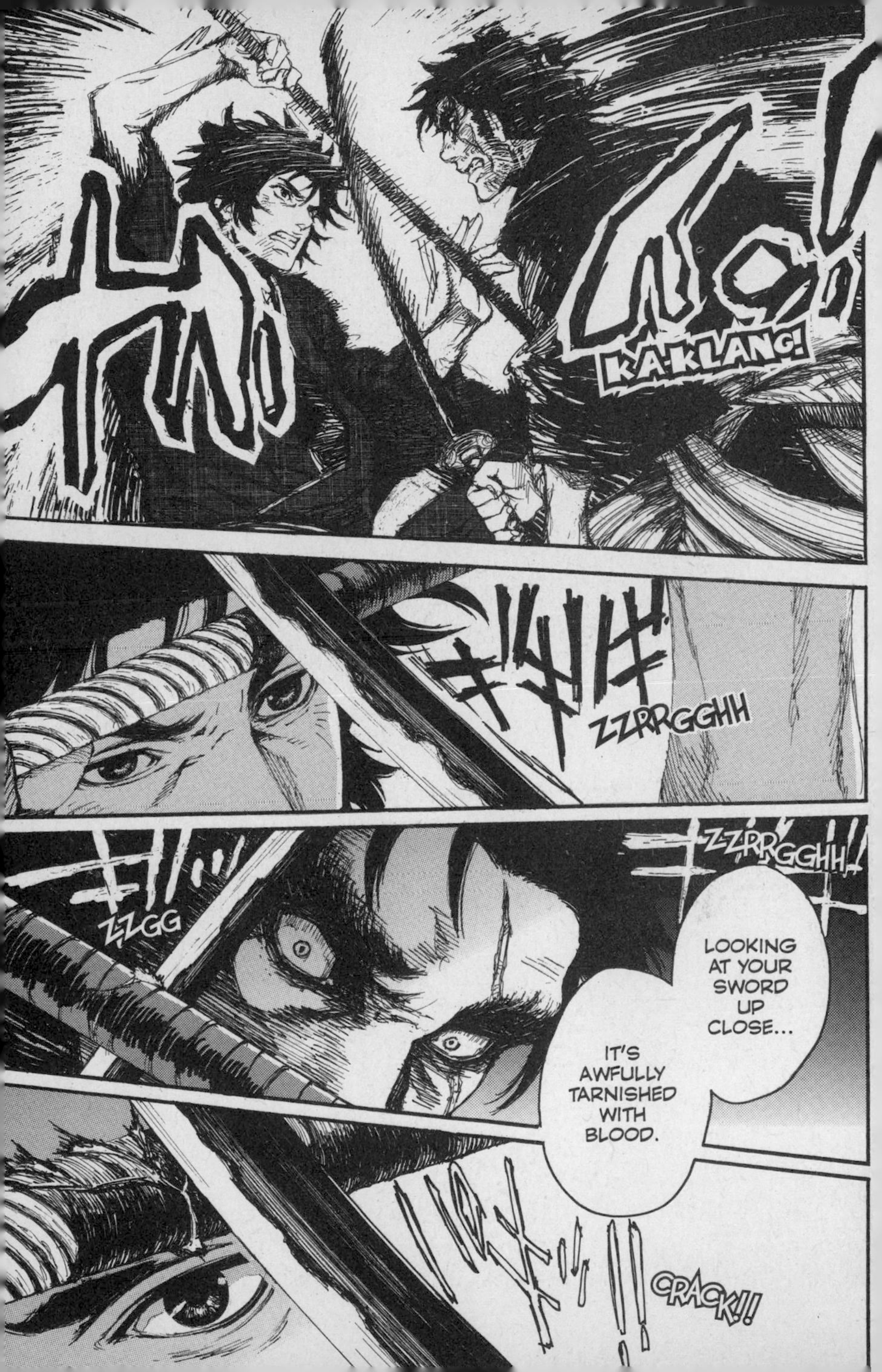
KAKLANG!
ZZRRGGHH
ZZRRGGHH!!
ZZGG
LOOKING AT YOUR SWORD UP CLOSE...
IT'S AWFULLY TARNISHED WITH BLOOD.
CRACK!!

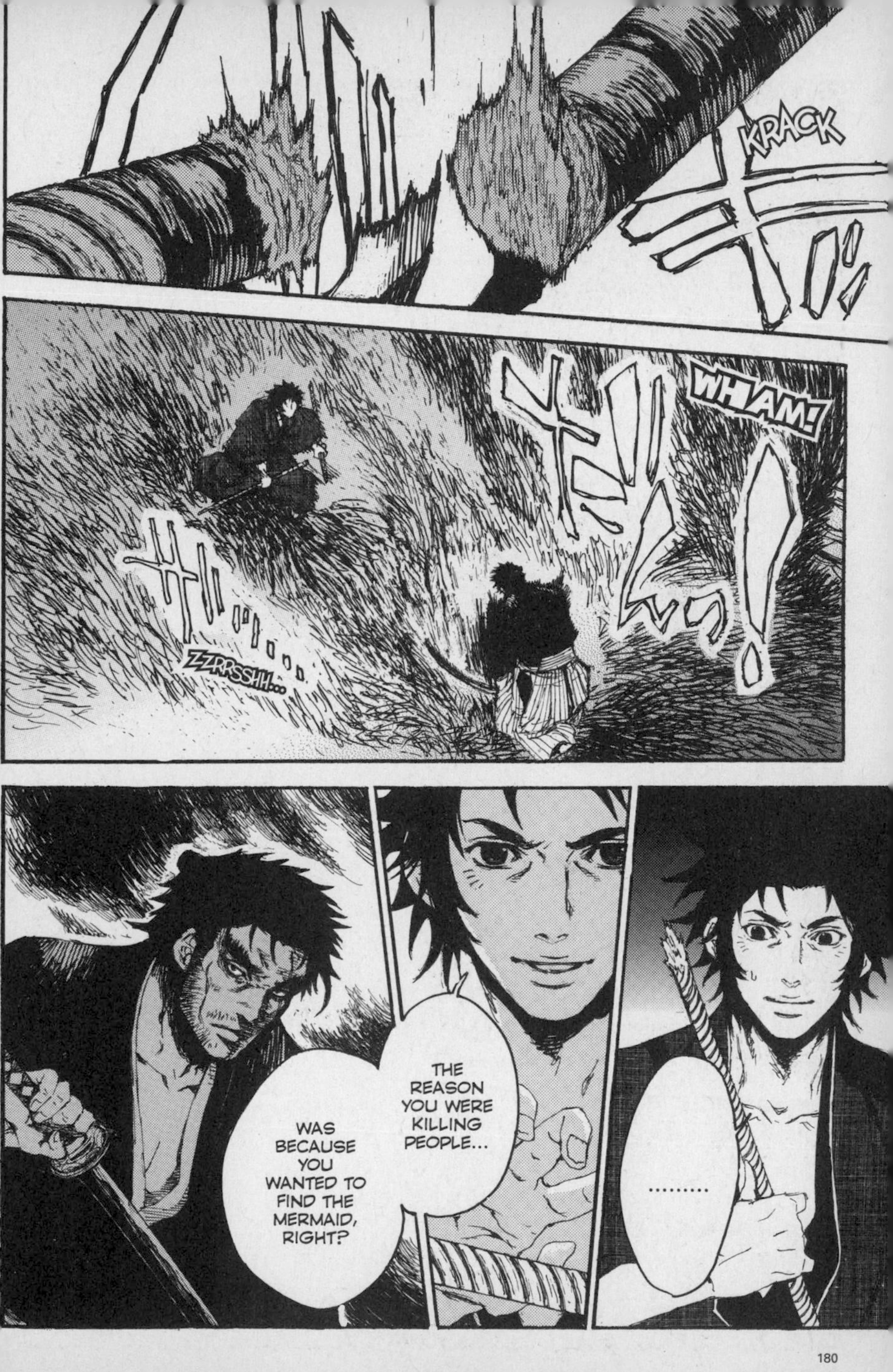
KRACK
WHAM!
ZZRRSSHH...
....
THE REASON YOU WERE KILLING PEOPLE...
WAS BECAUSE YOU WANTED TO FIND THE MERMAID, RIGHT?

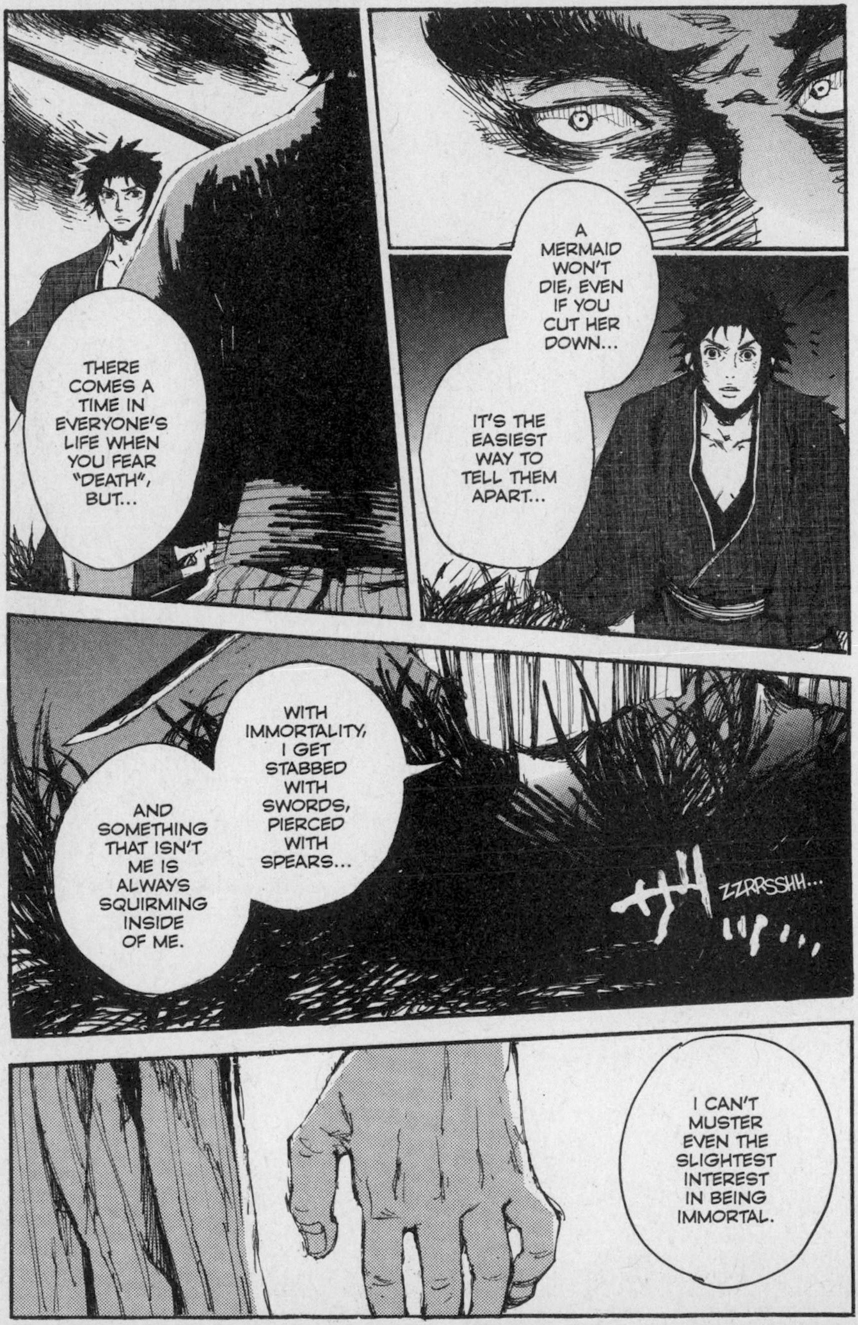
A MERMAID WON'T DIE, EVEN IF YOU CUT HER DOWN...
IT'S THE EASIEST WAY TO TELL THEM APART...
THERE COMES A TIME IN EVERYONE'S LIFE WHEN YOU FEAR "DEATH", BUT...
WITH IMMORTALITY, I GET STABBED WITH SWORDS, PIERCED WITH SPEARS...
AND SOMETHING THAT ISN'T ME IS ALWAYS SQUIRMING INSIDE OF ME.
ZZRRSSHH...
I CAN'T MUSTER EVEN THE SLIGHTEST INTEREST IN BEING IMMORTAL.

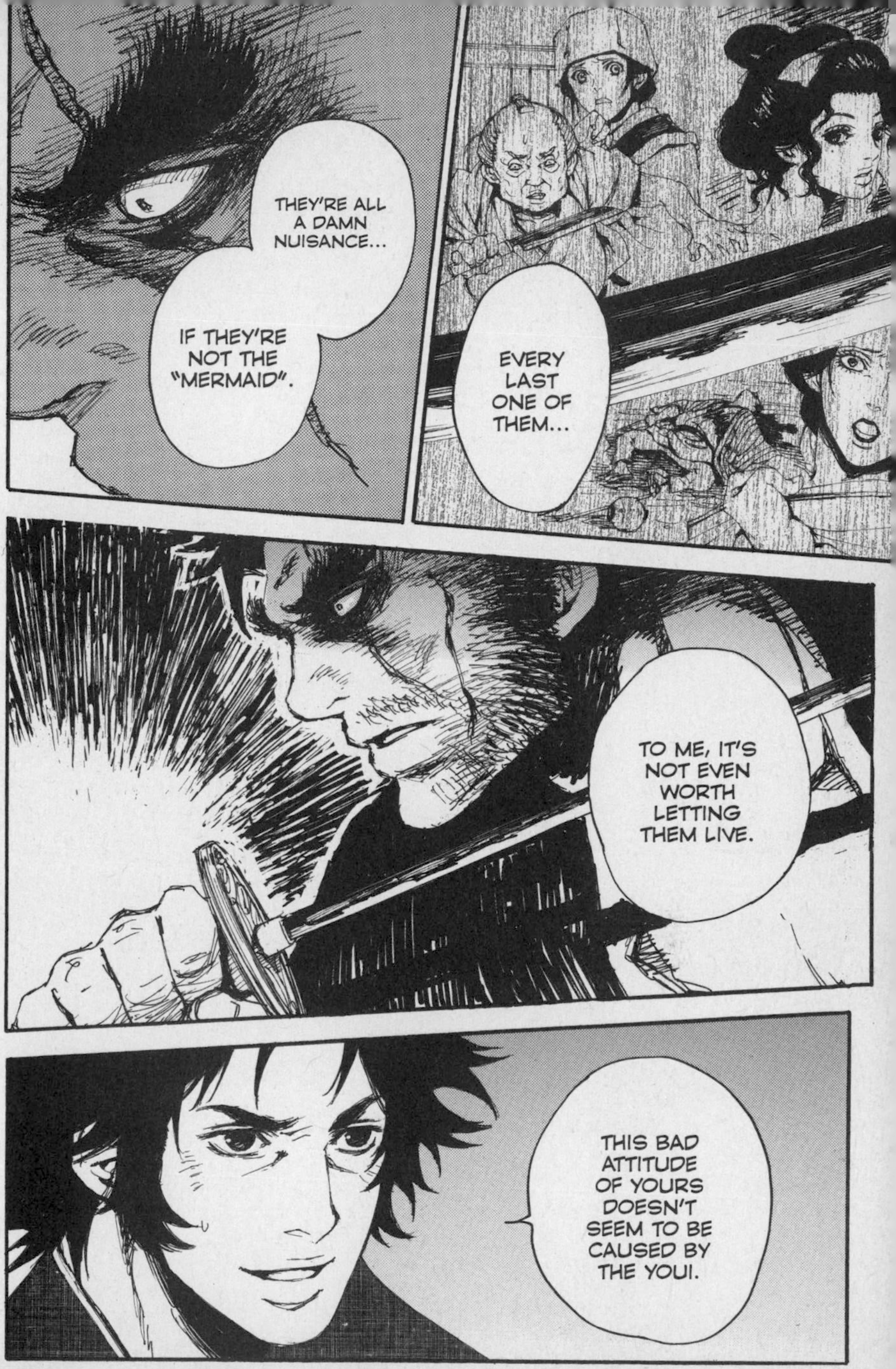
EVERY LAST ONE OF THEM...
THEY'RE ALL A DAMN NUISANCE...
IF THEY'RE NOT THE "MERMAID".
TO ME, IT'S NOT EVEN WORTH LETTING THEM LIVE.
THIS BAD ATTITUDE OF YOURS DOESN'T SEEM TO BE CAUSED BY THE YOUI.

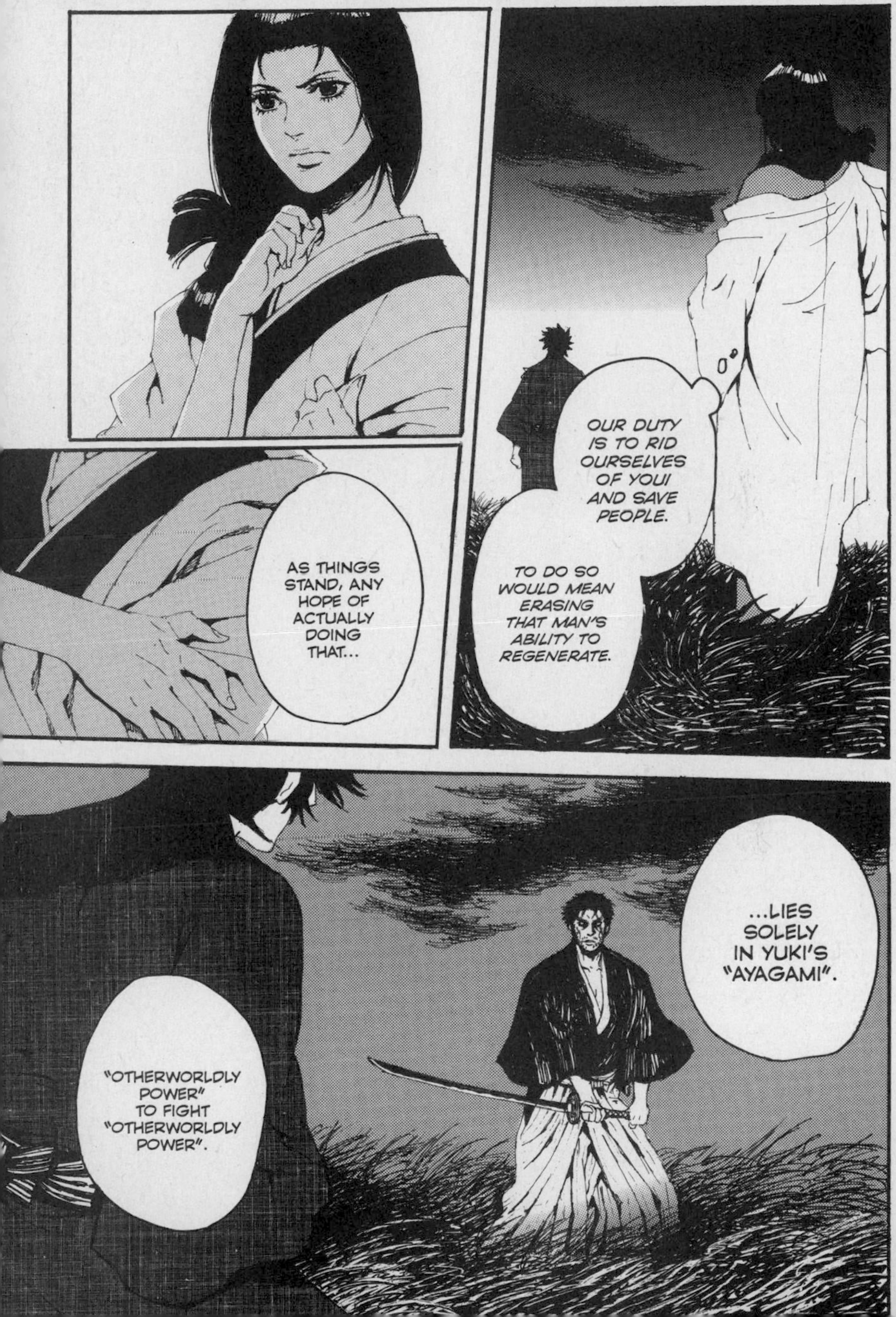
OUR DUTY IS TO RID OURSELVES OF YOUI AND SAVE PEOPLE.
TO DO SO WOULD MEAN ERASING THAT MAN'S ABILITY TO REGENERATE.
AS THINGS STAND, ANY HOPE OF ACTUALLY DOING THAT...
...LIES SOLELY IN YUKI'S "AYAGAMI".
"OTHERWORLDLY POWER" TO FIGHT "OTHERWORLDLY POWER".

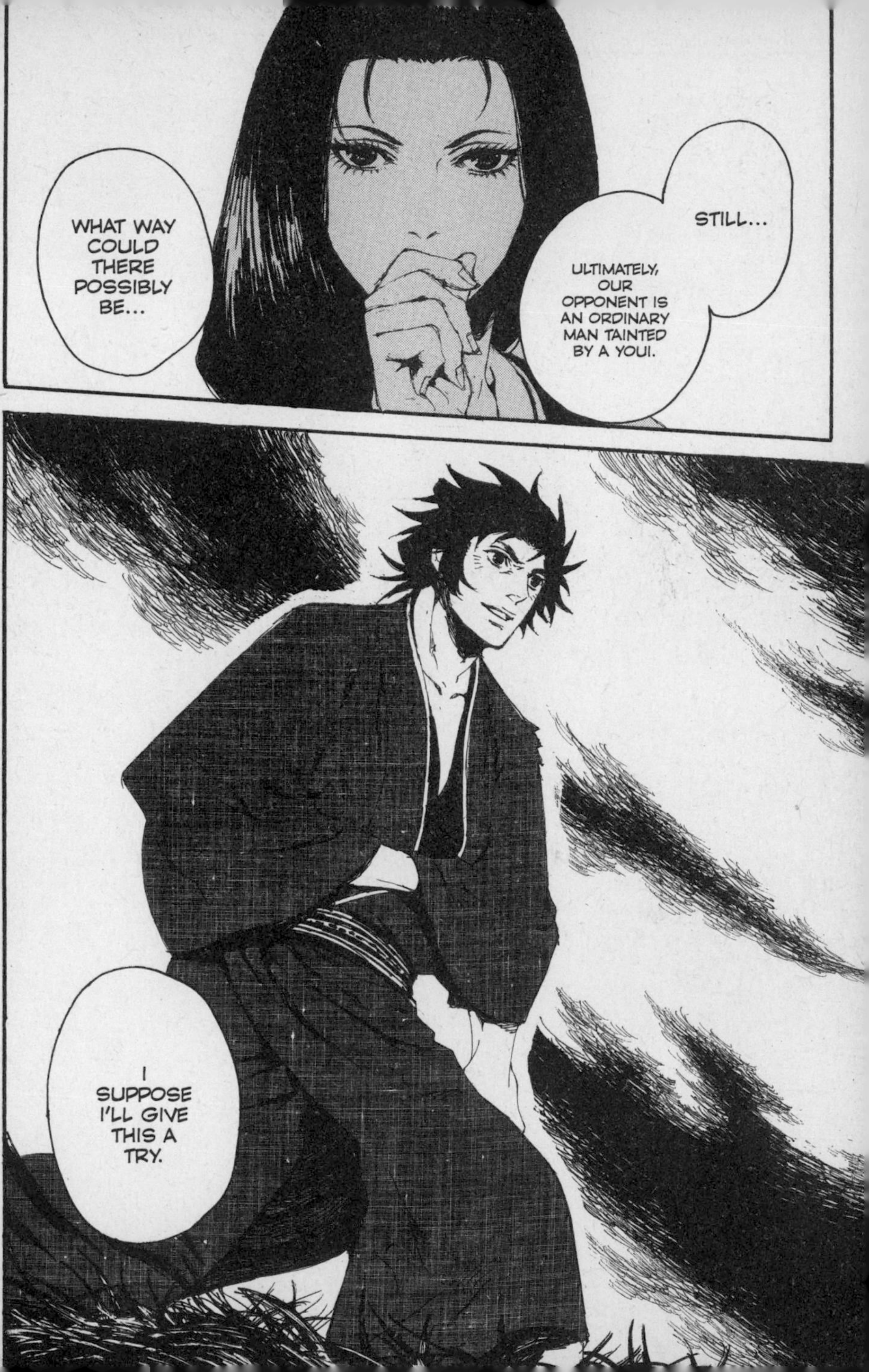
STILL...
ULTIMATELY, OUR OPPONENT IS AN ORDINARY MAN TAINTED BY A YOUI.
WHAT WAY COULD THERE POSSIBLY BE...
I SUPPOSE I'LL GIVE THIS A TRY.

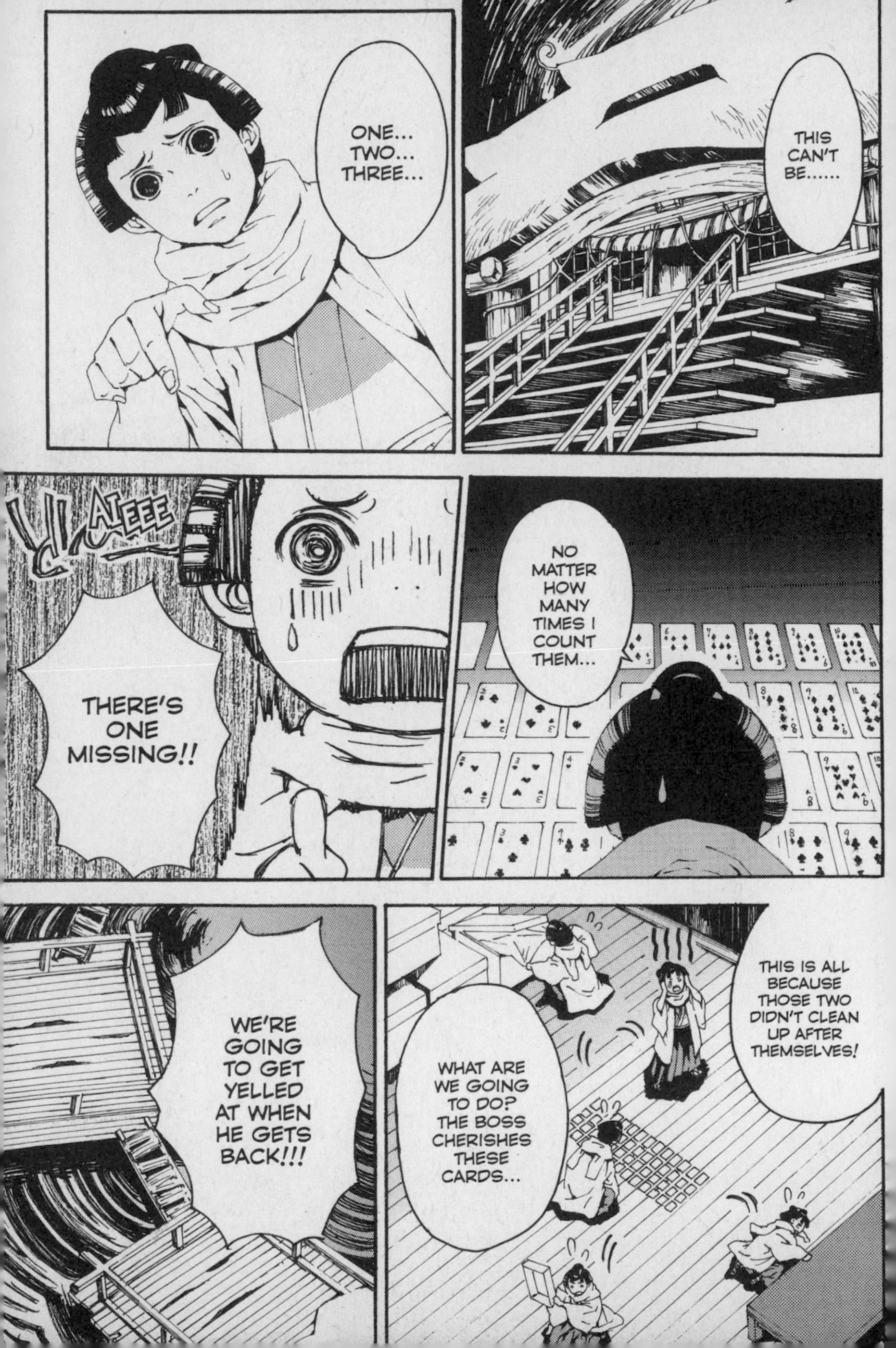
THIS CAN'T BE......
ONE... TWO... THREE...
NO MATTER HOW MANY TIMES I COUNT THEM...
AIEEE
THERE'S ONE MISSING!!
THIS IS ALL BECAUSE THOSE TWO DIDN'T CLEAN UP AFTER THEMSELVES!
WHAT ARE WE GOING TO DO? THE BOSS CHERISHES THESE CARDS...
WE'RE GOING TO GET YELLED AT WHEN HE GETS BACK!!!

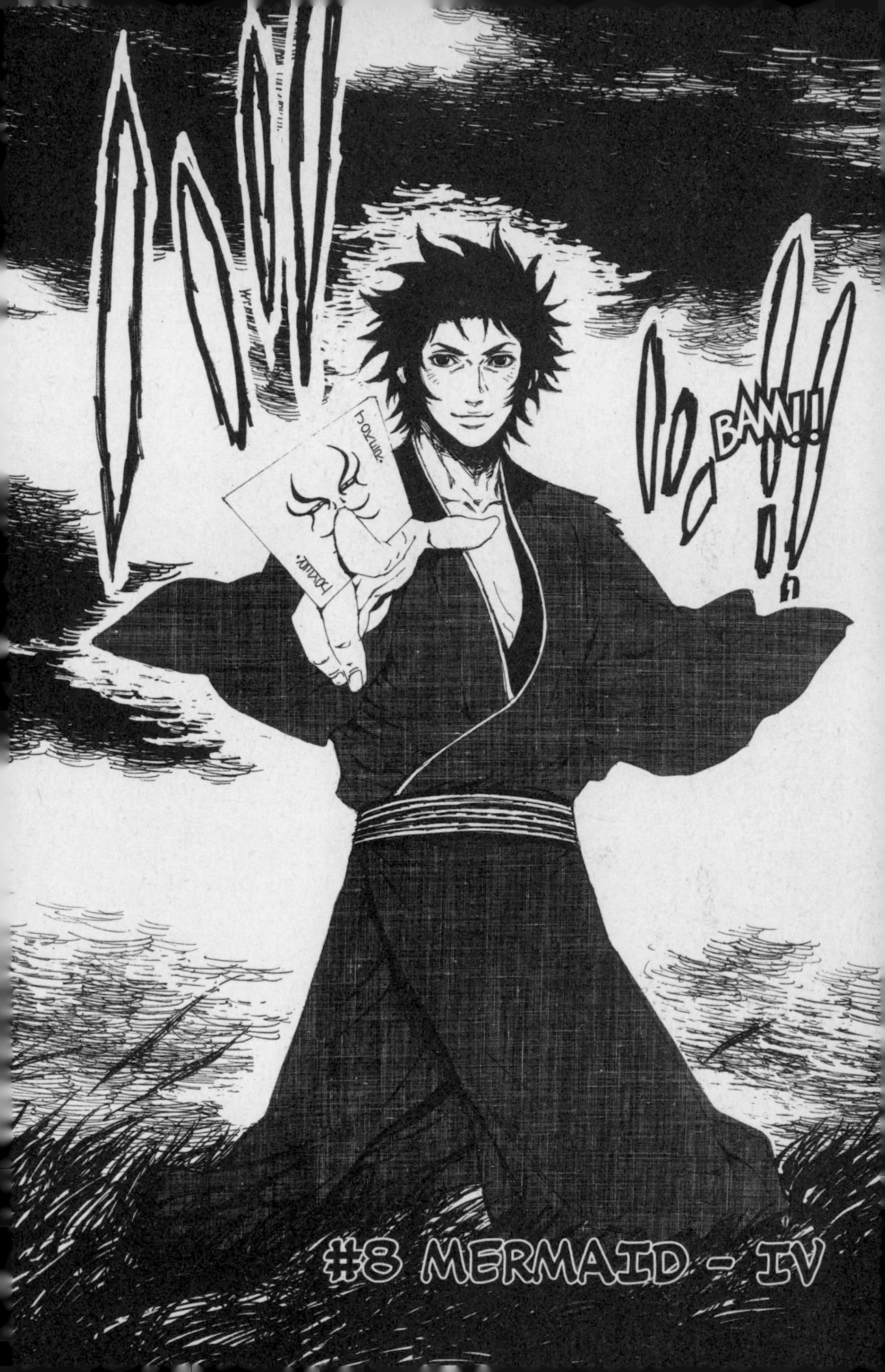
BAM!!
#8 MERMAID - IV

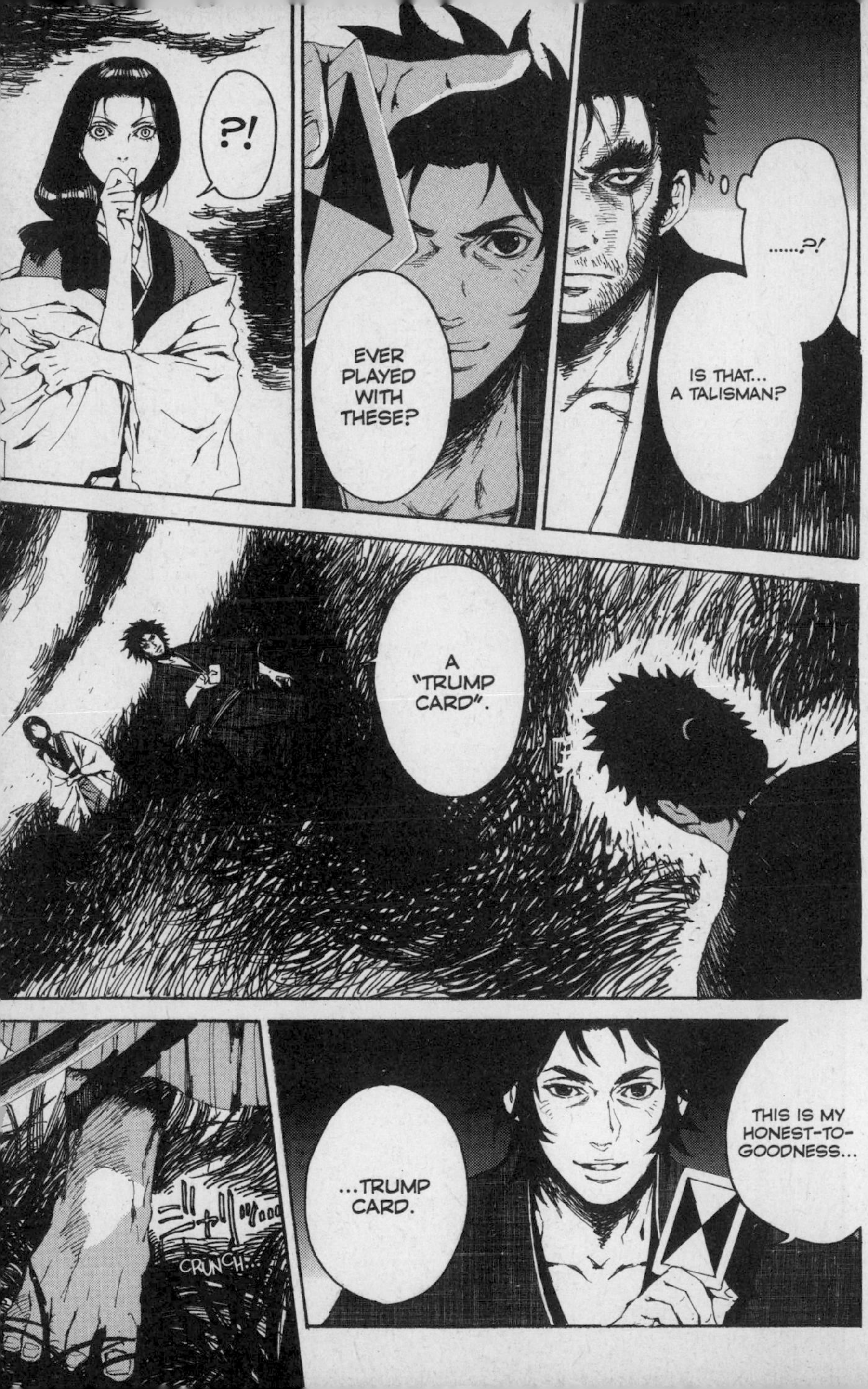
......?!
IS THAT... A TALISMAN?
EVER PLAYED WITH THESE?
?!
A "TRUMP CARD".
THIS IS MY HONEST-TO-GOODNESS...
...TRUMP CARD.
CRUNCH...

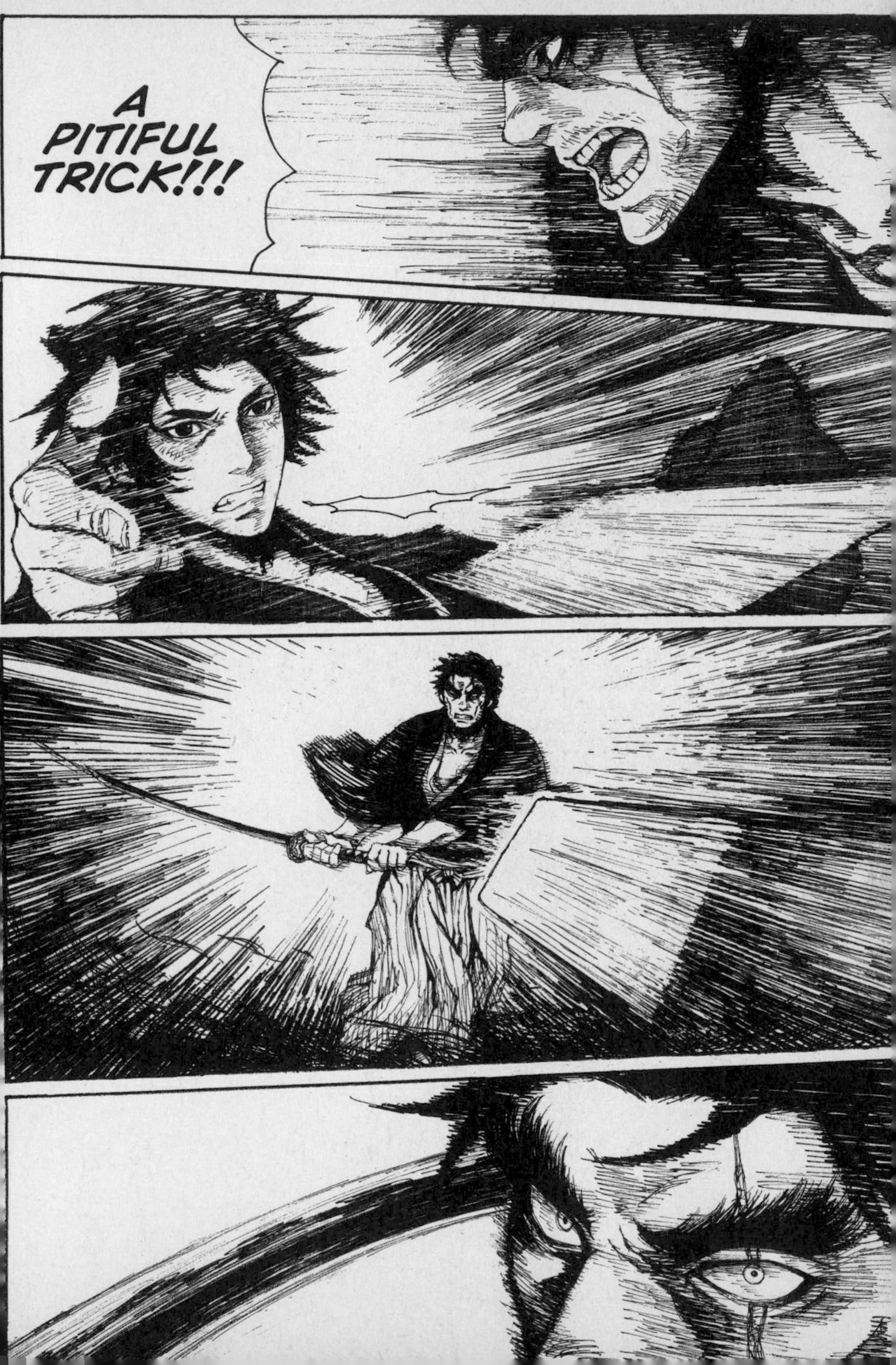
A PITIFUL TRICK!!!

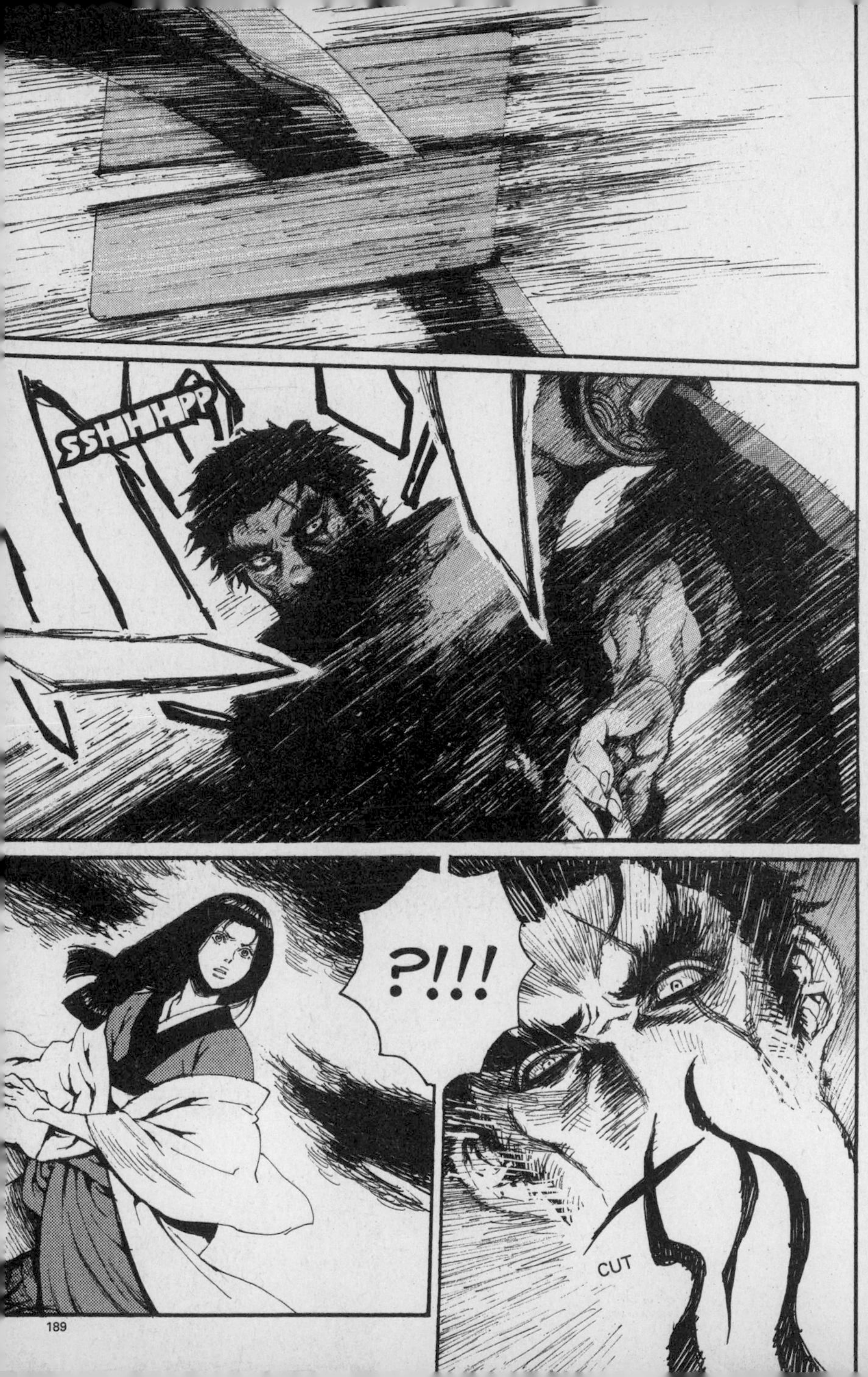
SSHHHPP
?!!!
CUT

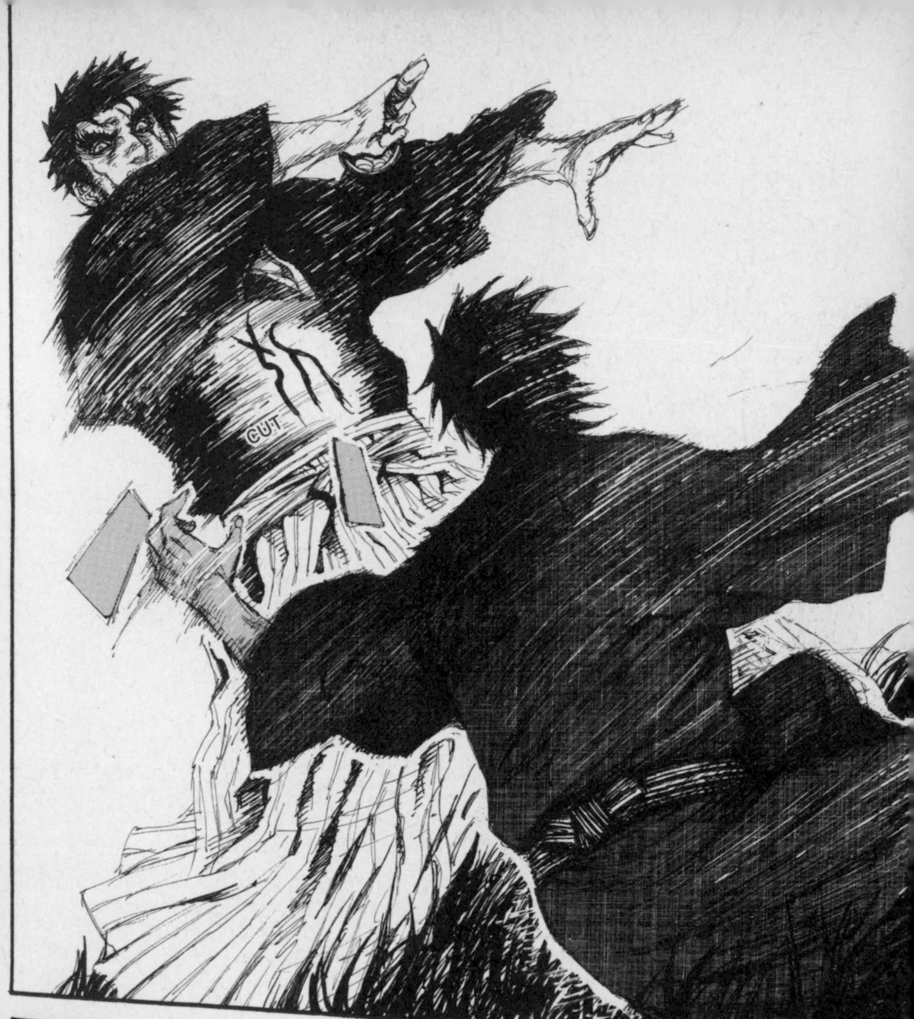
CUT

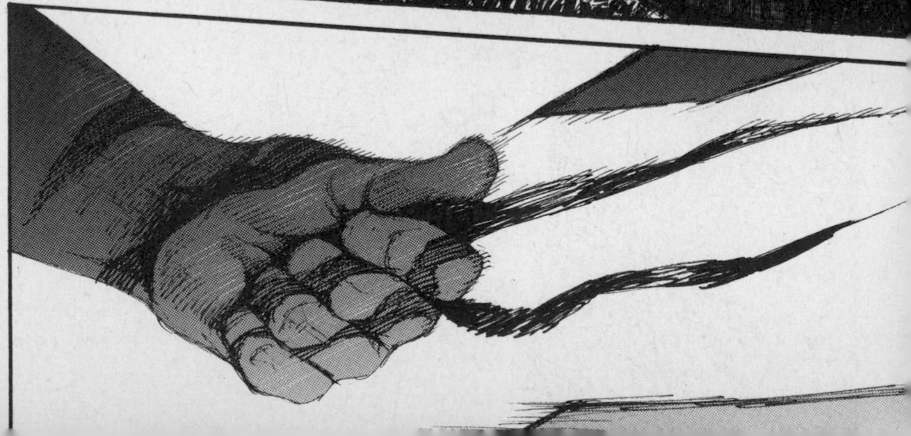

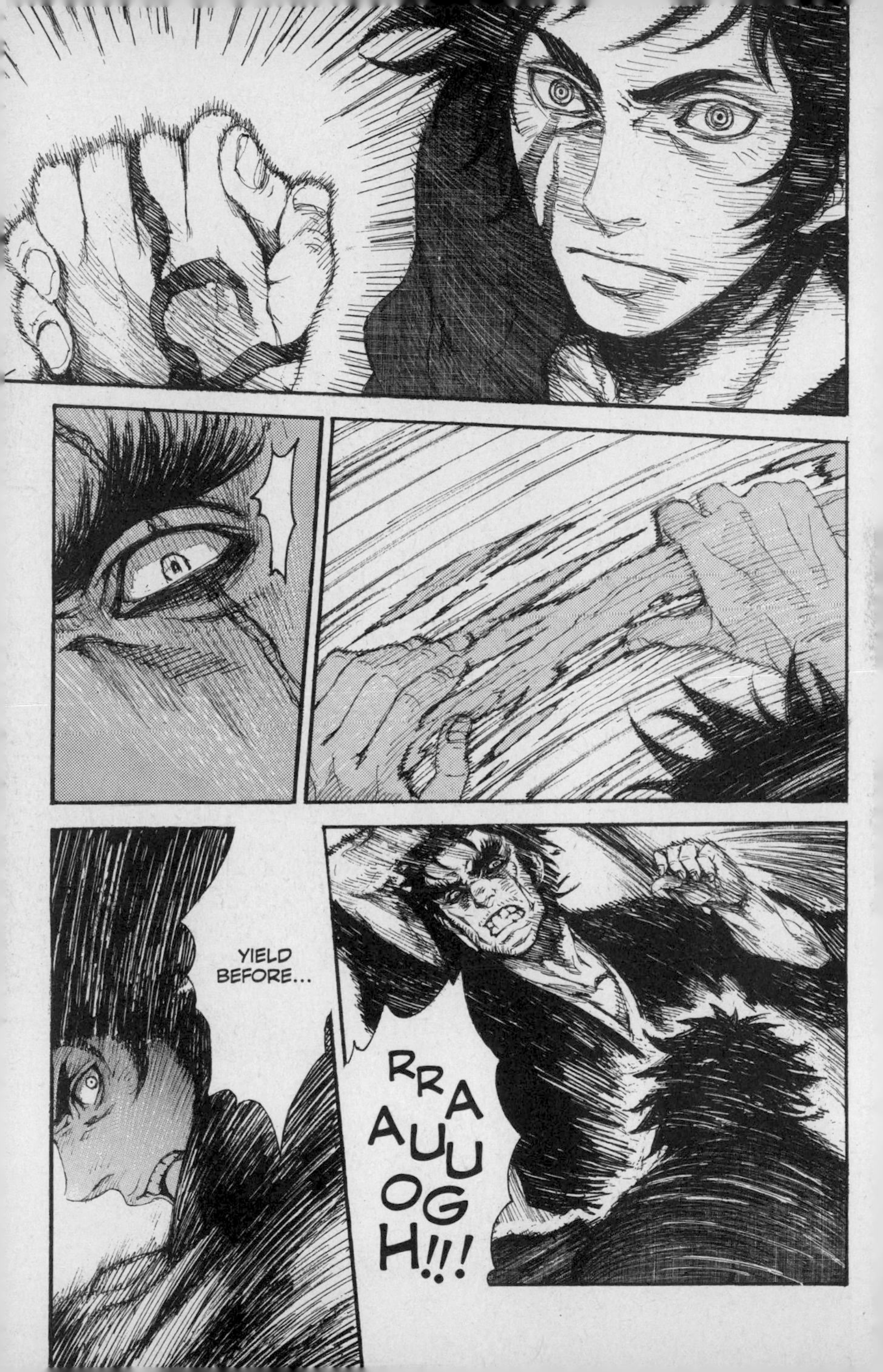
YIELD BEFORE...
RRAAUUOGH!!!

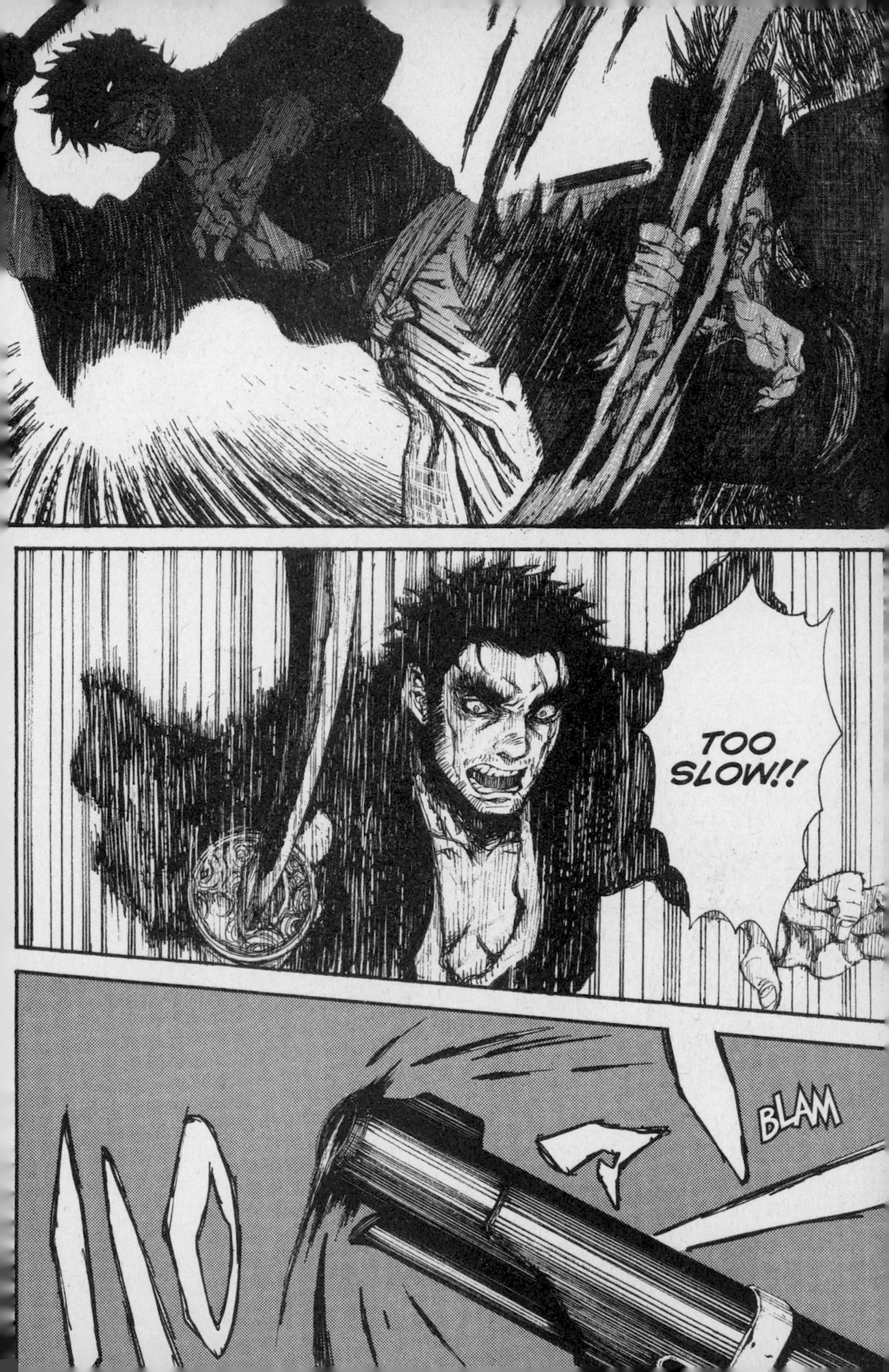
TOO SLOW!!
BLAM

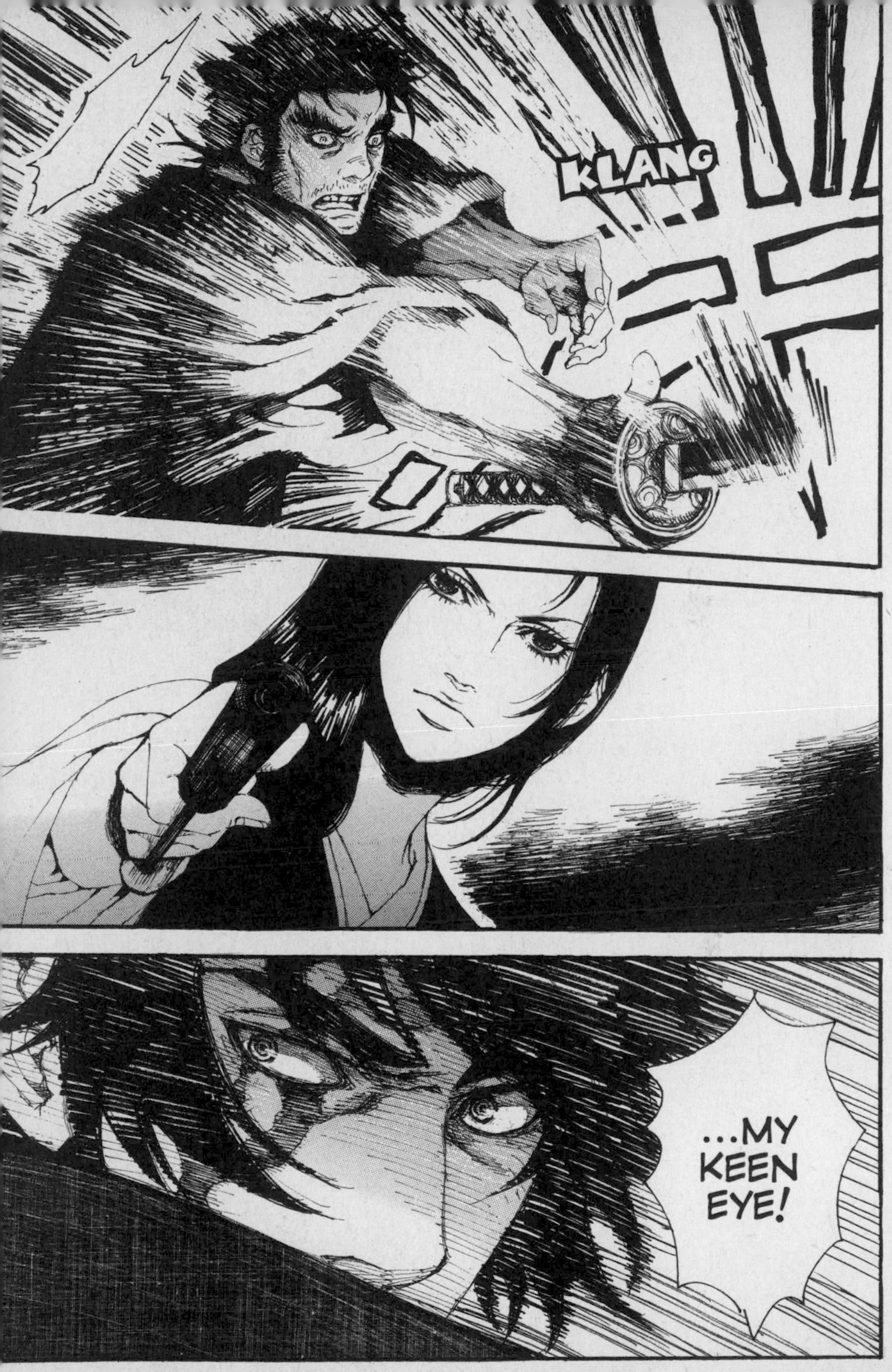
KLANG
...MY KEEN EYE!

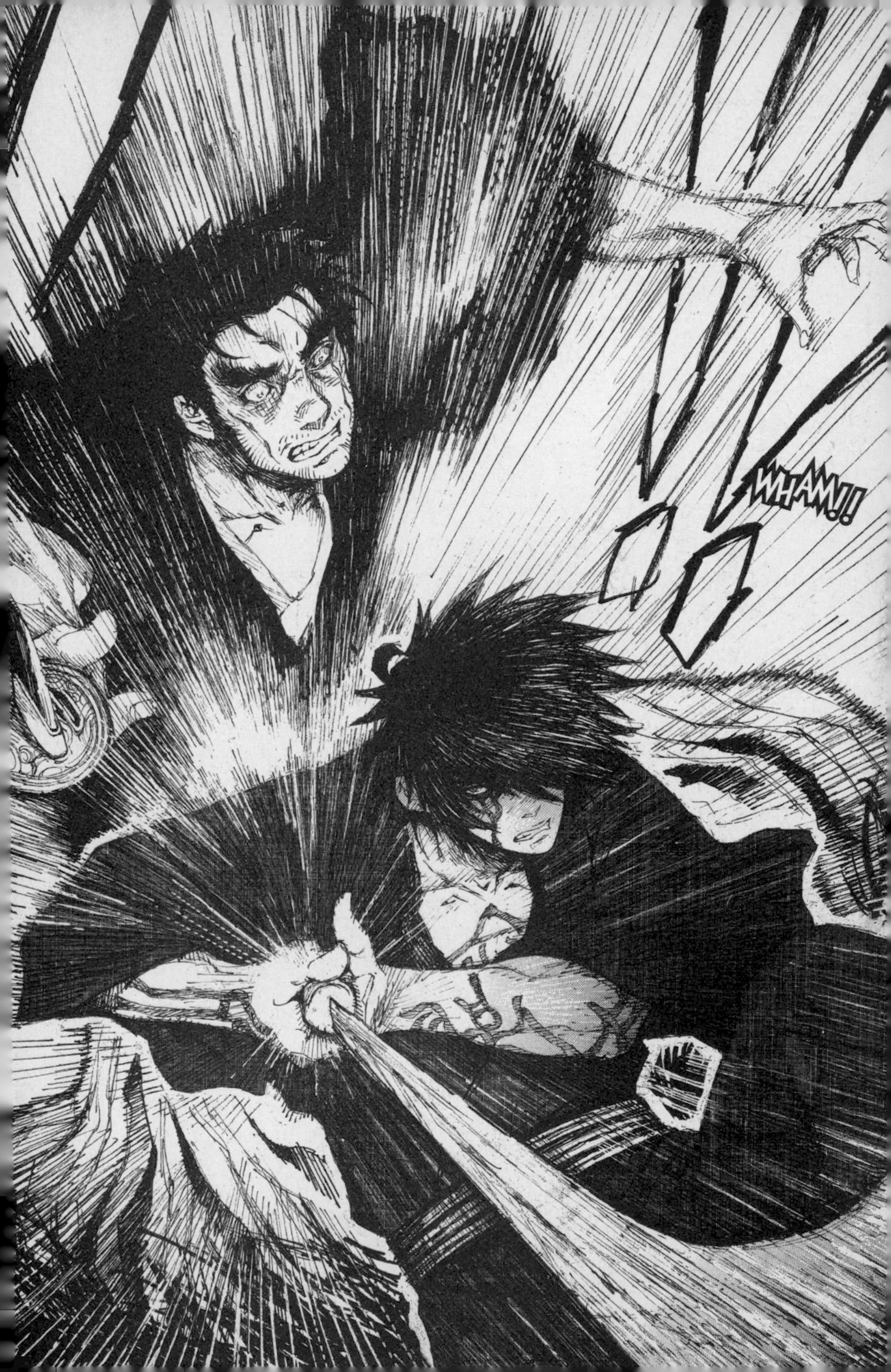
WHAM!!

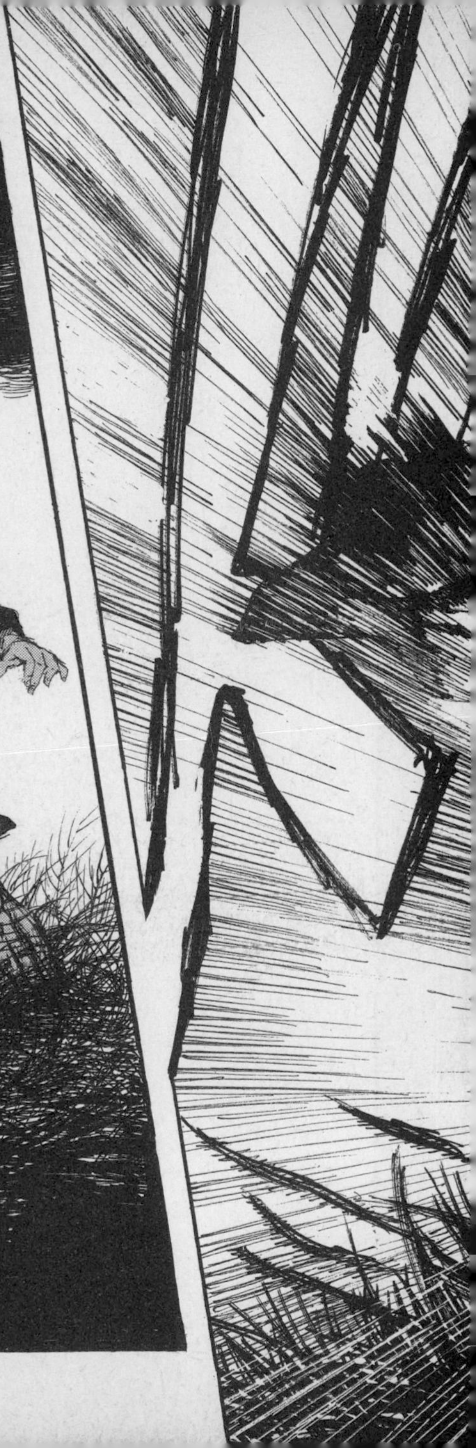

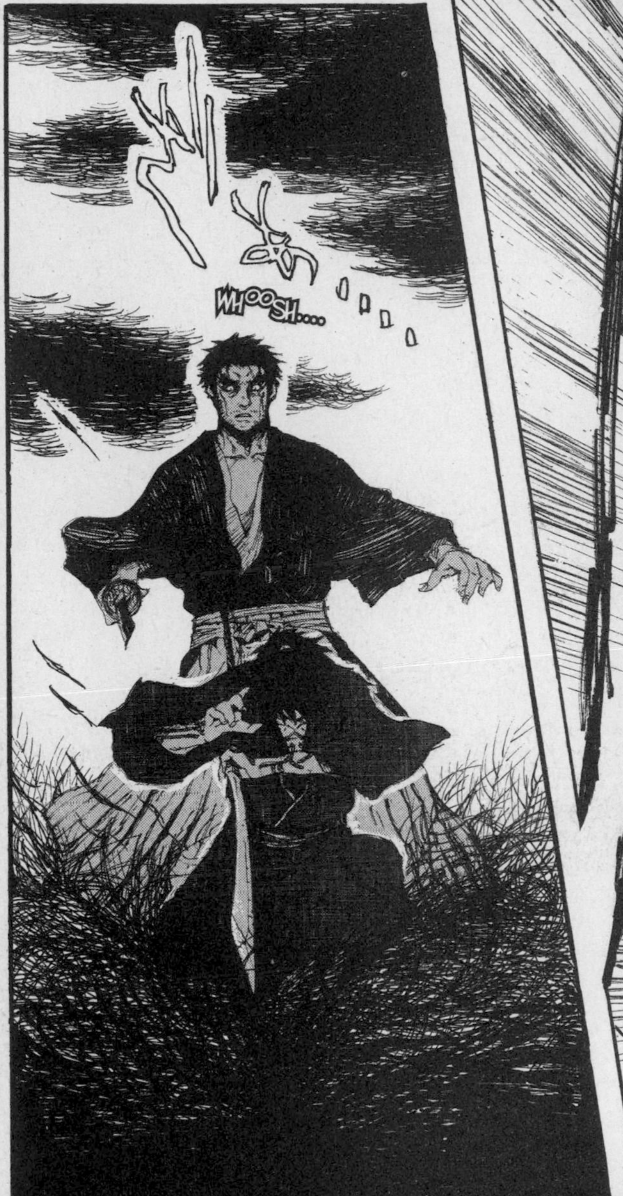
WHOOSH...

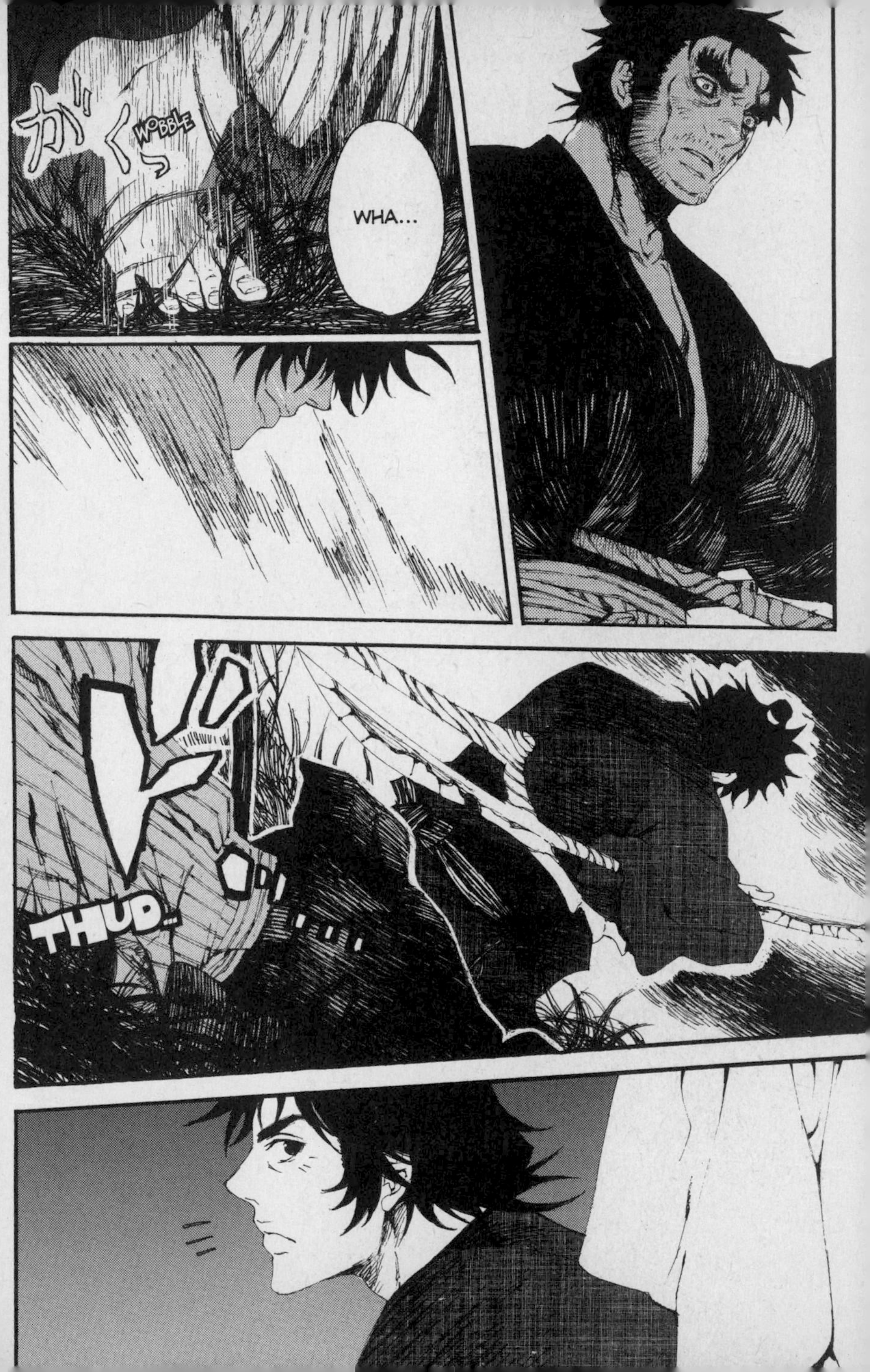
WHA...
がくっ
WOBBLE
ドッ
THUD..

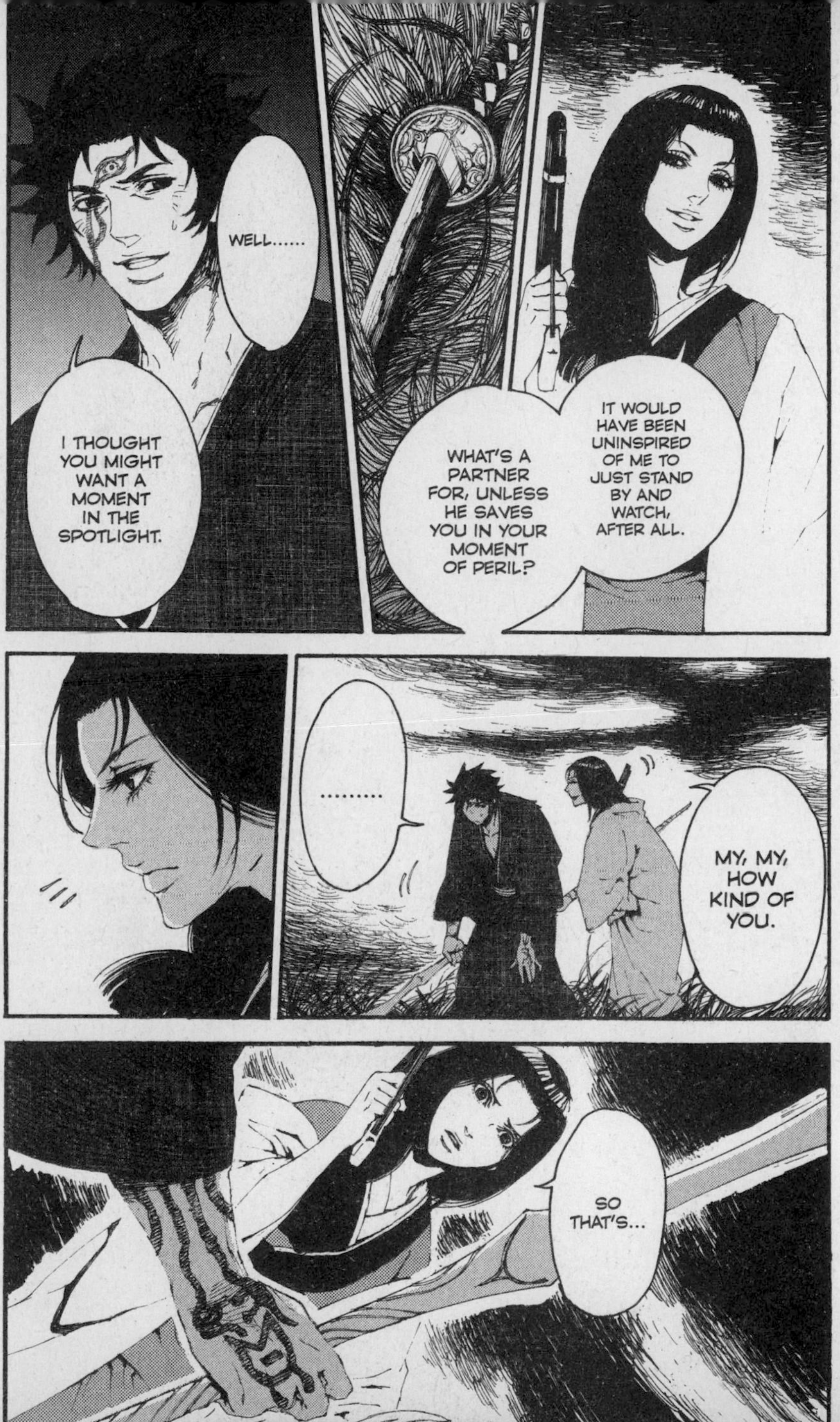
IT WOULD HAVE BEEN UNINSPIRED OF ME TO JUST STAND BY AND WATCH, AFTER ALL.
WHAT'S A PARTNER FOR, UNLESS HE SAVES YOU IN YOUR MOMENT OF PERIL?
WELL......
I THOUGHT YOU MIGHT WANT A MOMENT IN THE SPOTLIGHT.
MY, MY, HOW KIND OF YOU.
....
SO THAT'S...

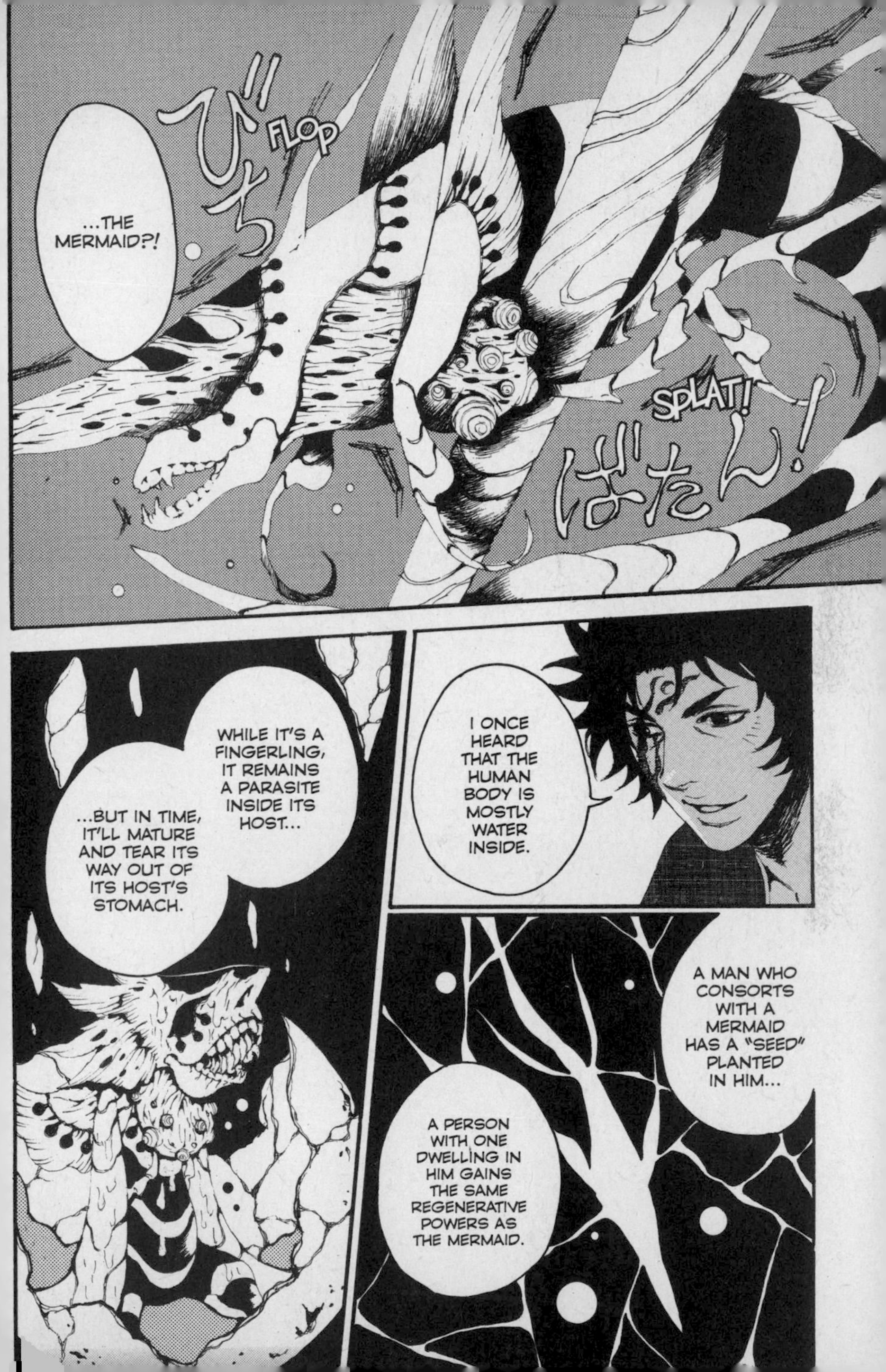

びち FLOP
...THE MERMAID?!
SPLAT! ばたん!
I ONCE HEARD THAT THE HUMAN BODY IS MOSTLY WATER INSIDE.
A MAN WHO CONSORTS WITH A MERMAID HAS A "SEED" PLANTED IN HIM...
A PERSON WITH ONE DWELLING IN HIM GAINS THE SAME REGENERATIVE POWERS AS THE MERMAID.
WHILE IT'S A FINGERLING, IT REMAINS A PARASITE INSIDE ITS HOST...
...BUT IN TIME, IT'LL MATURE AND TEAR ITS WAY OUT OF ITS HOST'S STOMACH.

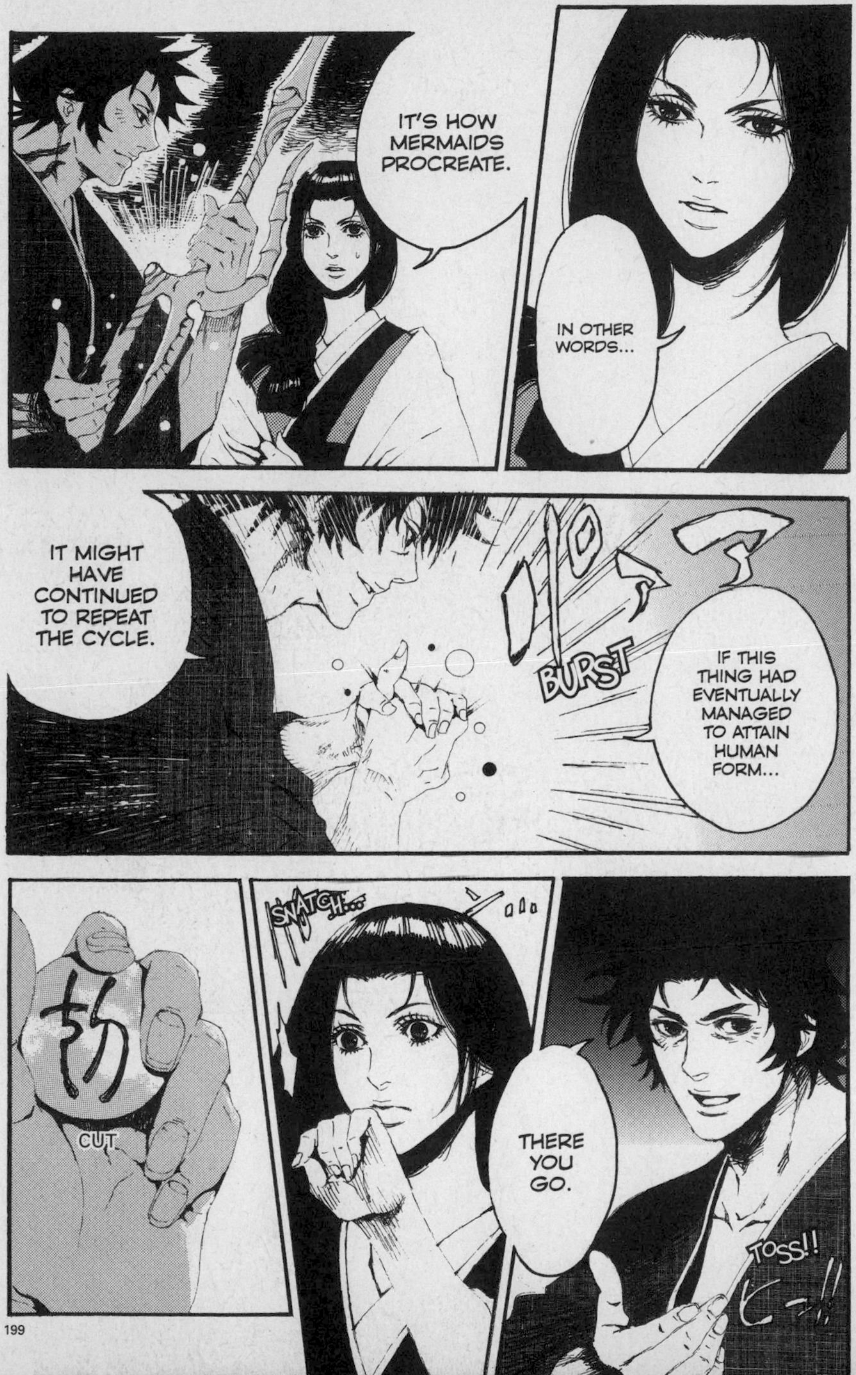
IN OTHER WORDS...
IT'S HOW MERMAIDS PROCREATE.
IF THIS THING HAD EVENTUALLY MANAGED TO ATTAIN HUMAN FORM...
BURST
IT MIGHT HAVE CONTINUED TO REPEAT THE CYCLE.
THERE YOU GO.
TOSS!!
SNATCH...
CUT

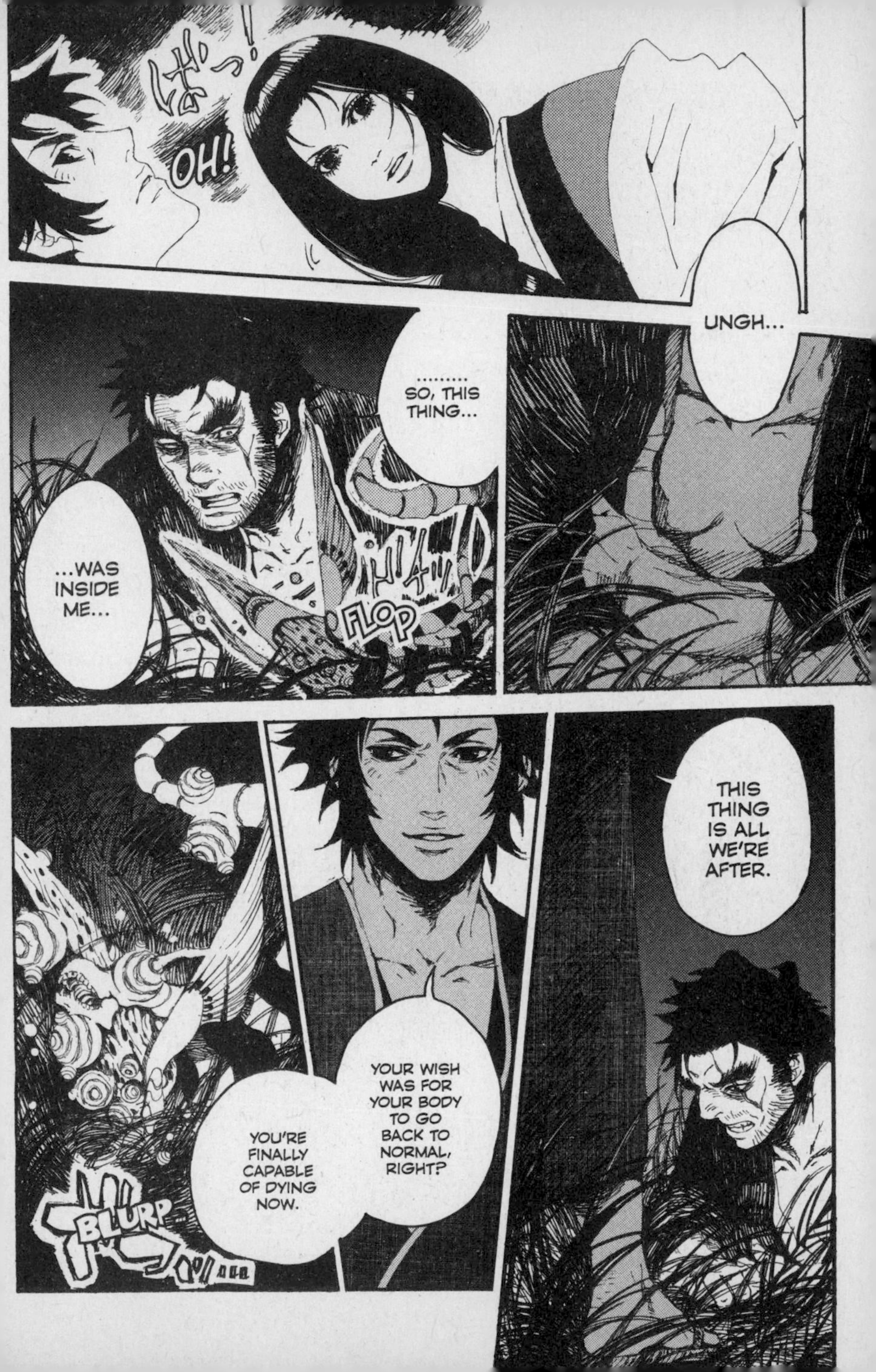
ばっ!
OH!
UNGH...
....
SO, THIS THING...
...WAS INSIDE ME...
FLOP
THIS THING IS ALL WE'RE AFTER.
YOUR WISH WAS FOR YOUR BODY TO GO BACK TO NORMAL, RIGHT?
YOU'RE FINALLY CAPABLE OF DYING NOW.
BLURP...

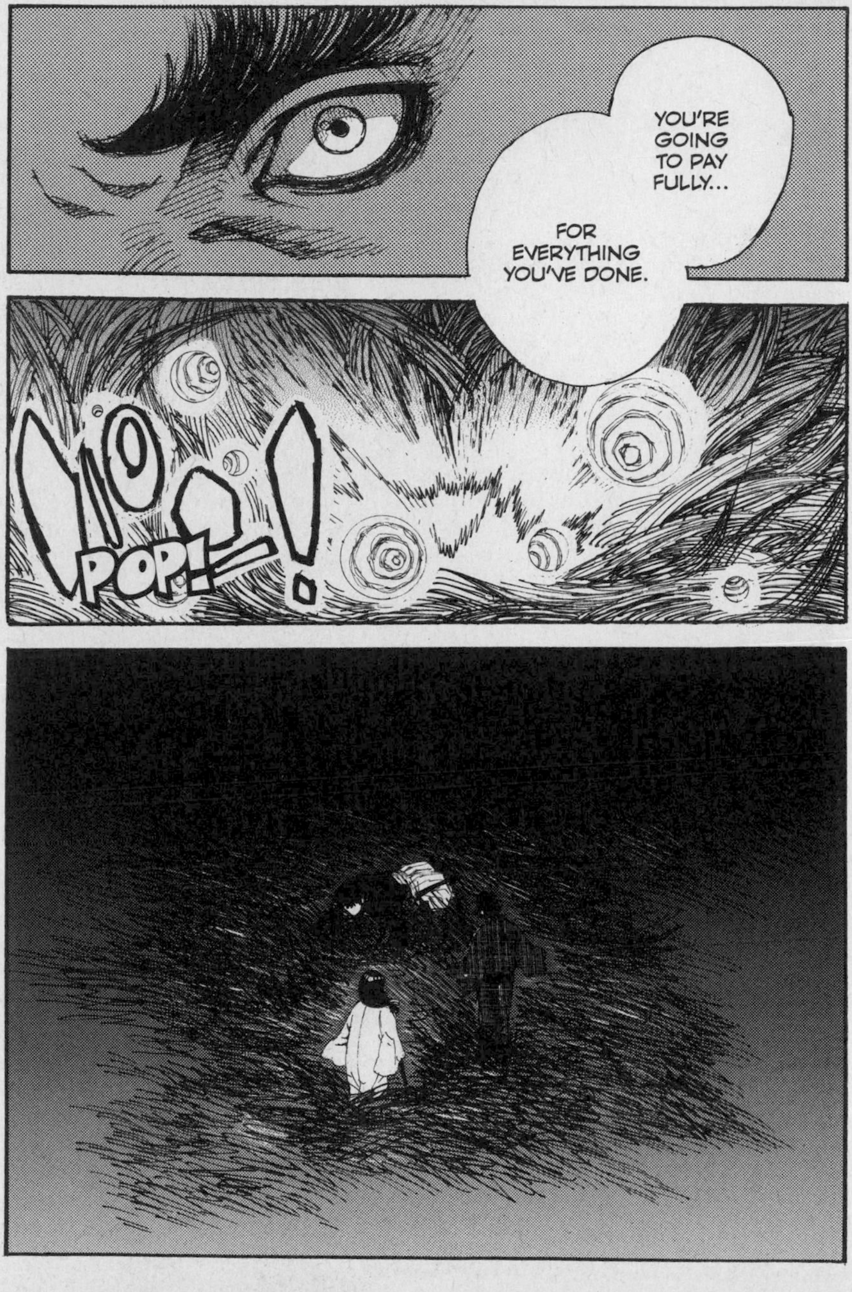
YOU'RE GOING TO PAY FULLY...
FOR EVERYTHING YOU'VE DONE.
POP!

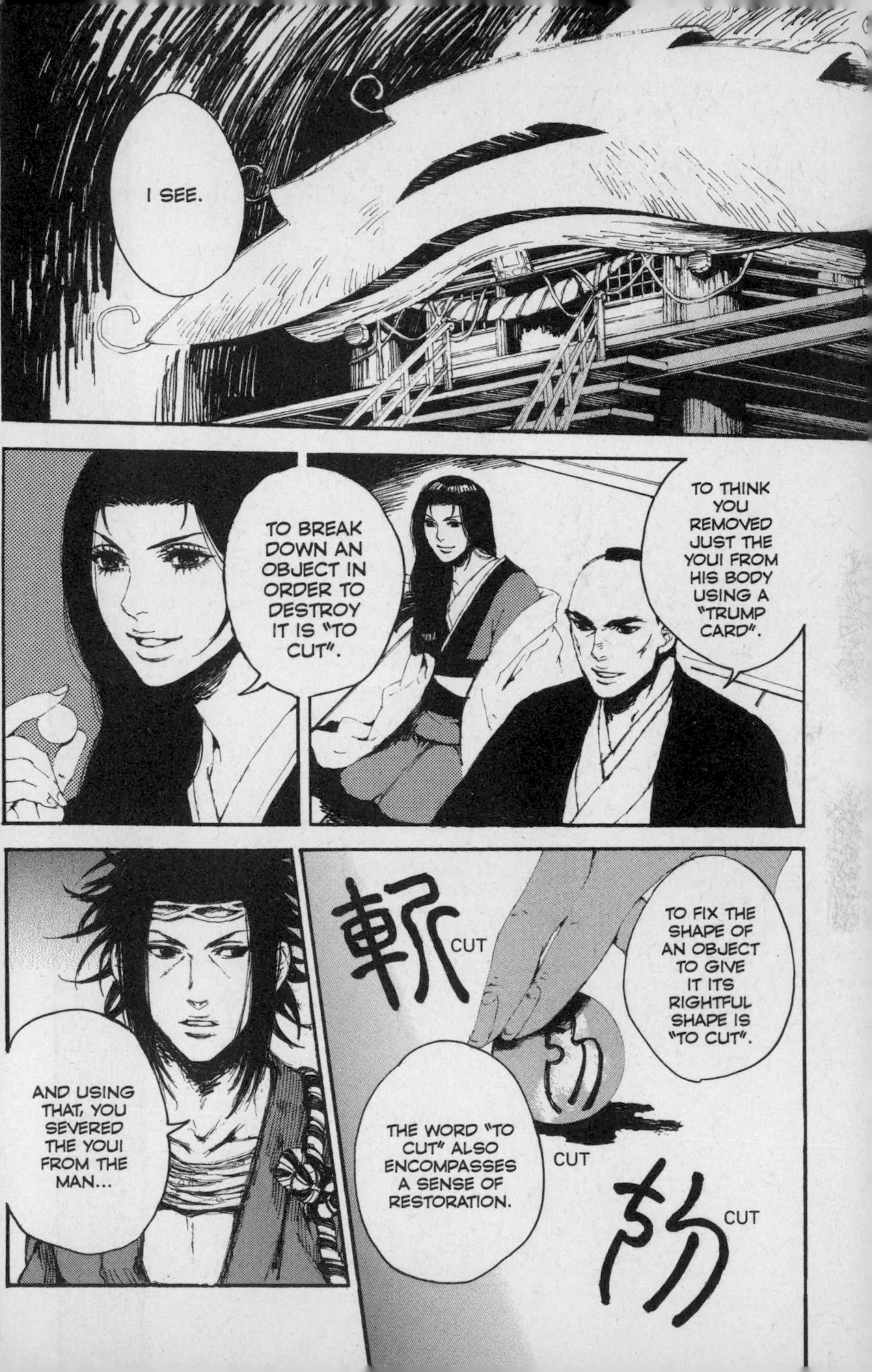
I SEE.
TO THINK YOU REMOVED JUST THE YOUI FROM HIS BODY USING A "TRUMP CARD".
TO BREAK DOWN AN OBJECT IN ORDER TO DESTROY IT IS "TO CUT".
TO FIX THE SHAPE OF AN OBJECT TO GIVE IT ITS RIGHTFUL SHAPE IS "TO CUT".
斬 CUT
THE WORD "TO CUT" ALSO ENCOMPASSES A SENSE OF RESTORATION.
CUT
CUT
AND USING THAT, YOU SEVERED THE YOUI FROM THE MAN...

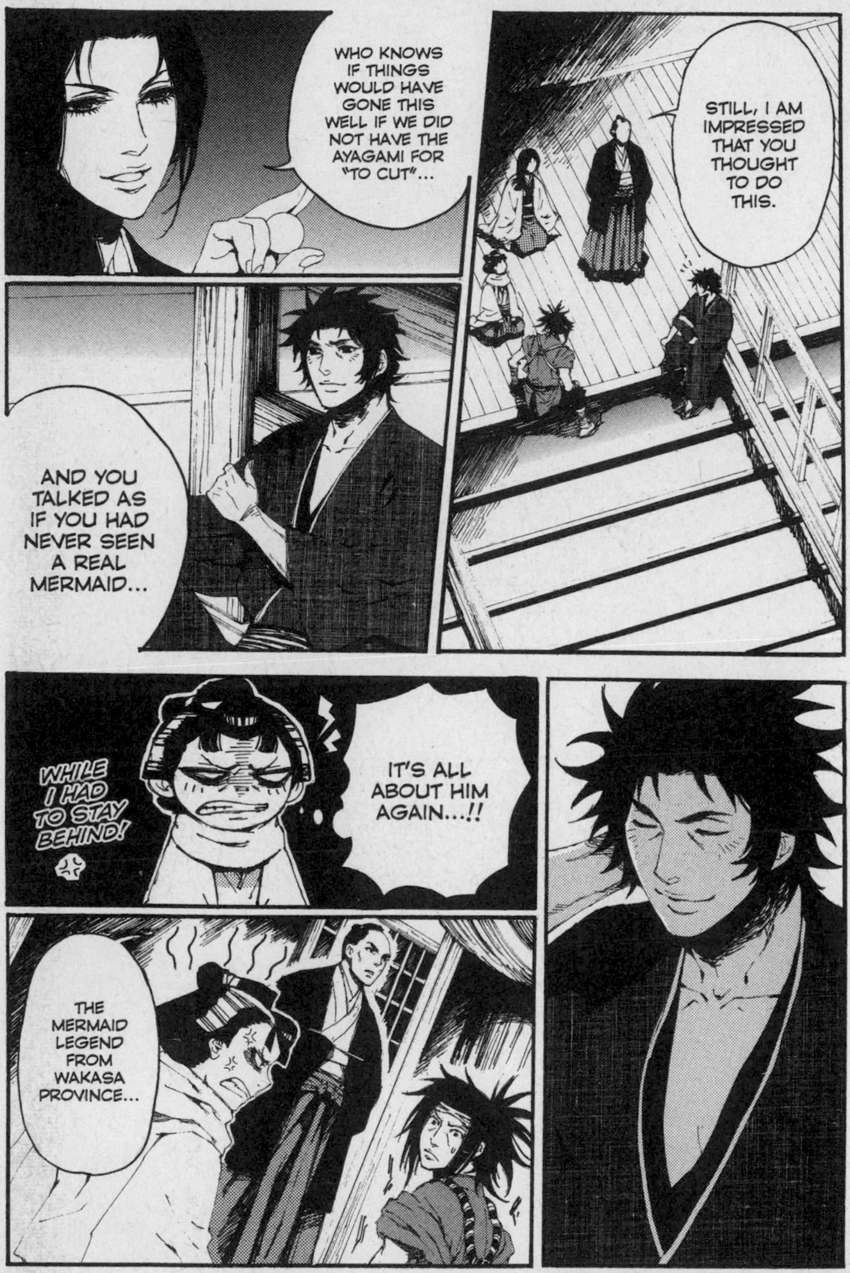
STILL, I AM IMPRESSED THAT YOU THOUGHT TO DO THIS.
WHO KNOWS IF THINGS WOULD HAVE GONE THIS WELL IF WE DID NOT HAVE THE AYAGAMI FOR "TO CUT"...
AND YOU TALKED AS IF YOU HAD NEVER SEEN A REAL MERMAID...
IT'S ALL ABOUT HIM AGAIN...!!
WHILE I HAD TO STAY BEHIND!
THE MERMAID LEGEND FROM WAKASA PROVINCE...

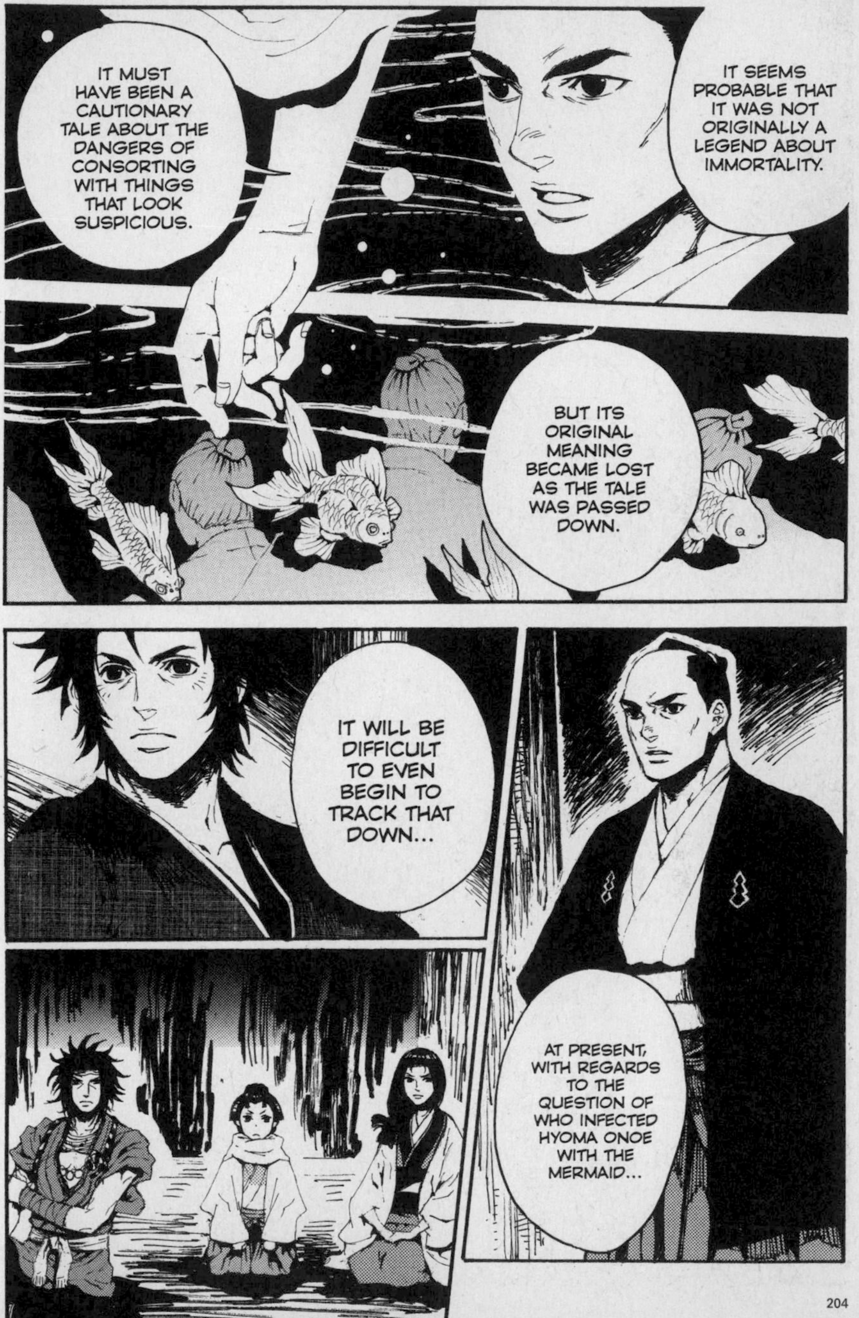
IT SEEMS PROBABLE THAT IT WAS NOT ORIGINALLY A LEGEND ABOUT IMMORTALITY.
IT MUST HAVE BEEN A CAUTIONARY TALE ABOUT THE DANGERS OF CONSORTING WITH THINGS THAT LOOK SUSPICIOUS.
BUT ITS ORIGINAL MEANING BECAME LOST AS THE TALE WAS PASSED DOWN.
AT PRESENT, WITH REGARDS TO THE QUESTION OF WHO INFECTED HYOMA ONOE WITH THE MERMAID...
IT WILL BE DIFFICULT TO EVEN BEGIN TO TRACK THAT DOWN...

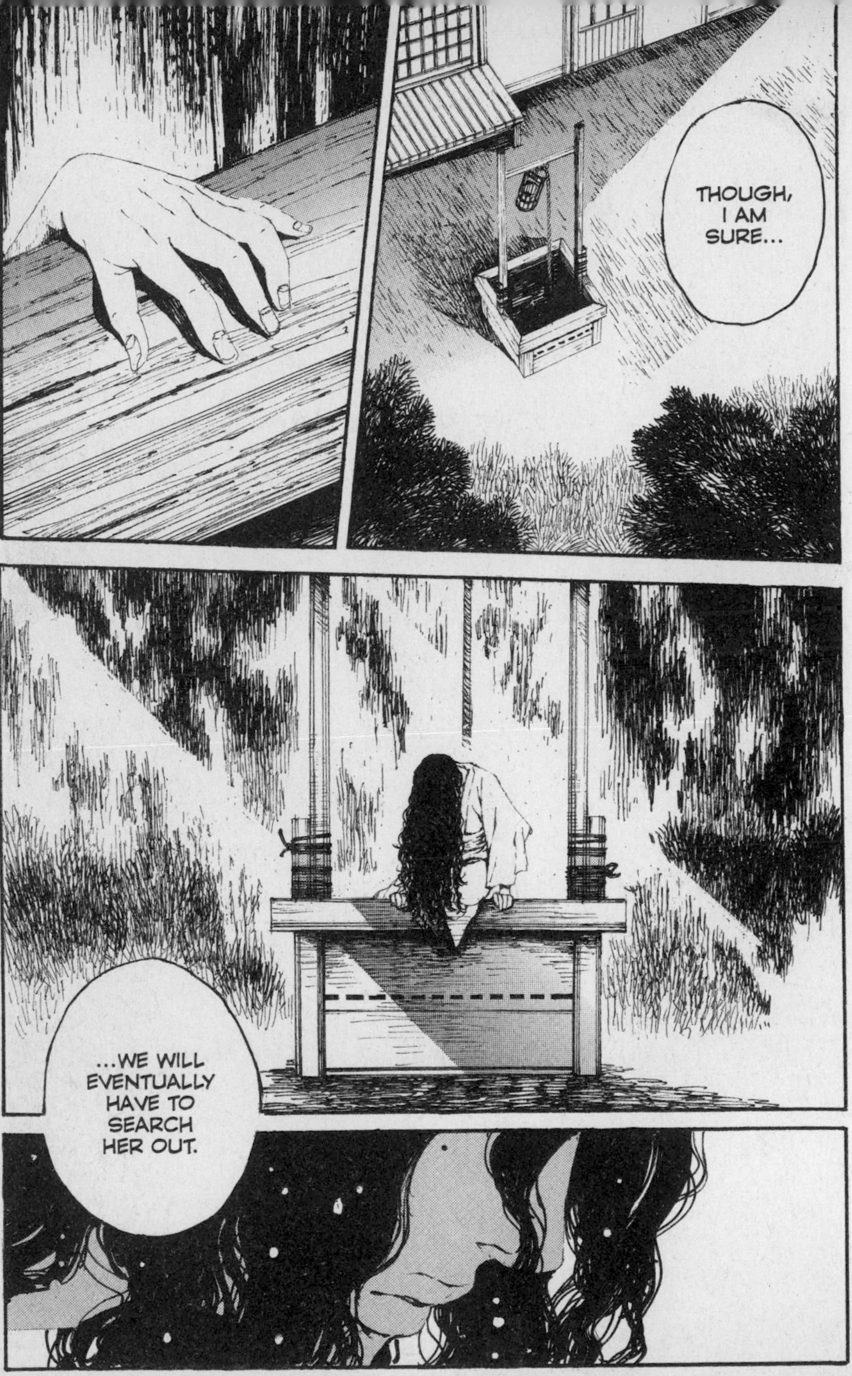
THOUGH, I AM SURE...
...WE WILL EVENTUALLY HAVE TO SEARCH HER OUT.

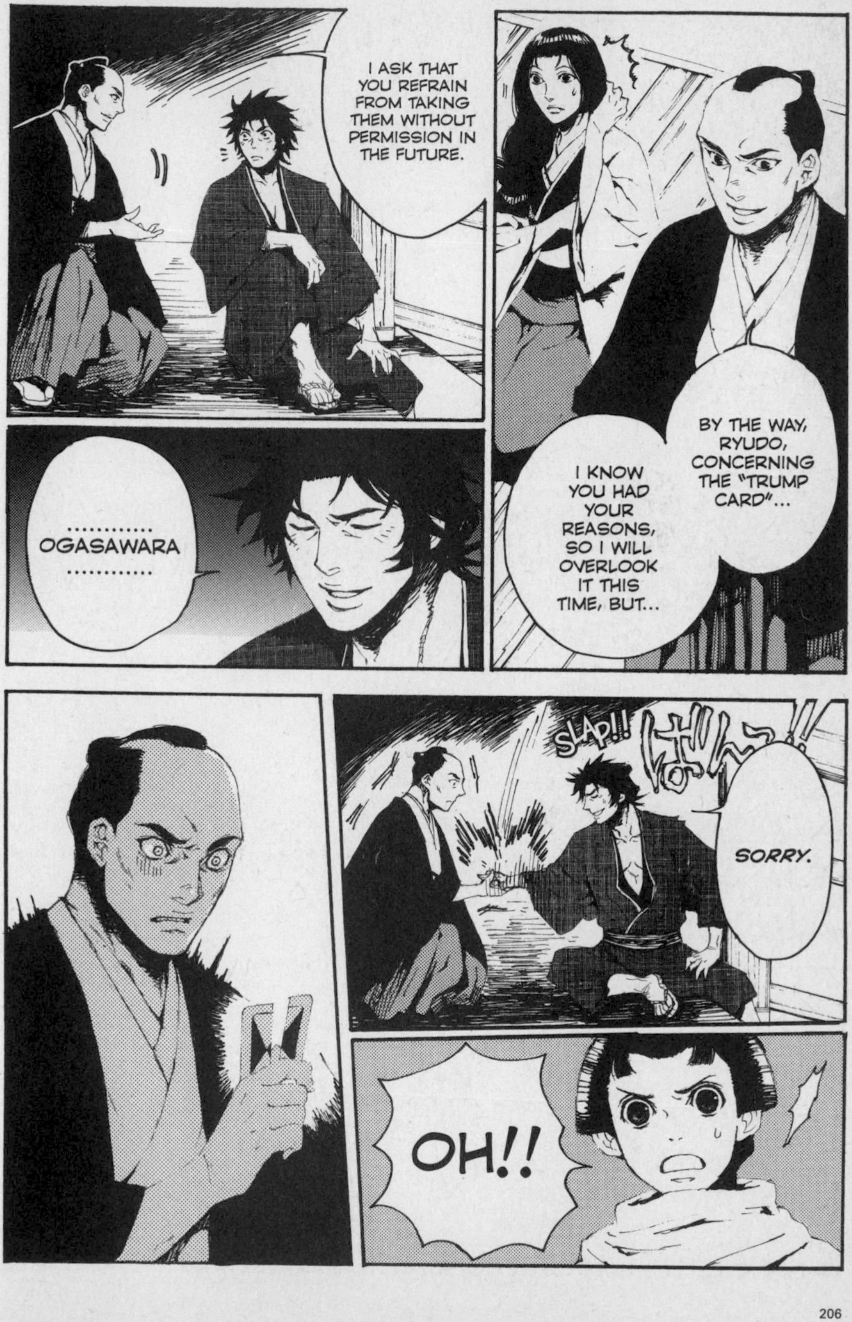
BY THE WAY, RYUDO, CONCERNING THE "TRUMP CARD"...
I KNOW YOU HAD YOUR REASONS, SO I WILL OVERLOOK IT THIS TIME, BUT...
I ASK THAT YOU REFRAIN FROM TAKING THEM WITHOUT PERMISSION IN THE FUTURE.
.... OGASAWARA ....
SLAP!!
SORRY.
OH!!

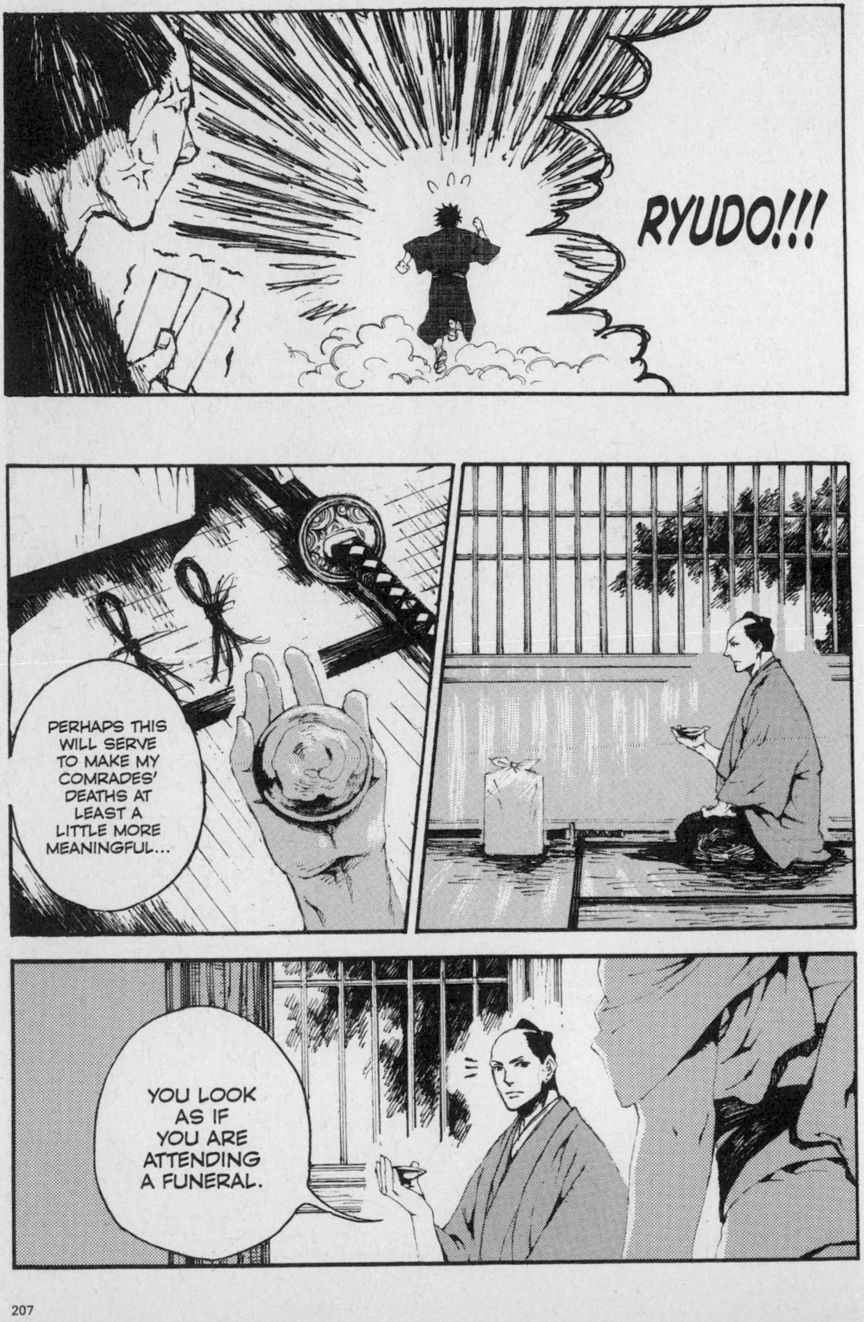
RYUDO!!!
PERHAPS THIS WILL SERVE TO MAKE MY COMRADES' DEATHS AT LEAST A LITTLE MORE MEANINGFUL...
YOU LOOK AS IF YOU ARE ATTENDING A FUNERAL.

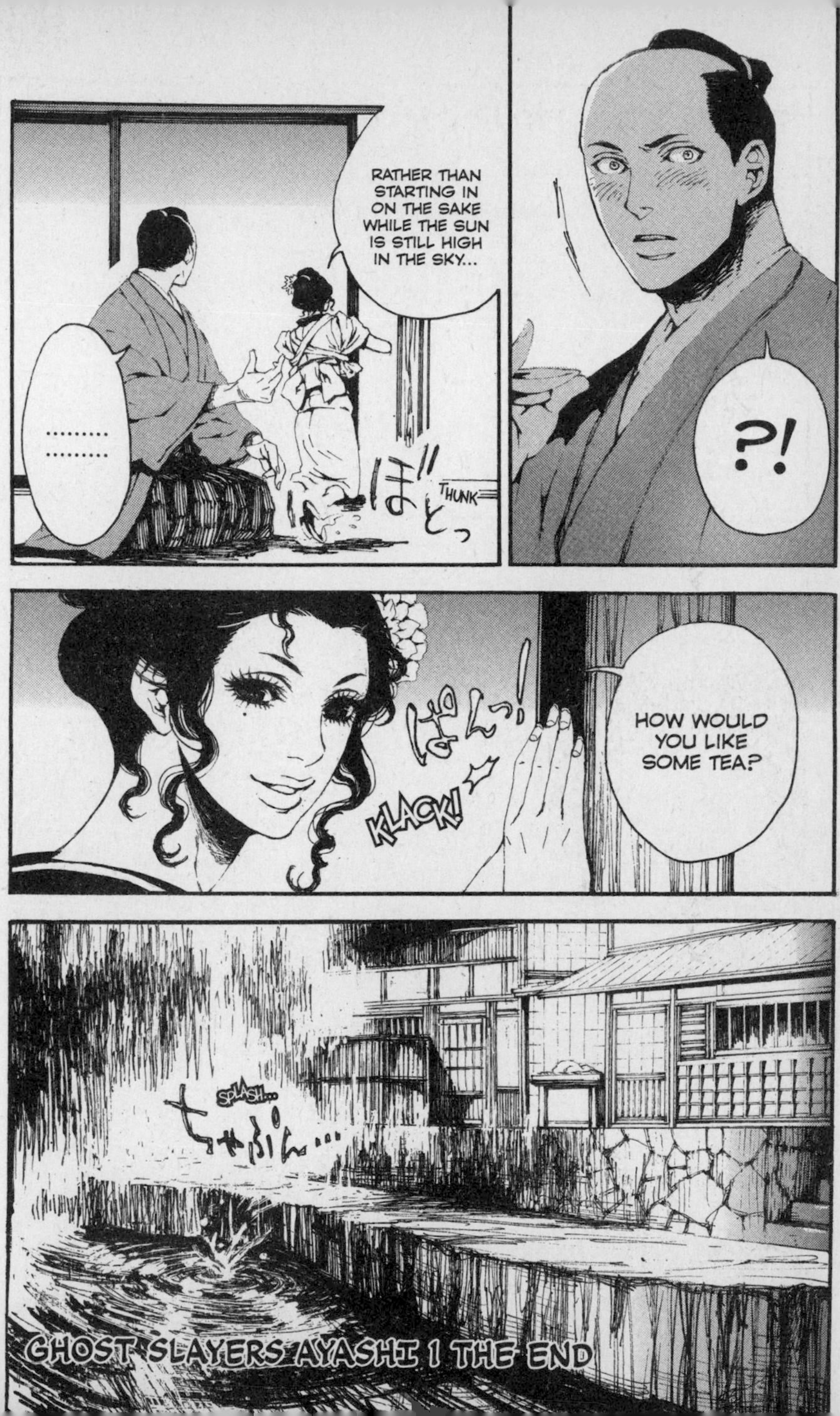
?!
RATHER THAN STARTING IN ON THE SAKE WHILE THE SUN IS STILL HIGH IN THE SKY...
....
....
THUNK
ぼとっ
HOW WOULD YOU LIKE SOME TEA?
ぱんっ!
KLACK!
SPLASH...
ちゃぷん...
GHOST SLAYERS AYASHI 1 THE END

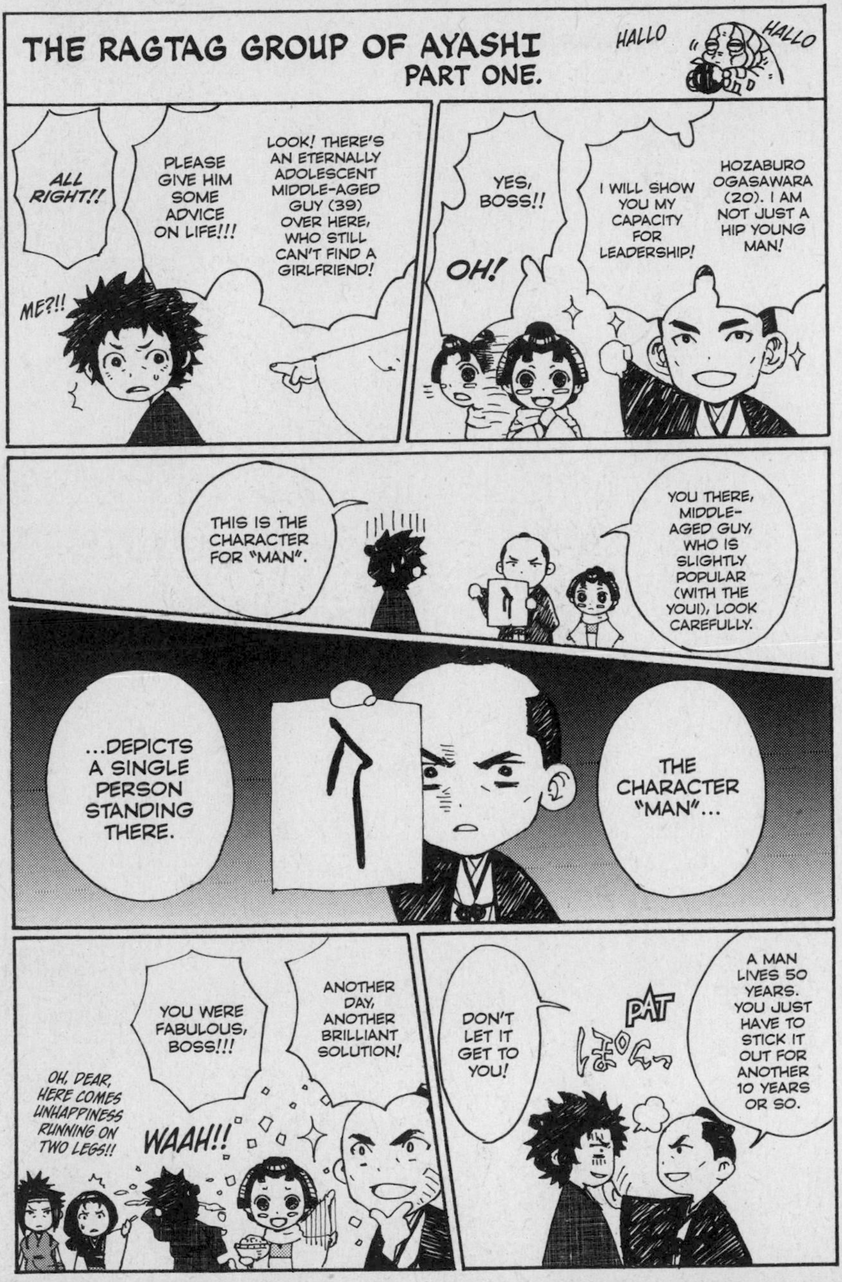
THE RAGTAG GROUP OF AYASHI
PART ONE.
HALLO
HALLO
HOZABURO OGASAWARA (20). I AM NOT JUST A HIP YOUNG MAN!
I WILL SHOW YOU MY CAPACITY FOR LEADERSHIP!
YES, BOSS!!
OH!
LOOK! THERE'S AN ETERNALLY ADOLESCENT MIDDLE-AGED GUY (39) OVER HERE, WHO STILL CAN'T FIND A GIRLFRIEND!
PLEASE GIVE HIM SOME ADVICE ON LIFE!!!
ALL RIGHT!!
ME?!!
YOU THERE, MIDDLE-AGED GUY, WHO IS SLIGHTLY POPULAR (WITH THE YOUI), LOOK CAREFULLY.
THIS IS THE CHARACTER FOR "MAN".
THE CHARACTER "MAN"...
...DEPICTS A SINGLE PERSON STANDING THERE.
A MAN LIVES 50 YEARS. YOU JUST HAVE TO STICK IT OUT FOR ANOTHER 10 YEARS OR SO.
PAT
DON'T LET IT GET TO YOU!
ANOTHER DAY, ANOTHER BRILLIANT SOLUTION!
YOU WERE FABULOUS, BOSS!!!
WAAH!!
OH, DEAR, HERE COMES UNHAPPINESS RUNNING ON TWO LEGS!!

GHOST SLAYERS
Ayashi

ONE

STORY BY
SHO AIKAWA · BONES

ART BY
YAEKO NINAGAWA

TRANSLATION BY
SHOKO OONO

PRODUCTION BY
JOSE MACASOCOL, JR.

EDITED BY
ROBERT PLACE NAPTON

PUBLISHED BY
KEN IYADOMI

First Bandai Printing SEPTEMBER 2008

Printed in Canada

10 9 8 7 6 5 4 3 2 1

TRANSLATOR'S NOTES

PAGE 3: "GUOOONG GUOOONG"

THE SOUNDS HERE IN JAPANESE LITERALLY ARE "GO-O-N," WHICH IS PRONOUNCED SIMILAR TO "GONE", NOT "GOON". SOME CHARACTERS REFER TO IT AS THE SOUND OF THUNDER, BUT THIS IS NOT NORMALLY HOW THE SOUND OF THUNDER IS RENDERED. THE JAPANESE HERE SOUNDS MORE LIKE THE TOLLING OF A LOW-PITCHED BELL. THIS IS PROBABLY BECAUSE THIS IS THE SOUND OF A YOUI, WHICH IS MEANT TO SOUND LIKE NOTHING ELSE.

PAGE 7: "WILY FOX TAMAHEI THOUGHT IT WAS SUSPICIOUS."

THIS DESCRIPTOR FOR TAMAHEI IN JAPANESE LITERALLY MEANS "LIVE HORSE TAMAHEI," IN REFERENCE TO A METAPHOR THAT GOES "SWIFT ENOUGH TO TAKE A LIVE HORSE'S EYES OUT", WHICH IS USED TO DESCRIBE A CUT-THROAT NATURE. IN THE ANIME, THERE IS SOME WORD PLAY, NECESSITATING SOME AWKWARDNESS TO MAKE THE JOKE WORK, BUT SINCE THAT JOKE DOES NOT APPEAR IN THE MANGA, IT GIVES US THE OPPORTUNITY TO GO WITH SOMETHING MORE NATURAL-SOUNDING.

PAGE 9: "I'VE GOT THE FUKAGAWA SPECIALTY, FRIED SWEET BISCUITS HERE!"

THE MAN IS SELLING "KARINTO," WHICH ARE A KIND OF JAPANESE SWEET, WHICH ARE TRADITIONALLY SMALL STICKS OF DOUGH FRIED TO A CRISP AND COATED WITH A SHELL OF BROWN SUGAR.

PAGE 102-103: *BURST...*

THIS SOUND EFFECT IS A SORT OF MAGICAL PEACEFUL BUBBLE BURSTING.

PAGE 120: "YOU HAVE MOST DEFINITELY DELIVERED IT INTO MY CARE."

GENBATSU IS MALE, IN SPITE OF HIS APPEARANCE AND THE WAY HE DRESSES.

"THEY SAY THAT THE CHARACTER FOR "FATHER" WAS ORIGINALLY A PICTOGRAPH OF A HAND HOLDING AN AXE."

THE TWO SYMBOLS BELOW THE ABOVE LINE SHOWS THE PROGRESSION OF HOW THE CHARACTER CAME TO LOOK THE WAY IT DOES NOW.

PAGE 149: "THE SWORD WOUNDS ON THOSE BODIES..."

THERE WAS A CLAN CALLED OBAMA. THERE IS UNFORTUNATELY NO WAY AROUND THE FACT THAT IT IS SPELLED THE SAME AS THE NAME OF THE POLITICIAN. PLEASE NOTE THAT THE "O" REALLY IS A SHORT "O" AND THIS CANNOT BE SPELLED AS "OHBAMA" OR "OOBAMA."
LATER, THERE IS A CHARACTER NAMED SHINJIRO, WHO IS ONE OF THE CLANSMEN, BUT BASED ON THE ART, IT SEEMS LIKE SHINJIRO MAY BE THE ONE IN THE BOTTOM FRAME, WHO DOESN'T SAY ANYTHING. AND THE PERSON SPEAKING HERE IS NEVER GIVEN A NAME.

PAGE 151: "......... THE STORY ABOUT HOW A WOMAN DEVOURED MERMAID FLESH AND BECAME IMMORTAL?"

NORMALLY, THE WORD TRANSLATED AS "DEVOUR" WOULD BE "EAT" OR "CONSUME," BUT IN THIS CASE, IT NEEDS TO WORK WITH THE MERMAID'S LAST LINE ON THE PAGE, WHERE THE WORD ALSO NEEDS TO IMPLY INTIMATE RELATIONS.

"JUST LIKE YOU ARE DEVOURING RIGHT NOW, MASTER SAMURAI."

AS IN "JUST LIKE YOU ARE DEVOURING MERMAID FLESH RIGHT NOW," BUT SHE LEAVES IT DELIBERATELY CRYPTIC, AS HYOMA'S RESPONSE SHOWS.

TRANSLATOR'S NOTES (CONT'D)

PAGE 185: "WHAT ARE WE GOING TO DO? THE BOSS CHERISHES THESE CARDS..."

BACK IN THOSE DAYS, WESTERN PLAYING CARDS WOULD HAVE BEEN RARE IMPORTED GOODS.

PAGE 189: "CUT"

IN JAPANESE, A "TRUMP CARD" IS "KIRIFUDA," WHICH LITERALLY MEANS "THE CUTTING CARD." THUS, THE AYAGAMI OF "CUT (KIRU)" APPEARS. ("KIRU" IS "TO CUT" AND "KIRI" IS A MODIFIED READING, BECAUSE IT IS COMBINED WITH "FUDA" TO CREATE THE WORD "KIRIFUDA.") THE FACT THAT THE CARD GETS CUT HERE IS IRRELEVANT AND A COMPLETE COINCIDENCE, DONE FOR COMIC EFFECT LATER WHEN YUKIATSU HAS TO RETURN THE CARD TO HOZABURO.

PAGE 202: "TO BREAK DOWN AN OBJECT IN ORDER TO DESTROY IT IS 'TO CUT'."

IN JAPANESE, THERE ARE TWO CHARACTERS THAT BOTH MEAN "CUT" AND ARE BOTH PRONOUNCED AS "KIRU," AS IN FROM "KIRIFUDA." HOWEVER, THE ONE DESCRIBED HERE IS THE ONE MOST OFTEN USED TO DESCRIBE DESTRUCTIVE CUTS WITH A SWORD.

TO FIX THE SHAPE OF AN OBJECT TO GIVE IT ITS RIGHTFUL SHAPE IS "TO CUT."

AND THIS IS THE ONE THAT APPEARED IN ALL THE PREVIOUS INSTANCES OF THE AYAGAMI, AND IS USED IN MORE MUNDANE SITUATIONS, SUCH AS CUTTING WITH SCISSORS. HOWEVER, THEY TAKE THE DISTINCTION FURTHER FOR PLOT PURPOSES.

GHOST SLAYERS Ayashi

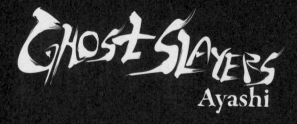

VOLUME TWO

HERE'S A SNEAK PEEK OF GHOST SLAYERS AYASHI VOLUME 2 IN JAPANESE! THE OFFICIAL ENGLISH VERSION WILL BE AVAILABLE FROM BANDAI ENTERTAINMENT ON DECEMBER 2008!